TROUBLESHOOTING GUIDE TO RESIDENTIAL CONSTRUCTION

The Diagnosis and Prevention of Common Building Problems

From the Editors of The Journal of Light Construction

Cover Photos: Carolyn Bates, Ron Whitaker

Editor: Steven Bliss
Production Editors: Josie Masterson-Glen, Ursula Jones
Article Editors: Sal Alfano, Ted Cushman, Clayton DeKorne, Dave Dobbs, Don Jackson, Carl Hagstrom

Production Manager: Theresa Emerson
Graphic Designer: Lyn Hoffelt
Illustrator: Tim Healey

International Standard Book Number
ISBN-13: 978-1-928580-23-2
ISBN-10: 1-928580-23-8

Library of Congress Catalog Card Number: 96-079909
Printed in the United States of America

A Journal of Light Construction Book.

The Journal of Light Construction is a tradename of Hanley Wood LLC.

The Journal of Light Construction
186 Allen Brook Ln.
Williston, VT 05495

INTRODUCTION

"If we learn so much from our mistakes, I must be a near genius by now." — unknown builder

In home building and remodeling, as in many other professions, the important lessons are learned on the job. To a great extent that means learning from our own mistakes — which is good up to a point. Some mistakes, however, we'd just as soon not experience personally. We don't want to crack a foundation, start an electrical fire, or drop a set of trusses, the learning experience notwithstanding. These are things we'd rather learn some other way — preferably from someone with solid, first-hand experience.

This book was put together in that spirit — to help readers tap into the vast pool of hard-won knowledge that exists on job sites across the country. To that end, we looked over the past ten years of *The Journal of Light Construction* and gleaned all the best material on product and material failures, structural trouble spots, and other problems that lead to customer complaints and callbacks. As in *The Journal*, you, the readers, are the primary source of the information; we just help put it to work.

We hope the book works for you and helps you prevent a significant building problem or solve one you already face. First-hand experience may in fact be the best teacher, but the experience of others can be a pretty close second if we pay attention — and it's a whole lot cheaper.

Steven Bliss
Editorial Director

TABLE OF CONTENTS

FOUNDATIONS & SITEWORK

- Preventing Basement Leakage

- Foundation Settlement and Frost Heaves

- Building on Fill

- Controlling Cracks in Slabs

- Retaining Walls

- Septic Systems: Remodeler's Guide

PREVENTING BASEMENT LEAKAGE

Wet basements and crawlspaces are the most common problems I see as a consultant, followed by attic moisture problems. And sometimes the two are related. But there is no excuse for a wet foundation in a new house.

The marketplace is full of waterproofing systems, all of which are relatively expensive. But there is a system available to builders everywhere that is inexpensive, easy to apply, and foolproof. It requires no special skills, and causes no delays in delivery. It's simply a combination of standard materials, good sense, and careful drainage details.

The Usual Way

The excavation hole is usually backfilled with loose, disturbed material that will settle over time as water puddles on it. But where is this water to go once it reaches the bottom of the excavation? It's trapped between undisturbed soil and concrete.

Even if a perimeter drain has been provided and run to daylight or to a sump, it will soon silt up and become useless (Figure 1). Water will build up against the walls. If the drain has no outlet — as is too often the case — water will build up that much faster. When it does, the water pressure often finds relief through joints and cracks in the walls.

If the walls are reasonably watertight, the weight of saturated soil can crack and buckle the foundation. In very cold climates, this process is aggravated by frost.

Figure 1. Drain tile filled with roots (left) or silt (below) is worthless. The combination of a properly detailed gravel bed and filter fabric will keep out both.

Those who build in areas with coarse and sandy soils have an easier life — but not necessarily without problems. I have been called a number of times to diagnose buckling foundation walls in sandy areas. Every single case was caused by rain or melting snow — with temperatures near the freezing point during the day and below freezing at night. The sandy soil didn't have time to drain and the water froze, putting pressure on the foundation. Over the course of the winter, the situation got worse until finally the foundation gave way.

So how can these problems be prevented?

A Better Way

First, you need to build houses with foundations that stick up far enough above the natural grade to permit proper final grading that drops away from the house. For instance, if you now excavate about 8 feet deep so that your houses hug the ground when completed, try going down only 6 1/2 feet. You'll save on dozer time and won't have as much dirt to store and handle.

Next, if you build with poured foundations, you must ensure that the concrete cures properly. And, finally, you must carefully follow a strict procedure to build and protect the foundation drain, backfill, and final grade.

As soon as the wall forms come off, knock off the ties and cover the foundation walls — inside and out — with 6-mil clear plastic. Don't use black plastic except in winter pours, as it can cause the concrete to overheat.

Keep the number of joints in the poly to a minimum, overlap them substantially, and tape them with duct tape. Let the plastic drape over and cover the footings, and hold it in place with shovelfuls of crushed stone. This will prevent dehydration of the concrete and thus allow complete curing, which takes 28 days. The end result will be rock-hard walls that are less prone to shrinkage cracks or water penetration.

Leave the outside plastic on permanently; you may remove the inside plastic after a month.

Footing Drains

If you plan on insulating the foundation from the outside — which I highly encourage — this is the time to do it. Then pin a strip of filter fabric (Typar, Mirafi, etc.) to the bank of the excavation (see Figure 2). Make sure the strip is wide enough to cover the entire perimeter drain that you are about to install.

The filter fabric must extend from the bottom of the trench all the way to the foundation wall with a few inches to spare. This will keep the footing drains from silting up. Don't be stingy; backfilling makes the fabric "shrink."

Spread a couple of inches of 1½-inch crushed stone on the bottom of the trench outside the footings. Next, lay the perforated pipe (holes face down) around the perimeter on the crushed-stone bed. The pipe doesn't need to be sloped; sloping the pipe is impractical and could endanger the footing, since its lower end would have to be below the footing. Water rarely runs in the pipe, anyway. Except in flood-like conditions, the 2 inches of stone below the pipe will handle the water. (Sites that need to use the perforated pipe regularly should probably not have been developed in the first place.)

Now cover the pipe with enough crushed stone to cover the entire footing plus the bottom 4 to 6 inches of the foundation wall. Drape the filter fabric over the stones and turn it up the foundation wall. Then proceed carefully with backfilling.

Backfilling

Backfilling should be done only with coarse material such as bank-run gravel or coarse sand. Do not use silty or clayey soils, because they will quickly plug up the pores of the filter fabric and render the drain useless.

I strongly recommend that you backfill up to, or almost to, natural grade with this coarse material. This not only provides excellent percolation for any water that penetrates the surface, but also gives good protection against frost pressure. Also, the bank-run gravel or coarse sand is dense enough that it won't silt up from the topsoil.

Where the excavation trench around the foundation is quite wide, it is easy to reduce the amount of coarse material needed by gently dumping a band of it against the foundation and following with native soil pushed over the lip to even out the level. These procedures should be alternated until you reach the top.

You will now have about 2 feet of foundation sticking out of the ground. Use the native soil to build the grade up to several inches below the siding. The slope of this final grading is necessary to shed water away from the building; shoot for a slope of about 2 inches per foot. Generally, you will use most of the native soil to accomplish this, and will have to haul away little or none.

There's another advantage to this system. In subdivisions — or where

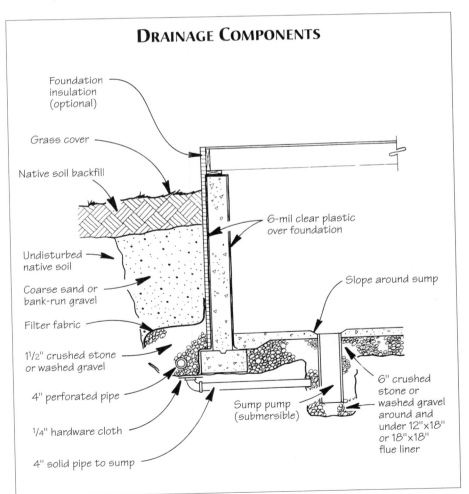

DRAINAGE COMPONENTS

Foundation insulation (optional)

Grass cover

Native soil backfill

Undisturbed native soil

Coarse sand or bank-run gravel

Filter fabric

1½" crushed stone or washed gravel

4" perforated pipe

¼" hardware cloth

4" solid pipe to sump

6-mil clear plastic over foundation

Slope around sump

Sump pump (submersible)

6" crushed stone or washed gravel around and under 12"x18" or 18"x18" flue liner

Figure 2. The gravel bed and footing drains remove subsurface water. The filter fabric keeps out silt, and the coarse sand keeps the filter fabric from clogging up. The sloped finish grade and grass keep most water out from the start.

DRAINAGE TO DAYLIGHT

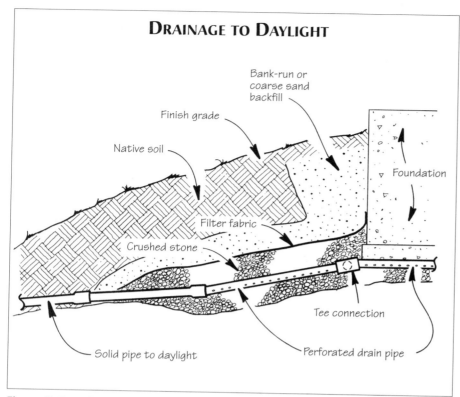

Bank-run or
coarse sand
backfill

Finish grade

Native soil

Foundation

Filter fabric

Crushed stone

Tee connection

Solid pipe to daylight

Perforated drain pipe

Figure 3. Run the footing drain to daylight, if possible. The outlet should be capped with hardware cloth to keep out rodents.

you build two or more houses on flat, contiguous lots — you can vary the grade and create interesting contours, while providing swales between houses that will conduct water to main disposal channels.

If you provide landscaping, don't stick shrubs or flower beds directly against the foundation (put them 4 to 6 feet away). Advise your customers that if placed closer these would trap water and could damage the waterproofing system. Instead, plant grass or lay sod around the foundation. Grass next to the foundation is one of the best insurance policies against water problems you can buy. It will shed a lot of water, and most of the rest will be caught in its deep root mat and re-evaporated.

To Sump or Daylight

If these steps are carefully followed, surface water should never reach the perimeter drain. In many

areas, however, *subsurface* water might be a problem. To function properly in either case, the drain must have an outlet.

If you are building on a lot that permits the footing drain to flow to daylight, the following procedure is recommended. At the point where you tee the drain into the outlet, excavate a sloping (minimum 1 inch per foot) shelf that extends from the footing drain to 10 feet away. Connect a 5- to 10-foot section of perforated pipe to the tee, and lay it in a heavy bed of crushed stone that is covered with filter fabric (see Figure 3). Connect solid pipe to the single section of perforated pipe, and run solid pipe to daylight. This will allow water to drain away from the foundation perimeter into this collection basin and be carried away, thereby keeping the soil under the footing dry.

Cap the daylight outlet with removable hardware cloth to keep rodents from nesting inside this

secure shelter, and build a loose-stone culvert around it to keep grass and soil from closing it up.

When building on a flat site, connect the perimeter drain to a solid pipe that goes under the footing to a sump inside the basement or crawlspace. The pipe should turn up and terminate level with the bottom of the footing, and be covered with hardware cloth to keep out the crushed stones. The sump should pump to the exterior, for example through a band joist, with a check valve at the base of the hose to prevent drain-back. The water should strike a splash block and drain away from the foundation on a sloping grade.

To handle a rising water table under the slab, spread 4 to 8 inches of crushed stone under it, and connect this stone layer to the exterior perimeter drain with a solid pipe that runs through the footing. In the case of a sump, surround the sump with crushed stones so the water can drain into it. I should mention that for a sump I always use — and recommend — a large clay flue-liner section that is set on and surrounded by 6 inches of crushed stone.

I use the term "crushed stone" for a reason. In some areas, gravel means washed round gravel, and it can be obtained in about $1\frac{1}{2}$ inch diameter. But in other areas, gravel means bank or river gravel, which is not suitable for the fast movement of water. Crushed stone should go around the footing drains; bank-run gravel or coarse sand goes above.

Carefully follow this prescription and you'll have an inexpensive and effective — indeed, foolproof — foundation waterproofing system that will ensure crack-free walls and an unblemished reputation.

By Henri deMarne, a home inspector and nationally syndicated columnist from Waitsfield, Vt.

FOUNDATION SETTLEMENT AND FROST HEAVES

Most builders fail to recognize that the soil surrounding a foundation is responsible for the majority of foundation failures. Even foundations built with good materials and first-rate workmanship will fail if poor soil conditions are not considered.

The five leading causes of foundation callbacks in cold climates, listed in order from the most to the least frequent, are
1. Frost-related damage
2. Settlement problems
3. High water-table problems
4. Leaky basements
5. Soil contaminant problems

Preventing Frost-Damaged Foundations

Water expands in volume by about 10% when it freezes, and can exert pressures of up to 80,000 pounds per square foot as it expands. If wet soil below a footing is allowed to freeze, significant heaving will occur, causing damage to the structure above.

For frost heave to take place, three conditions must be present: a frost-susceptible soil, a source of water, and freezing temperatures. Eliminate any one of these conditions and you'll eliminate frostheave.

To avoid frostheave in colder climates, footings are placed below the frostline. But this alone doesn't prevent frost problems altogether.

Adfreezing

Severe damage to the foundation wall can result from adfreezing, or side grip, of the soil to the wall (Figure 4). This phenomenon happens much more frequently in unheated buildings, like garages (Figure 5). As the soil surrounding the wall freezes and expands, it exerts an upward thrust on the foundation walls, which can result in costly damage.

Since soils such as clay, fine sands, tills, and silts are susceptible to frost action, they should not be used to backfill around unheated structures.

A practical method that prevents adfreezing is to provide a "slip plane" at the surface of the foundation wall. Many builders create this slip plane by placing two or more layers of 6-mil construction-grade polyethylene between the soil and the surface of the wall. The durability of polyethylene has improved

dramatically over the past few years, and the builders I've talked to have reported good results.

Pier or sonotube foundations are a cheaper alternative for seasonal homes in my area. Since these foundations are even more susceptible to adfreezing, it's critical that a slip plane be provided.

Uninsulated basements in heated buildings will typically leak enough heat to keep the surrounding soil from freezing. However, placing

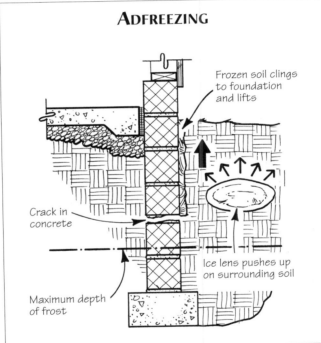

ADFREEZING

Frozen soil clings to foundation and lifts

Crack in concrete

Ice lens pushes up on surrounding soil

Maximum depth of frost

Figure 4. As the soil around an unheated building freezes and expands, it can "grip" the foundation and lift the wall apart (left). Although block walls are particularly susceptible, poured concrete walls can also be damaged (below).

insulation on the interior of basement walls will reduce this heat leakage and contribute to adfreezing. The only instances of this full basement adfreezing that I've observed have occurred where concrete block walls were used. Again, two layers of 6-mil poly on the exterior of interior-insulated foundation walls will prevent this type of adfreezing from occurring.

Other frost-related problems can occur when improper winter construction methods are used. If a foundation is built in subfreezing weather and the soil below the footings (or surrounding the walls) freezes, frost heave can effectively destroy the foundation. If you can't avoid building during winter conditions, be sure to protect the foundation and keep the temperature in the basement above 40°F.

Preventing Settlement Problems

Most settlement problems are caused by "problem" soils — soils that do not have the bearing capacity to carry structural loads without specialized engineering design (Figure 6). These soils are typically soft clays, including volatile, expansive, and lead clays.

If there are any doubts about the suitability of the soils where you intend to build, make a call to a geotechnical consultant. These experts are often aware of "problem pockets" in the region and can advise you how to proceed with a soils investigation. The Soil Conservation Service is another source for soils information.

Soft clays can often be recognized by probing with a piece of rebar: If soft clay is present, the rod will penetrate the soil easily. Builders should also note any unusual soil profiles or signs of soft clay uncovered during excavation. Keep in mind that in some cases the soil observed in the excavation may be adequate, while the underlying soil may be a soft clay or contain some other buried monster.

If a problem soil is discovered or suspected during excavation, have a soils engineer dig an auger test hole to check the underlying soil within the house excavation. A possible alternative to the auger test hole is to have a backhoe excavate outside the house foundation area. These tests can determine soil strength, which is critical for the proper design of your foundation.

Once the soil strength is determined, engineered footings and the foundation can be designed. Solutions may include a raft or pile foundation, preloading of the site to consolidate weaker soils, or the use of engineered fill.

These measures may add $4,000 to $5,000 to the cost of the foundation, but I consider that a good buy. I've seen situations where it cost more than $60,000 to repair improperly built foundations on problem soils.

Poorly Compacted Fill

Many foundation problems are due to improperly compacted fill material. Soil that is too wet or too dry will not compact properly. Builders should bring in a qualified engineer who will advise (and document) proper compaction techniques.

Be aware that when a foundation hole is "overdug" and excavated soil is returned to the foundation hole to raise the final level, the same compaction rules apply. Whenever possible, avoid using excavated material to raise the level of a foundation hole. By pouring thicker footings or building taller foundation walls, an engineered solution can sometimes be avoided.

High Water Tables

A high water table may result in insufficient foundation support. Excavations below the water table will create a wet hole, which will lead to poor-quality concrete in the footings. If gravel fill is used, the migration of fines will cause foundation settlement.

Figure 5. Unheated garages are prone to damage from adfreezing (left). Two layers of 6-mil polyethylene placed on both sides of the foundation wall provides a slip plane that prevents freezing soils from bonding to the foundation wall (right).

Figure 6. The foundation of this factory home (left) was built on unstable soil. Settlement caused extensive foundation damage (below), which required complete excavation and engineered underpinnings (bottom left and right).

To avoid the problem, check the local groundwater levels and always build above the groundwater table. If disturbance does occur in the foundation soil, do not dig deeper, as additional hydrostatic pressures will occur, causing further loosening of soil. In these cases, consult a geotechnical engineer.

Some areas have a seasonal water table that is highest in the spring and lowest in late summer. In these areas, it's important to establish an "average" water table, and base building decisions on that.

Get Accurate Information

The best no-cost measure for preventing foundation problems is to look at any available soils maps and to check with municipal planning/building departments before starting the job. On larger projects, seek out any geotechnical reports that may have been provided by the developer. The soil type and water table levels are usually analyzed before a subdivision goes in. Geotechnical consultants often have a database of local soils, including known problem areas. Look for a proven track record from the consultant and make sure he or she has liability insurance.

Make sure all geotechnical reports and foundation inspections are certified by a geotechnical engineer and in compliance with local codes. This can be valuable information to present to the home buyer.

In the absence of expert information (or in addition to it), local well drillers and — in more rural areas — farmers have a wealth of knowledge about local water table levels and soil types. The important point is to collect this information as early as possible in the building design process to avoid costly problems or delays.

By Rob Marshall, a civil engineer and building science specialist in Ontario, Canada. Photos courtesy of Ontario New Home Warranty Program.

BUILDING ON FILL

Few foundation topics generate as much confusion as does building on filled sites. Many homeowners and contractors — and even some engineers — assume that filled sites offer good foundation support, particularly for residential or light-commercial structures. The assumption is that if someone took the time to fill a site, it must be better than it was before. This contrasts sharply with my experience, so my first reaction to a filled site is generally, How bad is the problem?

When dealing with a filled site, a prospective developer or contractor should keep in mind the roadside signs that say "Clean Fill Wanted." These signs exemplify the uncertainties you face with a filled site: how was the site filled, and what happens when it is later developed?

There are probably as many different reasons for wanting fill as there are signs. The fill may be needed to provide a level area for parking cars or storing material, or to provide space for a garden or play area. In some instances, a site is filled to cover up a swampy depression or poor soil, such as peat. Some people mistakenly believe that hiding the problem solves it.

The range in the quality of fill is even wider. People take what they can get: loam, silt, wood, ash, building rubble from demolition projects — sometimes even sand and gravel! The homeowners, farmers, and others who do the filling are often unaware that engineering is required, or they are unwilling to spend the money to construct an engineered fill. At any rate, the result rarely conforms to good construction practice.

An Engineered Fill

What is an engineered fill? While each site and building must be assessed individually, when planning an engineered fill you should generally do the following:

- Have a geotechnical engineer assess the underlying soils.
- Know the nature of the structure to be built on top of the fill.
- Establish criteria for fill materials and the degree of compaction.
- Remove organic soils or other deleterious material before placing the fill.
- Place the fill on top of appropriate subgrade soils in thin lifts that are mechanically compacted to the specified densities.
- Have a geotechnical engineer monitor and test the fill materials and the degree of compaction.

Unfortunately, many people involved in filling undeveloped sites don't take these steps. The questions that then arise are:

1. What soils are present below the fill?
2. What fill materials were used?
3. Was the fill compacted?

First, determine *why* the area was filled. Poor quality soils frequently lie under the fill. So even if the fill satisfies all the other requirements of an engineered fill — a rare case — poor subgrade soils could still result in damage to the foundation.

In terms of fill quality, the terms "clean," "solid," or "good" are ambiguous and have no technical meaning. The developer should assess the quality of the material that was used. Trash, wood, stumps, cinders, and ash, for example, are not appropriate for use below structures, even if compacted.

A growing concern is whether environmentally hazardous materials are present in the fill. Contaminated soils may require removal at

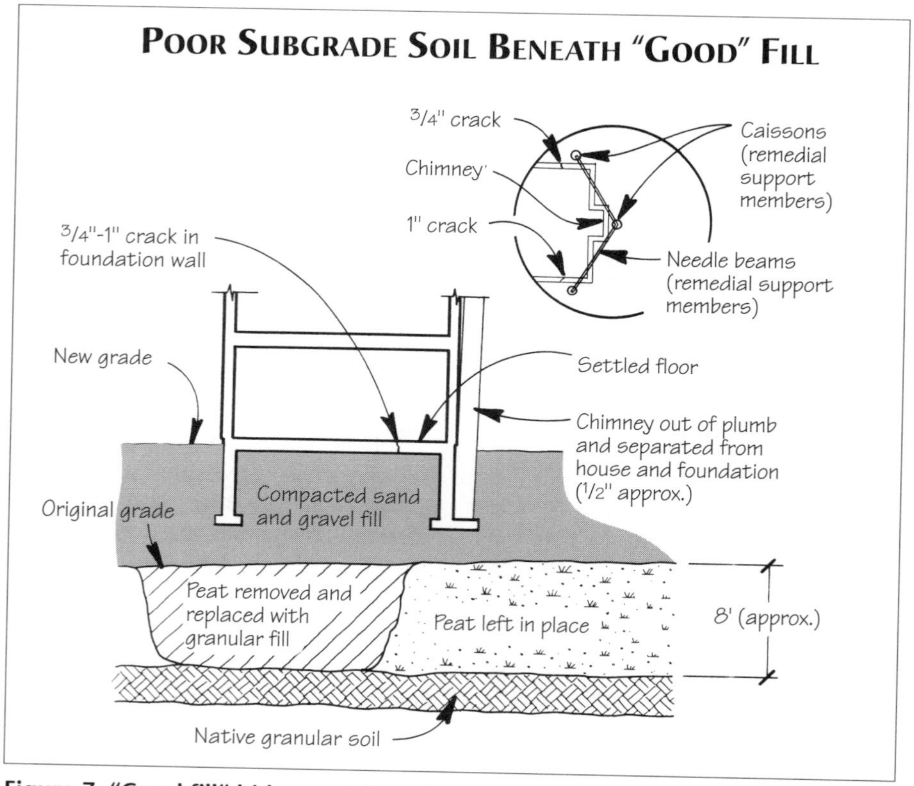

POOR SUBGRADE SOIL BENEATH "GOOD" FILL

Figure 7. "Good fill" hid a peat deposit up to 8 feet thick that supposedly had been removed from this site. But part of it remained and cracked the foundation, which later had to be stabilized with caissons and needle beams.

costs far greater than the value of the entire project. Prospective developers should test for hazardous materials when purchasing the property — and, in fact, many mortgage lenders now require this. "Clean fill" has begun to take on a whole new meaning.

Compaction

I am frequently asked, "The fill has been there for a year (or ten years): Is that enough compaction?" In almost all instances, the answer is no. Natural processes do not provide enough compaction for fill to support structures.

"Ponding" (or "flooding") the fill area is not a recommended method of compaction. This procedure cannot be systematically controlled, and its effectiveness is hard to gauge. Most fills have not been systematically compacted, and should be considered inadequate unless proved otherwise.

Assessing compaction *after* the fill has been placed is expensive and time-consuming. Moreover, it is fraught with unknowns because, under the best of circumstances, only a small fraction of the fill can be tested. There's no guarantee that the tested area represents the entire fill. And a small, uncompacted area can significantly damage a structure.

Unknown Fill

So far, this discussion has assumed that the prospective developer knows that the site was filled. Often, however, contractors are not aware that they are building over fill. In some cases, it is difficult to distinguish between fill soils and natural soils.

To guard against problems, you must research the site. Possible sources of information are old topographic site plans, USGS topographic maps, previous owners, neighbors, or local contractors.

Have a geotechnical engineer monitor explorations on all sites where fill is suspected. In fact, a pro-

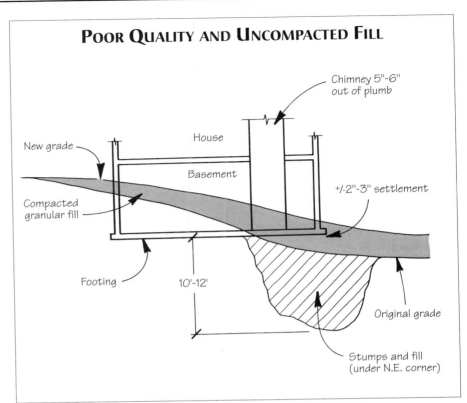

Figure 8. In leveling the site, the excavation contractor was told to bury the stumps at the far end of the lot. Unfortunately, they ended up under one corner of the house — cracking the foundation and shifting the chimney.

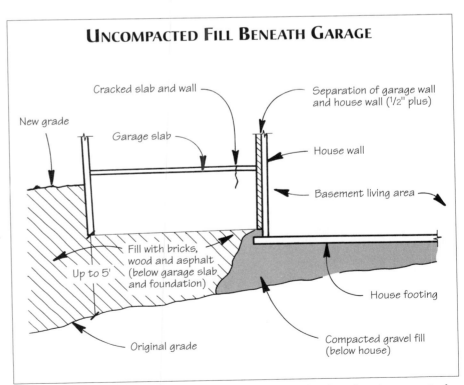

Figure 9. In leveling this site, fill material was properly placed and compacted under the house. But under the garage, the fill was sloppy. It later consolidated — and the slab and walls cracked.

fessional review of soil conditions is a good idea on all house sites — and is required by code in many areas.

Case Studies

A common attitude in residential construction is "It's *only* a house, with no real load on it." This is shortsightedness — particularly in filled sites.

The severity of the problems vary, but in all of the following cases it would have been cheaper to build the foundations right in the first place than it was to repair them later (and, in some cases, pay for the lawyers).

Case one. Compressible soils — frequently peat or other organic soils — that are left below fill are probably the most common cause of problems on filled sites. The fill frequently appears to be good quality "gravel," which misleads the contractor into assuming that the bearing conditions are good. But the problem is still present *below* the foundation.

In this case, a peat deposit — 8 feet thick in places — was supposedly excavated from the site, and the exca-

GETTING GOOD COMPACTION

When a field test shows inadequate compaction, chances are good the problem is caused by soil gradation, poor compacting techniques, or moisture.

Choose the right soil. While every soil can be adequately compacted, the amount of effort

Figure A. Soil that's moist enough to compact well should hold shape when you ball it up in your hands. But the only sure way to determine optimum moisture content is to have the soil tested.

required varies greatly. Choose coarse, granular soils above silt and clay. Their moisture content is easier to manipulate, and they respond well to vibratory compactors. Given a choice, most earthwork contractors know instinctively that they would rather compact gravel than clay.

Between gravel and clay is a range of silt, silty sands and gravels, and clayey silts. Although silt is more permeable than clay, it's difficult to control the moisture content of both soil types. Generally speaking, the lower the percentage of silt and clay particles in the soil, the easier it will be to compact.

Under no circumstances should topsoil, roots, or other organic materials be incorporated into the fill. These materials will decay and decompose over time, eventually causing settling even in well-compacted soil.

Also be alert to changes in grain size in the fill material. If soil grada-

Figure B. The large surface area of a vibratory plate compactor works well with sand and gravel. Here a worker moistens dry sand to speed compaction.

tion changes, so will the optimum dry density. In some cases, gradation changes will be visually obvious, but the tip-off is usually field test results that don't make sense.

Compact shallow lifts. You should compact soil in layers from 6 to 10 inches thick. Even heavy rollers don't have much effect at depths over a foot.

A common mistake in backfilling foundations is to place a 3- or 4-foot-thick layer and then try to salvage the situation by pounding on the surface until it looks great. This might compact the top 8 inches, but 18 or 24 inches down the percent compaction is still low. In this case, the fill will settle unless it is removed, and replaced and compacted in thin lifts.

Moisture matters. Moisture plays a major role in the compaction process. If the soil particles are absolutely dry, there's a lot of friction to overcome when trying to push the particles together, making the process difficult and inefficient. On the other hand, if the spaces between particles are full of water, the water absorbs some of the compaction energy — like a shock absorber. Then the soil particles don't get the full brunt of the compacting impact, and a lot of energy gets wasted.

Sand and gravel dry out quickly in hot weather. Before compacting this type of soil, it may be necessary to use hoses or a water truck to sprinkle the soil with water to increase the moisture content, bringing it closer to optimum.

vation was backfilled with sand and gravel fill (see Figure 7). The contractor had performed test borings before construction, and presumably verified that the peat had been removed. A shallow foundation was built bearing on the sand and gravel backfill.

Less than a year later, one end of the house had to be underpinned with caissons and needle beams to stabilize a 3/4-inch crack in the foundation. Although the footings were on the sand and gravel, peat still remained under part of the house. It is not known whether this problem resulted from improperly locating the house over the excavated area, or from inaccuracies in the boring logs.

Case two. Poor fill *material* can also cause settling in light structures.

On this site, the ground originally sloped 10 or 12 feet across the lot. To level the site, the lot was filled with material from nearby areas. In addition, the earthwork subcontractor was told to bury the stumps at the far end of the lot.

When the basement area was excavated, it extended into both natural soils and fill. Because the soils

---

On the other hand, prolonged, heavy rain can create a quagmire in less permeable silt and clay. Once these soils are saturated, it's pointless to attempt compaction. The result is usually surface weaving, rutting, and the kind of disturbance that loosens up even previously compacted soil. Waiting out the wet weather is usually the only answer. Eventually, the moisture will slowly percolate downward and, when the sun reappears, evaporate. Opening wet clay soil to aeration by discing will help speed up the drying process. To keep wet soil stable, you can sandwich in layers of dry sand or gravel.

To judge whether or not the soil you are using is near the optimum moisture content, try forming a handful into a ball (Figure A). If it crumbles easily, the soil is probably too dry; if moisture oozes out, it's too wet.

Avoid frozen soil. When temperatures dip below freezing, all bets are off. Frozen sand or gravel acts just like dry material because the moisture no longer acts to overcome friction. If there's enough moisture in the soil, it will freeze solid. The same is true for fine-grained soils. Once frozen, they can't be moved, let alone compacted. And when silt freezes, it can expand and heave, negating the effect of compaction.

Use the right equipment. Heavy drum rollers, rubber tire rollers, and sheepsfoot rollers work well when compacting clay. A jumping jack will also work in tight quarters. Vibratory rollers and plate compactors work best on sand and gravel (Figures B and C), although

rubber tire rollers and even loaded dump trucks can do the job.

A common error with hand-operated compactors is traveling too fast over an area and making too few passes. The more you pound on a particular spot, the better compacted it will be. The only way to be sure the soil is properly compacted is to test each lift.

Choosing the right equipment for a particular site and soil condition is important. Read the manufacturer's literature before you buy or rent a compactor. Discuss your needs with equipment suppliers and distributors. They usually have people on staff who can match the right machine to the problem at hand.

Test the soil. If you're placing more than a foot or two of fill that will support a structure or a slab, have it tested. First, get a sample of the proposed fill material to a testing lab (to find a lab, look in the Yellow Pages under "Laboratories — Testing" or "Engineers — Testing"). Have the lab perform a Proctor test (named after the engineer who introduced the concept of optimum dry density in the 1930s). The Proctor test subjects a sample of soil to a fixed compaction pressure at varying moisture contents and yields the optimum dry density, the benchmark against which to measure field compaction. Then have the in-place fill tested by someone from the testing lab or by an engineering firm. It's not an expensive process: $200 should cover the cost of a few hours on the job site plus the Proctor test.

If for some reason you can't test

Figure C. The small footprint of a jumping jack does a good job of compacting, particularly in tight spaces.

every lift, at least test compaction in the first lift so that if it's not right, you can adjust the compacting effort before it's too late. There's nothing more discouraging that finding out after 5 feet of fill is placed and compacted that the effort wasn't good enough. The only remedy at that point is to remove the fill and start over.

Keep a shovel handy during the field test. The technician should dig a few shallow test holes to verify that the fill matches the soil on which the Proctor was performed. Test holes are also a good way to check for organics, which should always be removed when detected.

By Roger Dorwart, P.E., president of Knight Consulting Engineers, Inc. in Williston, Vt.

were similar, the contractor didn't realize that part of the house was built on top of fill.

The result was substantial settling of the foundation and slab. The chimney separated from the house, and one corner of the house settled and cracked. Subsequent investigation revealed stumps below the corner of the house to depths of 10 to 12 feet. Figure 8 shows the soil profile below the house.

Case three. The final case shows what can happen when fills are not compacted.

A house and attached garage were located on a sloping site (Figure 9). According to the owner, the main area of the house was built partially on a granular fill that had been

properly placed and compacted in thin lifts by the contractor.

The garage, however, was built over an uncompacted mixture of topsoil, subsoil, sand, silt, asphalt, and other materials. Later, the foundation walls and slab at the rear of the garage significantly settled and cracked, due to the consolidation of the uncompacted fill. Apparently, the contractor had considered the garage foundation less important than the main house foundation — but the owners didn't share this view.

Buyers Beware

In summary, prospective developers should approach filled sites with a skeptical and critical eye. A general recommendation is to avoid build-

ing on top of any fill that cannot be proved to be an engineered fill.

Beyond that, developers must be aware that the risk of finding hazardous wastes in soil or groundwater is real — and clearly greater in filled sites. This should be considered when evaluating the feasibility of a project.

Finally, these foundation problems on small construction projects demonstrate the fallacy of the "it's only a house" philosophy. Because a structure is small or lightly loaded does not mean that an engineering evaluation of a site is not warranted. An ounce of prevention, in these cases, could have saved pounds of costly callbacks.

By M. Daniel Gordon, a consulting geotechnical engineer from Newton, Mass.

CONTROLLING CRACKS IN SLABS

When it comes to concrete slabs, there is one fact that must be faced by homeowners, contractors, and concrete subs alike: Concrete will crack. Period. The challenge for the concrete sub is to work with the material and make it behave in a way that is acceptable to both the customer and the contractor. The key to success is to control

where the concrete is going to crack, and prepare the customer for the inevitable.

Brittle Behavior

Concrete does its best work under compression. It's great for driving cars on, rolling shopping carts on, even for raising elephants on. But it doesn't have great tensile

strength. Picture a glass table cover at a restaurant: It works fine when it's in full contact with the table top. You could probably dance on it without any damage to the glass. Your reputation might be shot, but the glass would be okay. But if you hold one edge of the glass off the table and apply pressure to it, the glass shatters.

Concrete behaves the same way. It's this lack of tensile strength, or brittleness, that most often causes the cracking found in residential slabs. A new slab shrinks as it cures, setting up tensile stresses throughout the slab. When the tensile stresses caused by the shrinkage exceed the tensile strength of the concrete, the concrete surrenders, and a crack appears.

And the cracking's not over when the slab is fully cured. A slab expands as the temperature rises and contracts as the temperature drops. This thermal fluctuation guarantees that the slab will always be subjected to tensile stresses.

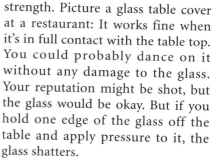

Figure 10. To prevent settlement cracks, the subgrade must be compacted properly. Here, a worker uses a vibratory plate compactor to correctly prepare the subgrade.

There's not much you can do to control the shrinkage and external forces at work on the slab. But there are other causes of cracking that can and should be avoided.

Compact Before You Pour

Proper subgrade preparation is essential. If the subgrade isn't compacted properly, the slab will settle and sink. If the slab settles and sinks, you'll be asking it to perform like the glass table top that's extended over the edge of the table, and cracking will occur. To prevent a slab from settling, the subgrade should be a minimum of 4 to 6 inches of well-drained and uniformly compacted material (Figure 10).

Never pour concrete on a frozen or heavily frosted subgrade. Water expands as it freezes, and when a frozen subgrade thaws out, the slab will settle.

The problem with plastic. A plastic vapor barrier is often specced as part of the subgrade preparation. The plastic keeps ground moisture from coming back up through the slab and affecting floor coverings and creating damp conditions. That's the good side. But vapor barriers can also increase the amount of shrinkage cracking in a slab. That's bad.

Once the concrete is out of the truck and in place, the water in the mix starts to evaporate. If the concrete is poured directly over plastic, the water has just one avenue of escape — through the surface. Once the top of the slab has dried, this subsurface water will cause shrinkage cracking to occur as it forces its way through the surface of the concrete. Fortunately, most shrinkage cracks are more cosmetic than structural, so if the floor is going to be covered, some cracking may be acceptable.

To reduce the chances of shrinkage cracking, cover the vapor barrier with 3 inches of compacted sand before placing the slab. This sand

Figure 11. The best way to guarantee concrete slump at the site is to perform a cone slump test (left). The wetter the concrete, the higher the slump (right).

Figure 12. Here, 3-inch strips of asphalt-impregnated expansion board isolate a slab from wood framing. The flatworkers can also use the expansion board as a guide for finished slab height.

ISOLATION JOINTS

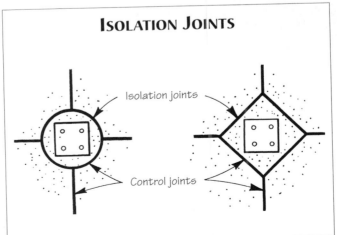

Isolation joints

Control joints

Figure 13. Columns should be isolated from the slab using blockouts. When forming square blockouts, the points of the square should be positioned to meet the control joints.

can be compacted by a thorough wetting the day before the pour.

Thickness, Strength, and Slump

Before you prepare the subgrade, you'll need to decide how thick the slab should be. The American

Figure 14. Sawn joints are cut with a power saw equipped with a diamond blade. They should be cut soon after the surface hardens.

Concrete Institute (ACI) has broken nonstructural concrete floors into five classes and lists design criteria for each class, including thickness, strength of the mix, and maximum slump (see the table, "Recommended Slab Thickness").

Concrete subcontractors should pay more attention to slump (Figure 11). It's controlled by the amount of water in the mix: The more water, the higher the slump and the weaker the concrete. When concrete is poured at a high slump because of excessive water in the mix, the ingredients in the mix don't stay together. The water and some of the cement go one direction, the sand and the rest of the cement go another direction, and the stones end up alone in their own pile. To produce strong, durable concrete, all of the ingredients need to be uniformly distributed so the concrete performs as a homogeneous material.

Exceeding the recommended slump can also result in excessive bleed water. Bleed water is the water in the mix that migrates to

the top of the slab immediately after placement. If this bleed water is not allowed to evaporate but is instead troweled back into the slab, it will create a weakened surface layer that will encourage shrinkage cracking, dusting, and possible crazing of the finish surface (see "The Finisher's Art").

Keeping it together. There is a very common misconception that the addition of wire mesh or rebar in the slab will eliminate cracking. It won't. Steel placed in the middle of the slab section will only limit the width of cracks, preventing them from opening up into canyons.

The highly touted fiber mesh that many concrete suppliers offer won't stop cracking, either. I once had an opportunity to pour two 40-yard slabs side by side, one with wire reinforcement and the other with fiber mesh added to the mix. The slab with the wire cracked where predicted, but the slab with the fiber mesh cracked randomly. (I think the mesh additive makes the concrete look stiffer as it comes

THE FINISHER'S ART

I have an immense amount of respect for good concrete finishers. Part athlete and part artisan, a finisher develops a sense of feel and timing that can only be gained by years and years of hard work and practice. I wager a claim that this is some of the toughest work in the trades. So it is only respectfully and carefully that I suggest some areas where finishing crews need to pay attention.

The water valve. Adding water to the concrete mix opens the door to problems. When a mix is designed, it is based on the relationship between the water and the cement, and the Portland Cement Association has established acceptable limits for this water/cement ratio. When water is added to the mix, strength and surface hardness decrease while shrinkage and crack-

ing increase. The bleed rate also increases and so does the chance for dusting and crazing. Concrete designed to be poured at a 4-inch slump should be poured at a 4-inch slump. If you are not familiar with what a 4-inch slump really looks like, I'll bet money that your ready-mix supplier would trip over himself to show you.

Bleed water. Troweling bleed water back into the concrete weakens the finished surface layer of the slab by raising the water/cement ratio. Since the very top of the slab gets all of the attention as well as all of the traffic, it should be as strong and durable as possible.

Air entrainment. In most areas of the country, if the concrete is expected to live outside, it's air entrained. Air entrainment creates billions and billions of microscopic

air bubbles in the mix. This gives moisture someplace to hang out during periods of freezing and thawing. Without air in the mix, the surface layer of concrete, which is exposed to cycles of freezing and thawing, will deteriorate much more quickly than air-entrained concrete. Be sure to ask if your supplier provides air entrainment.

Tools to avoid. I have yet to see a situation where a vibrator was needed when pouring a nonstructural slab. Likewise, the jitterbug should only be used on very low slump placements. The reason that it makes finishing easier is the same reason that it makes the surface much, much weaker: It pushes the large aggregate well below the surface and creates a weak plane where there needs to be a strong one. — *D.G.*

down the chute, so contractors often add additional water to compensate for what they think is an overly stiff mix.)

Isolation Joints

Since you can't prevent cracks altogether, the best approach is to control them with proper joint design and installation. There are two kinds of concrete joints: isolation, or expansion, joints and control joints.

Slabs are a bit antisocial — they don't interact well with the structural elements of a building. Nonstructural slabs must be allowed to expand, contract, and move up and down independent of surrounding walls and columns.

Installing expansion joint material where the slab meets adjoining walls effectively isolates the slab from the wall. Fastened to the wall before the pour, this material, typically an asphalt-covered fiber board, also serves to establish the finished concrete level (Figure 12).

Columns must also be blocked out and isolated from the rest of the slab. The blockouts at column bases should be round or square. If they're square, they should be positioned so that the points of the square meet the control joints (Figure 13).

Control Joints

This is where you step in and tell the slab where you want it to crack. If you don't, the concrete will crack at random. The most common types of control joints are sawn joints and tooled joints.

Sawn joints should be cut as soon as possible after the concrete hardens. This can be a real judgment call on the part of the finisher, but it's generally a few hours after the final finish has been applied (Figure 14). If stones pull out when sawing begins, you're too early. If random cracks begin to occur before sawing has begun, you're too late.

Tooled joints are formed using a hand-held grooving trowel and are "cut in" immediately after the bleed water has left the slab.

Plastic extrusions are pressed into the wet concrete as the pour progresses to form control joints. One of the most popular is the "zip strip" type, a two-piece tee-shaped extrusion. The 10-foot lengths are tapped into the slab with the butt of a hand float and the top portion of the tee is "zipped" off, leaving the remaining vertical section 1/8 inch below the surface of the slab (Figure 15). Check with your concrete supplier for availability in your area.

No matter which method you use to create control joints, you should follow a few rules of thumb:

- Control joints should be no less than one-fourth the thickness of the slab in depth. This ensures the concrete will crack where you put the joint.
- Joint spacing should equal slab width. Slabs that are rectangular in shape tend to crack in the middle (Figure 16).
- Maximum joint spacing for 4-inch slabs is between 12 and 18 feet (Figure 17).

Where random cracking is better. There are some situations where random cracking is actually preferred. If the slab is going to serve as the base for a tile floor, a random crack will

Figure 15. Two-piece plastic control joint materials are popular on residential sites. The tee-shaped extrusion is pressed into the wet concrete (left), then the top, horizontal piece is "zipped" off, leaving an invisible control joint (right).

RECOMMENDED SLAB THICKNESS

Floor Class	Application	Minimum Thickness	28-day Strength	Slump
1	Residential or tile covered	4"	3,000 psi	4"
2	Offices, churches, hospitals, schools, ornamental residential	4"	3,500 psi	4"
3	Drives, sidewalks for residences, garage floors	4"	3,500 psi	4"
4	Business or commercial walks	5"	3,500 psi	4"
5	Light industrial & commercial	5"	4,000 psi	3"

JIM ALLOR

Figure 16. Rectangular slabs tend to crack in the middle. Control joint spacing should equal slab width.

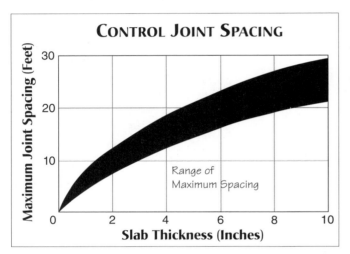

CONTROL JOINT SPACING

Figure 17. The maximum spacing for control joints depends on the thickness of the slab. The shaded area of the graph indicates the acceptable range.

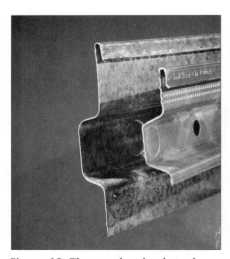

Figure 18. These galvanized steel forming materials create a "keyed" control joint — essentially a tongue-and-groove — that helps keep adjacent slab sections in a flat, horizontal plane.

often do less damage to the tile than a poorly aligned control joint. Ideally, a tile joint should fall directly over the control joint, but this is difficult to achieve in the real world.

Keyed Joints

This method is probably the most reliable jointing method for the conscientious concrete crew because it vertically aligns adjacent slab sections. These tongue-and-groove joints are most easily formed by using a manufactured galvanized piece of "keyway" material whose width matches the thickness of the slab (Figure 18). Most suppliers of forming accessories stock this item.

The galvanized strip is typically installed just below the surface of the slab. Once it's in, you're done — the

crack will appear above the strip. No gas-powered saws to worry about, no expensive diamond saw blades to fret over. During the pour, however, the crew has to realize that the keyway shouldn't be kicked, tripped over, smacked with a shovel, or otherwise moved.

Construction joints. All a construction joint actually does is draw the line where the concrete placement ended on a given day. For thin, lightly loaded floors, a straight-formed "butt joint" is adequate. For more heavily trafficked and loaded applications, a keyed joint may be more appropriate.

Cure It Before It Ails You

Proper curing is essential for controlling cracks as well as for producing strong concrete. Cement and water have a kind of love/hate relationship. When placing fresh concrete, too much water can cause a variety of problems. But once the slab is poured and finished, moisture should remain in the slab as long as possible.

The cement needs the water to complete the chemical process of hydration. If the water in the slab is allowed to evaporate too quickly, the rate of shrinkage — and shrinkage cracking — will increase. Curing is the process of ensuring that the water stays a part of this codependent relationship. It's important to plan on a method of curing before you pour.

If it sounds like a quality slab requires a whole lot of planning and a bushel of effort, you're right. Pouring a first-rate slab requires hard work and concentration from the time the project is conceived until the time that it becomes a rock-hard reality. But when the job is done properly, the rewards can last almost forever.

By Dennis Golden, a former concrete contractor and ready-mix quality control technician. He currently works for the Department of Public Works in Buckley, Wash.

RETAINING WALLS

In most parts of the U.S. you don't have to look far to find failed or failing retaining walls. They can lead to callbacks, unhappy customers, and even worse, damage to property or even serious injury.

Catastrophic failure (walls tipping over completely) is unusual, partly because the process often progresses slowly and corrective action is usually taken before the catastrophe can occur. But that's not always true. One rainy afternoon in about 1960, the harmless-looking wall in Figure 19 suddenly and spontaneously tipped over. Fortunately my three sisters and I were inside playing Monopoly instead of out playing in the yard. The shock of the impact of five tons of masonry against our house, followed by twenty tons of mud, was something none of us will ever forget.

What made that wall tip, and why so suddenly? The answers are really pretty straightforward. First, the wall was a simple — and very poorly designed — gravity wall that had only a very small footing and no reinforcing steel. In short, it was not much different from a tall stack of blocks. During a period of prolonged heavy rains, the soil behind the wall soaked up a lot of water, and became heavier and more fluid, increasing the force behind the wall. At the same time the ground under and in front of the wall became soft and slippery, undermining the stability of the footing and offering little resistance to the tipping wall (Figure 20).

Clearly, water was the biggest factor in this failure. What could have been done differently? The single most important thing would have been to prevent the accumulation of water in the soil behind and beneath the wall. As the photograph in Figure 19 shows, there were occasional blocks placed sideways as well as gaps between blocks

in the bottom course. These well-intended features, like the drain holes frequently seen in the face of retaining walls, were inadequate because water-retentive native soil was used as backfill.

Soils with more than a minimum of clay content (5% fines by weight) are generally water retentive and should not be used as backfill. Instead, place gravel or clean sand behind the wall, with footing drains

Figure 19. This block wall, which on its face looks sturdy and well-built, collapsed during heavy rains because it had no reinforcing, too small a footing, and was backfilled with native soil.

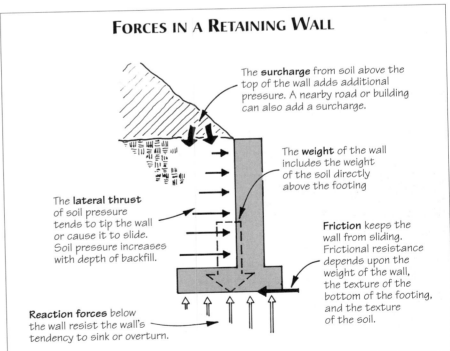

FORCES IN A RETAINING WALL

The **surcharge** from soil above the top of the wall adds additional pressure. A nearby road or building can also add a surcharge.

The **weight** of the wall includes the weight of the soil directly above the footing

The **lateral thrust** of soil pressure tends to tip the wall or cause it to slide. Soil pressure increases with depth of backfill.

Friction keeps the wall from sliding. Frictional resistance depends upon the weight of the wall, the texture of the bottom of the footing, and the texture of the soil.

Reaction forces below the wall resist the wall's tendency to sink or overturn.

Figure 20. The greater the depth of the wall, the greater the total lateral force of the soil. This exerts an overturning force that is resisted by the weight of the soil over the footing and the weight of the wall itself. Friction at the base of the footing keeps the wall from sliding.

MASONRY RETAINING WALL DETAILS

Concrete Block

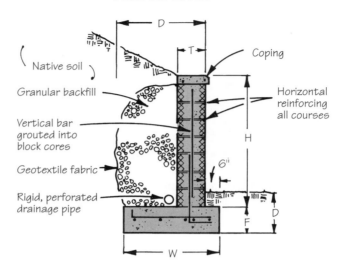

Native soil

Granular backfill

Vertical bar grouted into block cores

Geotextile fabric

Rigid, perforated drainage pipe

Coping

Horizontal reinforcing all courses

Poured Concrete

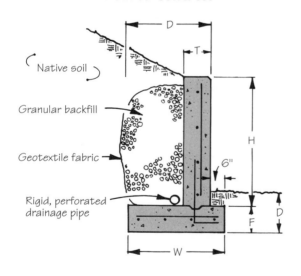

Native soil

Granular backfill

Geotextile fabric

Rigid, perforated drainage pipe

Mortared or Dry-Laid Stone

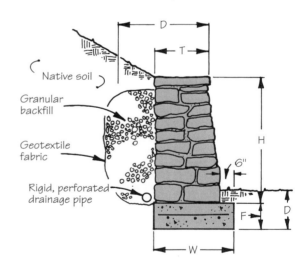

Native soil

Granular backfill

Geotextile fabric

Rigid, perforated drainage pipe

RECOMMENDED DIMENSIONS FOR LOW MASONRY RETAINING WALLS*

H	W	Steel Rebar	Bar Spacing	F	T	D
2'	20"	#3 ($^3/_8$")	2'-0" o.c.	9"	8"	Local
3'	25"	#4 ($^1/_2$")	2'-0" o.c.	10"	8"	frost
4'	32"	#5 ($^5/_8$")	2'-0" o.c.	11"	10"	depth or
5'	42"	#5 ($^5/_8$")	1'-6" o.c.	12"	12"	12"-18"

*Suggested details for walls no higher than 5 feet where dense, coarse-grain soil exists below footings. Not for loose or soft sand, peat, or clay.

similar to common foundation footing drains. Good practice is to separate the backfill from the native soil face of the excavation with geotextile fabric, often nothing more unusual than "weed mat."

Freeze Damage

The case described above was unusual in two regards: It ended in catastrophic failure, and the prime cause of failure was not freeze damage. In the northern half of the country at least, most retaining wall problems result from the expansion of wet soil when it freezes during cold weather. This type of failure is still an indirect result of backfilling with water-retentive soil and/or the lack of good drainage, but it is frost action that causes the damage.

Figure 21 shows retaining walls suffering from tipping brought on by frozen soil. This kind of damage often occurs over a period of years. With each freeze, the soil expands and pushes the wall outward a little bit. Then, as the soil thaws, it settles down to take up the extra space. I call this frost ratcheting, as it progresses in small increments, and never reverses itself.

The best solution for frost damage is to use gravel or sand backfill and footing drains. In some cases, you may be able to use 2-inch extruded polystyrene foam insulation to help retain ground heat and thereby prevent freezing. Put the foam directly against the back of the wall from the footing to just below grade at the top of the wall, and horizontally across the top of the granular backfill, again just below grade. This strategy is appropriate where a large amount of granular backfill cannot be accommodated, such as a tight site where excavation is limited. Consider foam insulation anywhere you don't have room to place backfill all the way to frost depth.

To paraphrase from an engineering text, the forces exerted by freez-

TIMBER RETAINING WALL DETAILS

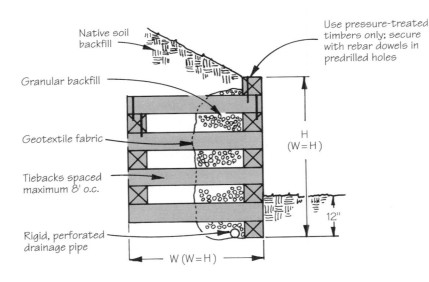

Native soil backfill

Use pressure-treated timbers only; secure with rebar dowels in predrilled holes

Granular backfill

Geotextile fabric

Tiebacks spaced maximum 8' o.c.

Rigid, perforated drainage pipe

H (W=H)

12"

W (W=H)

RECOMMENDED DIMENSIONS FOR LOW TIMBER CRIB WALLS*

Timber Size	Dowel Size	Spacing of Tiebacks
6x6	1/2" (#4 bar)**	6'-0" max
8x8	3/4" (#6 bar)**	8'-0" max

* Details apply to walls no higher than 5 feet.

** In acidic soils, increase by 1/4" or use hot-dipped galvanized.

Figure 21. In northern climates, the freeze-thaw cycle is the primary cause of retaining wall failure. Wet soil expands as it freezes, exerting enormous force against the wall, pushing it outward. As the soil thaws, it settles into the space against the wall and the cycle is set to begin again with the next frost. With poured concrete walls, the entire wall often tips as a whole (left). In the case of block walls (center) or mortared stone walls (right), cracks and bulges may appear as sections of the wall tip.

ing ground are too great to be resisted by any practical structural design. The only prevention is to eliminate the conditions which lead to freezing: water and cold.

Shear Failure

Figure 22 shows a relatively unusual condition known as shear failure. In this case, the upper part of the wall has managed to slide forward without tipping, along a failed mortar line. Mortar is not an effective glue; it usually fails under load unless there is a large compressive force such as the weight of a house sitting on it.

Sometimes the slippage occurs between the footing and the soil beneath (usually with clay soils), in which case the shear failure is also called a slipping failure. That's why you should always set footings 12 to 18 inches below grade and compact any fill between the toe of the footing and the footing excavation.

Other Problems

Look at Figure 23. Is this freeze damage or is it the tree? In a case like this it is hard to tell, because the forces exerted by growing tree roots

are nearly as irresistible as the force of freezing ground. Don't plant large or fast-growing trees near retaining walls.

Figure 24 illustrates classic bad design, frost damage, and material deterioration. How could anyone expect a stack of railroad ties spiked together to resist ground forces? The leaning end of the wall should have been secured to the corner of the foundation or anchored with timber or steel deadmen back into the earth behind. If that had been done, and properly drained backfill used, this wall would still be serviceable. The drainage would also have helped retard the decay visible in the top tie.

When building timber crib walls, dowel the timbers together with lengths of rebar. Driving spikes is ineffective and often splits the timbers, sometimes long after the wall is built. Instead, drill holes the same size as the rebar dowels you are using. Be sure to treat all cut ends and holes with a preservative.

How To Avoid Failures

Like anything else you build, to avoid failure in low retaining walls

you must design the wall right and build it accordingly. Here are the basic guidelines for walls no higher than 5 feet:

- Always use durable materials on sound footings. For poured concrete walls, use a 3,500 psi mix. For timber walls, use only pressure-treated timbers.
- Take into account local frost depth.
- Provide well-drained granular backfill with geotextile separation from native soil.
- Make the footings wide enough (see "Retaining Wall Details").
- Don't ever place footings on fill, no matter how much you compact it.
- Use proper reinforcement with masonry walls and tiebacks in the case of timber walls.
- Wherever you need to add fill in front of a footing, use good quality, compacted granular fill. This may help the footing resist slipping. However, to get any design "credit" for resisting slipping, you must pour the footing against the undisturbed face of the excavation trench.

Figure 22. Shear failure occurs when the force of the soil causes the retaining wall to slide along a mortar joint, but without tipping over.

Figure 23. Tree roots can cause retaining walls to lean; keep large or fast-growing trees away.

Figure 24. Railroad ties stacked and spiked together, but without tiebacks into the earth behind, cannot resist the force exerted by wet or frozen soil. Poor drainage also accelerates rotting.

Modular concrete an option. There are several excellent modular concrete block retaining wall systems that incorporate geogrid anchorage into the backfill, including Keystone Retaining Wall Systems Inc. (Minneapolis, MN; 800/747-8971; www.keystonewalls.com), Unilock (800/864-5625; www.unilock.com), and Versa-Lok (Oakdale, MN; 800/770-4525; www.versa-lok.com). These products are similar in principle to the timber crib walls, and generally require more excavation and backfill than concrete walls. Where this can be accommodated, modular walls will probably be a competitive option. As with all retaining walls, success depends on good footings and drainage. Since they are unmortared, modular block walls are a little more forgiving than solid masonry to minor settlement or frost action.

By Robert Randall, P.E., a structural engineer in Mohegan Lake, N.Y.

Septic Systems: Remodeler's Guide

Many suburban or rural remodeling projects can involve a confrontation with a septic system when a contractor does any one of the following:

• increases the amount of sewage generated by changing the use of the building or adding facilities;

• changes the footprint of the building, interfering with the location of septic tanks, pipes, and absorption wells or fields;

• provides for delivery of materials or the passage of heavy construction equipment over a portion of a septic system.

In order to avoid problems, either with code violations or with septic system operation, it's wise to have a basic understanding of septic system fundamentals.

Sewerage systems were originally just holes in the ground that were blocked up with stones, bricks, blocks, wood, etc., to provide a cavity where all household waste could enter and be absorbed into the ground. When one of these *cesspools* failed, another one was usually added after it (Figure 25), and then another and so on. Then came the modern septic system, which generally consists of two basic components to handle household waste, a *septic tank* which acts as a settling and digestion chamber and a *leaching system* which returns

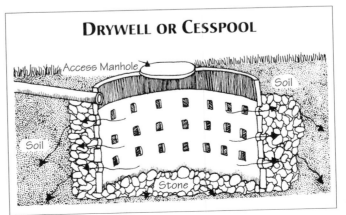

DRYWELL OR CESSPOOL

Figure 25. Cesspools and drywells are identical in construction. The only way to tell the difference is by what's going into it: fresh sewage (cesspool), or clarified effluent (drywell).

the *clarified effluent* to the ground.

In many states, the bottom of the leaching system must be located a minimum of 4 feet above the seasonal high groundwater level in an attempt to provide proper treatment of effluent before it reaches the water table. This requirement has resulted in the "elephant mounds" (raised leach beds) so common now on poor soils. It also often requires a *pumping station* to get the effluent up to the field. (Refer to the "Septic System Glossary," page 26, for explanations of septic system terminology.)

Let's look at some situations where septic systems should concern a remodeling contractor and what he should to do save himself expense and aggravation.

Increasing Load

It is often necessary to demonstrate to code-enforcement people that an existing system is adequate to handle increased loads. In many states, verification of the existing system is required whenever the number of bedrooms (not bathrooms) in a dwelling is increased. Bedrooms rather than fixtures determine occupancy. Verification is also required when the use of a dwelling changes, such as from seasonal to year-round use. If a system is shown to be inadequate for the increased flow (which is often the case), a new one will have to be designed, approved, and installed.

Adding a hot tub, a dish or clothes washer, or a garbage disposal onto an older system may *not* require a septic system upgrade by code. However, increased usage of a system built to handle the water consumption of 30 years ago will probably create a problem.

Solutions. Where it's permissible, I add a separate drywell or a leaching line for a washing machine or hot-tub drain to avoid introducing excessive soaps and bacteria-killing chemicals into an existing system. The *grey water* from these two fixtures is likely to cause more upset to a functioning system than any other wastewater we could add.

Dishwashers and garbage disposals can also cause problems. They should be discharged into septic tanks in order to separate and trap solids and greases, separating them from the wastewater. This protects the absorption surfaces of leach fields or drywells.

Although septic systems designed in recent years are *supposed* to be able to handle all of these appliances, many systems have proven marginal. Some states, such as New Hampshire, are starting to require larger septic tanks, or some means of reducing or separating kitchen-wastes input, whenever a garbage disposal is installed.

Low-volume appliances. Water conservation, where permitted, is a realistic option for offsetting increased demands on a septic system. Reducing the volume of water a flush toilet uses from over 5 gallons to less than 1 1/2 could make it possible to install other water-consuming fixtures or provide relief for a marginal system. Low-volume sink and shower aerators are also available. (Some states permit a considerable reduction in leach field size for such systems.)

Figure 26. High-tech comes to the rescue. This hand-held wand can locate a small transmitting "mole" taped to the end of a snake. Here the snake is about to be inserted through the tank outlet to locate the leach field or drywell.

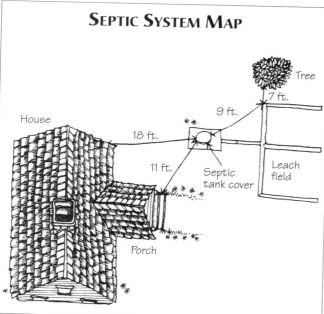

SEPTIC SYSTEM MAP

House
18 ft.
9 ft.
7 ft.
Tree
11 ft.
Septic tank cover
Leach field
Porch

Figure 27. Map out the septic system before starting an addition or deck. Check clearances to basements and slabs allowed by code in your area.

In short, it's best to check with the appropriate state agency, the local building inspector, or a septic designer familiar with local codes to be sure that you are covering yourself for any of these upgrades. When working in an unfamiliar town, keep in mind that local codes can be more strict than state codes.

Changing Footprints

Many building codes ignore the existing septic system for any project that does not change use or flow as discussed above, even when plans involve adding onto the building. In these cases, it's completely up to a builder to locate and identify septic system components at the planning stage to avoid later conflict, either with the system or the owner. Special tools are available to help you locate underground components (Figure 26).

No one wants to have the top of their septic tank become the thermal mass of their new sunspace. Septic tanks generate offensive and explosive gasses during normal operation and can, in some cases, leak their contents into the surrounding ground. For this reason, codes require septic tanks and leach fields to be a safe distance from basements and slabs — typically 10 to 35 feet depending on the type of foundation and whether it has perimeter drains (Figure 27).

These and other distance requirements can be supplied by your designer or inspector. Some jurisdictions may grant waivers in certain cases where it is impossible to meet requirements and the solution is deemed appropriate.

Let's consider what we might do when it becomes impossible to construct an addition without interfering with some part of a septic system.

Moving or replacing a system. Surprisingly, it's not really difficult to move a concrete septic tank. Most septic tank companies should be willing to lift and reset a tank for $200 to $300 given reasonable access to the site and a tank that has been almost completely emptied and unearthed all the way to the bottom. Tanks over 1,000-gallon capacity may be a different story, as they are generally delivered in two halves (most septic truck hoists cannot lift an assembled 1,500-gallon tank), and once they are in place for some time they are hard to get apart. Fortunately, they aren't commonly used for most residences.

Moving a steel septic tank would be an unlikely consideration, as most steel tanks last 30 years at best, and should be replaced by concrete tanks when relocated. Don't plan to replace a 500-gallon steel tank with a 500-gallon concrete tank, however, even if code permits (which is unlikely), and the smaller tank is available. The cost difference between even a 750-gallon and a 1,000-gallon tank is only about $50. The larger tank is a better value because it does a better job.

Plastic tanks (a more recent innovation) would be well worth moving, especially because of their high cost (around twice that of concrete). Because of their ease of handling, they may provide a good replacement alternative for hard-to-reach sites. As for reusing fiberglass tanks, I've heard stories about them deteriorating, so I would assess the tank's condition before moving. In all cases, call a pumper to have the

---

THE SEPTIC TANK

Untreated household sewage will quickly clog all but the most porous gravel if released directly into the soil. The function of the septic tank is to condition the sewage so that it can percolate into the ground without clogging the soil. Within the tank, three important processes take place:

1. The heavier, solid particles in the sewage settle to the bottom of the tank forming a layer of sludge. Lighter materials, includ-ing fat and grease, float to the surface forming a "scum layer."

2. Bacteria living in the septic tank break down some of the organic solids into liquid components, helping to reduce the buildup of sludge in the tank.

3. Sludge and scum are stored within the septic tank rather than being allowed to flow out into the leaching system where they would quickly clog the soil.

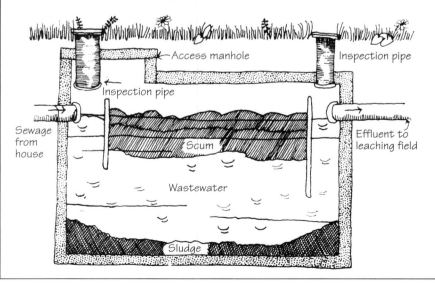

TROUBLESHOOTING NOTES

1. ***Check lowest fixture or drain.*** If problem is septic blockage, water should back up through any drain which is below level of toilet when flushed. Check washing machine outlet, floor drain, bathtub, downstairs apartment, or remove cleanout plug carefully (to avoid a flood). If not backup, problem is probably with toilet or other household plumbing only.

2. ***D-Box problems.*** If distribution box for side-hill trench system is out of level, one trench may be taking all water and "failing." Re-level pipes and block outlet to overload trench for several months. Roots may also be blocking one or more pipes. Remove roots and seal joints where roots enter if possible.

3. ***Pumps and floats.*** Exercise care handling pumps as they have 110- or 220-volt supply lines, which may not have GFIs. Some float systems (which turn pump and alarm on and off) may also contain full line voltage. Use insulating rubber gloves and follow procedures with a disinfecting hand wash for sanitation. Or call licensed plumber, if required by code.

4. ***Snake safety.*** Exercise care using snake in cleanouts or drains as some waterborne diseases can be transferred through contact. Use rubber gloves and surgical mask and follow with disinfecting wash. Stiff garden hose can sometimes be used in place of snake. Disinfect after use.

5. ***Failed field.*** Usually means soil plugged due to age, overuse, underdesign, lack of maintenance, or a combination of these. Requires field replacement or rest. (See "alternating fields" in Septic System Glossary.)

6. ***Failed drywell.*** Same reasons as (5) above. However, drywells can sometimes be excavated around and repacked with crushed stone to create a new soil surface for absorption. Check codes.

7. ***Pipe problems.*** Settling, breaking, crushing, pulling apart, and back-

sloping are installation related. Freezing, plugging at joints, and root plugging (though also caused by poor installation) can occur later. Insulating, replacing, releveling, sealing joints, and properly backfilling will resolve most problems.

8. ***Find septic tank.*** If homeowner does not know exact location of septic system or have accurate plan to follow, start looking for septic tank outside of house where waste pipe exits basement wall. (Note pipe direction through wall.) If plumbing exits below slab, check side of house with roof vent, especially if most of plumbing is on that side of house. Look for spot on the ground where snow melts first, grass turns brown, or there is a slight depression or mound. Steel tanks will sometimes bounce slightly when jumped on, but be careful, steel lids rust out!

A thin steel rod with a tee handle makes a handy probe. Drive probe until achieving several "hits" at the same depth to indicate tank top. A metal detector can help. Even concrete tanks and cesspool covers generally have steel reinforcing within. Another trick is to insert a snake in house cleanout and push it until it stops. Gently sliding snake against inlet baffle can often send a shock that can be heard and/or felt at ground surface by second person. (Note that sometimes a snake can curl up within a septic tank or, particularly, in a cesspool, sometimes making this technique useless.)

If snake hits obstruction but cannot be felt at surface, remove it from cleanout and measure its penetration. Draw an arc the distance of snake penetration from the house and try again with the probe. Remember that the pipe from the house may not be heading straight towards the tank.

If all else fails, locate and uncover the waste pipe where it leaves the house and again every few feet until the tank is located. Or ask previous owner, neighbor, or septic pumper who may have serviced the system in the past.

Note: Devices are available that transmit a radio signal along a snake or from a tiny "mole." Signal is traced by a receiver wand as snake is pushed through waste pipe.

9. ***Determining the type of tank found.***
• ***Primary/secondary septic tank.*** Two or more tanks are used in some installations for better settling and detention of solids. First tank should have fresh waste entering directly from house. (Flush colored paper towel down toilet and watch it enter at inlet manhole.) Second tank should have a little floating grease and scum, with some settled sludge at bottom. Note that septic tank always has an outlet unless it is being used as a holding tank.
• ***Cesspool or drywell.*** Likely has no outlet and seldom has an inlet baffle. Liquid level could be low in a septic tank if tank is rusted out (steel tank) or if center seam leaks (concrete tank). If fresh waste is present, see Glossary, "cesspool." If no fresh waste is present, see Glossary, "drywell."
• ***One of a series of cesspools*** (see Glossary, "cesspool").
• ***Greasetrap.*** Found in restaurants, inns, markets, etc. (see Glossary).
• ***Pump tank*** (see Glossary). If water runs back into septic tank from the outlet pipe when the tank is pumped out, system has probably failed. See (5) or (6) above.

10. ***Inlet/Outlet problems.*** Plugging often occurs from scum buildup within baffles, roots entering through poorly sealed joints, tanks installed out-of-level or backwards, or pipes sticking into the tank too far and nearly hitting baffles, blocking waste. Correct as needed.

11. ***Locating field or drywell.*** Follow directions for finding septic tank (8), except start at septic tank outlet rather than at house. Snake will not hit a baffle within drywell as there is none. It may or may not hit side of D-Box but could pass through into one of outlet pipes.

SEPTIC SYSTEM TROUBLESHOOTING GUIDE

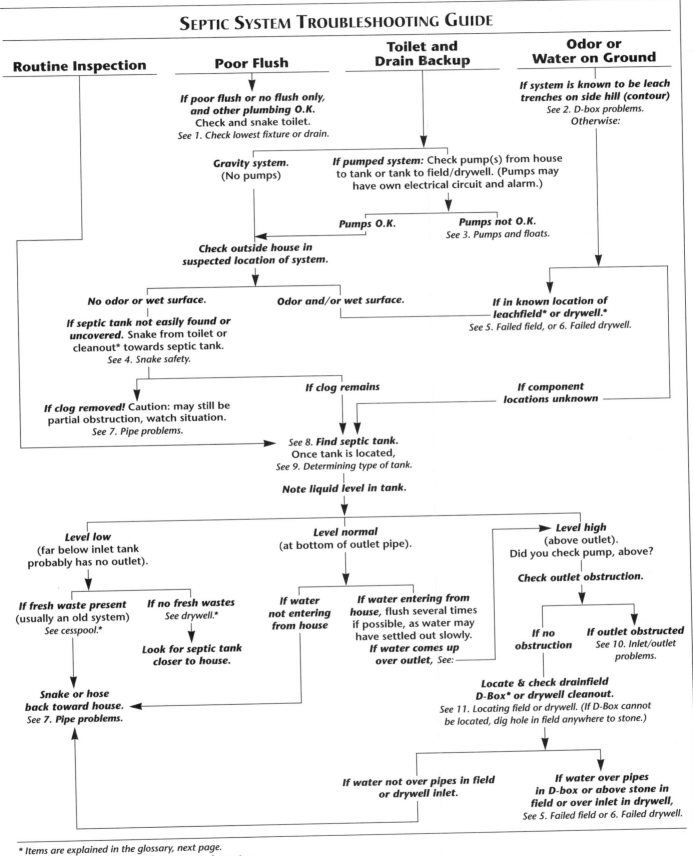

Routine Inspection

Poor Flush

Toilet and Drain Backup

Odor or Water on Ground

If poor flush or no flush only, and other plumbing O.K. Check and snake toilet. *See 1. Check lowest fixture or drain.*

If system is known to be leach trenches on side hill (contour) See 2. D-box problems. Otherwise:

Gravity system. (No pumps)

If pumped system: Check pump(s) from house to tank or tank to field/drywell. (Pumps may have own electrical circuit and alarm.)

Pumps O.K.

Pumps not O.K. *See 3. Pumps and floats.*

Check outside house in suspected location of system.

No odor or wet surface.

If septic tank not easily found or uncovered. Snake from toilet or cleanout* towards septic tank. *See 4. Snake safety.*

Odor and/or wet surface.

If in known location of leachfield or drywell.* See 5. Failed field, or 6. Failed drywell.*

If clog remains

If component locations unknown

If clog removed! Caution: may still be partial obstruction, watch situation. *See 7. Pipe problems.*

See 8. **Find septic tank.** Once tank is located, *See 9. Determining type of tank.*

Note liquid level in tank.

Level low (far below inlet tank probably has no outlet).

Level normal (at bottom of outlet pipe).

Level high (above outlet). Did you check pump, above?

Check outlet obstruction.

If fresh waste present (usually an old system) *See cesspool.**

*If no fresh wastes See drywell.**

Look for septic tank closer to house.

If water not entering from house

If water entering from house, flush several times if possible, as water may have settled out slowly. *If water comes up over outlet, See:*

If no obstruction

If outlet obstructed See 10. Inlet/outlet problems.

Locate & check drainfield D-Box or drywell cleanout. See 11. Locating field or drywell. (If D-Box cannot be located, dig hole in field anywhere to stone.)*

Snake or hose back toward house. See 7. Pipe problems.

If water not over pipes in field or drywell inlet.

If water over pipes in D-box or above stone in field or over inlet in drywell, See 5. Failed field or 6. Failed drywell.

---

* Items are explained in the glossary, next page.
Numbered items are explained in accompanying notes.

tank cleaned out beforehand, both for ease of handling and for inspection of the tank and its baffles.

Moving a leach field is quite a different story. There is no practical way to reuse much of anything from an old leach field, except perhaps the distribution box (and I'm not sure that there are many folks who would want to handle a used "D-box"). Because of the life expectancy of an average leach field, it would probably be best to rebuild the field in a different location if it is over ten years old anyway, especially if the system has been poorly maintained.

I suspect that most states will require a new system approval if the leach field is being moved more than just a few feet or if it is within 75 feet of surface water or wells. If possible, eliminating a portion of the existing leach field to meet distance requirements and adding a second alternating leach field to fulfill size requirements would be best.

If a leach field or drywell must be replaced, the materials excavated from the old field or well will be quite offensive at first and should be handled with caution, but a few hours of good sunny weather will dispel the odors amazingly well, and the result-ing material spread out below a few inches of clean topsoil will provide a good base for a lawn. Keep this material 75 feet from water supplies, and the customer's and neighbors' wells. (Check your local codes, please!) If the old field or drywell has begun to fail, that is, wastewater is standing in the system, it is best to have it pumped out first. Try to find a patient and understanding licensed septic hauler to help you out.

Avoiding Vehicle Damage

It's prudent to know the exact location of a septic tank and other components if you are expecting the

Septic System Glossary

Alarm: An electromechanical device that provides audible and visual indication that the water level in a pump or holding tank is above what it is supposed to be.

Alternating leach field: One of two or more leach fields designed to be used while the other(s) rest. They are generally fed via a manually operated diverter valve located in the line from the septic tank.

Baffles: Pipe tees or partitions within a septic tank, which reduce turbulence at the inlet and prevent floating greases and scum from escaping into the leaching system at the outlet. (They are usually the first part of a steel tank to rust away, leaving the leach field or dry-well unprotected from excessive solids overloading.)

Cesspool: The original type of sewerage system, often still in use in older homes. They were simply a single hole in the ground loosely blocked up with locally available materials — stone, brick, block, or railroad ties — and capped either with ties covered with a layer of old steel roofing or a cast-in-place concrete lid with a cleanout hole near the center. All

household wastewater entered and the liquid portion was absorbed into the ground. When the soil plugged, a new cesspool was added. Wiser installers placed an elbow, or better still, a tee in the outlet pipe from the first cesspool, creating a baffle to hold back the floating greases and scums (see **Baffles**).

In a sense, this created the first type of septic system, because the first cesspool in the line, sealed by its own demise, served as a septic tank and the subsequent tank provided a greater degree of settling and separation of soil-plugging solids and some absorption. (Owners often have the first tank pumped out to maintain system operation.)

Chambers or ameration chambers: Open-bottomed precast concrete or plastic structures, which are placed next to each other in an excavation to take the place of crushed stone in a leach field. Unlike leach fields, heavy-duty chambers can be driven over.

Cleanout: A removable plug in a "wye," or a "tee" in a sewer line, where a snake can be inserted to clear a blockage.

Distribution box or D-Box: Usually a small square concrete box within a leach field from which all pipes lead to disperse effluent within the field. Newer boxes should be marked at the surface to protect from vehicle traffic.

Drywell: Constructed identically to a cesspool and differs only in that the clarified effluent from a septic tank or the wastewater from a washing machine or other grey water may enter. Modern drywells are often precast perforated rings surrounded by crushed stone to increase the absorption area.

Drywells are not commonly installed today because of laws requiring the bottom of a leaching system to be 4 feet above the seasonal high-water table.

Effluent: The liquid that flows out of the septic tank after the tank has "taken out the big pieces."

Grease trap: An in-ground chamber similar to a septic tank, usually used at restaurants, markets, and inns to trap grease from the kitchen wastewater before it reaches the septic tank. Unusual to find in private homes.

delivery of heavy materials or will be operating heavy equipment on site, even if only on the driveway. (I've seen more than one drywell or old steel septic tank under the middle of a driveway.) Because some tanks may weaken with age, and modern trucks and equipment are often much heavier than older models, it would be well to know what you are dealing with to avoid costly "pitfalls."

It may be possible to brace the lid of a tank that must be driven over with thick steel plates, railroad ties, or other materials once you know its location. A leach field should never be driven over and would be consid-erably more difficult to protect because of the greater area involved. Use good judgment, discuss liability with the owner, and perhaps seek the assistance of a local installer or pumper willing to help you assess the situation.

Building On Top

Setting a Sonotube on top of a con-crete septic tank to support a deck would probably cause little harm as long as the inlet, cleanout, and outlet openings on top of the tank were not obstructed by either the tube or the deck. (Indeed, this footing would probably be the most substantial of the whole job.) Supporting a heavier load might warrant keeping a tube close to the edge of a tank unless it were a heavy-duty variety. The same principles would apply to drywells. (In all cases, check codes.)

Avoid setting anything on steel tanks because they cannot support much weight. If a steel tank is that close to an addition, it should be replaced while work is being done anyway because of its limited life expectancy and the possibility of reduced access to replace or main-tain it in the future.

As for setting a Sonotube or other building component over a leach

---

Grey water: All liquid wastewater except for the toilet wastes (sink, shower, washer, etc.).

Leaching system: The part of a septic system that returns water to the ground for reabsorption. Could be a drywell, leach field, trenches, chambers, etc.

Leach bed: A leaching system which consists of a continuous layer of crushed stone about a foot deep, usually in a rectangular layout, with perforated pipes laid level throughout to disperse efflu-ent as evenly as possible over the entire bed.

Leach field: Term often used to describe either a leach bed or leach trenches.

Leach trenches: Built essentially like beds, except that each pipe is in its own stone-filled level trench, usu-ally 3 feet wide. Each trench can be at a different level than the other trenches. Well suited to sloping ground.

Mound (or raised) system: A leach bed built on a mound of fine to medium-grained sand to elevate it above the seasonal high water table and/or to accommodate a system on a hillside.

Percolation test: A shallow, hand-dug hole saturated with water, per-formed as a part of a septic design to determine the soil's permeability — the rate at which water is absorbed by the soil — which dic-tates the system size.

Pump station, pump tank: A watertight container, usually (but not always) separate from the septic tank, into which effluent flows by gravity and is then ejected by a submersible electric pump through a pressure line to the leaching system. Pump tanks often are hooked to an alarm to warn of pump failure.

Seasonal high water table: The highest elevation that groundwa-ter reaches within the year (usually in the spring). Many states require the bottom of a leaching system to be at least 4 feet above this point.

Septic tank: A watertight chamber, which all household wastewater enters for settling and anaerobic digestion of greases and solids. Original tanks were made of asphalt-coated steel. Modern tanks are made of concrete, fiberglass, or plastic. All tanks should have a set of baffles, which are critical to their operation.

Most tanks have an inspection hatch at both the inlet and the outlet and some have a third hatch in between for pumping access. Locations of each of these should be recorded and/or marked. Steel tanks often have one round lid that covers the entire tank.

Septic tanks should be pumped every three years or so in normal operation. They should not be treated with any additives and should be protected from receiving any of the harmful chemicals used in many homes and commercial workshops. This includes disinfec-tants or bleaches, which can kill bacteria in the tank, and solvents, darkroom chemicals, or other materials that could pollute the water supply.

Septic design: Usually consists of a topographic survey, test pit, and perc test plus information about the water supply and subdivision and a filing fee to the state pre-pared by either a licensed designer or the owner.

Test pit: A hole dug to determine soil type, seasonal high water table, and depth to ledge. Some states require a test pit of specific depth (to determine that ledge is a minimum number of feet below bed bottom) while others require only a shallow pit to determine depth to hardpan soils.

field, most states do not permit anything to be built over the field except lawns and gardens (no trees or shrubs).

Note that decks installed over shallow septic tanks or pipes can create freezing problems by keeping the insulating layer of snow from reaching the ground. A couple of inches of extruded polystyrene over tanks and pipes can help prevent problems.

Documentation

Perhaps the easiest part of this whole task, yet the part that is most often overlooked, is making a record of the work for future reference. At the least, a customer should be provided with accurate measurements of all known parts of his system for maintenance needs and the dates when work was done. A simple plot plan hung on the cellar wall next to the plumbing can provide great assistance to a homeowner in a future emergency.

By Russ Lanoie, a licensed septic system designer and installer in New Hampshire.

CHAPTER 2

WOOD FRAMING

- Wall and Floor Framing

- Wood I-Joists

- Roof Framing

- Truss Bracing

- Shed Dormers

- Details for Wood Shrinkage

WALL AND FLOOR FRAMING

Over the past 17 years, first as a builder and then as a representative of the Western Wood Products Association, I have traveled extensively, talking to builders and code officials to see how framing is done throughout the country. While I've found regional differences, I've also found a few serious framing problems that tend to crop up everywhere, again and again.

All of these problems are covered by the model building codes. A given problem might occur because the builder doesn't know better, or because framers are paying more attention to other construction needs. Either way, these framing defects not only cause trouble with code officials, but cause problems big and small down the line.

Here are some of the most common framing errors I come across, along with code-approved, structurally sound solutions.

Framing Openings Cut in Floors

A common problem occurs with floors when subs cut through joists to make room for plumbing runs, hvac ductwork, or other mechanical elements. The loads these cut joists supported must be properly transferred to other joists. You can do this using header joists, end-nailed across the cut ends of the interrupted joists, to carry loads to the adjacent trimmer joists. Where the header has to span a space less than 4 feet wide, a single header end-nailed to the trimmer joists will do.

Things get more complicated if the header must span more than 4 feet, as in Figure 1. If that's the case, both header and trimmer joists should be doubled. The doubled trimmer joists must be nailed together properly (with spaced pairs of 16-penny nails every 16 inches) so that they act as beams. The header joists must be appropriately anchored to the trim-

mers. End nails will do for header spans up to 6 feet; beyond that, use hangers. Any tail joists over 12 feet should also be hangered.

When you're framing the floor, check the blueprints to see where any such openings might go, and header off any joists that might be in the way in advance. It's much easier than trying to work from underneath the subfloor later.

Holes and Notches

Whenever you cut a hole or notch in a joist, that joist is weakened. You (and your subs) should avoid this whenever possible. And when you absolutely have to cut or notch, you should know the rules for doing it in the least destructive manner.

Figure 2 shows proper guidelines for cutting holes and notches. Straying from these guidelines weakens the joists and risks a red tag from the building official. Trying to fix such problems can be very costly, since it usually involves redoing the plumbing and electrical work along with replacing or doubling the joists.

When Notch Becomes Rip

Occasionally, what might be thought of as a notch turns into a rip, such as when floor joists at the entry of a home are ripped down to allow underlayment for a tile floor (Figure 3). Unfortunately, ripping wide dimension lumber lowers the grade of the material, and is unacceptable under all building codes. You should frame these areas with narrow joists of a higher grade or stronger species, making sure they can carry the load.

Bearing Walls on Cantilevers

How far can a conventionally framed cantilever extend and still support a bearing wall?

Most of the confusion about how far a cantilever can extend beyond its support stems from an old rule of

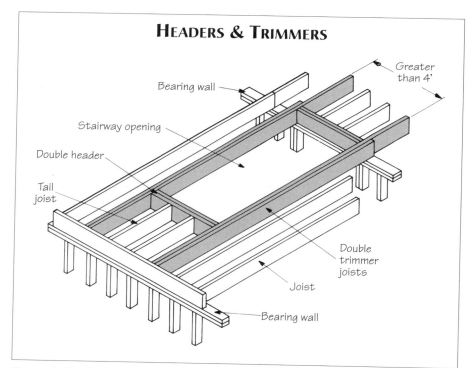

HEADERS & TRIMMERS

Bearing wall

Stairway opening

Double header

Tail joist

Greater than 4'

Double trimmer joists

Joist

Bearing wall

Figure 1. Head off interrupted joists to transfer their loads to adjacent joists. If the header spans more than 4 feet, it must be doubled and the loads transferred to double trimmer joists.

thumb used by builders and code officials alike: the rule of "one-to-three." This states that a joist should extend back inside the building at least three times the length of the cantilevered section — if the cantilevered section hangs 2 feet out, the joists should extend at least 6 feet in.

This rule works fine for nonbearing situations. But it does *not* apply to a cantilever that supports a bearing wall. In this situation, the maximum distance that joists can be cantilevered without engineering them is a distance equal to the depth of the joists, as in Figure 4. So if you are using 2x10 floor joists, the maximum cantilever for those joists supporting a bearing wall is $9^1/4$ inches. Beyond this distance, shear becomes a serious factor, as does the bending moment at the support. This combination could eventually cause splitting of the cantilevered joists. The only way to work around this problem is to have it engineered.

Broken Load Paths

A similar alignment problem relates to maintaining vertical load paths. All loads start at the roof and transfer vertically through the building to the foundation. If they aren't transferred properly, you can end up with cracking of interior finishes or sagging framing. Many cracking problems written off to "settling" are actually due to what might be called broken load paths — paths that end up putting loads on areas not meant to carry them. This is one of the most common framing errors I see, and one to which many building inspectors pay close attention.

Misaligned bearing walls. In other instances, loads carried by bearing walls or posts must be transferred through floor systems. If the bearing wall or post above doesn't line up closely enough with a bearing wall, post, or beam below, the floor joists in between can be overstressed, causing severe deflection. This can even-

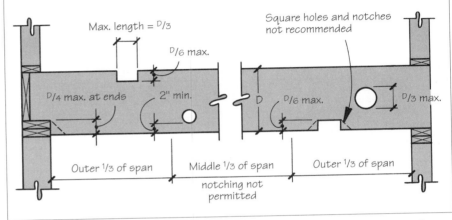

GUIDE FOR CUTTING, NOTCHING, AND BORING JOISTS

Joist Size	Maximum Hole	Maximum Notch Depth	Maximum End Notch
2 x 4	None	None	None
2 x 6	$1^1/2$	$^7/8$	$1^3/8$
2 x 8	$2^3/8$	$1^1/4$	$1^7/8$
2 x 10	3	$1^1/2$	$2^3/8$
2 x 12	$3^3/4$	$1^7/8$	$2^7/8$

Figure 2. In joists, never cut holes closer than 2 inches to joist edges, nor make them larger than one-third the depth of the joist. Don't notch the span's middle third where the bending forces are greatest. No notch should be deeper than one-sixth the depth of the joist, nor one-quarter the depth if the notch is at the end of the joist. Limit the length of notches to one-third of the joist's depth. Use actual, not nominal, dimensions.

Figure 3. Ripping long notches in floor joists, such as to make room for grouted entry floors, weakens the joists unacceptably and violates all codes. Instead, you need to use smaller dimension milled lumber of a higher grade, or set the joists closer together. If necessary, you can fur at the ends to bring non-grouted areas up to level.

tually split the joists, as well as cause finish cracking problems.

How closely must they align? Bearing walls supported by floor joists must be within the depth of the joist from their bearing support below (just as with cantilevers), as in Figure 5.

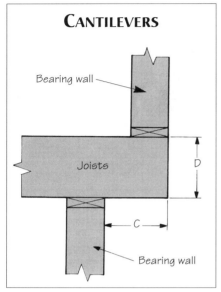

CANTILEVERS

Bearing wall

Joists

D

C

Bearing wall

Figure 4. When a cantilever supports a bearing wall, the distance it extends beyond its support (C) should not exceed the depth of the joist (D).

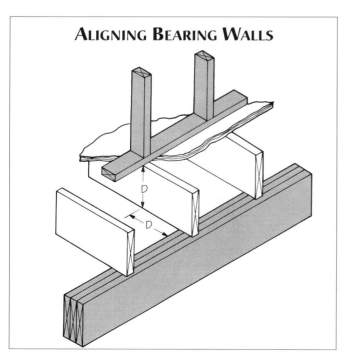

ALIGNING BEARING WALLS

D

D

This code requirement applies only to solid-sawn wood joists. Engineered products such as wood I-beams are required to have the loads line up *directly* over each other, and special blocking is required. Special engineering of either dimensional or engineered lumber may allow placing loads at other locations, but you shouldn't try it without consulting an engineer first.

Bringing columns to foundation properly. If you use a column to support a beam or other member, make sure it bears on something that can in turn support it. A common mistake is to rest one on the floor, without extra blocking or support beneath. Doing this can crush the underlying joists. Columns shouldn't rest on unsupported floor joists; they should run continuously to the foundation, or (if you must have a clear space beneath) to an engineered beam or header to transfer the load out to other columns or bearing members.

Columns shouldn't rest on rim joists either, for similar reasons. If you need to rest a column at the rim, add full-depth vertical blocking inside the rim joist the full depth and width of the column base, so

Figure 5. If a bearing wall doesn't line up with the support below, it should lie no farther away than the depth of the joists (D). If the joists are engineered lumber, the walls and support must align exactly.

that the load is transferred through the blocking to the foundation.

Puny Hangers

A simple but common framing error is hanging a three-member beam (such as three 2x10s nailed together) from a double joist hanger. This usually occurs because triple hangers are hard to find. But if only two of the three members are supported, then only two carry the load. The third member just goes along for the ride. Toe nails or end nails are not going to make it carry the load.

If you're going to use a hanger, use one that holds everything, and use the right size and the correct nails. Undersized hangers and inappropriate nails will weaken the system.

The correct hanger is necessary to carry the vertical load as well as to laterally support the member to prevent rotation. And without the correct nails, the hanger doesn't mean much. Eight-penny galvanized nails or roofing nails won't do. You can buy regular joist hanger nails that are heavy enough to handle the shear stress, yet only 1 1/2 inches long so that they won't go clear through the lumber and possibly cause a split.

Of course, the best way to support a beam is from beneath. When possible, use a beam pocket or a column directly under the end of the beam. Be sure the full bearing surface of the beam is supported clear to the foundation.

Tapering Beams and Joists

It's sometimes necessary (or at least convenient) to taper the ends of ceiling joists or beams to keep them under the plane of the roof, as in Figure 6. But by reducing the depth of the joist or beam, you reduce its load-carrying capacity.

If you must taper-cut the ends of ceiling joists, make sure the length of the taper cut does not exceed three times the depth of the member, and that the end of the joist or beam is at least one-half the member's original depth.

With taper-cut beams, you should also check the shear rating. If you can't meet this criteria, you'll probably have to lower the beam into a pocket so that enough cross-section can be left, after taper-cutting, to carry the applied load.

Raising the Rafters

Another way to add room for attic insulation at the eaves is to set the rafters atop a ledger board running perpendicular over the ceiling joists, as in Figure 7. Unfortunately, builders who do this often fail to put in a rim joist or block the ends of the joists to prevent them from rolling over. The resulting design creates, in essence, hinges at the top and bottom edge of each joist. With a strong enough lateral force, such as a high wind or a strong tremor, all the joists could rotate and fall over — bringing ledger, rafters, and roof crashing down onto the now-flat joists.

To prevent this, install full depth blocking between all joist ends or a rim joist nailed against the ends of the joists. Either solution will also provide a baffle to prevent air from penetrating the ends of the batts and keep the batts (or blown-in insulation) from creeping into the eaves.

Blocking is also a good idea where joists lap over a center girder at foundation level or over a support wall at second-story level. If the centers are unblocked, the job of keeping the joists upright falls to the nails holding the floor sheathing to the joists. These nails just aren't designed to resist the strong sideways forces created by wind or earthquake. Full-depth 2x blocking over center supports will prevent the joists from rotating in such an event. The blocking also stiffens the floor, since it stops the rotation caused by deflection of the joists under load.

What if a few of these blocks get knocked out by mechanical contractors putting in ductwork or plumb-

Figure 6. Overtapering joists to fit beneath roofs creates inadequate joist depth at the plate (left). A proper cut (below) leaves at least half the depth of the joist.

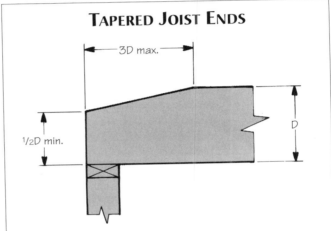

TAPERED JOIST ENDS

3D max.

1/2D min.

D

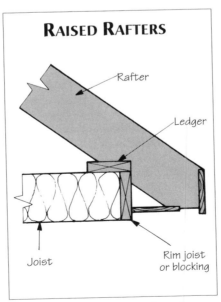

RAISED RAFTERS

Rafter

Ledger

Joist

Rim joist or blocking

Figure 7. When nailing rafters to a ledger over joists to make room for insulation, use a rim joist to keep the joists from rotating.

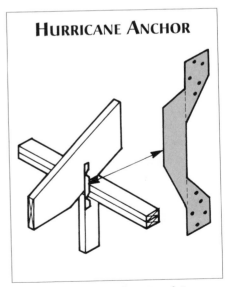

HURRICANE ANCHOR

Figure 8. Nailing rafters to plates, and plates to studs, is not always enough to resist high winds. Hurricane anchors at 4-foot intervals will securely tie rafters to studs.

ing? That's not usually a problem, as long as you don't remove consecutive blocks, so that each joist is blocked on at least one side.

Connecting Rafter to Wall

Conventional construction leaves too little connection between rafters and walls. Nails connect rafter to plate and plate to stud, but do nothing to connect the rafters to the wall itself. Such structures are subject to damage from the high, near-hurricane force winds that

sooner or later blow across virtually every roof.

As a result, the building codes are beginning to get more restrictive about how rafters and trusses are tied to the rest of the building. For example, the 1991 Uniform Building Code has added Appendix Chapter 25, which applies to high wind areas. Under its requirements, rafters or trusses must be tied not just to the top plate, but to the studs below at 4-foot intervals. This means using some kind of metal

connector to provide a positive tie to the studs.

The answer is the hurricane anchor (Figure 8). You don't need to face a hurricane to need it — winds of roof-damaging gale force blow in most parts of the country. If you build in an area subject to high winds (or seismic conditions), you should consider using these or other holddowns.

By David Utterback, a district manager for Western Wood Products Association and WWPA's designated code expert.

WOOD I-JOISTS

Builders who have used solid-wood 2x10s for 15 years know what they can and can't do; when they switch to wood I-joists, however, they're confronted with a relatively new product that has different structural characteristics. The product is often misapplied even by experienced builders.

Some of these errors are caused by poor design, while others are the work of subcontractors who alter the joists after they've been installed. Most of these mistakes could lead to squeaky or bouncy floors — problems that glue-nailed I-joist floors were specifically designed to solve. Other mistakes can cause more serious problems.

What follows are the most common problems I've encountered and ways to avoid them.

Misplaced Holes

The most common problem I see is misplaced and improperly sized holes in the web of the I-joist. With my company's I-joists, for example, you can cut holes up to $1\frac{1}{2}$ inches in diameter anywhere in the web, including right over a bearing point. Anything bigger than that risks compromising the web's shear capacity: The bigger the hole the bigger the problem, and the farther away from a bearing point it has to be.

Sometimes the problem is obvious. For instance, the hole cut for the ducts

in Figure 9 has completely destroyed the web, and with it the joist. (By the way, the problem was fixed by sliding a new I-joist next to the old and rerouting the ductwork.) Less obvious are properly sized holes drilled too close to the bearing point (Figure 10), which also compromises the strength of the joist. There's no need to guess about the location of holes in I-joists: Manufacturers supply hole charts with their I-joists. If you follow the chart, you'll avoid problems.

Hanger Problems

The next most common error is the improper use of joist hangers. The hanger in Figure 11 isn't tall enough to catch the I-joist's top flange. This leaves the top flange without lateral support, making it more likely to roll in the hanger. A worse problem is that the bottom flange had to be chiseled away to make it fit the seat of the hanger. This reduces the strength of the joist.

Sometimes I see hangers used that are wider than the joist flange. In this case, the carpenter has to nail across the gap between the hanger and the flange. If the joist ever moves at the bearing point, the nail will rub against the hanger and cause a squeak. Filling the space in the hanger with plywood blocking may

Figure 9. Routing five ducts through this I-joist meant removing the web, which effectively destroyed the joist.

stop the squeak, but hanger manufacturers say that this increases the stress on the hanger by loading it unevenly. The resulting deflection at the seat of the hanger could leave a void in the decking above and make a bulge in any drywall ceiling below. The bottom line is to use properly sized hangers.

Other common problems with I-joist hangers include:

- *No nails into joists.* I see plenty of hangers nailed to the supporting girder but not to the joist. The I-joist can then rub against the metal hanger and cause a squeak.

- *Too few nails into girder.* Face-mounted hangers need a nail in every hole, but sometimes installers leave some nails out. This greatly reduces the hanger's load-carrying capacity.

- *Wrong-size nails.* Hangers are typically nailed to I-joists by angling a nail down into the bottom flange. Though we recommend 1½-inch-long, 10d nails for this, some installers use 2½-inch-long nails, which go all the way through the flange, hit the bottom of the hanger, and curl under the joist. This can lift the joists slightly and cause a squeak.

- *Unnailed tabs.* Simpson hangers have tabs that bend over the top of the bottom flange to lock the joist to the hanger. It's very common for the nails to be left out of these; again, the penalty is a squeak.

The Two-By Rim

One of the main functions of a rim joist is to transfer loads from the wall above to the wall or foundation below. To accomplish this, the rim joist must be the same depth as the floor joists. A typical 2x10 is only 9¼ inches deep, so it doesn't match up well with a 9½-inch I-joist. Using the 2-by as a rim joist leaves a gap at either the top or bottom (Figure 12). Some manufacturers make 9¼-inch I-joists, but even here a "matching" 2x10 won't do. The 2-by will shrink

Figure 10. These large holes are too close to the end bearing point, so they compromise the strength of the joists. Follow the I-joist manufacturer's hole charts to avoid problems.

Figure 11. Because this joist hanger isn't tall enough to catch the I-joist's top flange, the joist may roll in the hanger. Also, the builder chiseled away the bottom flange to make it fit in the hanger, weakening the joist.

Figure 12. A 2-by rim joist is usually shallower than the I-joists; even if it's not, it will eventually shrink and leave a gap. This concentrates the structural load on the narrow joist webs, which aren't designed to support concentrated loads.

and the I-joists won't, so you'll still end up with a gap.

The trouble with this gap is that it puts all the loads on the joists themselves; in fact, it concentrates the load at the points where the thin I-joist webs meet the flanges. Depending on the web and flange materials, this concentrated force may either crush the web or cause it to knife through

the flange. The same bearing problem occurs where the I-joists cross a girder and support a bearing wall; in this situation, the blocking between the I-joists must be full depth.

The solution, of course, is to use a full-depth rim joist. This can be another I-joist, ripped strips of ¾-inch plywood, or an engineered rim joist. I usually recommend using engineered products because you can lag ledger boards for decks and porches into them without installing special blocking — something you can't easily do with I-joists or plywood. The two products I know of are Timberstrand LSL RimBoard (Trus Joist, 200 E. Mallard Dr., Boise, ID 83706; 866/859-6757), which is made from glued-up aspen chips, and Versa-Rim (Boise Cascade, P.O. Box 50, Boise, ID 83728; 800/232-0788), which is basically a 1-inch-thick LVL.

Joists Interrupted at Girder

Most I-joist systems are designed to run the entire width of the building, regardless of whether they cross an intermediate support. The main reason is performance: A 30-foot I-joist running continuously over an intermediate girder provides a stiffer floor than two 15-footers that break at the girder. This means that the floor in Figure 13 will be bouncier than it should be.

Ease of installation is also important: It takes less time to put up one set of 30-foot joists (a "continuous" span) than two sets of 15-foot joists (two "simple" spans). Using a single, continuous-span I-joist may also eliminate the blocking required where two simple-span I-joists meet above a bearing wall. (This blocking prevents the joist ends from rotating). Where there is a bearing wall above, however, full-depth blocking is always required to transfer the load to the girder.

An additional problem with Figure 13 is the nail in the I-joist's bottom flange. Because it was driven too close to the end of the flange, the nail caused a split. Splitting the flange reduces the allowable bearing stress because the web doesn't have as much flange to bear on; you need a minimum 1 3/4-inch bearing surface under I-joists. Nails should be no closer than 1 1/2 inches from the end.

Shear Destruction

Where I-joists meet rafters at an exterior wall, it's not uncommon for the joist bevels to be cut beyond the inside face of the bearing surface (Figure 14). Even with solid joists this isn't a good idea, because it reduces their effective depth.

Small loads and short spans are less worrisome than heavy loads and long spans, but other factors may contribute to the problem. Note, for example, the load-bearing wall on the left in Figure 14 — the exterior wall of a shed dormer. This wall raises the load on the already weakened joists, perhaps leading to a failure.

Our engineers fixed this problem by having the builder add plywood

Figure 13. Avoid breaking an I-joist at midspan over a girder, as the builder did here. Crossing the girder with a continuous-span I-joist will yield a stiffer floor. Note also the nail splitting the bottom flange, which reduces the joist's carrying capacity.

Figure 14. Beveling a joist beyond the inside of a bearing wall reduces its resistance to shear forces, which are greatest at the bearing. In this photo, the problem is made worse by the wall at the left, which rests on the joists with no bearing wall below.

Figure 15. Notching the flange of an I-joist seriously weakens it; the closer the notch is to the middle of the span, the worse the problem.

gussets to the webs. How far back these need to go depends on the situation and must be worked out by an engineer. It's better to avoid the problem altogether by designing the structure so that the rafter line is as high as possible, ensuring a small bevel cut on the joists.

Notched Flanges

It's not unusual for a plumber or hvac installer to notch part of a joist when installing pipes or heating ducts. With an I-joist, this might mean cutting the flange (Figure 15). I-joists have their highest-strength material in the top and bottom flanges. Cutting a flange seriously compromises the joist capacity and should be avoided at all costs.

The problem was fixed by cutting out the notched section and running a pair of headers between the two adjacent joists. Whether this would work in other cases depends on whether the two adjacent joists can handle the load. To find out, you'll need to go back to your designer or supplier so they can look at the original design. The best solution, of course, is to route mechanicals so as to avoid notching the joist in the first place.

Hollow Girder

Two I-joists that are doubled to serve as a header must be joined together with blocking at joist hanger locations. Without this blocking, one joist will have to support a load that should have been distributed between two (Figure 16). You could end up with a squeaky floor, or even with a lump in the floor. Where several I-joists are joined to form a girder, blocking between the members is even more important.

Attaching Sheathing

Most I-joist floors are covered with glue-nailed sheathing, and are designed to perform as a system. A bad sheathing job can cause squeaks and other problems. Common mis-

Figure 16. The absence of blocking here between the double joists means that the load at the joist hanger will be carried entirely by the I-joist it's attached to, instead of by the girder as a whole. The most likely result is a squeak or sag in the floor.

Figure 17. Notching an I-joist rafter over the inside edge of a wall leaves it bearing not on the heel, where it should, but on the toe. These rafters will split up the middle when loaded.

takes include the following:

- *Missed nails.* Often a nail will miss the joist and end up lying tightly against the side of the flange. When the sheathing moves up and down at that point, the nail rubs against the wood, causing a squeak.

- *Glue sets too soon.* Sheathing should be attached right after the glue is spread. Otherwise, the glue will set and the sheathing will not be properly attached. The problem here is not just squeaking. Most span charts assume that a floor is

properly glued and nailed. If it's not, it will have more bounce than it should.

Weakened Rafters

Toe-bearing is a common mistake with 2-by rafters, and I-joists are no exception. Never notch an I-joist rafter beyond the inside edge of the bearing wall: You risk splitting the web section of the rafter up its centerline (Figure 17).

Some roof framing problems are unique to I-joists (Figure 18). An I-

RIDGE CONNECTIONS

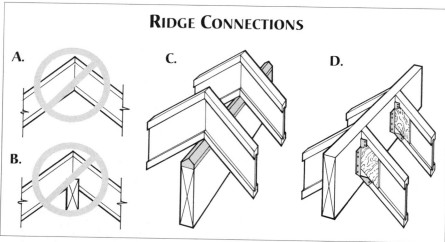

Figure 18. I-joist rafters can't be rested against each other at the ridge like 2-by rafters (A). Birdsmouths aren't permitted either (B). Instead, use a structural ridge and either rest the joists on a beveled plate (C) or hang them from the beam (D).

joist roof is like an I-joist floor in that it requires bearing at both ends. This means that you can't just bring the rafters together at the peak of the roof and expect them to hold each other up. To keep them from failing or sagging, you need to support the peak with a structural beam. You can't cut birdsmouths at the top of I-joist rafters, because this means cutting the bearing flanges. Instead, you'll need to either hang them off the face of the beam with joist hangers or cap the beam with a beveled plate and lay the rafters on top of this.

By Curtis Eck, P.E., a Seattle-based technical representative for Trus Joist MacMillan.

ROOF FRAMING

In recent years, houses have become larger and their roof systems more complicated. In light of this, it's worth revisiting the most common framing errors on both conventional and truss-framed roofs.

Toe-Bearing Rafters

A common error with low-slope rafters is excessive cutting of the rafter seat. This leaves the rafter bearing not on the heel of the seat cut, as it should, but on the toe. The seat cut may run straight from toe to heel, or there may be a deep birdsmouth at the inside edge of the wall — from a structural standpoint there's no difference.

There are two problems with this. One is that you no longer have the full width of the rafter to carry the load. Bearing on the toe effectively reduces the width of the entire rafter. The other problem is that the shear created by the flexing of the rafter can cause a split to start at the inside edge of the top plate. This is a particular problem with cathedral ceilings, where split rafters can lead to cracks in the ceiling drywall. The lumber's slope of grain will determine how likely it is to split, if at all.

But what if your roof is framed with 2x10s when, structurally, you only require 2x6s? Can't you safely overnotch the 2x10 to create an effective 2x6? The answer is no. For one thing, you still risk splitting the rafter. For another, lumber is graded to allow certain types of defects in certain parts of the lumber's cross-section. For instance, larger knots are allowed in 2x10s than in 2x6s. Turning a 2x10 into a 2x6 may put large knots close to the edge, ruining the board's structural integrity.

You can avoid all these problems by cutting the rafter so that it bears on the heel of the seat cut, rather than the toe. If that's not possible, try putting a ledger strip beneath the rafters to catch the heel, or support the rafters with joist hangers nailed into the top plates (Figure 19).

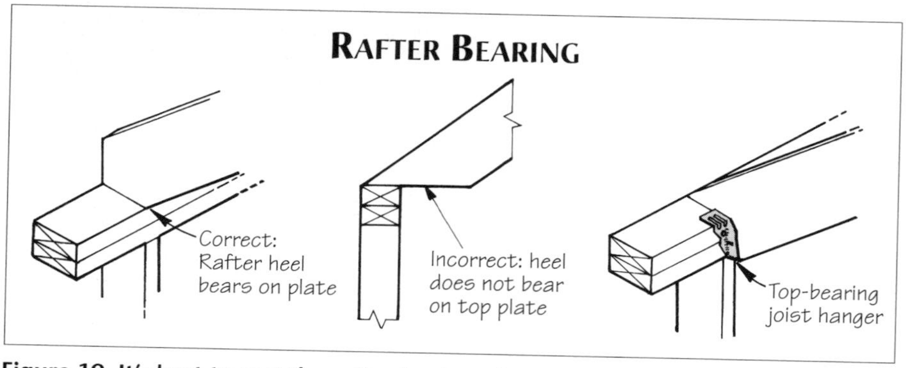

Transferred Loads

Another big problem with roof systems in today's large houses is

RAFTER BEARING

Correct: Rafter heel bears on plate

Incorrect: heel does not bear on top plate

Top-bearing joist hanger

Figure 19. It's best to rest the rafter heel on the plate (left), not on the toe (center). Where this isn't possible, you can sometimes support it with a joist hanger (right). The joist hanger also keeps the rafter from rotating, a job that normally requires ceiling joists or solid blocking.

load transfer. The complexity of some roof structures makes it hard to properly support some of the members. I see too many hips and valleys that are totally unsupported; sometimes these hips and valleys tie into lower ridges that are also unsupported.

Hip and valley rafters need to land on headers or doubled-up rafters sized to handle the loads. Headers around openings like skylights don't necessarily need to be plumb. But remember that the loads on a roof are vertical — not perpendicular to the rafters — and that lumber is strongest when placed on its edge. This means that, in most situations, the header should be put in plumb and its members stepped to follow the roof slope. A rule of thumb is that headers up to 4 feet long can be put in square with the rafters, while anything over 4 feet should be plumb. Header rafters more than 6 feet long should be supported by framing anchors.

Roof loads are also transferred by the purlins and struts used to break up rafter spans. Where I live, near Kansas City, every house has these — even inexpensive starter homes. Too often, the struts are not properly located. Diagonal struts must extend to bearing walls at less than a 45-degree angle from the horizontal. If the struts land on strongbacks set across undersized ceiling joists (Figure 20) or fall on nonbearing walls, the ceiling finish may crack or the doors in those nonbearing walls may bind and stick.

No Rafter Ties

Cathedral ceilings present special problems. If there are no ceiling joists, you must find another way to keep the rafters from pushing the exterior walls out. If not, symptoms can develop up to a year or two after the house has been built, and include cracks at the wall-ceiling intersection, cracks above headers, and walls

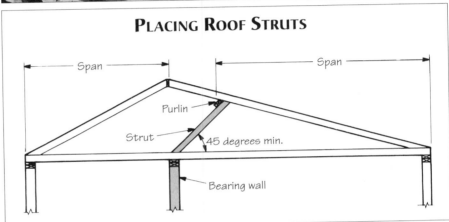

Figure 20. The rafters in this house (top) have been stiffened with a purlin that runs the length of the roof. Because the struts that hold the purlin bear on a set of unsupported ceiling joists, however, chances are that the ceiling will eventually crack. To properly support the roof, the braces need to go from the purlin to a bearing wall, and should not drop below a 45° angle as shown (above).

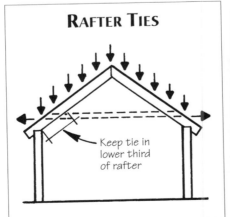

Figure 21. As rafters settle, their outward thrust pushes out on exterior walls. Rafter ties should be placed in the lower third of the rafter span (left) so they have enough leverage to resist this thrust. The ties in this photo (right) serve no structural purpose.

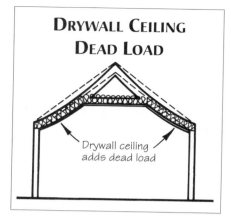

DRYWALL CEILING DEAD LOAD

Drywall ceiling adds dead load

Figure 22. Hanging a ceiling near the middle of the rafter span adds dead load to the rafter at its maximum bending point. Avoid this detail, or use a structural ridge to reduce the outward thrust of the rafters and design the rafters to support the additional dead load.

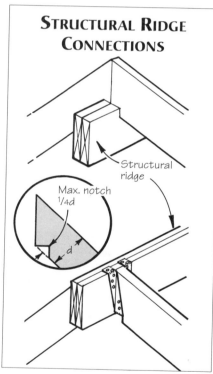

STRUCTURAL RIDGE CONNECTIONS

Structural ridge

Max. notch 1/4d

d

Figure 23. The most effective way to reduce outward roof thrust is to use a structural ridge beam. Either rest the rafters on top of a structural ridge (at top) or use joist hangers attached to the ridge beam (at bottom). The notch at the bottom of the plumb cut should be no deeper than one-fourth the rafter width.

that are greatly out of plumb. No builder needs callbacks on problems like these.

In rooms with attics above them, the ceiling joists or the bottom chords of the trusses create a tension tie between the outside walls. In a cathedral ceiling, open rafter ties can serve the same purpose if they're not placed too high. A good rule of thumb is that unless the roof structure has been specially engineered, don't place the rafter ties above the lower third of the rafter span (Figure 21); otherwise, they won't have enough leverage to resist the rafters' outward thrust.

You'll understand this if you think about the way a tree pruner works. Grabbing the handles at the end gives you plenty of leverage to cut off the limb; grabbing them near the cutter head makes the job considerably harder. Rafter ties do the same thing in reverse — instead of trying to squeeze the outside ends of the rafters together, the rafter ties keep them from moving farther apart. The closer the ties to the bottom of the rafter, the greater the leverage.

If you install ceiling joists near the center of a rafter span and hang drywall from them, you increase the dead load on the roof at the rafter's maximum bending point. This will cause the rafter to deflect and push out on the outside walls even more (Figure 22).

Ridge beams. You can also prevent cathedral ceiling rafters from pushing the walls out by using a structural ridge beam. By holding up the top of the rafters, a structural ridge lets the exterior walls carry the vertical loads applied to them by the rafters, but reduces the outward thrust. Keep in mind that a beam has to be sized to carry the load that will be imposed on it, and that the beam will have a limited span capability. It will also need proper supports at each end, and, if necessary, along its length. Too

often I see ridges that are neither properly sized nor properly supported. Many times the only thing holding up the ridge beam is the rafters themselves, which obviously defeats the purpose of the ridge beam. Designing a structural ridge is a bit complicated for the average builder, so get an engineer to do the calculations.

There are two ways to join rafters to a structural ridge: You can either butt the plumb cut to the ridge beam or you can cut a birdsmouth in the rafters and set them on top of the ridge. Either way is acceptable, as long as you follow the guidelines in Figure 23. A toe-nailed connection is not strong enough.

Trusses

As one would expect from engineered components, trusses present a different set of problems than solid lumber.

Field alteration. Don't try this on your own. Since trusses are engineered systems, they shouldn't be altered on the job site. To do so destroys the integrity of the truss. If you absolutely have to cut a truss, call the truss engineer.

Improper bearing. The average truss is designed to bear on the outside walls of a building and to clear-span everything between. One of the most frequent framing errors I see is nailing the bottom chords of roof trusses to interior partitions. A truss can be engineered with an additional bearing point along its bottom chord, but on the typical roof truss, creating an additional bearing point on the bottom chord will redistribute the loads through the truss. This can cause web members designed for tension to become compression members and vice versa. In extreme cases, the truss could fail.

Another problem with nailing to interior partitions is cracked drywall from truss movement. During the winter months, the uninsulated top chord picks up moisture from the air

Figure 24. Most roof trusses are designed to bear only at the exterior walls. Avoid nailing roof trusses to interior partitions (left); otherwise, as the bottom chord rises with changes in moisture content, it will move the wall with it and open up cracks in the ceiling drywall. Instead, use truss clips (bottom left), which allow the truss to move independently of the partition wall.

But once I tell them to measure the joists and check them for level, they find out that while the joists may contribute to the problem, something else is going on.

What can be done about rising trusses? First of all, don't shim under the wall. The trusses and the wall will nearly always come back down in the summer. If you try to prevent this from happening, you'll create that unwanted bearing point I mentioned earlier. You can also replace the nails holding the bottom chord to the wall with truss clips — metal connectors that let a truss move up and down without taking the wall with it (Figure 24). If you use truss clips, don't screw the ceiling drywall to the truss where it passes over the partition. Instead, hold your screws 12 to 14 inches back from the partition and screw the edge of the ceiling to 2-by nailers that have been fastened to the top plate between the trusses. This will let the drywall flex and prevent a crack from forming at the wall/ceiling intersection.

By David Utterback, a district manager for Western Wood Products Association and WWPA's designated code expert.

and expands. As it expands it arches, pulling the bottom chord up with it. If the bottom chord is nailed to an interior partition, either the nails will simply pull loose or the rising truss will pull the wall right off the floor, opening a gap below the baseboard. Most of the calls I get about this are complaints from builders that the floor joists are shrinking.

TRUSS BRACING

Using roof trusses lets you close in a building quickly and gives you flexibility in placing interior partitions. But except for some data published by the Truss Plate Institute (Alexandria, VA; 703/683-1010), there is little written information on how to install and brace trusses. The few books that do discuss the issue typically show the first truss located directly over the end wall and braced diagonally to stakes driven into the ground.

I can give three reasons why you should, or in one case must, support your trusses another way. First, depending on the building's height and the slope of the site, the length of a diagonal brace from the peak of a truss to the ground can measure more than 40 feet — too long a span for strong, rigid bracing. Second, in the case of a hip roof, the girder truss usually sits at least 12 feet inside the end wall, where it's impossible to brace it diagonally to the ground. Finally, braces running from the roof to the ground clutter the site, slowing the work and creating safety hazards.

A Different Approach

To avoid these problems, I use a different technique for installing roof trusses. First, I straighten and brace the exterior walls as usual. Then I beef up the bracing of one of the end walls — the end where I plan to start truss installation. But instead of starting directly above the end wall, I position the first truss 8 to 12 feet in, then brace it back to that wall (Figure 25). Here's how it works.

Before plunging into the stack of trusses, I mark the truss spacings (usually 2 feet on-center) on the top plates of the bearing walls. While I mark the layout, I have another carpenter prepare plenty of 2-by lateral braces by marking off the truss centers and starting a duplex nail at each mark.

Next, either with a crane or with lots of muscle, we raise the first truss and set it in position on the first layout mark farther from the end wall than the height of the truss. For example, for 7-foot-high trusses, we would position the first truss at the fifth layout mark (8 feet in for trusses 2 feet on-center). This ensures that all the braces from the top chord of the truss will be at less than a 45-degree angle, making them much stronger than braces at steeper angles.

Then, with the help of the crane or with braces from the end wall or the deck below, we hold the truss plumb while we position it exactly on the layout marks and toenail it to the plates.

At this point we pull a dry line from the front to the back plate and 6 inches in front of the truss. We position braces at 6- to 8-foot intervals from the top of the bottom chord to the top of the end wall. Depending on the distance between the end wall and the first truss, I've used almost everything from 2x4s to staging planks. *Never* use 1-inch stock for bracing.

We first spike each brace into the top of the bottom chord. Then, as one worker measures, his or her partner adjusts each brace and spikes it to the end wall when the truss's bottom chord is exactly 6 inches from the line.

Next, with either the crane or workers on the deck or end wall still steadying the truss, I climb an extension ladder to the peak and plumb the truss, using a 6-foot level and straightedge or a plumb bob. (For lower-pitch trusses, staging or a tall step or trestle ladder also works for getting to the peak.) When the truss is plumb, I nail a brace from the peak to the top of the end wall. Then I work down the top chord at 6- to 8-foot intervals, straightening and plumbing it, then bracing it back to the end wall.

The Rest Is Easy

With the first truss in place, straight and plumb, the rest of the trusses go more quickly. We nail the second truss in place; then, using the premarked lateral bracing, we secure it to the first truss.

For a standard house truss, say 24 to 36 feet long, we install at least one row of lateral bracing along the peak, one along the attic walkway, and one along the midpoint of each top chord. Larger trusses require more.

To be sure the trusses will withstand a windstorm, we connect all the trusses to one another with diagonal web bracing. We begin installing this as soon as the fourth truss is up.

Once we've set a dozen or so trusses, another crew can start the roof sheathing to help stiffen them. We keep the lowest lateral brace at least 5 feet up from the bottom edge of the truss so we don't have to remove it until the first row of plywood is nailed off. Meanwhile, the first crew continues across the building, setting trusses and installing the diagonal and lateral braces. When the entire roof assembly is anchored together, we nail two continuous 2x6

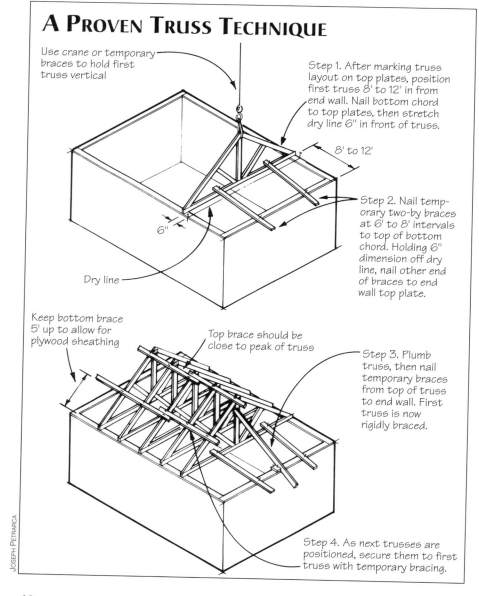

A PROVEN TRUSS TECHNIQUE

Use crane or temporary braces to hold first truss vertical

Step 1. After marking truss layout on top plates, position first truss 8' to 12' in from end wall. Nail bottom chord to top plates, then stretch dry line 6" in front of truss.

8' to 12'

6"

Dry line

Step 2. Nail temporary two-by braces at 6' to 8' intervals to top of bottom chord. Holding 6" dimension off dry line, nail other end of braces to end wall top plate.

Keep bottom brace 5' up to allow for plywood sheathing

Top brace should be close to peak of truss

Step 3. Plumb truss, then nail temporary braces from top of truss to end wall. First truss is now rigidly braced.

Step 4. As next trusses are positioned, secure them to first truss with temporary bracing.

JOSEPH PETRARCA

Figure 25. By starting truss installation several feet in from one end of the building and bracing back to the end wall, the author avoids using long bracing from the roof to the ground.

braces from the ridge to the floor in the form of an "X" or an "A."

To finish the roof, we remove the end wall braces to the first truss and work back to the end wall. Finally, we install the permanent bracing and metal tie-downs per the engineered bracing plan from the truss manufacturer.

By Paul De Baggis, an instructor at Minuteman Technical School in Lexington, Mass. and former builder.

SHED DORMERS

Shed dormers remain a popular remodeling project but they are often retrofitted without proper concern for whether the structure can handle the new loads. Below, we'll examine some of the structural concerns that must be considered before retrofitting a shed dormer to an existing roof. Of course, the same concerns and recommendations apply equally to new construction as well.

Shed Dormer Basics

Consider a basic frame roof, like the one in Figure 26. Assuming its members are correctly sized, this roof is a rigid triangle. The rafters lean against each other at the ridge with a force equal to their outward thrust, which is resisted by the ceiling joists. All vertical loads are transferred to the walls, which (we hope) safely carry them down to the foundation.

However, if you introduce a shed dormer on one side of this roof, you upset the balance of forces in this stable triangle. Unless proper precautions are taken, the roof will tend to deflect, as indicated by the dashed lines in Figure 26B. This kind of deflection is not usually apparent within weeks, or even months, of the completion of a shed dormer project. But my observations in the field have shown me

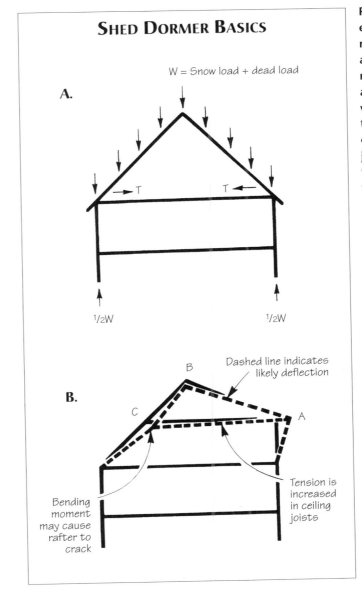

SHED DORMER BASICS

A. W = Snow load + dead load

T T

1/2W   1/2W

B.

B

C

A

Dashed line indicates likely deflection

Tension is increased in ceiling joists

Bending moment may cause rafter to crack

Figure 26. A properly built gable roof is a stable triangle (A). The rafters lean against each other with a force equal to the tension, T, carried by the joists, which resist the tendency of the roof to spread. Install a shed dormer, though, and the stable triangle is upset (B). The tension in the dormer ceiling joists increases considerably, adding bending stress at the rafter/joist connections. In situations where the triangle ABC is less than 4 feet in height, the author recommends two 1/2-inch carriage bolts each at connections A and C.

that over many years houses will experience this kind of movement. In several cases, I've seen exterior walls leaning out by as much as $1\frac{1}{2}$ inches, and in many cases I've seen sagging ridge lines that are noticeable from the street.

Undersized framing. There are several causes of deflection in shed dormers. A common one is that shed dormers are often added to roofs that already have undersized rafters. Many 19th-century capes — common choices for shed additions — have 4x4 rafters 3 or 4 feet on-center, often without a structural ridge beam. And many modern frame houses have 2x8 or even 2x6 rafters — where 2x10s or 2x12s should have been used.

In these situations, retrofitting a shed dormer without providing for the new loads is asking for trouble. These undersized rafters simply don't have any reserve strength to accommodate the bending loads which can be imposed by the dormer. Not only is a noticeable sag in the roof possible, but very high bending moments can create a real risk of cracking in the rafters.

Also, attic floor joists are usually sized smaller than main floor framing. With the addition of a shed dormer, the attic joists must support living space loads. And in many cases, the outside wall of the dormer

is set in from the outside wall of the house (Figure 27), bringing additional roof loads onto the joists. Often, a kneewall is incorporated somewhere near the eaves along the non-dormered side of the roof; this, too, transfers roof loads. All of these conditions can greatly increase bending loads on the attic floor joists, causing visible deflection — often as much as an inch — in the floor and the ceiling below.

Creeping deflection. Another reason that shed dormer roofs deflect is that creeping deflection takes place. Over the years the rafters develop a permanent sag from continued loading. This is especially true in snow climates. And since shed dormer roofs usually have a fairly shallow pitch, they tend to hold more snow.

Loosening connections. A third cause of deflection is that over time nails begin to slip and bend, loosening the connections. This is especially true of the ceiling joist/rafter connection at the shed dormer eaves.

Supporting Dormer Loads

There are some basic precautions you can take to make sure your shed dormer addition doesn't sag with time:

• Provide a continuous path to the foundation for all roof loads. This may mean adding structural elements.

• Use properly-sized framing members. For dormers where you're adding new loads onto existing framing, this may mean sistering new members to the old.

• Make strong connections. Adequate nailing, bolts, metal connectors, and plywood can all help here.

The simplest solution — on paper at least — is to fully support the new dormer loads all the way to the foundation. There are two common ways to do this: a structural ridge or a center bearing wall. Which you use depends on the design and layout of the particular house you are remodeling.

Structural ridge. Though they can be troublesome to retrofit, structural ridge beams can solve most of the loading problems associated with shed dormers (Figure 28). The structural ridge can either replace the existing ridge or be installed below it. The table in Figure 28 offers guidance in sizing structural ridges. The table is based on a 24-foot-wide house, with 30-psf snow loads.

Take special care to provide adequate support at ends of the structural ridge. In the case described in the table in Figure 28, two 2x4 studs in a plywood sheathed wall would adequately support each end of the ridge beam. Without the lateral support of plywood sheathing, however, more careful examination of stud buckling would be required. A triple 2x6 post, properly nailed, would suffice in any case. Be sure that the load path is continuous to foundation.

A structural ridge design requires nothing of ceiling joists, other than supporting the ceiling; they can be omitted if you like.

Center support wall. In many cases, interior support is provided by walls located at or near the center of the structure (Figure 29). The advantages are the same as for the structural ridge, but the need for a sturdy beam with double or triple 2x posts is eliminated.

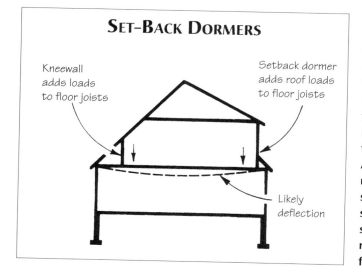

SET-BACK DORMERS

Kneewall adds loads to floor joists

Setback dormer adds roof loads to floor joists

Likely deflection

Figure 27. If you set back the front wall of a shed dormer for aesthetic reasons, make sure the floor joists can handle the additional roof loads. A kneewall on the non-dormered side of the roof shortens the rafter span but also adds roof loads to the floor.

As with the structural ridge design, continuity of load paths to the foundation is important. Ideally, the support wall should stand directly below the ridge line, and be in line with walls or girders all the way to the foundation. It's okay if the support wall is a few inches out of line with the wall below, but in this case you should align the studs over the floor joists or use a double sole plate. If the walls are more than a few inches out of alignment, have an engineer check the joists to avoid sagging and ceiling distress.

But Can I Do It Without Additional Support?

Admittedly, many shed dormers have been built in roofs without structural ridges or where no center support wall exists. And many of these dormers, which under engineering analysis with code loads would seem deficient, have fared well.

In many of these cases, the main factor that saves an otherwise troubled design is the relatively short length of the dormer (parallel to the ridge). Also, partition walls may provide some vertical support and even an existing ridge beam, if it's 2x8 or larger, may serve for spans between partitions of less than 12 feet. In general, a small shed dormer may work without a structural ridge or center bearing wall if the following conditions are met:

- Set the exterior wall of the shed dormer directly above the first-floor exterior wall (Figure 30). This ensures that at least half the dormer roof loads are carried safely to the foundation — assuming the wall below is well-built, with properly sized door and window headers.
- Include a kneewall at the rear (non-dormered side of the roof). This provides midspan support to the rafters on that side. Keep the horizontal distance between the

STRUCTURAL RIDGE

A.

Rafter hangers

Original rafters

Dormer rafters

Structural ridge installed in place of nonstructural ridge

B.

Dormer rafters

Original rafters

2x braces

Structural ridge retrofitted below nonstructural ridge

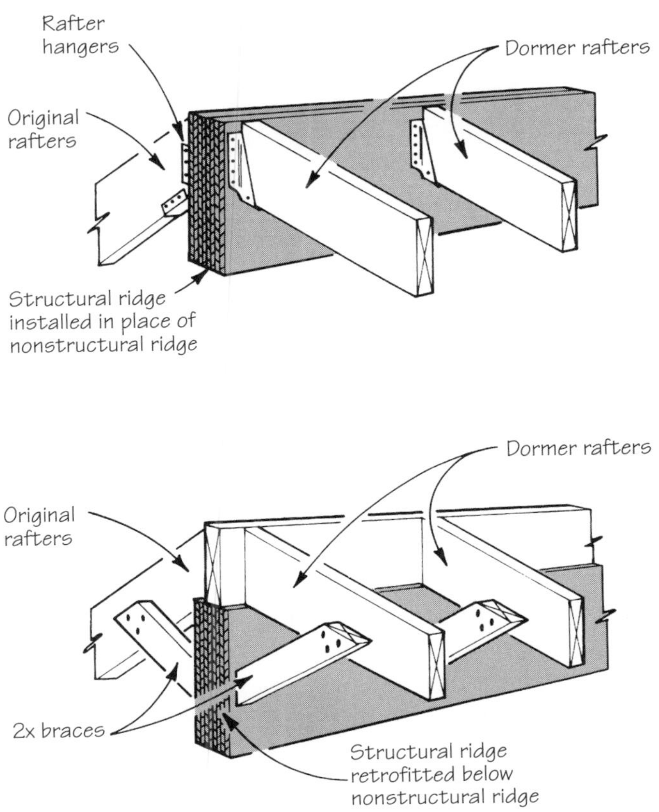

SIZING STRUCTURAL RIDGE BEAMS

Ridge length	LVL beam	2x beam*
8'	LVL 1³/₄ x 9¹/₂	(2) 2x10
9'	"	(3) 2x10, (2) 2x12
10'	LVL 1³/₄ x 11⁷/₈	"
11'	"	(2) 2x12
12'	"	(3) 2x12
13'	LVL 1³/₄ x 14	Not recommended
14'	"	"
15'	(2) LVL 1³/₄ x 14	"
16'	"	"

Note: This table is based on a sample house 24 feet wide (eaves to eaves), with design snow loads of 30 psf.
* Fb = 760 psi min. (new grading tables), or 1,000 psi with the old tables

Figure 28. Structural ridge beams are a good solution for the loads introduced by a shed dormer addition. The author prefers to install them in place of the nonstructural ridge (A), but they can also be retrofitted below the existing ridge (B). The table gives the author's sizing recommendations for LVL and laminated 2x ridge beams.

kneewall and the dormer's ceiling joist/rafter intersection to less than 4 feet, unless the rafters are 2x10s or larger. Also, make sure the floor joists below the kneewall are large enough — if less than 2x10, they will usually have to be sistered.

• The vertical distance between the ridge and the dormer ceiling should be 3 feet or more. The dormer ceiling joists act in tension to resist the roof spread. As they go higher, the tension increases, as does the bending moment at the connection. This increases the risk that the rafter will crack or that the connection will slip.

• Use perpendicular interior walls to brace the dormer's exterior wall against leaning out. This will not work well if the partitions are covered only with drywall. Sheathe these partitions with plywood and use strap ties to tie them to the top plate of the dormer's exterior wall, as shown in Figure 30.

• Use minimum 1/2-inch plywood roof sheathing, properly nailed, to develop diaphragm action in the dormer roof. Also, an existing ridge beam 2x8 or larger will help maintain ridge alignment.

Taken collectively, these features may prevent deflection problems, whereas any single feature would be inadequate.

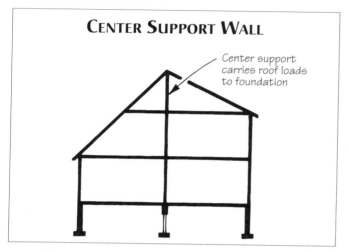

CENTER SUPPORT WALL

Center support carries roof loads to foundation

Figure 29. Center support walls are often the easiest way to handle shed dormer loads, but they must provide a continuous path to the foundation.

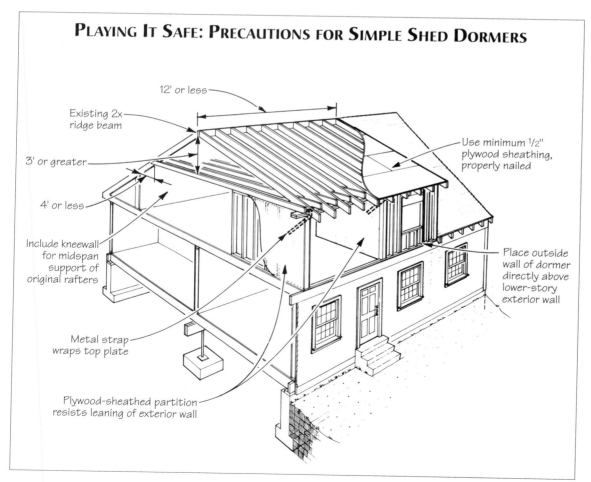

PLAYING IT SAFE: PRECAUTIONS FOR SIMPLE SHED DORMERS

12' or less

Existing 2x ridge beam

3' or greater

4' or less

Include kneewall for midspan support of original rafters

Metal strap wraps top plate

Plywood-sheathed partition resists leaning of exterior wall

Use minimum 1/2" plywood sheathing, properly nailed

Place outside wall of dormer directly above lower-story exterior wall

Figure 30. Although it's a safer practice to include a structural ridge or center support wall when retrofitting a shed dormer, it's possible to add a dormer without these structural elements as long as certain conditions are met, as shown here.

Other Design Considerations

There are many small variations on shed dormer design that have structural implications.

Supporting set-back dormers. As mentioned above, many dormer designs set the outside wall of the dormer back from the line of the main wall of the house for the sake of appearance. The problem common to these designs is the transfer of roof loads to the floor joists. Where the floor joists are 2x6s, this set-back design should not be considered without sistering the floor joists. Where 2x8 floor joists exist, a setback no greater than one foot is suggested. With 2x10 floor joists, a 2-foot set-back is probably reasonable. (Have your design reviewed by a licensed engineer to verify these recommendations.) Where you have a structural ridge or a center support wall, the setback distances can be increased somewhat.

Drop-ridge dormers. If aesthetic considerations lead you to drop the shed dormer ridge (because practical considerations are not likely to!), then all the previous guidelines still apply. Where you have a structural ridge or center support, this detail is easy. Just tie the dormer rafters in at the ridge or center wall and finish the roof off with short nonstructural rafters above the shed (Figure 31).

If you're retrofitting a dormer where there's no structural ridge or center support wall and you want to drop the ridge, an added challenge lies in making careful connections at the ridge. I would recommend two 1/2-inch carriage bolts at each connection.

Except for very small dormers, I would not recommend using a header between doubled rafters to support the top of drop-ridge dormer rafters. Although this practice is common, these headers are usually undersized and a sagging roof or cracked rafters can result.

Dormers over half-walls. Often the existing construction has second-story half-walls, either balloon-

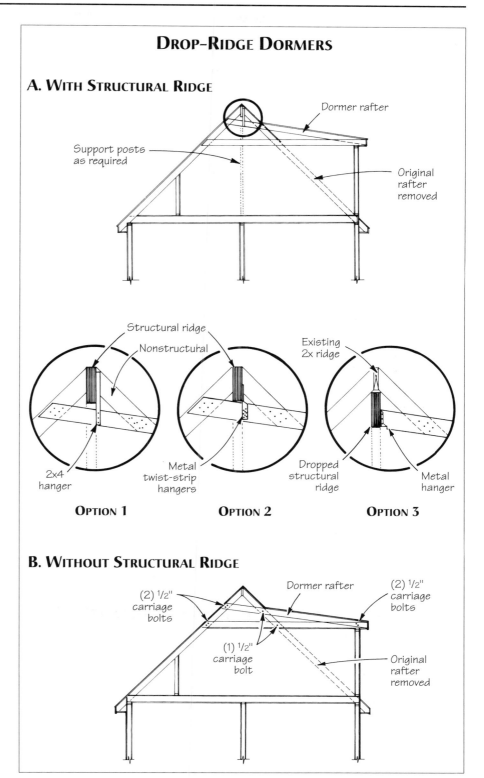

Figure 31. Shed dormer designs sometimes drop the shed ridge below the main ridge of the house. With a center bearing wall or structural ridge (A), this presents no problem; just tie in the dormer rafters and add short nonstructural rafters above. The drawing shows three options for tying the dormer rafters to the structural ridge. However, in situations without a structural ridge (B), special attention must be given to connecting the dormer rafters. The author recommends 1/2-inch carriage bolts at all connections.

BALLOON-FRAMED HALF-WALLS

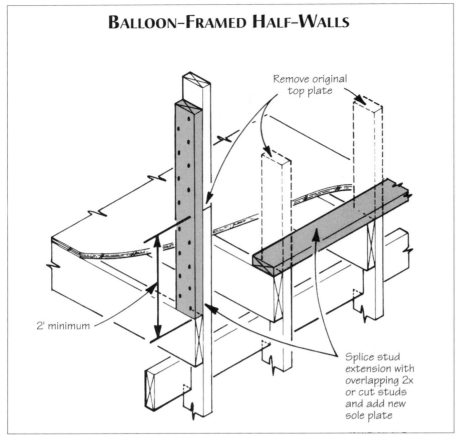

Remove original top plate

2' minimum

Splice stud extension with overlapping 2x or cut studs and add new sole plate

Figure 32. When adding a shed dormer above balloon-framed half-walls, don't build the wall extension directly on top of the balloon wall top plate. Instead, either remove the top plate and carefully splice on stud extensions or cut the balloon studs flush and build a new full-height stud wall.

framed or of platform construction (Figure 32). Resist the temptation to scab on to the half-wall when raising the shed roof — it's never a good idea to have a weak wall splice midway between floor and ceiling. Instead, remove the top plate of balloon-framed half-walls and add stud extensions, splicing them together with an overlapping 2x member. Or you can cut the balloon studs off flush with the floor deck and add a top plate, then build a new full-height stud wall on top. Remove platform-framed half-walls altogether and replace them with full-height stud walls.

There is another problem that can occur when a shed dormer is added over half-walls. Because a half-wall affords some access under the non-dormered side of the roof, the knee-wall on that side is often omitted,

leaving a clear-span roof and no load transfer to floor joists (good). Unfortunately, the resulting bending moments applied to rafters at ceiling joist connection points are likely to be unacceptable (very bad). In this situation it's best to provide a structural ridge or center bearing wall, or to seek the help of an engineer.

Hybrid dormers. In many cases, a long dormer may incorporate two or three of the basic designs described above, selected according to interior wall placement and available load paths below. There is really little to worry about with such combinations as long as each section, taken alone, is structurally adequate.

Final Precautions

Regardless of the type of dormer being built, it is important to verify

the strength of the existing framing beneath the new construction, and to consider flashing and ventilation details for the new roof:

- *Floor joists* may require sistering if the new construction adds significant bending loads to the floor. Two-by-sixes should always be sistered and 2x8s will often need to be. Two-by-tens may not need sistering if the new loads are not excessive.
- *Interior walls,* if used to carry vertical loads, should be inspected to make sure the headers are adequate. Check the alignment of support walls with walls and girders below. If more than a few inches of misalignment exists, seek professional review.
- *Girders* should be analyzed for the new loads. Examine them for signs of twisting, lateral instability, or excessive sagging or crushing of wood members at points of support.
- *Columns* should be checked for deformation at the top, for proper attachment, and for any settlement. Inspect steel columns for corrosion as well.
- *Footings* are usually adequate to carry additional loads, but should be inspected just in case they were poorly constructed in the first place.
- *Ventilation* may be needed where you're finishing previously unfinished attic space. Don't forget to pay proper attention to details of insulation and ventilation of the new roof.
- *Roofing* may require special thought, depending on the slope of the dormer roof. Shingles will not drain as well as they did on the original steeper roof. If the roof cannot be readily seen from the ground, or if the slope is less than 4:12, I recommend a single-ply material, such as modified bitumen. And regardless of the slope, you should incorporate an ice and water membrane for the first 36 inches of the roof above the eaves to avoid ice dams.

By Robert Randall, a structural engineer from Mohegan Lake, N.Y.

DETAILS FOR WOOD SHRINKAGE

Today, most builders frame with kiln-dried stock. But if you think that means you don't have to be concerned about wood shrinkage, think again: Kiln-dried lumber will definitely shrink. How much depends on its moisture content at the time of installation (see "Calculating Shrinkage," page 51). And as the lumber shrinks, it tends to twist and bow, causing humps and nail pops in walls, and bumpy, squeaky, out-of-level floors.

Understanding Wood Shrinkage

Moisture affects wood the same way it affects a sponge. If you take a sopping-wet sponge and wring it out, you'll remove some of the water, though not enough to change the sponge's size. But if you let the damp sponge dry out, it will shrink. And if you wet the dry sponge, it will swell back up until it reaches the point where it can't absorb any more water and can't get any larger.

In a piece of wood, moisture resides both in the cell cavities and in the cell walls. Green wood is like a sopping-wet sponge: As it dries, the moisture in the cavities is the first to go. But, as with the sponge, this doesn't cause the wood to shrink. The point at which there is moisture in cell walls, but not in cell cavities is called the *fiber saturation point*. Below this level, the wood (like the sponge) will shrink as it dries and swell as it absorbs moisture.

The amount of moisture in a piece of wood is referred to as its *moisture content* (MC). Moisture content is the ratio of the weight of the moisture in a piece of wood to the weight of the piece of wood if all of the moisture were removed. Because the water in a piece of green wood can easily outweigh the

wood fiber, wood can have a moisture content of more than 100%. The fiber saturation point of most wood species is 25% to 30% MC; kiln-dried framing lumber is supposed to have no more than 19% MC. Since this is well below the fiber saturation point, the wood will swell and shrink with changes in moisture content.

Wood stored at a constant humidity eventually reaches a stable MC, called the *equilibrium moisture content*. For most of the U.S., the

equilibrium MC of wood that's inside a building is around 8%. In arid climates like Arizona, it's closer to 6%, while in moist climates like Florida, it's closer to 11%. This means that a piece of kiln-dried lumber will lose 8% to 13% MC after installation.

Start With Dry Lumber

Kiln-dried framing lumber is stamped KD or S-DRY (surfaced dry). Lumber stamped S-GRN (surfaced green) has not been kiln dried.

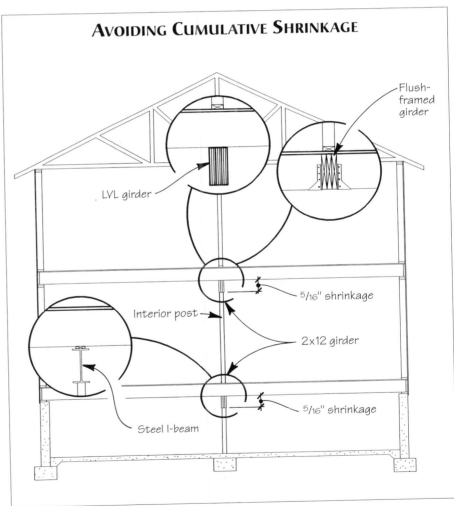

AVOIDING CUMULATIVE SHRINKAGE

Flush-framed girder

LVL girder

5/16" shrinkage

Interior post

2x12 girder

5/16" shrinkage

Steel I-beam

Figure 33. In the house shown here, the two built-up 2x12 girders will cause the center bearing wall to shrink much more than the exterior walls. This will result in a 1/2-inch drop at the second floor level — enough to cause nail pops and cracks in the finishes. Using a steel I-beam in the basement and engineered lumber or flush framing at the second floor will alleviate the problem.

Its MC was higher than 19% at the time it was milled — probably a lot higher. Avoid S-GRN lumber anywhere you're concerned about shrinkage. Also be aware that anything larger than a 4x4 isn't available in KD. The outside of these timbers may be somewhat dry, but assume that the inside is pretty green. When using a large solid beam, like a 6x6 or a 6x10, keep in mind that it will shrink a lot more than a comparable built-up beam made from kiln-dried stock.

You can minimize the effects of moisture swings by ensuring that all your framing lumber has the same MC. This means storing it up off the ground and protecting it from sun and rain with a tarp. It's just as bad to let the joists on top of the lift dry out in the sun as it is to let the bottom ones soak in a puddle. The idea is to make sure that all of the members in a given component — all of the joists in a floor, for instance — shrink the same amount.

Dry the Frame

Studs that are straight at 19% MC can do a lot of twisting and bowing as they dry to 8%. The U.S. Forest Products Lab (FPL) recommends that a frame be within 5% of its final moisture content before walls and ceilings are closed in. At the company I work for, we try to dry the frame to 10% or 12% MC before installing drywall or plaster. This gives us a chance to fix or replace any pieces that bow.

In cold weather, drying the frame may require some heat. A few winters back, I used a moisture meter to record how long it took the frame of a house I was working on to dry out. It was cold, but the humidity was low and the house was weathertight. After three weeks, most of the frame was stuck at 15%. We then set up an old gas furnace as a temporary heater. A week and half later, everything had dried to around 10%. Of course, it's not cheap to use heat to dry out a house. But if you're doing a high-end job, it beats coming back later to repair drywall, tile, and trim. And the heat doesn't have to be all that high. The FPL says that you need to keep the inside of the building only 10 to 15 degrees warmer than the outside.

Pay Attention to Framing Details

Even if you purchase high-quality framing lumber and protect it after it arrives, you still won't be able to prevent the wood from shrinking altogether. But if you use framing details that *allow* for the shrinkage, you will avoid most of the problems that can occur when the frame shrinks.

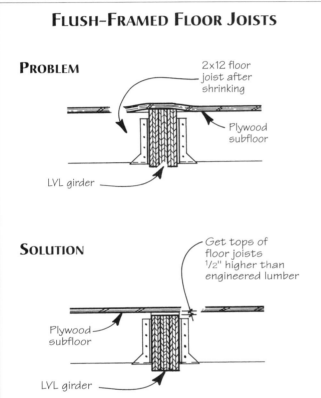

FLUSH-FRAMED FLOOR JOISTS

PROBLEM

2x12 floor joist after shrinking

Plywood subfloor

LVL girder

SOLUTION

Get tops of floor joists 1/2" higher than engineered lumber

Plywood subfloor

LVL girder

Figure 34. Floor joists laid flush with the top of engineered or steel beams will create a bump in the floor when they shrink. In these situations, install the joists 1/2 inch higher to accommodate the anticipated shrinkage (left). Where I-joists meet an engineered lumber beam (below), you can install them flush since shrinkage is not an issue with I-joists.

Problems occur when one side of the building has considerably more headers and plates than the other side, when there's an improper connection to masonry, or when solid lumber is mixed with steel or engineered lumber without compensating for the materials' different shrinkage rates. The symptoms include sloping floors, and lumps and dips in floors and walls. Although this sounds complicated, it's fairly easy to design a frame that will shrink evenly.

Avoid Lopsided Shrinkage

It's important to recognize situations when a structure will shrink unevenly. Look at the example in Figure 33. Here, the first-floor joists are supported by a built-up 2x12 girder. The upstairs features an open floor plan, with the second-floor joists also resting on a 2x12 girder.

The problem with this configuration is that the two girders may shrink as much as 5/16 inch each as the lumber dries from 19% moisture content to 8%. This is much more than the shrinkage that would occur in the exterior walls. The first-story ceiling and the second-story floor will then drop by 1/2 inch or more, wreaking havoc with the drywall finish and possibly leaving noticeable dips in the floor.

The solution is to use girder material that doesn't shrink — either steel or LVL — or to flush-frame the girders.

Whenever you're flush-framing a floor system where solid wood joists meet an engineered lumber or steel beam, don't set the tops of the joists exactly even with the top of the beam (Figure 34). Otherwise, when the joists shrink, they'll leave a bump in the floor. When I'm faced with this situation, I drop the beam approximately 1/2 inch in relation to the joists, so the joists can shrink without the top of the beam contacting the subfloor.

Foundation Details

Some designs call for the first-floor joists to bear on an interior foundation ledge, as in Figure 35. The problem here is that when the joists shrink, the ends pull away from the subfloor, leaving a slope at the exterior wall. I once installed a refrigerator in a kitchen that was framed this way; the floor sloped so badly that I couldn't level the refrigerator with the leveling feet.

A better detail is to keep the subfloor off the sill plate. When the floor joists shrink, the subfloor will move with them. When installing a wood floor, you can prevent a gap from opening beneath the baseboard

CALCULATING SHRINKAGE

Because wood shrinks and swells at a predictable rate, it's possible to calculate how much a building, or any part of a building, will shrink as it dries. Let's say we want to find out how much a kiln-dried Hem-Fir 2x12 at 19% MC will shrink if it's dried to 8% MC. We need something called the coefficient for dimensional change — the shrinkage coefficient — which expresses the percentage

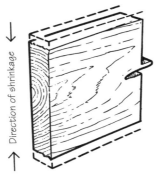

change in the size of a piece of wood for each percentage change in its MC. Although different wood species have slightly different shrinkage coefficients, an average number for flat-sawn framing lumber is .0025. You can safely use this to calculate the shrinkage for average 2-by stock.

With that in mind we can use the following formula:

Shrinkage (or swelling) =
Width of wood x change in MC
x Shrinkage Coefficient

So a typical 2x12 will shrink about 5/16 inch as it moves from 19% MC to 8% MC (11.25 inches x (19-8) x .0025). A 2x6 would shrink half as much (see chart, below). The formula can also be used to calculate how much wood swells as MC increases.

PREDICTED SHRINKAGE OF DIMENSION LUMBER

Lumber Size	Actual Width	Width @ 19% MC (at Delivery)	Width @ 11% MC (Humid Climates)	Width@ 8% MC (Average Climates)	Width @ 6% MC (Arid Climates)
2x4	3 1/2"	3 1/2"	3 7/16"	3 3/8"	3 3/8"
2x6	5 1/2"	5 1/2"	5 3/8"	5 5/16"	5 5/16"
2x8	7 1/2"	7 1/4"	7 1/8"	7 1/16"	7"
2x10	9 1/4"	9 1/4"	9 1/16"	9"	8 15/16"
2x12	11 1/4"	11 1/4"	11"	10 15/16"	10 7/8"

Note: Framing lumber shrinks primarily across its width; shrinkage along the lumber length is insignificant. Actual shrinkage varies depending on the lumber's moisture content when delivered and the area's climate.

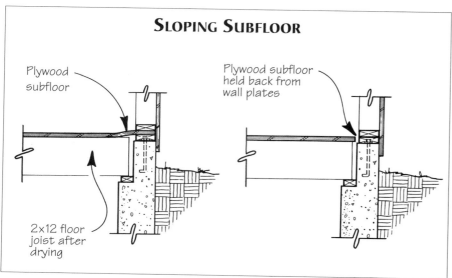

SLOPING SUBFLOOR

Plywood subfloor

Plywood subfloor held back from wall plates

2x12 floor joist after drying

Figure 35. Subflooring that is installed underneath the exterior wall framing (at left) will cause a slope as the floor joists shrink. Where floor joists bear on a foundation ledge, the subflooring should stop short of the exterior wall (at right). This allows the subfloor to move with the joists as they shrink.

by installing the flooring after the baseboard and using a shoe mold that's attached to the floor.

Where Wood Meets Masonry

If the framing isn't dry when a concrete hearth is poured, the framing will shrink so that the hardwood floor surface ends up slightly below the hearth. Because hearths are usually set late in the job, after the framing has had time to dry, this is seldom a problem. But if the hearth is set earlier — or if cold weather prevents the frame from drying — you should anticipate shrinkage and set the hearth a bit lower.

By David Frane, a contributing editor to The Journal of Light Construction *and* JLC's Tools of the Trade.

CHAPTER 3

WOOD & HARDBOARD SIDING

- Making Walls Watertight
- Wood Siding
- Wood Siding Over Foam
- Hardboard Siding
- Guide to Galvanized Nails

MAKING WALLS WATERTIGHT

I vividly remember the job where I learned that even properly installed siding isn't waterproof. It was a large, expensive gambrel on the peak of the highest hill in town. Start to finish, the job was a plum. The clients were overjoyed with my work and moved in ahead of schedule. But six months later, a wind-driven rain converted my plum into a prune. In a late-night phone call, the owner explained in detail how many drips-per-minute were falling from the head jamb of the east-facing double-mullion window.

I "fixed" the leak the next day, but it reoccurred once a year for three consecutive years. Each time there was a heavy east wind driving the rain directly against the window and the wall surrounding it. I caulked every joint and tightened every flashing connection on the east wall of the home in an effort to fix the leak, but with no luck.

When out of desperation I finally removed every course of bevel siding from the east wall, the problem was right in front of me. I had prewrapped the entire wall with 15-lb. felt and popped in the back-ordered window later. The problem was caused by the Z-flashing above the window head casing — I had attached the Z-flashing against the felt paper rather than tucking it under. Heavy winds forced rain water through the butt joints of the siding above the window, where it ran down the face of the felt paper, behind the window flashing and head casing, and dripped into the house.

Wind and rain can drive water through the smallest of cracks in any siding. All homes should have a second line of protection, especially those exposed to wind-driven rain (Figure 1). After investigating structural failures and repairing homes for many years, I have found that some failures are chronic. The details provided here will improve your chances of preventing leaks, even in severe conditions.

Housewraps

Too often, builders neglect to wrap houses with a water-resistant membrane before they apply siding.

Figure 1. To protect this oceanfront home from wind-driven rain and surf spray, the builder has covered the housewrap around doors and windows with a self-adhering bituminous membrane.

Figure 2. Water driven behind the siding can soak the sheathing and find its way into the house at gaps between upper and lower courses of housewrap (left), and at backwards overlaps (above).

This is especially true when the house will be sided with vinyl — many builders are convinced that nothing gets past vinyl siding. But vinyl siding isn't waterproof, as I learned while inspecting a house in frigid temperatures after a heavy, wind-driven rain. The sidewall had icicles protruding from beneath one section of the vinyl siding where rain had penetrated the siding and was frozen in its tracks trying to escape.

Patchwork. Poorly installed housewrap is just as bad as no housewrap. Figure 2 shows a combination of Tyvek and Typar on the same house. This is not a problem in itself, but the lack of consistency caught my eye. What concerns me is how the builder has cobbled together little scraps of housewrap; there are gaps, and in some cases the lower pieces overlap the upper pieces. If rain penetrates the siding on this house, it could easily find a path behind the housewrap.

Wrapping windows. Most builders wrap the entire house before installing windows or doors. In fact, manufacturers recommend wrapping over rough openings, then cutting an X into the window opening and folding the wrap inward. The windows are then installed over the housewrap. When I see this, I am always reminded of my leakage problem with the gambrel. When rain penetrates the siding on homes wrapped this way, it will find its way behind the window flashing and into the house.

Step flashing. Another problem area is a sloping roof that intersects a taller sidewall, as when the gable end of a garage is attached to the gable end of a two-story house. The garage roof shingles are usually step-flashed against the housewrap on the sidewall sheathing of the main house. But in cold climates, water from melting snowdrifts collects at this joint and will find its way through butt joints, knots, cracks, and other irregularities in the siding. The solution is to place the garage roof flashing directly against the bare house

sheathing, then make sure the housewrap overlaps the step flashing.

Corners

Not all leaks result in water dripping on carpets in plain view of nervous clients; some leaks slowly compromise the structural integrity of a building. Rip off the corner boards of enough old houses and you will see your share of rotting corner posts. In general, corners of buildings experience the greatest effects of wind pressure, so you should take special care to protect this area from exposure to rain water.

Last month I visited the construction site of a very expensive new home. Overall, the quality of construction was excellent, but one detail troubled me. The 1-by wood corner boards were applied directly over the plywood sheathing, with no housewrap underneath. Over time, the corner boards and the wood siding will shrink and expand, giving rain water a path to the sheathing and framing.

Many builders caulk between corner boards and siding, assuming this creates a watertight joint. In wood-frame construction, however, the bond between most sealants and wood deteriorates within a few years, faster in severe exposures. In my opinion, caulking only makes matters worse by retarding the drying process when water penetrates the corner joints.

A more forgiving corner detail is to extend whatever type of housewrap you're using around the corner before installing the corner board. And because corners of houses are often dinged and damaged during construction, I would also recommend that a second vertical spline of felt paper or housewrap be applied over wrapped corners just before the corner boards go on.

Windows and Doors

One of my first assignments as an apprentice carpenter was wrapping

Housewrap Checklist
- Use housewrap or felt paper on all houses, no matter what kind of siding you're using.
- The wrap should be continuous; avoid a patchwork of small pieces.
- Provide an unrestricted path down and out of the space behind the siding. Wall membranes should overlap by 3 inches horizontally and 6 inches vertically. Tape all seams.
- Protect all pathways into the building envelope by lapping housewrap over flashings.

Corner Board Checklist
- Install felt paper or housewrap at all corners.
- Double-wrap corners by applying vertical felt or housewrap splines under the corner boards.
- Don't caulk the joint between the siding and corner board; caulk deteriorates over time, providing a pathway for water to get into the frame and preventing trapped water from escaping.

Window Flashing Checklist
- Protect the top of the window flashing with overlapping wrap.
- Double-overlap housewrap around nailing fins of vinyl and clad windows.
- At sills, splines must direct water over underlying housewrap.
- At head, leave a 1/4-inch gap between the window flashing and bottom edge of siding to prevent wicking of moisture.

Siding Checklist
- Don't install board siding on a diagonal.
- For horizontal board siding, use top-grade boards with no knots, splits, or other defects. Install T&G and shiplap siding so that the joints between boards drain away from the sheathing.
- For panel siding, use housewrap over studs. Housewrap should overlap Z-flashing at the joint between panel courses.
- Protect wall sheathing close to grade with bituminous membrane.
- Siding should overlap sill-to-foundation joints by at least 2 inches.

window and door jambs. I would unroll a length of felt on the deck, cut 1-foot-wide strips (a little longer than the window and door openings), then fasten these "splines" along the sides of the window and door rough openings (Figure 3). I was taught that splines protect the sheathing from any weather that might penetrate the joint between the siding and window casings.

This makes sense, but there is a little more to this detail. Don't bury the bottom of the splines beneath a layer of housewrap. The bottom of the spline should be lifted and placed over the felt or housewrap that runs horizontally beneath the window. This will guide any water that penetrates the joint down the spline and over the felt or wrap that covers the wall.

Windows with nailing fins (vinyl, clad, and metal) have nearly replaced traditional wood-cased units on most job sites. When these units are properly installed, they offer more protection against water infiltration than wood-cased units, because the housewrap membrane can be double-overlapped in a weather-tight detail (Figure 4).

Head flashing is critical for window installations. The top edge of the window fin or Z-flashing should be protected by an overlapping membrane (Figure 5). When using a housewrap like Tyvek or Typar, it is not as easy to weave the flashing under the wrap as it is with felt. When using these wraps, you can prewrap the entire house, install the windows and flashing, and then tape the top of the flashing to the housewrap with 3M contractors tape (St. Paul, MN; 888/364-3577; www.3m.com). You can also wrap the walls before the windows are installed and slice the wrap above the window so you can slide the top of the window flashing beneath the housewrap.

Whatever method you use, be sure the splines don't lead rain water beneath the housewrap in any way (Figure 6). Be very careful at the window head: On windy days, water that collects on top of the window flashing will be blown sideways and may leak when it reaches the window's edge. Nailing flanges on clad windows provide good protection when double-wrapped, but make sure that Z-flashing leads water over the housewrap at the ends of the window. This may require carefully patching in with pieces of housewrap or felt at windows.

Siding

Many books have been written about siding, so I won't explain again how to prevent siding failures. But I will provide a sampling of some failures I've investigated in recent months.

Diagonal board siding. I don't like board siding that is installed at a diagonal. On rainy days, windward walls are covered by a thin film of water that's looking for somewhere to go. Gravity may pull it down; wind may push it sideways, upward, or even inward through breaches in the siding. Eventually, most of the rain water finds its way into the seams between adjacent siding boards. These seams act like gutters, collecting and channeling the water downward at an angle. The water is forced against the sides of windows, doorways, corner

Figure 3. When water gets behind window and door casings, correctly installed felt-paper splines keep water from wetting the sheathing.

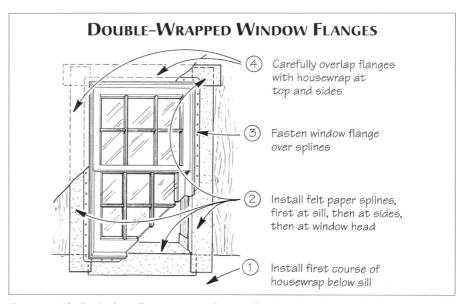

DOUBLE-WRAPPED WINDOW FLANGES

④ Carefully overlap flanges with housewrap at top and sides

③ Fasten window flange over splines

② Install felt paper splines, first at sill, then at sides, then at window head

① Install first course of housewrap below sill

Figure 4. Clad window flanges provide excellent protection against water penetration when double-wrapped with splines and housewrap. Make sure the upper course of housewrap overlaps the flanges at the top and sides of the window; at the sill, however, the spline and window flange should overlap the housewrap.

boards, and any vertical element that stands in its path. Without very careful detailing, the runoff will leak into the building at these points.

Horizontal boards. I'm not crazy for horizontal board siding in windy or exposed locations either. If the design calls for horizontally applied, tongue-and-groove or shiplap siding, be sure to install it with the tongues up so the joint will drain. Even when installed correctly, knots, splits, and other defects in the milled edges may allow water to pass through the siding, so good house-wrapping details are critical.

Panel siding. Problems typically occur with plywood panel siding at the joints between upper and lower panels. Often, plywood panel siding like T1-11 is used to economize, so structural sheathing is not installed beneath the siding panels and neither is housewrap. Typically, either Z-flashing is installed at the top of the lower panel or the top and bottom edges of adjoining panels are beveled to "prevent" leakage. These connections, however, are not weather-tight. The safest practice is to apply housewrap before installing the lower course of panels. Then install Z-flashing at the top of the lower panels and overlap the Z-flashing with the upper course of housewrap (Figure 7). Be sure to leave at least a 1/4-inch gap between panels to prevent capillary suction.

Splashback. We've all noticed siding that is discolored just above grade. This heavy weathering is caused by splashback — water bouncing off the ground and splashing back onto the siding — and is unavoidable on most homes. Regardless of the type of siding, this part of the wall will experience heavy exposure to water, so the sheathing just above grade must be carefully protected with a continuous layer of housewrap. Installing a strip of bituminous membrane like Ice and Water Shield under the siding at the bottom of the wall

Figure 5. To prevent leaks at window heads, lap felt paper or housewrap over the cap flashing.

Figure 6. Because this carpenter has stretched the housewrap over the splines at the bottom of the window, wind-driven rain will be able to run down behind the housewrap onto the sheathing.

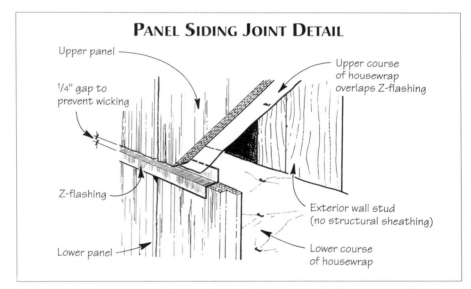

PANEL SIDING JOINT DETAIL

Upper panel

1/4" gap to prevent wicking

Z-flashing

Lower panel

Upper course of housewrap overlaps Z-flashing

Exterior wall stud (no structural sheathing)

Lower course of housewrap

Figure 7. Apply the lower course of panel siding over the housewrap, then overlap the Z-flashing with the upper course of housewrap before installing the upper panels. Leave at least a 1/4-inch gap between panels to prevent wicking.

may be a worthwhile investment.

The intersection of the sill to the foundation is critical. Be sure that water runs down the siding and is carried past this joint. Also make sure wind will not drive water under the sill — let the siding overlap the sill-foundation joint by at least 2 inches.

As is the case for all detailing, be conservative in your estimation of the

forces influencing your design. Plan on water penetrating your primary line of defense, and develop a plan that offers solid backup protection.

By Paul Fisette, a wood technologist and director of the Building Materials Technology and Management program at the University of Massachusetts in Amherst. Photos by author, except where noted.

WOOD SIDING

Many siding problems stem from selecting the wrong material for the job. Picking the wrong grade, size, or pattern can lead to a finished product that either doesn't look good, doesn't last long, or both.

Select a proper grade. Many siding problems occur because the grade is not adequate for the job. The chart "Standard Siding Grades" can guide you in speccing a suitable grade. If your lumberyard uses other terms for their siding grades, find out if they are equivalent to the standard grades established by industry trade associations shown in the chart.

Many mills or yards, for instance, use their own proprietary grades. And many use a hodgepodge of grades to compose their "knotty" grade of siding, also known as "STK"

or *select tight knotty*. Make sure any STK or knotty grade is composed of siding grades identified in the chart as acceptable for quality siding jobs. Otherwise you won't know what you're buying until it shows up on the job site. And if it turns out to be a pile of green wood with loose knots and a host of other defects, you'll have little recourse. You can't argue that it doesn't meet grade or request a reinspection if there are no written rules to be met.

Buying actual industry grades, such as "Select Knotty" or "Quality Knotty," is a lot safer. Another option is to use common board grades such as No. 2 or No. 3 Common, which give you the same knotty appearance and perform as well as siding.

Customers who want the highest quality appearance — and are willing to pay for it — will prefer the premium grades or some of the special cedar siding grades.

Don't forget moisture content. Nearly all wood siding shrinks somewhat after installation. If the wood's moisture content is too high when installed, shrinkage will be excessive and can lead to splitting, warping, or cupping, as well as paint checking. You can minimize these types of problems by specifying "S-Dry" material. S-Dry contains no more than 19% moisture. You should still stack the siding in a sheltered place on site for a week to ten days so it can acclimate to its surroundings. This will minimize the shrinkage after installation.

Premium grades are dried to MC 15, meaning that the wood has 15% moisture content or less (and that 85% of the pieces are dried to 12% or less). This wood should arrive at the site with close to its final installed moisture content.

"Alternate" grades follow standard grading rules but are unseasoned, with unknown moisture content. The same is true for ungraded sidings.

The importance of pattern. Many failures result from choosing the wrong pattern for the job. The least forgiving pattern is tongue and groove (T&G), because the pieces can come apart with relatively little shrinkage. Therefore T&G siding should be close to its final moisture content when installed and should be prefinished (see Figure 8).

As a rule of thumb, narrow patterns perform best because there is less movement from wet to dry periods, and from season to season. Thicker patterns are safer since they have less tendency to cup or split than thinner patterns. And the surface texture will affect how well the finish performs. Rough textures will

Figure 8. T&G is not a forgiving pattern. When installed green (left), it is bound to fail from excessive shrinkage. Even installed at 19% moisture content, the 1x10 siding (below left) opened at numerous joints. A better choice would have been 1x6s, acclimatized for at least a week before installation.

STANDARD SIDING GRADES

Product	Grade	Description	Moisture Content
Standard Clear Grades — Western Red Cedar			
Bevel Siding	Clear VG (vertical grain)	Free of knots and imperfections; for use where the highest quality appearance is desired.	MC-15 (15% or less — most pieces 12% or less)
	A Grade	Includes some mixed grain and minor growth characteristics.	
	B Grade	Includes mixed grain, limited characteristics and occasional cutouts in longer pieces.	
	Rustic	Similar to A grade, but graded from sawn face.	
	C Grade	Admits larger and more numerous characteristics than A or B grades.	
Boards (Finish, Trim)	Clear	Finest appearance with clear face, few minor characteristics.	MC-15 (15% or less — most pieces 12% or less)
	A Grade	Recommended for fine appearance. May include minor imperfections or growth characteristics.	
	B Grade	Permits larger and more characteristics, but may have short lengths of fine appearance.	
Standard Knotty Grades — Western Red Cedar			
Bevel Siding, Boards, Channel, T&G, etc.	Select Knotty	For fine knotty appearance.	19% or less
	Quality Knotty	Permits more pronounced characteristics and has occasional cutouts in longer pieces.	
Boards, Channel, T&G, etc.	Select Merchantable	Has fine appearance and includes knots and minor markings.	Unseasoned
	Construction	Limited characteristics allowed to assure high degree of serviceability.	
	Standard	Allows more characteristics than construction.	
Standard Softwood Grades (All species except redwood)			
All patterns	C select	Mixed grain, a few small knots allowed. For uses where a fine finished appearance is desired.	MC-15 (15% or less — most pieces 12% or less)
	D select	Mixed grain, slightly larger knots than allowed in C Select.	
All patterns	#2 common	Has fine appearance and includes knots and minor markings.	19% or less
	#3 common	Limited characteristics allowed to assure high degree of serviceability.	
	#4 common	Allows more characteristics than #3. Used chiefly for serviceability rather than appearance.	

Note: These grades apply to all lumber graded under the rules of Western Wood Products Assoc. (WWPA), West Coast Lumber Inspection Bureau (WCLIB), or National Lumber Grades Authority (NLGA) of Canada. The term "characteristics" refers to knots, wane, pitch pockets, irregular grain, etc.

typically hold a finish longer than smooth textures.

The chart "Wood Siding Patterns" suggests which products to use for various types of jobs and provides installation tips.

Pattern width. Finally, many of the problems we see are caused by siding that is too wide. Because wide pieces of siding move more, they are more prone to warp, cup, or cause checking in the finish. In general, patterns over 8 inches in width will probably cause you some problems.

In an effort to save time and money, many builders like wider patterns because they cover an area faster, thus reducing labor costs. But these savings are more often than not wiped out by callback problems later on. If you have experienced this problem, try using the same patterns, but in widths of 8 inches or less.

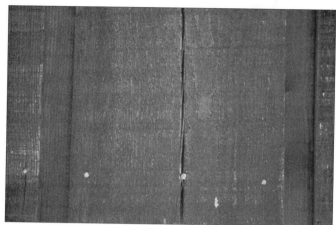

Figure 9. Nails at both edges and the middle of this wide piece of channel rustic (left) caused cracking. Two nails per board, 3 to 4 inches apart — with no nails through the overlap — is best. Bevel siding that is double-nailed is prone to cracking, particularly at the ends (below).

Figure 10. Use horizontal blocking at the joints in vertical siding. Otherwise, the end joints will pull loose and flap in the breeze — even with T&G, as shown here.

Putting It Up Right

Even if you start out with the right pattern, grade, and width, it will not perform well if you put it up wrong. The basics of siding installation are not complex, but following them is crucial.

Nailing. The most common problem is improper nailing. The chart "Wood Siding Patterns" gives nailing guidelines. One rule holds for any pattern and size: *Never double-nail solid wood siding.* That is, never nail through more than one layer of siding at a time. New siding is going to shrink as it acclimates to its new surroundings. If the siding is nailed at both the top and bottom edges (or left and right edge for vertical applications), the nails will restrict the movement of the siding and cause it to split (see Figure 9). With bevel siding, be sure that each nail is slightly above the top of the underlying piece.

Another common problem with bevel siding is overdriving. Drive the nails just flush. Overdriving can cause cupping or splitting.

Finally, make sure the siding nails hit solid wood, not just sheathing or air. On vertical siding, this means using horizontal blocking where two pieces meet (see Figure 10).

Proper overlap. A related problem stems from the amount of overlap. Some builders will use too wide a pattern for the amount of reveal they desire — say, a 6-inch-wide board when they want a 4-inch reveal. This leaves too much board under the overlapping board, forcing you either to double-nail (causing splitting) or to nail through the thin part of the board, causing cupping and

WOOD SIDING PATTERNS

Siding Patterns	Nominal sizes (thickness and width)	Nailing (Do not nail where siding pieces overlay)	
		6 in. and narrower	8 in. and wider
Bevel or Bungalow Bungalow (Colonial) is slightly thicker than Bevel. Either can be used with the smooth or rough-faced surface exposed. Patterns provide a traditional-style appearance. Horizontal applications only.	1/2 x 4 1/2 x 5 1/2 x 6 5/8 x 8 5/8 x 10 3/4 x 6 3/4 x 8 3/4 x 10	Recommend 1" overlap. One siding nail or box nail per bearing, just above the 1" overlap. Plain	Recommend 1" overlap. One siding nail or box nail per bearing, just above the 1" overlap. Plain
Tongue & Groove T&G siding is available in a variety of patterns. Vertical or horizontal applications.	1 x 4 1 x 6 1 x 8 1 x 10 Available with 1/4", 3/8", or 7/16" tongues. For wider widths, specify the longer tongue.	Use one casing nail per bearing to blind nail. Plain	Use two siding nails or box nails 3" to 4" apart to face nail. Plain
Channel Rustic Channel Rustic has 1/2" overlap and a 1" to 1 1/4" channel when installed. The profile allows for maximum dimensional change without harming appearance. Available smooth, rough or saw-textured. Horizontal or vertical applications.	3/4 x 6 3/4 x 8 3/4 x 10	Use one siding nail or box nail to face nail once per bearing, 1" up from bottom edge.	Use two siding nails or box nails 3" to 4" apart per bearing.
Board-and-Batten Boards are surfaced smooth, rough or saw-textured. Rustic ranch-style appearance. Requires horizontal nailers. Vertical applications only.	(4/4) 1 x 2 1 x 4 1 x 6 1 x 8 1 x 10 1 x 12 (5/4) 1 1/4 x 6 1 1/4 x 8 1 1/4 x 10 1 1/4 x 12	Recommend 1/2" overlap. One siding or box nail per bearing. 1/2" Board and Batten	Increase overlap proportionately. Use two siding nails or box nails, 3" to 4" apart. Board and Batten Board on Board

possibly splitting (see Figure 11). You should buy bevel siding 3/4 to 1 inch wider than the reveal you want. If you want a 5-inch exposure, buy 6-inch siding, not 8-inch.

Metal studs. Another fastening problem arises when attaching wood siding to metal studs. In this case, builders often nail the siding into the plywood or OSB structural sheathing. While plywood is good for lateral wall bracing, it's a poor nail base for siding. For good performance, siding

must be nailed into 1 1/2 inches of solid wood. This is supported by all the model building codes.

The best way to achieve this is to attach 2x nailers at each metal stud. An alternative is to fasten directly to the metal studs with stainless-steel or galvanized screws. But I doubt there's much cost difference between this approach and using 2x blocking and regular siding nails.

Rusty nails. Another problem that rears its ugly head time after time is

rusting fasteners or rusty streaks draining from nail holes (see Figure 12). This is a great way to ruin a nice siding job. To avoid it, always use corrosion-resistant fasteners — typically hot-dipped, galvanized nails. More costly alternatives include stainless-steel and high-tensile-strength aluminum nails. Do not use the nails galvanized through an electrolytic process, as the zinc coating can crack during installation and the nails will rust.

Keeping the weather out. Siding is a weather barrier, but it is not waterproof. Water can and will find its way in behind the siding at times, and if nothing else is there to stop it, it may eventually work its way through the wall to the inside of the building (see Figure 13). Some sheathings claim to be waterproof and say you can put siding directly over them. However, the industry recommendation is to use a building paper or a house wrap over all types of sheathing before applying the siding. This is the real waterproofing of your wall. We've also

Figure 11. The carpenter nailed this bevel siding too high up, where the boards are thin and unsupported. This can cup and split the siding. The maximum overlap should be one inch.

NAILING KNOTTY-GRADE

The key to successful installation of knotty-grade siding is to use non-corrosive nails that are long enough to resist withdrawal, and to place them so they don't restrict the siding as it moves seasonally. It sounds simple, but the problems I see most often as a field rep are caused by failing to follow these recommendations.

Nails. I'm amazed at how many builders and remodelers try to save $30 or $40 on nails only to end up with a project that is ruined by streaking within weeks. And the only way you can correct the problem permanently at that point is to pull the siding.

My first choice is stainless-steel nails, but they are very expensive. On budget-minded jobs you might consider high-tensile-strength aluminum nails. Both are available with color coating to help hide them.

Hot-dipped galvanized (HDG) are okay with a heavy body stain or paint. The zinc on HDG nails isn't as vulnerable as electrogalvanized (EG) coatings, which chip when you're driving the nails, and wear off quickly. However, you might consider stainless-steel or aluminum nails if you're using a clear preservative — a few problems have been reported in the field when galvanized nails were used with some of these finishes.

For knotty siding which is prone to greater wood movement, consider using spiral or ringshank nails. These are required to penetrate 1 1/4 inches into solid wood (for smooth-shank nails it's 1 1/2 inches). "Solid wood" means any combination of framing lumber and sheathing. But don't just nail into the sheathing.

Nails should be box or siding nails (see illustration) with *blunt*

rather than *needle* points to cut down on splitting problems. It's tempting to use casing nails because of their low head profile, but these lead to problems with "pull through" when the siding cups. They are recommended for blind nailing tongue-and-groove siding, but that's not something you should be doing in knotty grades on the exterior.

Nailing. Although it takes longer, hand nailing has real quality advantages over pneumatic nailing. You aren't as likely to "overnail" clapboards or drive the head of the nail below the surface of the wood, and it's a lot more accurate in putting nails just where you want them. If you have to use a nail gun, make sure you keep the air pressure adjusted so you're not overnailing, and never use staples.

Vertical siding should be nailed at a maximum of 36 inches on-found that the siding itself performs better when installed this way.

The use of building paper or a house wrap is particularly important behind any vertical or horizontal patterns, since those installations don't shed water as well as overlapping horizontal installations. It's a good idea on vertical installations to scarf any butt joints to prevent water penetration at these points. Make sure, however, that the scarfed joints are angled so they drain toward the exterior of the building.

The biggest problem with diagonal siding is that it channels water directly into door jambs, window moldings, or other joinery details on a structure. This means flashing and caulking details are critical. The best approach is to flash each side of the window with a cap molding (like the one used over the head casing).

Finishing Problems

Finally, many problems stem from choosing the wrong finish or applying it incorrectly.

First things first: Backprime. On most jobs, siding is finished after it is installed, so only the exposed face gets sealed. The back does not. This allows the back of the siding to absorb more moisture than the front, leading to cupping, warping, or even paint failure as the moisture looks for a way to escape. Backpriming equalizes the flow of moisture into and out of the front and back of the siding, minimizing these problems. For this reason I highly recommend backpriming or

prefinishing siding before installing it. This one step would prevent a large percentage of siding callbacks.

Let it weather? Some people choose to let the siding weather naturally, expecting it to turn that light gray color they've seen in pictures of houses on Cape Cod. The problem is, most places don't have Cape Cod's salty air to discourage mildew growth, so the unfinished siding ends up uneven in color. It tends to blacken in areas exposed to high moisture, while

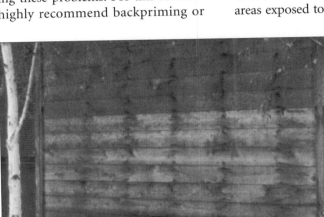

Figure 12. Rusting nails leave ugly streaks down the side of a building. The right nails are stainless steel or hot-dipped galvanized — not electrogalvanized.

center when face nailed, and 32 inches when blind nailed. (However, some building codes now require a 24-inch maximum spacing.) Horizontal siding can be nailed at a maximum of 24 inches on-center over sheathing, and 16 inches on-center without it.

But maybe the most critical rule is *never* nail through two courses of siding with a single nail, sometimes called "double nailing." On patterns 8 inches and up (except clapboards and Dolly Varden) you will need to drive two nails, spaced 3 to 4 inches apart, into each stud. But still, each piece is nailed independently of its neighbor.

Nailing two courses together may have developed in New England several centuries ago when the lower edge of a clapboard was nailed through the one below to help keep the wind out. Unfortunately, the practice is still common. Because of the void that is created when bevel siding is

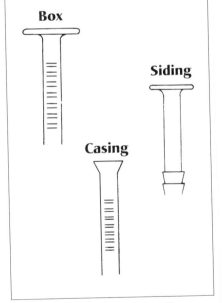

Box nails (left) and siding nails (right) will discourage the "pull through" common with casing nails (center), particularly with the wood movement common to knotty siding.

lapped, it's tempting to nail down toward the bottom edge where the lap makes it feel more solid. Although you may get away with this if you're using narrow, clear, vertical-grain siding in a climate that doesn't have a long drying season, you can end up with problems with knotty material.

All patterns should be fitted together without any gap or expansion space except board-and-batten, which calls for a 1/2-inch space between boards. Bevel siding (clapboards) should lap the previous course by only 1 inch so your nails don't end up going through the top of the course below. This means you'll get a 4 1/2-inch exposure from a 6-inch clapboard; if you want a narrower exposure, you'll need to rip the material down.

By Norm Sievert, Northwest field representative for the Western Wood Products Association.

protected areas, such as under eaves, remain the original color (see Figure 14). Some blackened areas eventually lighten up, but areas exposed to water splash stay dark for a long time.

To achieve that gray, weathered appearance quickly while adding some protection, use a bleaching oil. This preparation typically contains bleach as well as some light pigment

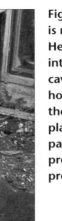

Figure 13. Siding is not waterproof. Here, water got into the wall cavity of a new home and rotted the studs and plates. Building paper would have prevented the problem.

Figure 14. The silver-gray, weathered look that some clients desire happens naturally only where there's plenty of sunlight and salty air to discourage mildew growth. Left untreated, cedar siding is more likely to end up dark and blotchy.

Figure 15. Solid-body stain applied directly to smooth siding has led to many failures. The solution: Use a primer first or put the rough side out. In either case, backbrush the finish if applied by spraying.

to help keep the coloring consistent.

Solid stains. Recently I have seen a number of problems with opaque stains when they were applied to smooth surfaces. These are sometimes called solid-color or heavy-body stains. Since they have more pigment than semitransparent stains, you might think of them as thin paints.

Since opaque stains form a thin film on the wood surface, they can flake and peel if the bond is poor (see Figure 15). Consequently these stains are not recommended directly over smooth surfaces. If you choose to use this type of finish on smooth siding, the wood should be primed first.

Brush it in. Speed is often the top priority when it comes to painting or staining siding. For this reason, many finishes are sprayed on. But spraying leaves the paint or stain sitting on the surface without penetrating into the wood. Eventually, it will start to flake off, even on a rough-textured surface. For that reason, spray-applied finishes should be backrolled or backbrushed to work them into the wood fibers.

The natural look. Many customers want their wood siding to look brand new and "natural" forever. Unfortunately, the natural process is for the wood surface to oxidize and break down. A number of clear finishes containing fungicides and mildewcides can delay the weathering process and keep the wood looking young for several years. But these generally require reapplication every year.

A better approach, I feel, is to apply a semitransparent oil-based stain with pigments that match the color of the natural wood. This allows the grain to show through, but keeps the color true. As the wood is periodically refinished, the color can be restored indefinitely.

By David Utterback, midwestern regional manager for the Western Wood Products Association.

WOOD SIDING OVER FOAM

As early as 1976, problems were reported with horizontal wood and hardboard siding applied over foam sheathing on the exterior of homes. Hardboard siding typically failed between nailing points, primarily because of expansion, which caused the boards to bow out. Wood siding, primarily redwood and cedar, failed because of cupping, which caused nails to pull out and boards to split.

The failures follow a fairly characteristic pattern. For all types of siding, failure is most severe on the east and south exposures of a building. Fewer problems exist on the west exposures, and almost none on north exposures.

For hardboard siding, the failures occur between the nails as the fibers expand and the siding buckles, creating a bowed-out "wave" pattern between each nailing point. Wood sidings generally cup and split — severely enough at times to cause siding boards to actually fall off.

The overall problem cannot be attributed to any single cause. Several factors — including the characteristics of rigid plastic foam itself, the wood siding involved, the use of sealers, the type of nails, and the method of installation — all play a role.

Characteristics of Rigid Plastic Foams

The same characteristics that make rigid plastic foams ideal for thermal insulation — their light weight, softness, and resistance to heat and moisture — can cause moisture problems when foams are used under wood sidings.

The softness of the foams increases the likelihood that the expansion and contraction of the wood, as well as the nailing of the siding, will dent the sheathing slightly and loosen the connection between the siding and

the foam. This leaves larger gaps in which moisture can collect.

In addition, the foam provides less support for nails. Thus, as the siding expands and contracts longitudinally, the nails move back and forth and loosen.

The foam's resistance to heat and moisture also creates a moisture buildup between the foam and the siding. In fact, this moisture buildup on the back of the siding is considered the major contributor to the siding problems.

All sidings undergo a series of wet and dry cycles, during which the moisture within the wood as well as from the air is driven to the back side of the siding. At the same time that moisture is accumulating on the back side, the front of the siding is being dried by exposure to the sun and the air. These cycles are exacerbated by the presence of foam sheathing.

The more severe failures on east and south exposures of homes result partially from the increased drying of the siding exterior by the sun, and also partially from the heat of the early morning sun, which heats the space between the sheathing and the siding. This causes dew points to be reached and thus moisture to collect on the back of the siding. Again, the foam's resistance to heat and moisture intensifies the situation.

Type and Size of Wood Siding

The type and size of wood siding installed also affects the seriousness of the problem at the foam and siding interface.

Wood sidings that are thicker (greater than 1/2 inch) and narrower (6 inches or less wide), for example, better resist the wet-dry cycles and the resulting cupping failures. And shorter boards (that is, less than 6 feet long) show less longitudinal expansion and contraction and thus

Figure 16. The use of redwood siding and rigid plastic foam has spelled disaster for the owner of this home, which has been plagued with pulled-out nails and split and cupped siding.

cause less stress on nails.

Finally, of course, wood siding should be at a stable moisture content before installation. This always is a major factor to consider for wood siding, whether it is installed over foam sheathing or not.

For hardboard siding, the most critical material-related factor appears to be its density. The most dense sidings tend to resist breakdown from moisture better than the less dense ones.

Color and Sealers

Color and sealers also play a role in the problem. Darker colors attract more heat into siding and intensify the problem. The use of a lighter color can create a considerable difference in temperature.

It now is recommended that wood and hardboard sidings be treated with sealers on all sides — but especially on the back — before installation. A sealer certainly will make any siding more resistant to moisture. Over time, however, sealers also will fail under continued intense heat and wet-dry cycling.

Nail Type and Size

The type and size of nails also can have an impact on the problem. Manufacturers recommend the use of galvanized or stainless-steel nails with improved grip and the use of nails with a blunt point for wood siding.

In addition, a $1\frac{1}{2}$-inch penetration into the wood stud is considered critical. For hardboard, a needle-point nail will reduce ripping as it passes through the back of the siding. While secure nailing is important for hardboard siding, it is not as likely as wood siding to fail at nailing points, so it is not as critical an item.

Recommendations

To minimize the chance of failure when installing wood siding over foam, follow closely all manufacturers' recommendations for installation as well as the following:

- Drive nails carefully to avoid denting the foam;
- Use thicker, narrower, and shorter siding pieces;
- Pay attention to the proper storage and stabilized moisture content of the wood;
- Select the proper type and size of nails;
- Apply sealers on all sides;
- Choose light-colored stains and paints;
- Choose proper locations for driving your nails; and
- Take care to achieve proper overall installation.

These recommendations, of course, treat the symptoms — moisture accumulation on the back of the siding — not the problem itself. The ultimate solution involves creating and venting a space between the sheathing and the siding in addition to following the above recommendations.

Furring strips to separate the foam sheathing and siding will allow the space to vent itself of heat and moisture and will reduce the heat and wet-dry cycles considerably. The space must be open at the top and bottom edges of the siding (insect screens are advised) to allow full movement of air.

By John Russo, an engineering consultant in Minneapolis, Minn.

HARDBOARD SIDING

Hardboard siding comes in forms imitating almost any other siding material you can think of. But most hardboard falls into two basic categories: lap and panel siding.

Lap and multilap. Lap and multilap siding, designed to look like

Figure 17. This hardboard has absorbed excessive moisture and expanded, causing buckling and bowing.

cedar, redwood, or fir clapboards, accounts for 60% of hardboard sales. It comes in sizes from 4-inch to 16-inch boards, and it is available in multilap versions that take care of several "rows" of siding at once to speed installation. Most lap siding is face nailed. Lap siding is especially prominent in the East, Midwest, and parts of the South — wherever clapboards are popular.

Panel siding. Hardboard siding also comes in 2x8-foot, 4x8-foot, and 4x9-foot panels. The panels imitate everything from board-and-batten construction and vertical rabbeted laps to stone and stucco. The large panels install quickly.

Panels are popular where the materials they imitate are common (stucco sells well in the Southwest, for instance) or where cutting costs is important, as in low-end mobile homes.

Different grades and thicknesses. Hardboard comes in five different grades and two basic thicknesses.

The better quality sidings are of "standard" or "tempered" grade. Tempered siding is impregnated with additives and/or heat treated to make it stiffer, harder, and more resistant to water and abrasion.

Siding comes in $7/16$-inch and $1/2$-inch thicknesses. Several of the builders and distributors I talked to said the $1/2$-inch product performed significantly better than the thinner versions.

Unprimed, primed, or prefinished. Unprimed hardboard siding is a rarity these days, because most installers want to reduce finishing time. Primed siding, which accounts for most of the market, comes ready to paint or stain. Most manufacturer warranties require finishing within 30 to 90 days of installation. Two coats of an acrylic latex paint or acrylic stain are recommended for hardboard.

Prefinished sidings are taking a steadily increasing share of the market — 10% and growing, according to the American Hardboard Association (AHA). Though more expensive, prefinished siding offers the advantage of quicker job completion. Both manufacturers and distributors say the extra cost is usually less than that of paying someone to paint primed siding.

Most finish warranties are for five years. But a few newer lap products that have blind nailing (nails hidden under the lap above) offer warranties up to 15 years.

Performance Promises

Hardboard promises a lot: the look, solidity, and insulating qualities of natural wood; a wide variety of types and patterns; resistance to impact; and a reasonable price.

But whether or not it delivers on these promises depends on several critical factors. Moisture absorption tops the list, followed by quality of installation, paint performance, and manufacturer support.

Moisture is bad news to hardboard — even more than to regular wood.

Dobbin McNatt, who has researched hardboard at the U.S. Forest Products Laboratory in Madison, Wis., for almost 20 years, says that by its nature, hardboard is vulnerable to moisture.

"Hardboard, as it comes out of the factory, is pretty dry," says McNatt. "If it's not equilibrated before it's put up, it will pick up moisture and expand. Since it's homogenized wood, it expands more in length than a piece of solid wood siding will. And it will buckle if it's nailed down when it expands."

This expansion from moisture absorption lies behind most hardboard siding failures. The industry standard allows an expansion of 2.4 inches for every 50 feet of siding. That's enough to cause severe buckling of the board — enough to pull nail heads through the board as it bows away from the wall. This expansion is even enough to move

studs out of line and cause cracking in interior surfaces.

Buckling and bending. Any break or weakness in hardboard's finish — an overdriven nail, an unpainted butt edge, an uncaulked seam — can lead to moisture problems (see Figure 17). Once moisture gets a toehold, a cycle sets in. Breaks in the finish caused by pulled nails, for instance, invite more moisture infiltration, causing more expansion and more pulled nails, and so on. Moisture can also speed paint degradation, and as the paint comes off, more moisture comes in.

Bad enough to quit. Problems like that are driving some hardboard dealers and installers out of the business. Minneapolis siding distributor Marty Bennis, for instance, has sold and installed hardboard siding for 20 years. In recent years, however, he has begun to phase the product out of his sales.

"A lot of hardboard is good product, but it's inconsistent," says

Bennis. "You get what you pay for. We've just had too many problems over the years." Bennis says moisture "wicking" into the hardboard caused most of his problems, which included buckling boards and peeling paint (see Figure 18).

Tim Melgren, operations manager at Inner Mountain Lumber in Missoula, Mont., tells of similar problems.

"It's pretty dry here," says Melgren, "but we've still had expansion problems, swelling and shrinking. Where you have long runs on a wall, you get swaying and buckling. It'll pull nails and swell up over the heads. We've also had some shrinkage problems, where the gap opens and the caulk pops off."

Melgren blames some of these failures on builders who butt the boards too tightly or fail to caulk and paint adequately. But, he says, "We're seeing some problems even when people follow the installation guidelines strictly… and the problems are

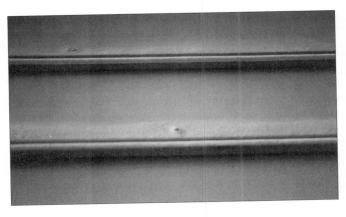

Figure 18. Overdriving nails into hardboard siding invites trouble. The broken surface gives an inroad to moisture, leading to cracking and further moisture absorption. Overdriven nails should be caulked.

Figure 19. Undersized corner boards have aggravated the expansion problem on this installation by allowing moisture access to the ends of siding panels. Corner boards should fully cover the ends of the siding.

bad enough to discourage us from using it." As a result, says Melgren, he now sells hardboard "reluctantly." When possible, he steers his customers to the OSB product Inner-Seal made by Louisiana-Pacific instead.

It's not just the humidity, it's the heat. Hardboard fares worst in areas that have big swings in humidity and temperature and does best in areas that are dry year-round. Louis Wagner, technical director of the American Hardboard Association (AHA), says "you'll very rarely see a rot or buckling problem in Arizona, but in Louisiana or Mississippi or across the South where you've got high summer temperatures and high humidity, you tend to see more problems with linear expansion. And in the North, where you get condensation from inside, you tend to get more problems with rot. There's a band in the central part of the country where you don't see problems very often."

Proper installation crucial. Along with weather, quality of installation is a crucial factor in hardboard's performance. To stray from the manufacturer's installation guidelines is to ask for trouble.

Installation guidelines vary only slightly from one manufacturer to another (see "Hardboard Do's and Don'ts"). Most companies void the warranty if certain guidelines aren't followed. Generally, key guidelines include:

Hardboard Do's and Don'ts

Always follow the manufacturer's recommendations for the specific hardboard product you use. Failing to do so risks product failure and voiding the warranty. Most manufacturers' guidelines are similar to the ones described here, which are compiled from American Hardboard Association (AHA) literature, manufacturers' instructions, and conversations with builders, suppliers, and researchers.

If the product doesn't come with instructions, call the manufacturer and have them send you a copy.

Pre-Application
Hardboard performs best if you take a few precautions and do a little planning before you install it.

Get it used to the place. It's best to get hardboard siding a week early and store it at the job site to let it adjust to the site's humidity. That should minimize expansion or shrinking after application. Store it flat on stickers in an unheated, covered building or under tarps. Keep it away from moisture.

Some manufacturers recommend "splintering" the bundles (breaking them up and restacking them with stickers placed between every few layers of siding) to help this stabilizing process. In fact, splintering is the only way to ensure the siding will reach the proper humidity level.

Let the place dry first. Don't install hardboard siding when a building's concrete foundation is still drying. The moisture released by the foundation may condense on the back side of the hardboard. If you have no choice, says AHA technical director Louis Wagner, "Make sure that you find other ways to dispose of that water vapor — leave a window open — and make sure you're getting some outdoor air exchange." Leaving the interior unheated as long as possible will also help.

Installation
The instructions below are fairly representative, but you should follow your manufacturer's guidelines to protect your warranty.

Use a warm-side vapor barrier. The hardboard industry requires warm-side vapor barriers — if you don't use one and have problems, you'll probably strike out trying to get a warranty settlement.

Use a vapor retarder rated at one perm or less (this includes polyethylene film, kraft paper, or foil-backed gypsum board). Some manufacturers will accept foil-backed fiberglass batts.

These requirements generally apply to retrofit jobs, too. If you can't provide a suitable interior vapor barrier on a residing job, some manufacturers will accept exterior foam sheathing. Some will also accept an exterior vapor barrier with strapping between it and the hardboard; however, in cold climates, an exterior vapor barrier could trap moisture within the wall cavity. Either solution may require you to extend the window and door trim as well.

Cut it correctly. Use a fine tooth saw. Always cut into the face of the board: that is, place boards face up when using a hand saw, face down when using a circular saw.

Stay clear of the ground and roofs. Don't install hardboard siding closer than 6 or 8 inches to the ground (many codes require an 8-inch clearance) or closer than 2 inches to roofs. If you're in an area where it snows a lot, you might want to leave a 4- or 6-inch gap above roofs.

Gap all butt ends. To allow for expansion, follow the manufacturer's recommendations for spacing between boards. Usually this is $1/16$ inch or $1/8$ inch; a few recommend $3/16$; some recommend different gaps for board-to-board and board-to-trim spaces. If you use H-strips, you may need to leave an even bigger gap.

Seal the gaps. You can either caulk the gaps or install "H-strips" manufactured for sealing them. Use an acrylic or urethane-based caulk — silicone won't take paint. You'll need to leave a larger gap between boards — up to $1/2$ inch — when using H-strips.

Builders are divided on whether caulk or H-strips perform better. Some feel the caulk makes for a smoother look; others feel that H-strips look okay and are worth the protection they give from caulk

- Installing a continuous warm-side vapor barrier.
- Leaving gaps of about 1/8 inch between butt ends of boards and between boards and trim. The gaps must be caulked or covered with a special "H-joint" (see Figure 19).
- Using only galvanized box nails driven flush with the board's surface.
- Finishing the siding within a certain period, usually 30 to 90 days after installation.

Leaving out any of these steps opens the door to moisture and expansion problems, and later to warranty disputes. So knowing and following the guidelines is crucial.

Unfortunately, not all manufacturers do a good job of getting these guidelines to builders. Builders unaware that special instructions exist might easily put the siding up incorrectly — only to run into problems with warranty claims later.

Paint: Another Sticky Subject

Hardboard's need for frequent painting is another source of complaint from builders and homeowners. Jim Adams, who used to use hardboard for the 400 homes his Good Value Homes builds in the Minneapolis area every year, quit using it primarily because it required painting so often.

"We just had too many claims from clients," he says. "The freeze/thaw cycle was rough on the paint, and it

---

bulging or falling out when boards expand and contract.

Use proper corner boards and trim. Corner boards and trim must be thick enough to completely cover the ends and edges of the siding. Leave a gap of about 1/8 inch between board and trim and caulk this (see illustration). Where boards run over the top of a door or window trim, use a proper flashing and caulk.

Use the right nails, and don't overdrive them. Use galvanized box nails of the recommended size; usually it's a 6d, 8d, or 10d nail. Nails should penetrate at least 1 1/2 inches into the studs.

Drive the nails just flush with the surface. An underdriven nail will loosen; an overdriven nail breaks the surface of the siding, opening an avenue for moisture infiltration. If you overdrive one, caulk the hole.

Finishing

To protect the wood and the warranty, you must finish with the thoroughness of a tax auditor.

Use the right primer and paint. Hardboard manufacturers leave the back side of their siding unprimed and unfinished, and they recommend that you do the same. According to AHA's Wagner, this is done to give moisture some means of escape.

For unprimed siding, use oil/alkyd primers. Over the primer or on primed siding, apply two coats of a high-quality acrylic latex paint or acrylic stain that is *recommended for use on hardboard*.

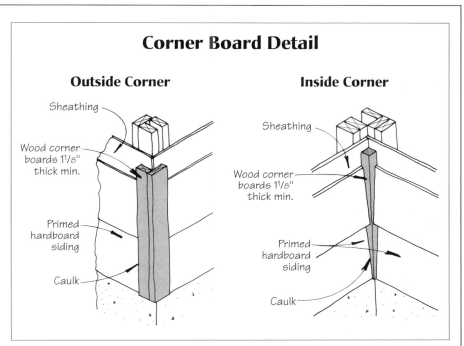

Corner Board Detail

Outside Corner

Sheathing

Wood corner boards 1 1/8" thick min.

Primed hardboard siding

Caulk

Inside Corner

Sheathing

Wood corner boards 1 1/8" thick min.

Primed hardboard siding

Caulk

Corner boards must be thick enough to cover ends or edges of siding, with a caulked gap of about 1/8 inch between boards and siding.

Products not recommended may not adhere as well or last as long. Don't skimp on the paint; if necessary remind your client that cheap paint will likely mean a new paint job a lot sooner.

It helps to use a paler color, preferably with a lot of white in it. "The whiter the color, usually, the longer it'll last," says Wagner. "There are some colors that don't last well at all — yellow, for example. Titanium dioxide makes a stable color, and will last longer than anything else." Titanium dioxide content is highest in white or off-white paints.

Don't take any "holidays." Painters call a missed spot a "holiday." Don't take any with hardboard siding. Hit every spot, paying special attention to the butt edges along the bottom of each board. This will mean getting down low to hit the bottoms of the lower boards, which will need protection the most.

Emphasize maintenance. Clients need to keep an eye on the siding and look for popped caulk, missing H-joints, or nail holes that open. These should be caulked and refinished immediately. — *D.D.*

would crack. You have to repaint every two or three years. Then we got a batch with some bad primer and the paint wouldn't stick, and that was the frosting on the cake for us."

According to construction consultant Paul Cove, Adams' problem with frequent painting isn't unusual. "Hardboard has to be painted more often than wood," he says, because cracked or peeling paint opens the way to moisture infiltration.

A few of the newer hardboard products address this issue, offering longer finish warranties. MacMillan-Bloedel, for instance, recently came out with a blind-nailed product that carries a 15-year finish warranty, and Masonite offers its blind-nailed "Colorlock" with a 15-year warranty.

Such products might ease many of the industry's problems. According to manufacturers, blind-nailing makes the product both more durable and more attractive. In face-nailed sidings, nail holes usually offer moisture its first entry; hiding the nail holes under the lap above removes this entryway. The absence of visible nails also gives the siding a much cleaner look.

By David Dobbs, a freelance writer from Montpelier, Vt.

GUIDE TO GALVANIZED NAILS

Builders typically use galvanized nails for framing decks, for applying wood siding, and for installing exterior trim. But not everyone knows that "galvanized" can have more than one meaning when you're talking about nails. All galvanized nails are made of steel and coated with zinc. The zinc coating is what protects the nail from rust. But how much zinc is on the nail, and how the zinc is applied, make a big difference in how well the nail will resist rust.

Hot-Dipping

The traditional way to coat steel nails with zinc is "hot-dipping." In the hot-dipping process, the nails are immersed in a bath of molten zinc, like french fries in a pot of oil. The intense heat of the zinc bath causes the zinc and the steel to bind together in an alloy layer that acts as a base for a heavy zinc coating and provides long-lasting protection against rust.

"Double hot-dipped" galvanized nails are actually dipped twice in molten zinc, and are processed for uniformity between dips. The second dip is designed to fill up any pinholes and adds thickness to the outer layer of zinc (Figure 20).

Electroplating

Steel nails are electroplated by immersing them in an electrolytic solution. An electric current in the bath deposits a thin film of zinc from a zinc anode onto the surface of the nails. With their smooth, shiny coating, electroplated nails work well as collated nails in mechanical nail guns — and they look beautiful when they're brand-new. But the thin zinc coating commonly applied to nails in commercial electroplating oxidizes away rapidly when exposed to weather, and the nails then begin to rust (Figure 21). Siding trade associations warn against using these nails in exterior applications.

Hot-Galvanizing

A lot of the galvanized nails sold in lumberyards are coated by "hot-galvanizing." Nails produced this way are labeled "HG," while nails produced by hot-dipping are labeled "HD." Because the labels are so similar, carpenters looking for hot-dipped galvanized nails are often sold hot-galvanized nails. But even though the terms sound similar, there is a significant difference in the nails. In hot-galvanizing, also known

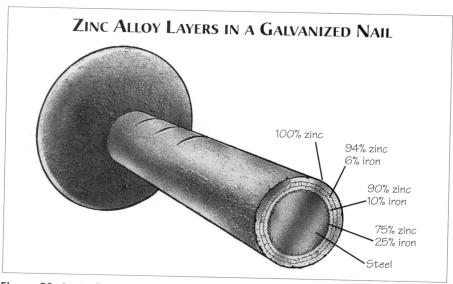

ZINC ALLOY LAYERS IN A GALVANIZED NAIL

100% zinc
94% zinc
6% iron
90% zinc
10% iron
75% zinc
25% iron
Steel

Figure 20. According to the American Galvanizers' Association in Aurora, Colo., hot-dip galvanizing creates a series of protective alloy layers around a steel nail. The outer layer is 100% zinc, while inner layers contain progressively less zinc and more steel. If the zinc and alloy layers are scratched and some steel is exposed, zinc in the outer layers will corrode before the steel does, preventing rust formation.

Extractive Bleeding & Wood Staining

Builders who install wood siding and leave it natural or use a clear finish frequently notice staining of the wood around nail heads. This staining is often blamed on the nails themselves. But if wood contains moisture when installed or gets wet after installation, stains often occur around nail heads even when the galvanized layer is still intact, and even when stainless-steel or aluminum nails are used. In these cases, the source of the problem is extractive bleeding.

All wood contains a certain amount of naturally occurring substances like pigments, tannins, oils, and resins. These substances are called extractives because they can be drawn from wood by various solvents, including water. The water-soluble extractives are sometimes brought to the surface of the wood by moisture inside the wood — whether from the wood's inherent moisture, from moisture inside a dwelling that migrates into the siding because there is no vapor barrier, or from moisture that penetrates the wood from outside. This migration of extractives is intensified by the "drawing effect" of the sun. Extractive bleeding often stains the wood, and can also discolor applied finishes, whether paint or stain. Extractive bleeding is a risk any time wood siding is used. Beautiful woods like cedar and redwood, which are durable because they contain the most extractives, have the highest risk of bleeding.

Extractive bleeding often occurs around nail holes. A poor-quality nail makes the problem worse because tannins react with unprotected iron to form a blue-black stain that spreads around and below the nail head.

To prevent extractive bleeding, pay close attention to construction details. Protect wood siding from water before, during, and after

"Extractive bleeding" has streaked these shingles below the nail holes (top). Iron in nails can react with natural wood tannins to make bleeding worse. Bleeding stains can also emerge from wood grain, even on stained or painted siding (middle). Bleeding is caused by exposure to water — note that the shingles protected by the eaves show less staining (bottom).

installation. Proper drying of lumber, moisture control within the building, effective finishing, and careful flashing and caulking are all important. And keep in mind that painted or stained siding requires periodic refinishing to retain its beauty. — *T.C.*

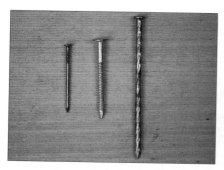

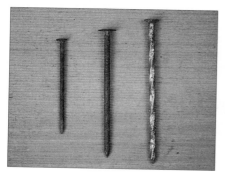
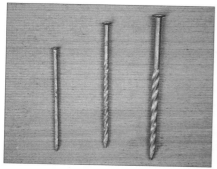

Figure 21. Electroplated nails (top) are bright and shiny, but have a relatively thin zinc coating. Peen-plated nails (second) also have a thin zinc coating. "Hot-galvanized" nails (third) are not hot-dipped, but coated with zinc chips in a hot tumbler, a process that can yield an uneven coating. Double hot-dipped galvanized nails (bottom) have a thick zinc alloy coating. High-quality hot-dipped nails outperform all other types of galvanized nails in exterior applications.

as "tumbler galvanizing," zinc chips are sprinkled on top of cold nails in a large barrel, then the barrel is rotated in a large furnace to melt and distribute the zinc. Like buttering popcorn, the results are uneven. Some nails receive too much zinc, and others not enough. It is hard to deposit enough zinc on and under the nail heads by this method, and globs of zinc tend to clog the threads of ring- and screw-shank nails.

Unlike hot-dipping, the hot-galvanizing process does not create a uniform alloy layer between the steel nail and the surface layer of pure zinc. Lacking this metallurgical bond between the nail and the coating, some percentage of hot-galvanized nails will be prone to rusting if used on the outside of a building. Often you can spot the rust on these nails in their shipping cartons, even before they are used.

Mechanical Plating

Mechanically plated nails are also called "peen-plated." In this relatively new process, the cold nails are rolled around in a drum containing zinc dust, tiny glass BBs, and an activator fluid. As the drum rotates, the BBs hammer, or "peen," the zinc dust onto the nails.

Mechanical plating works well for adding a zinc coating to screws or ring-shank nails, because the thin zinc coating applied does not clog the threads or rings. Mechanical plating is also commonly used to apply a zinc coating to hardened nails like the concrete fasteners used in powder-driven nail guns (hot-dipping is unsuitable for hardened nails because the intense heat of the molten zinc bath would soften the tempered nails). But mechanical-plated nails typically lack the thickness of zinc found on a hot-dipped nail, and they do not have the alloy layer that hot-dipped galvanized nails have. Most mechanically-plated screws or nails are less corrosion-resistant than hot-dipped nails.

Stainless Steel and Aluminum

Galvanized nails are not the only rust-resistant nails available. Stainless-steel nails are a more costly but very effective alternative. Stainless steel is a steel-nickel-chromium alloy that provides excellent rust protection, even when exposed to substances that might ultimately corrode a hot-dipped galvanized nail. Stainless-steel nails are definitely worth the extra expense in seashore environments, below-grade applications, or when cedar or redwood trim or siding is left natural or given a transparent finish.

Most stainless-steel nails found in lumberyards are labeled either "304" or "316." The 316 stainless nails contain higher levels of the alloy metals. You should use 316 stainless nails in rough environments like the seashore.

Aluminum nails are also available for use on exterior siding. They will not usually rust or corrode when exposed to the weather, but they may cause corrosion in other metals.

The Western Wood Products Association, the California Redwood Association, and the Western Red Cedar Lumber Association all recommend stainless-steel nails for installing natural wood siding on homes — especially in corrosive environments like coastal sites. But in most applications, all those associations agree that a galvanized nail can give excellent performance — as long as it is a high-quality, hot-dipped galvanized nail. Other methods of applying zinc to nails, they say, are not usually as resistant to corrosion.

By Ted Cushman, an associate editor at The Journal of Light Construction.

CHAPTER 4

BRICK, STUCCO & MASONRY

- Brick Veneer

- Brick Masonry Restoration

- Caulking Masonry Joints

- Leak-Proof Chimney Flashing

- Retrofit Chimney Flashing

- Patching Stucco

- EIFS Performance Review

BRICK VENEER

Many home buyers like the low maintenance and quality look of a brick veneer home. The veneer will never need painting; it will protect the house from wind (Figure 1); and if the work is done right, the veneer will last the lifetime of the house.

But contractors with a carpentry background may not understand the finer points of masonry-veneer construction. Mistakes made in foundation construction, in design, and even in homeowner maintenance can undermine long-term performance of brick veneer.

The brick veneer layer behaves differently than the structural wall behind it. Wood begins to shrink the moment a house is finished; concrete does too. But brick actually *expands* as it ages.

And unlike structural components, brick veneer can only support its own weight; in fact, *it* must be supported (Figure 2). Think of veneer as a stack of dominoes; the higher the stack, the more unstable it becomes. A stack on a slanted surface is extremely unstable.

Finally, the brick skin isn't completely waterproof. Water squeezes through small cracks in the mortar, and the brick itself can absorb water. Small amounts of water evaporate without causing problems, but if brick is exposed to a downpour or to water-saturated soil, it can be damaged.

Four simple concepts will help you avoid problems and help you understand the details that follow:
- Support the brick on a stiff, stable ledge.
- Tie the brick securely to its back-up.
- Leave room for expansion.
- Use flashing to keep water out.

Vertical Support

If you support brick veneer properly, you're off to a good start. The foundation, the brick ledges, and the lintels all have to support the brick without moving or deflecting.

Firm footings. Contractors know they should build on undisturbed soil. This minimizes building settlement. Settlement is not necessarily bad for a structure, however. If a building settles uniformly, you probably won't see cracks in brick veneer.

A major problem *will* show up if a building settles at different rates across its foundation area. If differential settlement occurs, step cracks will occur and will follow the mortar joints (Figure 3). The crack pattern will grow larger as it goes from the bottom to the top of the wall.

Even though uniform settlement probably won't hurt the wall, you don't want to take chances. The only way to guarantee that settlement won't damage the veneer is to make sure the underlying soil has been properly compacted. Don't throw in an extra shovelful of dirt just to save a little on concrete. In parts of the country where soil has a high expansive-clay content (like Texas), you may have to take special precautions. These can include subsoil foundation watering or foundation drainage systems.

Sometimes homeowner maintenance can cause problems with

Figure 1. A brick veneer goes right over insulating board and wood studs. The veneer protects the house from wind.

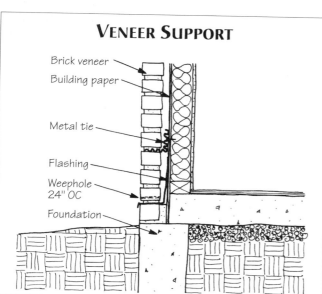

VENEER SUPPORT

Brick veneer
Building paper
Metal tie
Flashing
Weephole 24" OC
Foundation

Figure 2. The foundation supports the veneer. Elastomeric or metal flashing comes through the wall above the first brick joint. Metal ties connect the brick back to the structure.

veneer. If you're brought in to repoint a cracked veneer, you should look for the cause. Poor drainage of surface water away from the foundation can cause settling. More often the problem is caused by a downspout spilling water against the foundation wall (Figure 4).

Downspouts frequently end at the corner of the house. Water gathers around the foundation and percolates down to the footing or foundation slab. The moving water washes away fine particles of silt, creating voids in the soil and undermining the slab or foundation footing. Eventually, the weight of the house causes the soil to collapse, and a corner of the slab can crack off. In an extreme case, the foundation tips because the footing is undercut.

After you've repaired the damage, make sure you build up the soil level around the house so water drains away. Otherwise, you may be blamed if the crack opens again. Make sure all downspouts use extensions or splash pans.

Ledge. If you're sure the foundation's on solid footing, concentrate on getting a good brick ledge to support the veneer. The brick ledge should be large enough so that it will support two-thirds of the width of the brick.

Sometimes the contractor provides a 3$\frac{1}{2}$-inch ledge, thinking this is adequate for the masonry. However, the contractor may also install 1-inch rigid insulation, taking the ledge down to 2$\frac{1}{2}$ inches. The mason also needs finger room behind the brick. Without this finger room the mortar would push the veneer away from the wall. After taking away finger room, the mason is left with only 2 inches — less than the minimum needed. The mason's not going to stop work if you didn't leave enough room. He'll build it anyway. It's up to the general contractor to provide a minimum of 2$\frac{1}{2}$ inches *plus finger room* for the veneer.

Brick veneer can be added to an existing building — even if no brick

Figure 3. Spray-paint was used to highlight differential settlement cracks on the inside of this foundation. You can imagine what the brick outside looks like.

Figure 4. This conductor pipe spills water down the foundation wall and excavates a trench below the footing.

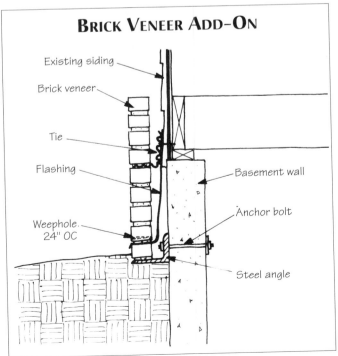

BRICK VENEER ADD-ON

Existing siding
Brick veneer
Tie
Flashing
Weephole. 24" OC
Basement wall
Anchor bolt
Steel angle

Figure 5. When adding brick veneer to an existing building, the angle of the support shelf and the number of bolts tying it to the building must be figured by an engineer.

Figure 6. Deflection of a wood window frame caused the triangular chunk of brick above the window to drop. The brick was only supported by the window frame.

ledge was provided originally (Figure 5). But you will need to make a ledge from steel angle attached to the existing foundation. Place the angle at or below grade, and make sure it's corrosion-resistant. Also make sure you get an engineer to look at the angle size, foundation strength, and bolt

size and spacing.

Lintels. Poor lintel design is common. Lintels over garage openings or wide windows should be designed to minimize deflection (Figure 6). With wood lintels, you should limit deflection to $1/600$ of the span length or a maximum of 0.3

inch. This will prevent cracking of the supported brick veneer. Or, use steel lintels for openings that exceed 8 feet. Make sure you leave extra room at the ends of the lintel where it is supported on the masonry. Steel expands, and you need to leave space for expansion. Otherwise the expanding steel will induce high stresses and cause the surrounding brick to spall (Figure 7).

For smaller openings, steel angles or reinforced-masonry lintels may be adequate. However, some builders leave out lintels over basement windows altogether. This is a poor practice that will lead to future window and veneer problems.

Tie It Tight

The brick veneer receives its vertical support from the foundation

BRICK VENEER DETAILS

Figure A. Because flashing was never installed below this window sill, the brick became saturated with water and efflorescence has occurred.

Figure B. This parapet wall, capped with numerous small bricks, created many joints and greater vulnerability to water damage. A better design would have used large stone, continuous metal, or glazed tile coping.

Of all the essentials of brick veneer construction, none is more important than proper detailing. Most problems involve wood shrinkage and inadequate flashing. Caulking and sealants for sills, jambs, shelf angles, lintels, and parapets also need special attention. If the detailing is well thought out and construction is done according to plans, the problems of efflorescence, water penetration, brick cracking and spalling, and wall bowing can be virtually eliminated.

Wood shrinkage. Wood shrinks far more along its width than it does along its length. Floor joists, for example, shrink more across their width than studs do along their length. With a two-story, split-level house, you may have as many as three platforms. If you're using a brick veneer, you need to allow for shrinkage of the wood and expansion of the brick.

For instance, problems often occur beneath windows. Leave room for the window to come down to the brick. If you don't take shrinkage into account, the window frame can come

or from stiff horizontal lintels. But the veneer must also be supported laterally. This is the job of the tie-support system. The wall ties transfer the horizontal wind loads on the building into the structural system and ultimately into the foundation. The ties must be strong enough to resist tensile and compressive forces.

Follow these rules of thumb in low-rise construction:

- Use one tie for every $3^{1}/_{4}$ square feet of wall area, with a maximum spacing of 24 inches on-center, or approximately one tie per stud every sixth or seventh course.
- For a concrete masonry back-up, use continuous horizontal joint-reinforcement with U-tabs or individual Z-ties.
- For wood framing, ties should

Figure 7. Expansion of the steel lintel caused this brick to spall.

be corrosion-resistant corrugated metal, at least 22-gauge, $^{7}/_{8}$ inch wide, and 6 inches long.

Engrave these numbers in your mind — maximum spacing of *24 inches on-center*. Put a tie about

every *6th or 7th course*. You see a lot of veneer installed with no wall ties. The mason might tell you ties aren't needed for a one-story building, but they are. Winds whip across the prairie and along the coasts, and even an occasional high

down hard on the brick. The window will jam and become inoperable.

A similar problem occurs with half-height veneer on a single-story house. When the wood shrinks, the siding can come down tight onto the veneer. If the soldier course has been flashed, the flashing tips towards the house, causing water to drain towards the inside. Even if no flashing is used, the siding will frequently be so tight that it will begin to buckle or rot. To avoid this, leave room between the flashing and siding for shrinkage, but tuck metal flashing behind the siding so that the gap does not allow water to penetrate.

Depending on the height of the building, you could get as much as $^{1}/_{2}$ to $1^{1}/_{2}$ inches of shrinkage in the wood frame. You can try to overcome the shrinkage problem by using balloon framing. If you do, however, make sure you also use balloon framing for interior walls as well.

Another way to tackle shrinkage on multi-story buildings is to support the veneer with shelf angle at each floor level. Leave an expansion joint below the shelf angle. Use a foam neoprene pad in the joint, and face the joint with backer rod and sealant.

Figure C. Be sure to seal the joints on a parapet wall. If sealant is not maintained, mortar deteriorates and efflorescence occurs.

Flashing problems. Brick needs flashing to stop the flow of water. In Figure A, flashing was left out below the sill. Notice the efflorescence. This is salt that rises to the surface as brick goes through wet/dry cycles. The surface efflorescence shows that water has entered the wall at the sill. Over time, through freezing and thawing, there is a good chance the brick will begin to spall.

Parapets are another place where it's easy for water to get in. Parapet design should be considered carefully before construction begins. Notice how the wall in Figure B was

capped. The numerous brick joints allow water to enter the wall. Instead, the wall should have been capped with large pieces of stone, continuous metal, or glazed terra-cotta tile coping. These materials create fewer joints and therefore fewer potential headaches. But remember to properly seal the coping joints with sealant. Figure C shows what happens if the sealant is inadequate or omitted. The mortar has begun to fall apart. Not only will wall damage eventually occur, but efflorescence will result as well. — *R.B. and R.R.*

wind can put unacceptable stress on a veneer wall.

Make sure the ties are *corrosion-resistant*, particularly in coastal climates or in areas where rainfall is high. Also, if you're building in winter, heat your water and materials instead of using an admixture. Admixtures can cause tie corrosion and veneer failure.

Leave Room for Expansion

Walls are subjected to movement. Thermal expansion and contraction, moisture absorption, material shrinkage, or building loads may cause movement of the building components. Provide room for this movement so it won't damage the veneer. The main way to handle movement is with expansion joints.

Expansion joints. Expansion joints look like long, vertical slices down a brick wall. You'll see them near corners of large buildings. Expansion joints are placed in brick masonry construction to prevent overstressing of the veneer. Expansion joints prevent cracking due to thermal movement, moisture-absorption, and load effects. Since the brick is exposed to the outside, temperature and moisture changes can be significant. A south-facing wall, for example, can experience temperature swings of 140°F in a day.

In residential construction, most walls are relatively short. Accumulated movements are usually not large

enough to warrant expansion joints. However, long walls — 75 feet or more — can have problems. Problems also occur where there are abrupt changes in wall geometry. If you're building a long ranch house, with the brick veneer facing the sun, you may need to use expansion joints.

The approximate amount of expansion from the various sources can be calculated by an engineer. When you build an expansion joint, however, you'd better make sure the joint is about twice as large as the anticipated movement because the mason will fill this joint with sealant. If you don't provide enough room for the volume of the sealant, it will squeeze out of the joint during maximum expansion, and the water seal may break. In repairing a wall that has cracked because of wall movement, you should never seal the crack with mortar. Always repair with a compressible sealant to prevent further distress.

Keep Water Out

The fourth concept is probably the hardest to accomplish in practice. That's because there are many ways for water to enter a veneer wall. And in residential construction, masons do not always follow recommended industry practice. For example, it's common for masons to leave out base flashing. But base flashing is one of the most important safeguards against water damage.

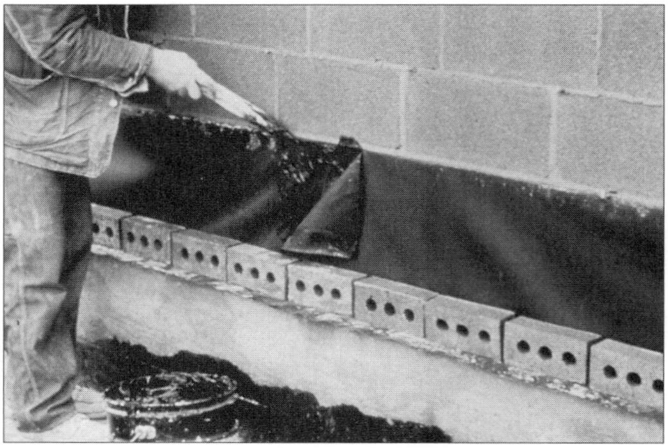

Flashing. Although many masons don't use base flashing, it's very important and *should be used*. Even when it is used, it is often torn or damaged during construction. Figure 8 shows how to do the job right. The bricklayer is lapping and sealing the flashing to ensure a continuous membrane. He has also extended the flashing beyond the exterior face of the brick. This will direct water that enters the wall to exit on the exterior face. Water won't accumulate in the cavity between the block and the veneer.

Weep holes. In case water should get into this cavity, the mason must provide channels for it to escape. Put weep holes every 24 inches on-center directly above all flashing. Some contractors incorrectly place weep holes several courses above the flashing. This can cause problems since it allows water to accumulate from the flashing up to the exit point. The water may freeze, and the resulting ice can put pressure on the brick, causing cracking or spalling.

Also, the mason should make sure the mortar droppings do not clog the weep holes. One way to keep weep holes free is to use short lengths of cotton sash cord. Place the cord where the weep holes should be, but make it long enough so it will stay above the mortar droppings. Water will wick out the sash cord. When the sash cord eventually rots, the weep hole will be free.

Another way to provide weep holes is to leave out every third brick in the base course. As the wall goes up, the brick mason can have a helper clean out the mortar droppings. When the wall is finished, the mason mortars in the missing brick, leaving out the head joint (the joint at the side of the brick). You'll have weep slots right where you need them.

The masonry contractor should also flash any horizontal brick ledge or surface. Suppose, for example, the brick veneer is only half the height of the wall. A flat soldier course will

Figure 8. The bricklayer laps the flashing and seals the joint. Loose bricks hold the flashing in place and ensure that it won't get bunched up in the wall or torn during construction.

collect water. The soldier course should either be flashed or sloped to shed water. It's best to avoid flat soldier courses altogether.

Mortar and brick quality. The quality of brick and mortar can affect how much water gets into a wall. On the one hand, porous brick absorbs water. On the other hand, very hard-fired brick may not bond as well with mortar. Without a good mortar joint, the wall may leak, even though the brick is not porous. Brick with about 6% to 9% water absorption by boiling (ask for bricks that conform to ASTM C216) provides good bonds.

Mortar quality is also critical. The mason should be using mortar made from portland cement and Type S (fully hydrated) lime. Cement makes the mortar strong, and lime makes the mortar "plastic." Lime mortars fill in small cracks that could otherwise allow water to penetrate the wall.

Make sure the temperature doesn't fall below freezing until the mortar cures because ice crystals can form in mortar. The mortar may eventually cure, but the crystalline holes will be embedded in the joints. Even a normal rain will get through the joints and leak into the house.

By Robert J. Beiner, P.E., director of technical services for the International Masonry Institute in Washington, D.C., and by Robert Rhault, New England regional director of the International Masonry Institute.

BRICK MASONRY RESTORATION

The masonry rehab techniques described below are in compliance with the *Standards for Rehabilitation* approved by the National Park Service for projects seeking rehab tax credits. However, they are good guidelines for any masonry rehab where high-quality, durable workmanship is desired.

Many projects have been denied rehab tax credits due to poor or inappropriate work — specifically masonry work. This means: Do not sandblast masonry, replace water-struck brick with extruded wire-cut units, or repoint with portland cement mortar and expect to get approval.

Why Repoint?

There are several possible reasons why any particular building needs to be repointed. These are listed with the most common reason first, the rarest last. If buildings were built and maintained better the sequence would be reversed:

Poor workmanship — past or current. Not only may past work be visually inappropriate, but it can actually speed up the deterioration

Figure 9. This brick was sandblasted and then repointed with hard portland-cement mortar. Deteriorating brick and protruding mortar joints resulted. Old soft brick and new portland cement mortar don't mix for reasons shown below.

LIME VS. CEMENT MORTAR

Flexible Mortar (Lime)

Hot — Bricks expand Mortar compresses

Cold — Bricks contract Mortar flexes

Inflexible Mortar (Cement)

Hot — Bricks expand Spalling

Cold — Bricks contract Cracks open up

Figure 10. It makes no sense to bid a repointing job until the type and condition of mortar is known. Test patches yield this information along with data on how best to strip and clean. The brick under this deteriorated paint turned out to be in excellent condition.

of the brickwork. For example, sand-blasting can cause the masonry to crumble. The use of portland-rich mortar can lead to spalling brick and visually unacceptable patches (Figure 9). These problems are very costly to repair.

Work rejected by an owner or architect may also need to be redone — at substantial cost to the contractor or mason. Masonry work may be rejected because it is just plain bad work, but often it stems from inadequate specifications: the scope of work does not provide an adequate standard of reference for the job.

Structural deficiencies. Structural problems may be caused by faulty

DETAILS FOR GOOD JOINTS

A. REMOVAL OF OLD MORTAR

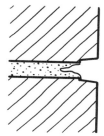

Incorrect
Mortar is not cleaned out to a uniform depth. Edges of brick are damaged by tool or grinder, which creates a wider joint.

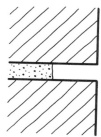

Correct
Mortar is cleaned out to a uniform depth — about 1" deep. Edges of brick are undamaged.

Old mortar should be removed to a minimum depth of two-and-a-half times the width of the joint — about 1 inch deep for most brick joints — to ensure an adequate bond (Figure A). Any loose or disintegrated mortar beyond this depth should also be removed. Joints should be cleaned with care since damage to the bricks can affect not only the appearance, but can also lead to accelerated weather damage.

Where existing mortar has been removed to a depth greater than 1 inch, these deeper areas should be filled first, compacting the new mortar in several 1/4-inch-thick layers to reduce overall shrinkage. It is important to allow each layer time to harden before applying the next layer, since most of the shrinkage occurs while the mortar hardens.

The rate of hardening can be controlled by dampening the brick

B.

construction (possibly altered during renovations), deteriorated structural members, or hydrostatic pressure. Whatever the case, a builder must determine if there is active movement. This will require evaluation — possibly by an engineer — to determine the cause, present activity, and corrective treatment needed. This may require substantial work before starting the masonry restoration.

Water damage. Change in grade, splashback, deteriorated flashing, missing gutters, colorless coatings, and sandblasted brick can all cause or contribute to water-related damage. Well-maintained masonry itself will seldom fail prematurely. If there is spalling, efflorescence, or mildew, suspect water as the culprit. Eliminate the source of damage before undertaking any masonry restoration.

To fix water-related damage may require a lot of related work: regrading, roofing, flashing, cornice repair, and new downspouts. Even if all of this is beyond the scope of your work, be certain to inform the owner/architect of these essentials. Otherwise your best work — backed by a guarantee — may prematurely fail through no fault of its own or yours.

Deteriorated masonry. This means the normal, anticipated erosion of mortar that is to be expected after about a hundred years. Under these conditions, work is typically limited in scope and should not require 100% repointing. In fact, the rule is to repoint only where required.

Putting Masonry to the Test

Too often, contractors are expected to bid on masonry repairs based on poorly developed specifications, no test patches, and materials defined by phrases like "or equal." In these instances, the burden falls on the contractor to do the impossible; for example, to "match existing" mortar that is obscured from vision.

The only way to develop meaningful specs is to test first. Initial testing should be done during a preliminary evaluation of existing conditions (Figure 10). The results

---

and old mortar before filling the joint, but avoid free water or excessive wetting. Too much water will delay the tooling or cause excessive shrinkage; too little water will reduce bond strength.

When the final layer of mortar is thumb-print hard, the joint should be tooled to match the historic joint (Figure B). Proper timing of the tooling is important for uniform color and appearance. If tooled too soft, the color will be lighter than expected, and hairline cracks may occur. If tooled too hard, there may be dark streaks called "tool burning," and you won't get good closure of the mortar against the brick.

If the old bricks have worn, rounded edges, it is usually best to recess the final mortar slightly from the face of the bricks. This will help avoid a joint wider than the actual joint width, which would change the character of the original brickwork. It will also avoid the creation of a large, thin feathered edge that is easily damaged (Figure C).

If the repointing work is done carefully, the only cleaning required will be a small amount of mortar brushed from the edge of the joint with a stiff bristle brush following tooling. This is done after the

C. Tooling the Joint

Incorrect
Joints are filled too full. Wide feather edge is susceptible to spalling.

Correct
Joints are slightly recessed, which makes a durable joint.

mortar has dried, but before it is fully hardened (one to two hours). Mortar that has hardened can usually be removed with a wooden paddle or, if necessary, a chisel. Further cleaning is best accomplished with plain water and bristle brushes.

New construction "bloom" or efflorescence occasionally appears within the first few months after repointing and usually disappears through the normal weathering process. If the efflorescence is not removed by natural processes, the safest way to remove it is by dry brushing with stiff natural or nylon-bristle brushes and water. Muriatic acid is generally ineffective and should be avoided. In fact, it can deposit salts which can lead to additional efflorescence.

Adapted with permission from Preservation Brief 2: Repointing Mortar Joints in Historic Buildings, *published by the National Park Service, Preservation Assistance Division.*

should be incorporated into the specifications for the scope of work, materials, and methods. These specs must be available to the contractor at the time of the walk-through prior to bidding the project.

After the initial scope of work is established, it may need to be updated as more information becomes available during the course of the project. For example, the degree of repointing needed on painted or badly stained masonry cannot be determined until the entire building is stripped or

cleaned. The contractor should make allowances in the contract for the additional work anticipated and allow time in the schedule to complete the work.

Testing includes test patches on the building, mock-up panels, and work samples. By testing we mean *non-destructive* testing. There have been a number of cases where poorly executed test patches posed more problems than the surrounding work. For example, sandblasting to remove paint, or using electric grinders to remove mortar profiles can cause more damage in

one hour than a building has sustained in 100 years.

Matching Materials

Repair work may require several ranges of brick from various manufacturers (if existing bricks are no longer made); mortar ingredients from different lime/cement companies; a range of sand aggregate for color and texture; and two or three mortar colorings to properly "age" the new to look old. Also, the use of properly slaked quick-lime is worth considering on brick structures built before 1850 where the mortar

---

JOINT PREPARATION: A JOB FOR PNEUMATICS

Proper joint preparation is at least as important as the actual repointing work. Joint preparation consists of carefully removing deteriorated or inappropriate mortar from between the masonry or stone units. Deteriorated mortar, by nature, is not difficult to remove: The challenge is to remove it *carefully* to a sufficient depth. Inappropriate mortar, on the other hand, is typically hard portland-rich mortar, which can cause irreversible damage to the surrounding masonry.

There are two prevalent methods of raking out mortar joints: the hand method and the use of electric grinders. You would do well to consider a third option: We've had great success with certain pneumatic carving tools described below.

Hand tools. Many contractors consider the use of hand tools — a mason's hammer and chisel — the best way to remove mortar. If you are among those, you'll have plenty of time to consider other options while using this slow, imprecise method. Laborious hand tooling is not only a matter of time and expense, but also of worker fatigue. A weary body and mind are prone to mistakes, here in the form of irreversible damage.

Electric grinders. At this point, electric grinders might seem a viable option. Perhaps they are, but

only on moderately wide horizontal joints that are uninterrupted by decorative elements such as brick window lintels or decorative terra cotta. And only if you have the skill to match the power of this tool.

Rotary electric grinders are frequently dangerous to both the building and the builder. Work cannot be properly viewed under the clouds of dust and fast-moving debris generated by a blade spinning at speeds as high as 6,000 rpm.

A major limitation of electric grinders is that they tend to over-cut into neighboring courses when used on vertical mortar joints. Also the depth of removal is limited by the working radius of the blade. A 4-inch blade offers only $1^1/2$ inches maximum raking depth. Yes, grinders have their place, but only in conjunction with the preferred methods described below.

Pneumatic tools. The use of pneumatic tools has had a tremendous impact on historic masonry restoration. Why? Exactly because of the precise manner and controlled impact of these air-powered instruments. They remove mortar by causing it to crumble and fall.

We're not talking about the implements used to remove mufflers from cars, or to drill post holes into sidewalks for "no parking" signs. These pneumatic tools are

totally unacceptable for any restoration work.

The tool we're describing is made by the Trow and Holden Company, a firm that has specialized in tools for the stone industry since 1890. Trow and Holden's pneumatic carving tool was designed as a precision sculpting instrument and has been used by the arts and industry since 1890. If the tool is precise enough to sculpt the face of Abraham Lincoln, why shouldn't it be able to rake out loose mortar from masonry?

Unlike the "muffler remover," the Trow and Holden tool has neither a retainer nor a throttle. This unconventional design provides for some unique control characteristics.

For instance, this tool has a chisel with a round shank, hand-held in place in the carving tool. A round shank permits the chisel blade to be oriented independent of the tool, an essential feature that is impossible with square-shank tools. The absence of a retainer, or any mechanical connection, enables the mason to defeat the power of the tool immediately by simply pulling the chisel away from the piston. One hand operates the tool while the other controls the chisel.

The chisel blades are tempered and available with carbide tips. They can be custom-made to any length or width. Even very thin

contains lime specks.

For matching mortar, dozens of samples may be needed to match the structural properties and texture of the original joints. Ingredients will include various aggregates, mortar dyes, cement, and lime. Do not use ready-mixed mortar, latex additives, or anti-freezing agents. Each sample should be carefully labeled, accurately proportioned by volume (coffee cans work well), and documented. These must be allowed to dry naturally before a perfect match for color and texture can be achieved.

A single building can have substantial differences in mortar from elevation to elevation. Over a dozen different mortar mixes may be required on one side of a two-story house. We know of one project, however, where the test results for two mortar samples served as the basis for restoring mortar on a 200,000-square-foot mill constructed over a period of 50 years.

Raking Out Mortar

There are several techniques for raking out mortar and removing masonry units. What is excellent for one job, however, can be disastrous for another. The methods include:
- Hand raking (hammer and chisel)
- Mechanical/electrical raking (tuck-point grinders)
- Mechanical/pneumatic raking (small grinders, reciprocating hammers)

In many cases, a combination of techniques is useful. For example, most historic masonry with soft lime mortar will require a combination of hand and mechanical/pneumatic techniques. On newer structures — with hard portland mortar —

The Trow and Holden pneumatic chisel was developed for sculptors (left), but can also remove old mortar quickly and with little fatigue to the worker. The worker maintains precise control by manipulating the loose-fitting chisel (center), and controlling the pneumatic back-pressure with his other hand. Vertical joints are easily cleaned (right), without harming adjacent brick — a real problem with grinding equipment.

"butter" joints can be cleaned, and a joint whose width is the distance between the lines on this page can be easily raked out. As with other raking tools, the width of the chisel should not exceed three-quarters of the width of the mortar joint.

Once mortar joints have been carefully raked out, any remaining debris can be easily cleaned with a regulated, light application of compressed air.

The Trow and Holden pneumatic carving tool is about three times faster than hand raking in removing loose mortar, hard mortar, and damaged bricks. Keep in mind that the object of masonry restoration is to restore only that material which actually requires work, with as little "intervention" as possible.

As with any instrument, it takes time and practice to master the correct use of this tool and its potential. For product and technical information, contact: Trow and Holden Company, Inc., 45 South Main Street, Barre, VT 05641; 800/451-4349 (out of state), or 802/476-7221. — *M.W. and P.M.*

grinders are predominantly employed but the fine work is done using pneumatics.

Proper selection and testing of tools will also help you match the original mortar-joint condition and depth of joint. The right tool can also make a major difference in efficiency (see "Joint Preparation," previous page).

Repointing Techniques

Aside from matching the color, texture, and physical properties of the mortar, the application, tooling, and cleaning all must be done correctly to match the original work. This will often involve a study of the joint profile to determine the original — and present — tooling. If the original tool is no longer manufactured, this might require making a special tool.

The time allowed between tuckpointing and tooling (dwell time) is critical. This will affect how deep the tool penetrates, and the mortar's viscosity and density. It also affects the texturing techniques used at the end (for example, brushing, burlapping, or water/air spraying).

Final cleaning must be done carefully and, again, after testing. Various materials react differently with a common chemical. Improper cleaning can lead to problems such as efflorescence, erosion, and burning of the mortar joint.

New Materials

The need to match the original materials exactly is the single most overlooked element of masonry restoration. With the range of materials available today — cement, lime, aggregate, dyes, brick, and stone — you can meet almost any job requirements. These elements, in the hands of a skilled individual, can produce work that's virtually impossible to tell apart from the original.

By Michael J. Watson, owner of Green Mountain Restoration Company in Shaftsbury, Vt., and by Philip C. Marshall, an architectural masonry conservator and an associate professor in the historic preservation program at Roger Williams University's School of Architecture in Bristol, R.I. Photos by Philip C. Marshall.

CAULKING MASONRY JOINTS

When it's done skillfully, caulking — or joint sealing — is almost invisible on a masonry exterior. But when it's botched, it can create a real eyesore. Worse, a poor caulking job can allow water into a building — with resultant damage, callbacks, lost time and money, and poor customer relations.

Masonry joint sealants are called for in three situations: in an expansion or control joint, in a joint between dissimilar materials, and at the perimeter of an opening in the masonry surface (Figure 11).

For the small general contractor, a single-family home or remodeling job that involves exterior masonry probably won't require enough caulking and sealing to make it worth hiring a specialty sub. But any joints, such as window and door perimeters or seams where brick meets wood siding, should be correctly sealed against water penetration. At least one person on your crew should understand the fundamentals of caulking.

While face brick is probably the most common masonry finish the caulker encounters, the same principles and similar procedures will apply for sealing joints in other materials — block, precast concrete, stone, stucco, and EIFS (exterior insulation and finish systems).

Size and Shape

A very tight joint — say, a joint less than $1/4$ inch wide — is fairly easy to caulk, especially if it's a right-angle joint. This is usually the case with a window in a masonry opening. You are simply gunning the sealant and tooling it into a corner. The two perpendicular surfaces will guide the tip of your gun and your finishing tool.

However, because tight tolerances are hard to achieve in masonry work, you will typically encounter joints that are $1/2$ inch wide or greater. And because a control or expansion joint needs to be fairly wide in order to tolerate the expansion, contraction, and movement in the masonry wall, it's not uncommon to come up against joints $3/4$ inch, 1 inch, or even $1 1/2$ inches wide. It's a real challenge to make a larger joint look good and provide a good seal.

The design of details should take joint sealants into account. If two dissimilar materials meet, there needs to be enough length of parallel return inside the joint so that backer rod will stay in place (more on backer rod below) and so that the joint sealant will have sufficient bonding surface.

Joint Prep

To achieve proper bonding on the two sides of the joint, some surface preparation may be necessary. Joint surfaces should be dry, sound, and free of dust, dirt, and loose or foreign material. Be prepared to scrape, chip, and dust the inside of the joint or even blow it out with compressed air. Depending on the conditions and the manufacturer's instructions, you may have to clean the joint with solvent or apply a primer.

If you have the unenviable job of recaulking an older building, you will need to check with the sealant manufacturer for special procedures to thoroughly cut out the old caulk. Old caulk can be pretty stubborn stuff, so you may need a special saw and a machine grinder. You also might have to prime every surface to be sealed.

Joint Sealants

The joint sealants that are most often specified for construction work are polyurethanes, silicones, and polysulfides. Silicones usually come in tubes. Polyurethanes and polysulfides can come packaged in tubes or in bulk. All joint sealants should be finished with a steel tool.

If you're a beginning caulker, tube caulk is much easier to work with. Keep in mind, though, that masonry caulking can use up a large number of tubes. For a 1/2-inch or 3/4-inch joint you may only get about 10 feet per 10.5-ounce tube. Also, tube sealants are air-cured and can take a week or longer to cure.

Bulk sealants are mixed with an activator before application, so they are chemically cured and can cure in a day or two. To work with bulk materials, you'll need a bulk gun, a large drill (at least 1/2 inch), and a special mixing paddle (Figure 12). Once you get it down, you can do a lot more caulking and save money on materials using bulk sealant. But you'll have a messier job and more cleanup, and you'll have to work with some unpleasant solvents.

Joint sealants come in a variety of standard colors. It's even possible to have the factory make up custom colors. Color decisions should be made well ahead of time, as some colors are hard to get and have to be special-ordered.

For a light-colored surface, I like a lighter sealant color; a darker surface calls for a still darker sealant color. For example, on a regular reddish brown brick wall, I often use a somewhat darker "Redwood Tan" sealant color to good effect. On a light gray block wall, a lighter "Off-White" looks good.

With this kind of scheme, the caulk line doesn't stand out so much.

Backer Rod

Backer rod is made out of foam and looks like long strings of spaghetti. It comes in sizes as thin as 1/4 inch and as thick as 2 inches and up. If you choose backer rod that's just a little larger than the joint you have to caulk, you can insert it under a slight compression so it will stay in place and allow you to control the depth of the sealant.

The main purpose of backer rod is to keep sealant off the back of the joint, thus preventing back-bonding, or three-sided bonding. To properly expand and compress, the joint sealant should be bonded to only two sides of the joint. If the joint is too shallow to fit backer rod, you can apply bond-breaker tape to the back of the joint to prevent back-bond-

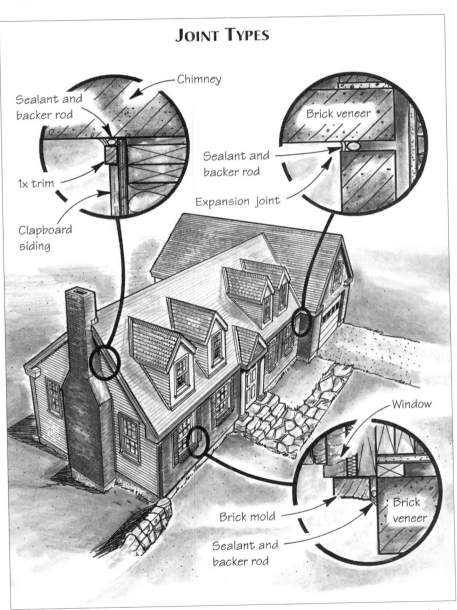

JOINT TYPES

Chimney

Sealant and backer rod

Brick veneer

Sealant and backer rod

1x trim

Expansion joint

Clapboard siding

Window

Brick mold

Brick veneer

Sealant and backer rod

Figure 11. To create longlasting joints in masonry, use the tools and materials found in commercial work, such as backer rod and polyurethane, silicone, or polysulfide sealants. Three typical joint types found in residential work are shown.

Figure 12. Two-part bulk sealants have to be mixed with a drill and paddle (left). Using a bulk caulking gun (center and right) allows you to do high-volume caulking more cost-effectively, but is messy.

ing. Bond-breaker tape comes on a roll and looks like cellophane tape.

You can buy backer rod from joint sealant suppliers. Backer rod comes in open cell and closed cell form. Open cell compresses more and is easier to work with. However, some architects don't like it because it's like a sponge and can absorb water, while closed-cell backer rod is impervious to water.

Whichever type you're using, push the backer rod into the joint gently, using a blunt tool that won't pierce or tear it (Figure 13). A piece of wood shingle makes a good backer rod tool.

Applying Joint Sealants

Joint sealants have both a functional and an aesthetic purpose. In sealing a joint, you are trying to provide a seal against penetration by

water and air, and you are applying a finish detail. The aesthetic aspect is affected mostly by your tooling method, but several factors will affect the water-tightness of a joint.

In sealing joints, don't think of yourself as just filling a crack. Be aware that you are providing a flexible seal between the surfaces of two independent building components, which move and shift in relation to

---

CAULKING TIPS

Good caulking requires a great deal of skill and a certain amount of artistry. I've found that not just anyone can be trained to do caulking. You need aesthetic sense, patience, an eye for detail, and a real concern for the integrity and appearance of the finished product.

Here are some little tricks that might help improve your sealant work.

Tube caulking. Cut the nozzle of your tube at an angle and slightly smaller than the size of the joint. If the joint size varies, have two or three tubes going at the same time, each with the nozzle cut at a different size.

Cold weather. Keep your material warm. You can even buy an electric heat chest to keep your tubes or bucket in. Use gloves with the fin-

gers cut off to keep your dexterity.

Steel tooling. Use long, steady strokes. Attempt to tool every run only once rather than dabbing at it repeatedly. Rather than tooling towards your previous work (as if you were painting), pull away from the last section you tooled. Press the sealant firmly, so that it fills the joint and bonds to the sides.

Spatula. Provide yourself with a selection of various sizes. For any given run, choose a spatula slightly smaller than the width of the joint.

Keeping your tool clean. At the beginning of your work day, take a newspaper and rip it into pieces about 4x4 inches. Use these pieces to keep your tool clean.

Tools. Wear a tool belt or nail apron to carry your various spatulas, scrapers, other tools, and your

pieces of newspaper. Don't use your favorite carpenter tool belt for caulking, as it will get pretty messy.

Sturdy caulking gun. Get a good sturdy caulking gun made for production work. Get a hook attachment so you can hang it on the staging or ladder. Use a gun with a release, so you can stop the flow of sealant quickly.

Backer rod. Rather than struggling to cram large backer rod into a small joint, keep a variety of sizes on hand for different sizes of joints.

Annoying details. When you're working on a section of a building, take note of things that weren't ready to be caulked the first time you went through. Have a plan for getting back to them later, especially if they are high up, hard to get to, and easily overlooked. — A.B.

Figure 13. Compressible foam backer rod fills the back of a joint and helps the caulk perform properly. Use a size slightly thicker than the crack and insert it gently with a blunt tool.

Figure 14. Caulk should be applied to a joint in a smooth, even bead. When applying tube caulk to a joint whose thickness varies, carry several tubes with various size openings.

Figure 15. To properly finish a joint, smooth it in a continuous motion with a steel caulking tool or spatula. The author sometimes custom-fabricates a tool from a wooden tongue depressor.

one another. The dimensions of that seal must be carefully controlled. It can't be just a thin skin, but neither can it be a thick gob.

If your joint sealant is not applied properly, it will not expand and compress with the movement of the joint. Instead, it may split or rip away from one of the two joint surfaces.

Most polyurethane joint sealants are designed to tolerate up to 40% extension and 25% compression. However, they will not achieve that degree of movement if the joint is too deep. For example, for a joint 1/2 inch to 2 inches wide, one sealant manufacturer requires that the joint depth be no more than 1/2 inch.

When gunning sealant into the joint, try to achieve a smooth, even flow (Figure 14). Don't try to just zip down a skin. Fill — but don't overfill — the joint, placing sufficient sealant to achieve proper joint depth.

Tooling

Correct tooling is critical to creating a sealant joint that's tight and looks good (Figure 15). The best tool is a steel spatula or sculptor's tool that is slightly smaller than the width of the joint. Try to achieve a smooth, even appearance, without squeeze-out on the sides. Good tooling takes a lot of practice.

For special circumstances, I have on occasion made a custom-sized wooden tool by whittling down a tongue depressor. I have also seen plastic joint tools. Unless the joint is very small, don't try to tool with your finger. It slows you down and makes a mess. Also, manufacturers' instructions usually discourage using water or solvent to tool a joint.

Planning a Caulking Job

On the surface, caulking can seem pretty simple. It's rarely on the "critical path" of a project plan. However, one key aspect of joint sealing guarantees complications: Often, the sealant is being used to treat the joint between two dissimilar materials, and these materials are often installed by different trades and at different times.

If the caulking work is to be done off the staging, make sure that it will be left up long enough. Because staging is often rented, there's a lot of pressure to get it off the job quickly.

Don't forget conditions on the ground. How steep is the grade — not the finished grade, but the grade as it will be when you're doing the caulking? Will it be safe for a ladder? Will a boom lift be able to operate

in the area? Keep in mind that a boom lift won't work if the grade is too steep.

Identify the scope of work. What gets caulked and what doesn't? Will one party be responsible for all caulking on the job? Or will each trade be responsible for caulking its own work? (This is a strategy that often yields poor results, in my experience.)

Weather and temperature affect caulking work. You can't caulk a wet surface, so allow flexibility in the schedule. And, although you can caulk in cold weather (check the manufacturer's limitations), sometimes ice or frost will collect in a joint and can be very hard to detect.

The application of joint sealants is a little-known construction specialty. But it can make a big difference in the integrity and life span of a masonry building. If you take care to apply the materials properly and give attention to detail, this is a trade that can add to your profits — and give the satisfaction that comes with doing fine work.

By Al Bredenberg, of Cornwall, Conn., a former contractor who writes frequently on construction topics. Photos by Carolyn Bates.

LEAK-PROOF CHIMNEY FLASHING

What is a flashing job required to do? The obvious requirement is to seal the opening around the chimney where it goes through the roof. Second, the flashing should provide a sliding connection that will allow the building to move independently of the chimney. The third, not so obvious requirement is to prevent the transfer of water, absorbed by the masonry above the roof, into the masonry below the roof. The flashing should meet these requirements for the life of the chimney.

Most of the masons I've seen lately prefer to use lead flashing in their masonry. Lead is the easiest metal to work, which makes up for its higher cost over aluminum and galvanized metal in time saved. Copper is the most expensive flashing, but it will probably last longer than lead. Since it too is difficult to form, copper flashing has to be formed in a metal shop. This shop work adds to the cost, so you usually see copper only on more expensive homes where it is specified by the architect.

On the average home, the mason sticks the ends of the lead an inch or so into the mortar joint and leaves it hanging down around the chimney. The roofers arrive, shingle up to the chimney, fold the flashing down between shingle courses, and nail the ends to the roof. If they are more conscientious than usual, they may slap some tar on the end of the flashing before they lay the next shingle.

The above scenario creates a number of problems. All wooden structures shrink in height as they age and shift slightly with seasonal changes. The chimney, however, does not move. The shifting and shrinkage of the frame structure stresses the flashing, causing the ends of the shingles to lift, breaking the tar seal and eventually tearing the flashing. Sooner or later, but usually within the first ten years, leaks will begin around the chimney. Also, since the problem of water transfer through the masonry units was not addressed

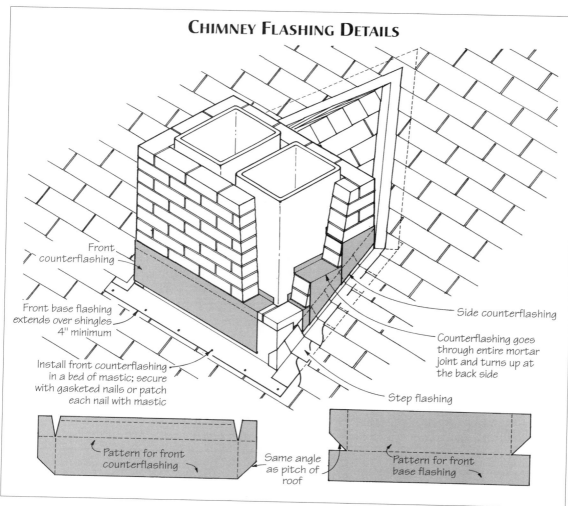

CHIMNEY FLASHING DETAILS

Front counterflashing

Front base flashing extends over shingles 4" minimum

Install front counterflashing in a bed of mastic; secure with gasketed nails or patch each nail with mastic

Pattern for front counterflashing

Same angle as pitch of roof

Side counterflashing

Counterflashing goes through entire mortar joint and turns up at the back side

Step flashing

Pattern for front base flashing

Figure 16. When flashing a chimney, never attach a flashing to both the chimney and the roof. The base flashings are attached to the roof only, the counterflashings to the chimney only. This creates a slip membrane, allowing the house to move independently of the chimney.

at all, the chimney begins transferring moisture into the house with the first good rain. This is because masonry units, whether brick, block, or stone, are not waterproof or even water-resistant; they can transfer gallons of water into a house. Doing the job right in the beginning can save the builder the headache of trying to fix a "leak" that no amount of tarring or reflashing can solve.

Three Trades Involved

Flashing a chimney involves workers from three trades: Usually at least one, and sometimes all of them, does not do the job correctly.

The carpenter. A good flashing job begins with the carpenter who makes the opening in the roof. If you're the carpenter on a chimney job, you must find out, preferably from the mason, the exact dimensions of the chimney at the point where it exits the roof. Codes usually require that the framing for the opening be kept 2 inches away from the masonry. If the roof sheathing is extended into the opening 1 1/2 inches on all sides (leaving a hole 1 inch larger than the dimensions of the chimney) the mason can then drop plumb lines from the corners to position the chimney at its base. You must also make sure that the roof opening lines up with the openings for the chimney in any floors or ceilings below and that the opening size is corrected for the roof pitch. These things may seem obvious, but mistakes are common.

The next step is to build the cricket. All chimneys, even small ones, should have a cricket unless they go through the roof directly at the ridge. The cricket should be no wider than the up-roof dimension of the chimney and should be constructed like the roof of a small dormer, with both sides the same pitch as the main roof. If the chimney is close to the ridge, the pitch of the sides may have to be less than the roof pitch to avoid extending the cricket above the ridge.

Tack the completed cricket to the roof in its intended location. (The mason may want to move it to facilitate his work, but he will need the completed cricket to correctly position the flashing in the masonry.)

The mason. Preventing the water transfer problem mentioned above is the responsibility of the mason. If you are the mason building the chimney, you may have to make a minor, but very important, change in the way you place the flashing pieces in the chimney. Instead of sticking them into the mortar joints only an inch or so, you must place the flashing so it passes completely through the mortar joint and turns up on the back of the masonry unit. This does not weaken the chimney because the flashing goes in at different levels of mortar joints as it follows the pitch of the roof. If you place the flashing this way, there will be no transfer of water into the house through the masonry units.

The roofer. The roofer's part of the job requires the most attention. If you are roofing around a chimney, a critical point to keep in mind is that you must *never* fasten any flashing connected to the chimney to the roof. The job goes as follows:

• On the down-roof side, or front, of the chimney, nail a continuous piece of flashing over the last shingle course and bend it up against the chimney to a height of about 3 inches. Take care to form this front flashing so that the first step flashing on each side can bend around it to prevent water from being funnelled into the building at this point (Figure 16). You may want to try Flash-Rite Corner Shingles (P.O. Box 23, Grabill, IN 46741; 219/627-6465) to give added protection at the corners. These are inexpensive prebent corner flashings, made of corrugated aluminum, that can be shaped to match your roof pitch (Figure 17).

• Next, beginning at the bottom and working up, install the step flashings where the end of each shingle course abuts the chimney.

• When you reach the up-roof side, or back, of the chimney, nail the cricket in place and shingle it as if it were a dormer roof, again using step flashings where the shingle courses abut the back of the chimney (Figure 18). It is usually easier to cover a small cricket with lead flashing rather than shingles. The step flashings may be lead, too, but on a large chimney it is easier

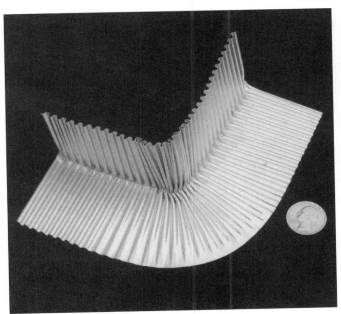

Figure 17. Install Flash-Rite corner shingles between base and counterflashings to protect the vulnerable spot at chimney corners. The corner shingles cost less than $2 each.

FLASHING THE CRICKET

Side Piece

Chimney piece

Counterflashing

Step Flashing

Plywood cricket

Figure 18. You can build the cricket from plywood and cover it with shingles or metal flashing (for a small chimney). The joint at the cricket is step-flashed and counter flashed like the rest of the chimney.

and quicker to use standard 5x7-inch preformed aluminum step flashings.

- To complete the job, fold the flashings attached to the chimney down over the step flashings and cut the ends in line with and slightly above the bends in the step flashing. As you fold down each piece, cement it to the previous piece at the vertical joint, using clear silicone caulk for mastic. The caulk will prevent a high wind from lifting the flashings and allowing water in. Also be careful not to cement the step flashings to the chimney or the counterflashing to the step flashing. You should not need mastic anywhere else.

When the flashing job is done this way it will last many decades and the builder will have no call-backs. Also, when the time comes to reroof, it is easy to remove the old shingles and install new ones, reusing the flashing embedded in the mortar.

By Peter Scripture, a builder of 30 years who specializes in building, repairing, lining, and cleaning chimneys.

RETROFIT CHIMNEY FLASHING

To prepare an existing chimney for counterflashing, a mason cuts a 1¹/₄-inch groove in the mortar joints using a gas-powered concrete saw.

Many contractors make the mistake of fastening the counterflashing to the side of the chimney, using masonry screws to secure the flashing to the side of the chimney, then applying a bead of caulk at the top edge of the flashing (Figure 19). As daily temperature changes cause the flashing to expand and contract, the adhesive bond of the caulk joint is constantly stressed. This type of flashing detail will fail — sometimes in less than a year. Roofing cement doesn't last any longer.

Properly installed counterflashing is "let in" to a groove in the chimney and overlaps the upturned sides of the base flashing. No fasteners are required. I've used these methods for both aluminum and copper flashing.

If you're working on an existing chimney, you've got no choice but to get out your goggles and dust mask and saw the joints in the chimney. You can use a circular saw equipped with a masonry blade, a heavy-duty concrete saw, or a hand-held grinder equipped with a diamond blade. The groove should be 1¹/₄ inches deep and the width of a saw kerf (Figure 20). Make sure you do your cutting before the new shingles are installed. Otherwise, you'll be cleaning masonry dust off the newly installed

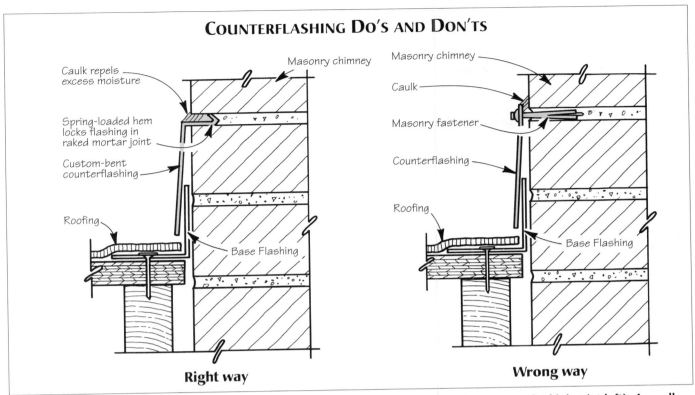

COUNTERFLASHING DO'S AND DON'TS

Right way

Caulk repels excess moisture

Spring-loaded hem locks flashing in raked mortar joint

Custom-bent counterflashing

Roofing

Masonry chimney

Base Flashing

Wrong way

Masonry chimney

Caulk

Masonry fastener

Counterflashing

Roofing

Base Flashing

Figure 19. The proper way to counterflash a chimney is to insert the counterflashing into a raked joint (at left). A small bend in the horizontal leg of the flashing ensures that no water can run behind the flashing. Caulk provides a secondary line of defense against moisture intrusion. Flashing fastened directly to the face of the chimney relies entirely on caulk to maintain a watertight joint (at right); in time, the caulk will fail, allowing water to penetrate the house.

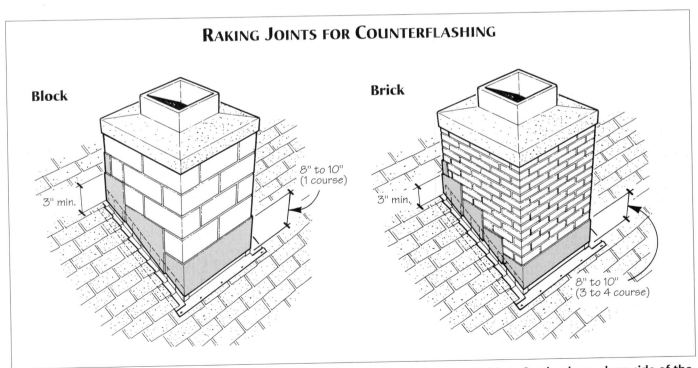

RAKING JOINTS FOR COUNTERFLASHING

Block

3" min.

8" to 10" (1 course)

Brick

3" min.

8" to 10" (3 to 4 course)

Figure 20. Rake the mortar joints to leave a 1¹/₄-inch-deep groove for the counterflashing. On the down-slope side of the chimney, choose a joint that is 8 to 10 inches above the roof deck (one course for block chimneys; three to four courses for brick). Rake the joint along the side of the chimney until the joint is about 3 inches above the roof deck.

Figure 21. The author cuts the upper and lower pieces of counter-flashing from painted-aluminum coil stock (.019 inches thick). The tapered cuts match the roof pitch; layout lines mark the folds at the chimney corners.

roof — a tough chore when working with dark-colored shingles.

Custom Counterflashing

For counterflashing, I like to use painted aluminum coil stock (.019 inches thick). If you have access to a break, forming the metal will be easier, but I've shaped flashing for more than one chimney using a 2x6 and a brick hammer.

To prepare the flashing, follow these steps:

- *Lay out the dimensions on the flashing stock and cut to size* before making any bends (Figure 21). Be sure to mark the fold lines where the counterflashing will turn the corner of the chimney.
- *Fold a ¹/₂-inch hem, then a 1-inch leg,* along the top edge of the counterflashing (Figure 22). Cut away a pie-shaped piece where the flashing must wrap around a corner of the chimney (Figure 23).
- *Pry open the hem to "spring-load" it.* This creates both a water stop and a mechanical "lock" that holds the flashing in place. Test-fit the flashing before opening the hem; removing the flashing once it's locked in place can be difficult.

THREE-STEP LOCKING BEND

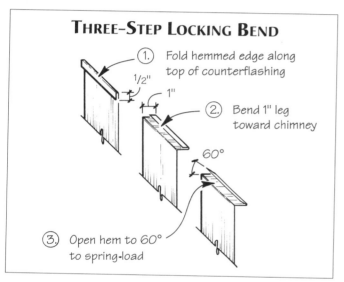

① Fold hemmed edge along top of counterflashing

½"

1"

② Bend 1" leg toward chimney

60°

③ Open hem to 60° to spring-load

Figure 22. First, make two simple bends along the top edge of the counterflashing, then pry open the hem to "spring-load" it: The V-shape will form a strong mechanical "lock" in the raked joint.

Before inserting the counterflashing, make sure the groove is free of debris, and is cut or raked out at least ¹/₄ inch deeper then the length of the angled leg. Then insert the V-shaped edge formed by the leg and the open hem into the groove (Figure 24) and seal the joint with caulk. I use Sikaflex-1a, a high-quality one-component polyurethane sealant available from Resource Conservation Technology (2633 N. Calvert St., Baltimore, MD 21218; 800/477-7724). It's gummy stuff, but forms a tenacious bond with masonry. Since the joint is watertight, the caulk serves to keep out excess moisture and wind-driven rain.

By Tom Brewer, a roofing contractor from northeast Pennsylvania.

Figure 23. The author cuts pie-shaped pieces in the folded hem so that the counterflashing can be bent around the chimney corner.

Figure 24. In this mock-up, the V-shaped leg of both the upper and lower pieces of counterflashing is locked into the joint between chimney blocks. A bead of caulk in the joint will keep out excess water and wind-driven rain.

PATCHING STUCCO

Stucco, when applied correctly in the first place, will not one day decide to fail of its own volition. Still, it's likely that all stucco homes will eventually require patching for one reason or another, whether to cover holes bored by blown insulation installers, or to repair heavy-handed demolition work done by carpenters adding onto the house.

The primary aim when patching stucco is to restore the integrity of the exterior cladding system — but that's the easy part. The challenge is to have the patch blend in well, rather than stick out like a sore thumb. It's a rare situation where you can make the patch truly invisible.

Novice attempts by homeowners or handymen to patch stucco are not only ugly to look at, but often compromise the structure's weather-resistance. In my work, I've seen patches done with everything from spackle and paint to Thorite, which has a compressive strength approaching that of stainless steel. I've seen cracks around windows filled in with what must have been dozens of tubes of caulk. These "bubblegum patches" look abysmal and have to be removed for a professional job to be done.

What follows is a description of how to patch the stucco in a wall where a window or door has been removed.

Preparing The Substrate

After adding the necessary studs, install new sheathing flush with the plane of the old sheathing. Carefully remove a swath of the existing stucco around the infill area, leaving at least 6 inches of the existing wire and paper intact. Saw cuts are not encouraged because they cut the wire, as well as leave a sharp edge that is difficult to transi-

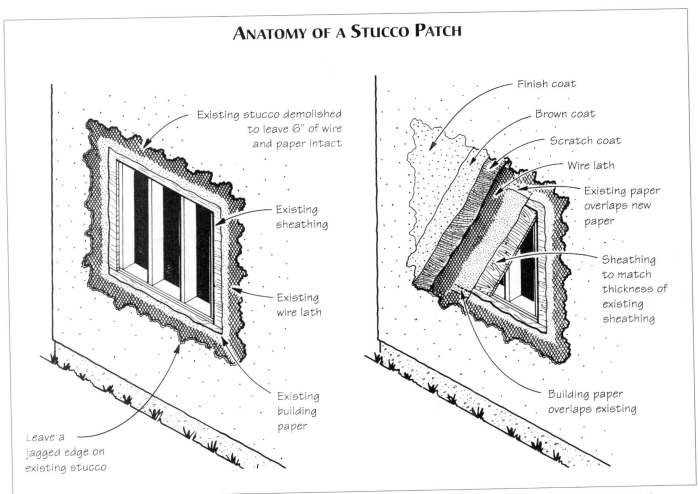

ANATOMY OF A STUCCO PATCH

Existing stucco demolished to leave 6" of wire and paper intact

Existing sheathing

Existing wire lath

Existing building paper

Leave a jagged edge on existing stucco

Finish coat

Brown coat

Scratch coat

Wire lath

Existing paper overlaps new paper

Sheathing to match thickness of existing sheathing

Building paper overlaps existing

Figure 25. When patching stucco, leave at least 6 inches of the existing lath and building paper exposed around the edge of the patch (left). The existing stucco should have a jagged edge, to create a less noticeable transition to the new stucco. Match the thickness of the existing sheathing (right), and make sure to lap the new building paper correctly — this guarantees a waterproof patch.

tion into. A jagged stucco edge is best (Figure 25).

Building paper. Next, cut a piece of asphaltic sheathing paper — Class D or better — that's slightly larger than the patch area. Carefully slip it behind the existing paper by at least one inch at the top and sides, and let it extend over the old paper at the bottom of the patched area. Remember that this paper protects the wall from the weather; lap it accordingly. Where the existing paper edges are destroyed, you can use duct tape to seal old to new. All stucco patches develop hairline shrinkage cracks around the perimeter, so great pains should be taken to ensure the paper is lapped adequately.

Lath. Cut the lath to completely fill the area to be patched. Remember that stucco requires a means of attachment to stay in place, and the grip the scratch coat gets on the lath is critical to a durable patch job. Use staples or galvanized roofing nails of sufficient length to get a good "bite" into the plywood or OSB sheathing. If you're installing the lath over foam sheathing, use longer nails and make sure you hit the studs.

The Mix

I can speak only for our company, but here in central Ohio, we use white waterproof cement, lime, bagged silica sand, and water. For our finish, we add iron-oxide pigment to achieve colors. We use bagged silica to ensure that there are no iron particles mixed in (from being loaded by a front loader which has been parked in the rain for three days), or rivets and nail heads found

---

FILLING STUCCO CRACKS

When asked to patch cracks in stucco, I often advise the homeowner to do the work himself using caulk, not stucco.

Houses are built primarily of wood. Wood is subject to expansion, contraction, racking, shifting, etc. The bulk of this movement occurs during the first couple of years after construction, as the house attempts to reach some kind of equilibrium.

Cement is intolerant of movement, which results in cracks. These cracks, ranging from hairline to 3/16 inch wide, are usually cosmetic only. If the building paper has been installed correctly, the house is protected from water damage.

If stucco is used to fill these cracks, not only will you be left with an expensive paint job, but the material will most likely crumble out as the building continues to shift.

For cracks 1/16 to 3/16 inch wide (leave hairline cracks alone), filling the crack with a caulk that matches the color of the wall is the best solution. OSI Sealants Inc. (Mentor, OH; 800/321-3578; www.stickwithpl.com), among others, makes a surprisingly wide palette of caulking colors. Have the homeowner determine which color most closely matches their stucco. Don't use silicone-based caulk, which will not hold paint.

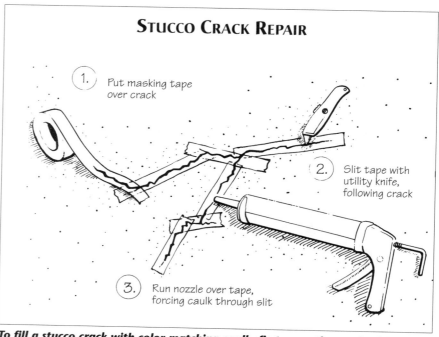

STUCCO CRACK REPAIR

1. Put masking tape over crack
2. Slit tape with utility knife, following crack
3. Run nozzle over tape, forcing caulk through slit

To fill a stucco crack with color-matching caulk, first cover the crack with masking tape, then slit the tape with a utility knife. Apply the caulk through the slit and remove the tape before the caulk sets up.

Don't open up or expand the width of the crack. Place masking tape over the length of the crack, then use a utility knife or razor blade to slit the tape, following the crack. Apply the caulk by running the nozzle over the slit, forcing the caulk through the tape into the crack. Finally, strip the tape before the caulk sets up. This approach keeps most of the caulk where you want it.

We've had good results with this technique. It makes a successful seal because the inherent flexibility of the caulk is able to tolerate later movement of the building. The customers make the decision on color, and their investment is minimal. They end up thinking we're heroes for giving them good advice and helping them to save money. — *S.T.*

in the less expensive "yard sand" available locally. We use the more expensive pigments because they won't fade in a couple of years like the cheaper pigments.

The American Society of Testing and Materials (ASTM) has published guidelines on what mixtures to use for various applications. This is a generic menu that will perform well in most situations. They also offer specific direction on lathing and its attachment, control joint placement, and other aspects of stucco work. This advice — however accurate or well intentioned — is routinely overridden at the field level because local contractors know what works best in their area. Stucco work routinely performed on the West Coast, for instance, has to stand up to seismic activity and therefore is different from work performed here in the Midwest.

The Scratch Coat

The first coat of "mud" is called the scratch coat, characterized by the marks left by the square-tooth trowel when it's applied. The scratch coat should be approximately 3/8 inch thick. Its job is to get a grip on the wire.

The scratch coat is composed of cement, lime, and washed mason's sand. The thickness of the mud should just cover the wire. Stucco (like concrete) derives its strength as a result of two factors: the relative strength of the mix and its drying time. A wet mixture will result in excessive shrinkage (often called checking), and a dry mixture or a stucco patch completed in very hot weather will dry rapidly and create a weak bond. If it's hot or the wind is blowing, you should lightly mist the walls a few times to retard the drying and produce a stronger first coat. If possible, avoid doing your work in direct sunlight.

The Brown Coat

The following coat, which is called a brown coat for some

unknown reason, is applied the day after the scratch coat. The brown coat is actually gray in color, but is composed of slightly more sand than the scratch coat mixture and is therefore a more manageable but a slightly weaker mix. It should be applied 3/8 inch thick, and if space permits, straight-edged and floated to ensure a flat plane held approximately 1/8 inch below the finished surface of the adjacent stucco. A pointer trowel should be used to work the stucco into the cracks where the new stucco meets the existing. You can lay a 2x4 or other straight edge across the patch (resting it on the existing wall surface) to measure the required thickness of the finish coat.

It's important that the brown coat be both flat and uniformly depressed below the level of the surrounding finish coat. An uneven brown coat will lead to an inconsistent thickness in the finish coat that will cause some areas of the finish coat to dry before other areas. If this happens, the finish coat will have color variations and excessive cracking. The result, if the finish coat is applied with pigment, will be splotchy or "mottled." If the finish coat is to be painted, there might be cracks that won't paint over easily.

The Finish Coat

How successfully the finish coat matches the existing depends largely upon the quality of the brown coat. Matching texture, and in the case of a pigmented finish coat, matching the color, are very difficult to accomplish. The mixture, drying conditions, and application method of the existing finish coat are all unknown. In the field you're left to your best judgment, but you'll almost never produce a perfect match.

The final coat is usually floated on, except in the case of machine-textured finishes. Most small patch jobs don't warrant the cost of bring-

ing a hoppergun and compressor onto the job site, when a skilled worker can apply a machinelike texture with a hand-thrown dash.

Sometimes a paint brush dipped in water is used to smooth the transition between a patch and the existing stucco. This helps to eliminate the sharp line between the two different textures. When painted, the seam between the new and existing is less noticeable.

There are products available for the purpose of strengthening the bond between the new and used stucco. These syruplike, brightly colored materials are expensive, and in our experience have done little to prevent cracking between the new and existing stucco. If the substrate is installed correctly, this will help keep cracking to a minimum. If the substrate isn't installed correctly, the movement in the wall will not be held back by a stucco bonding agent.

One-Coat Stucco

When a stucco patch is small and the homeowner wants to avoid the labor costs of three trips, a one-coat stucco material can be used. One-coat stucco, like standard stucco, is applied over paper and wire. These mixes are quite a bit more expensive, so they aren't cost-effective on larger jobs. We use Parex's *Monocouche* and *Greycouche* products (Parex Inc., P.O. Box 189, Redan, GA 30074; 800/537-2739), which are applied up to a 7/8-inch thickness according to manufacturer's instructions. Monocouche is white cement-based, and may be tinted using the same iron oxides used for stucco. Less expensive is the Greycouche, which is gray in color and suitable for patchwork if you're confident the area will eventually receive paint.

Besides the advantage of the single trip application, this "just-add-water" one-coat stucco shrinks less than standard stucco. But adhere to the manufacturer's temperature warnings when using these products.

Painting Stucco

When faced with a large patch like a patio door infill in a two-story, 40-foot-long wall, you have a problem: If the existing wall is composed of pigmented stucco, chances are very high that both the color and texture of the new stucco will not match. Regrettably, this patch occurs at eye level. One solution might be to rebrown and refinish the entire wall plane, which will render the patch invisible, but the job then lurches from a 42-square-foot patch to a 720-square-foot job requiring scaffolding, a lot more cement, lime, sand, etc. Plus, you'll need a mixer instead of a wheelbarrow.

My recommendation is to paint. Painting stucco is not only possible, but often advantageous to assure uniformity of color. It focuses the stucco worker on the goal of tying together the texture and plane of the new and the existing, and it's very likely that the paint will make the wall uniform in color.

Here are three tips on painting stucco:

- Newly applied stucco should be allowed about 30 days to cure, depending on the weather conditions.
- Existing stucco surfaces should be power-washed and allowed to thoroughly dry before painting. Do not use a water blaster, as its excessive pressure can do severe damage to the stucco.
- Stucco should only be painted with acrylic-based paints with adequate vapor transmission characteristics, so as not to create new moisture-related problems within the house. Oil-based, rubber-based, and latex paints all have their places, but none of them were intended for exterior stucco.

Client Expectations

When writing a quote for stucco work involving patching, I typically use phrases like: "In spite of our best efforts, this area will likely appear patched," or "Due to weathering of adjacent stucco surfaces, precise color and texture matching may not be achievable." These phrases are not meant to serve as escape clauses to condone bad work, but rather to alert the homeowner or contractor to the realities of stucco patchwork. We do occasionally hit it right on the head and achieve a perfect color and texture match, but this is the exception, not the rule.

The man who does our patch work (jobs less than 100 square feet) has been with us for 17 years. His dad worked here for 40 years. He still "misses" hitting a perfect match in most cases. One way I convey to clients the difficulty of the task at hand is with a clothing analogy: Imagine cutting a 4-inch-square patch out of one of your favorite shirts and then sewing it back in place. While it's exactly the same fabric filling in the exact hole from which it was cut, it will still be apparent as a patch, and not part of the undisturbed cloth surrounding it. The same is true of stucco patching.

By Steve Thomas, general sales manager for Reitter Stucco, in Columbus, Ohio.

EIFS PERFORMANCE REVIEW

The use of exterior insulation finish systems (EIFS) has grown dramatically in recent years, in both commercial and residential markets, accounting for more than 200 million square feet of building exteriors in 1991. The systems, sometimes called "synthetic stucco," are economical and give designers a lot of flexibility with colors and architectural details (Figure 26). In addition, they provide good insulation without thermal gaps and greatly reduce air infiltration.

Of the two generic types of EIFS, polymer-based (PB) and polymer-modified (PM), the PB systems are by far the more commonly used in the U.S. today. PB systems, some-times called "soft-coat," are typically thin (approximately $1/8$ inch total thickness), adhesively attached, and flexible, and they require few control joints. They cannot tolerate prolonged wetting.

PM systems, on the other hand, are typically greater than $1/4$ inch in total thickness, mechanically attached, rigid, and insensitive to moisture, and they require frequent control joints, similar to cement stucco. Sometimes called "hard-coat," PM systems do offer several significant advantages:

- They are mechanically attached, so 15-pound felt or similar moisture protection can be placed over the sheathing. This prevents any water that enters the system from damaging the sheathing and studs.
- They have greater puncture and abrasion resistance and better tolerate abuse from traffic at grade.
- They are more resistant to damage from internal moisture.
- They use metal or vinyl casing beads, which provide a more durable substrate for sealants.

PB systems, however, are far more popular, primarily because they cost less, allow for greater design freedom (because fewer control joints are needed), and have been marketed more aggressively by manufacturers. In fact, PB systems account for approximately 80% of the current

EIFS market. Because of its wide use, we will address only the PB type of system below.

The HUD Experience

Unfortunately, the increased use of EIFS has been accompanied by an increase in problems and failed applications. The U.S. Department of Housing and Urban Development (HUD) owns a large number of buildings finished with EIFS that have required extensive repairs or total replacement within ten years of installation. This high rate of early failure has caused HUD to reevaluate the acceptability of EIFS for use on HUD-funded construction. In the past, HUD required little more than a 20-year warranty and compliance with manufacturer specifications. Because of the high failure rate, however, HUD is in the process of reviewing the material and may establish new criteria for EIF systems.

As part of an ongoing study being conducted with the coopera-

Figure 26. Soft-coat synthetic stucco gives designers a lot of flexibility with colors and architectural details.

COURTESY OF RUSSELL BUILDING CO., BIRMINGHAM, ALA.

Figure 27. Mesh that's exposed on the surface of the base coat is likely to get wet and lose tensile strength. Once weakened, it will not provide adequate impact resistance.

EIFS LAWSUITS LEADING TO CHANGE

In 1995 a number of lawsuits were filed in North Carolina and South Carolina against EIFS manufacturers. The class-action suits claim that the systems are inherently defective, primarily because they do not allow water to escape once it penetrates behind the exterior skin.

In theory, water can penetrate an EIFS either by entering through the exterior skin or around it at openings and where the EIFS abuts other materials. However, our review of over 200 homes that had the EIFS removed revealed that — especially in coastal areas — water is penetrating via abutting components, not through the skin. The main causes of water penetration we observed in the Carolinas are described below:

Lack of sealant at window openings. Over 50% of the dwellings, even those at the ocean front, did not have any sealant between the edge of the EIFS and the window system. This was a major source of water penetration.

Roof/wall flashing. The flashing at the wall/roof intersection (step flashing) was, in most cases, installed so the flashing terminated behind the EIFS. Water that accumulated on the flashing was directed behind the protective skin of the EIFS. In some subdivisions, over 90% of the homes had this problem.

Window systems. We observed water penetration where window units were mulled together and where brick molds (locally manufactured) were used with wood windows. Water penetrated at center mullions, between the brick mold and sill, or between the brick mold and stile. Where two-piece sills were used, water penetrated into the EIFS once the sills split.

Recommendations. The state of North Carolina now requires that EIFS used with wood-frame construction have sealants at window and door openings, a secondary water barrier, and a positive method for draining water to the exterior. Based upon our involvement with EIFS and wood-frame construction over many years, we recommend that a secondary moisture barrier, such as 15-lb. building paper or membrane flashing, be used at all window openings, and that proper window flashing be required for EIFS and all types of wall cladding when used with wood framing and moisture-sensitive sheathing. One model code agency is considering similar requirements. — R.K.

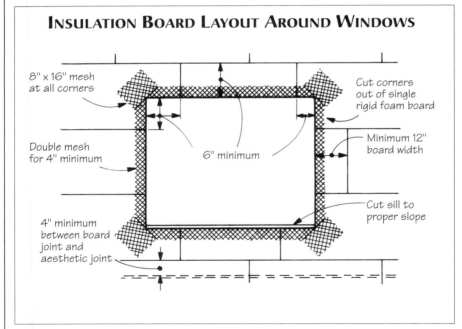

Figure 28. The sealant at this control joint failed within six months of installation, allowing water into the system. To prevent this, use a low-modulus sealant and apply it to the base coat, not the finish coat.

tion of HUD's Washington Office of Materials and Standards and the HUD area offices in Boston, Kansas City, and Pittsburgh, we reviewed a random selection of more than 30 buildings with EIFS exteriors, ranging from jobs under construction to buildings twelve years old. None of the buildings included in the study were known to have EIFS problems. The review included visual inspection, non-destructive moisture readings at random locations, and test cuts at a few buildings. The results to date strongly support

A BETTER EIFS

Despite the problems, we believe PB EIF systems can be modified to provide good durability and service life. The modified systems cost more than most current systems, yet still compare favorably with other exterior wall materials. The following requirements are, in our opinion, the minimum necessary to assure good durability, and they have been used successfully on a number of recent projects:

- The substrate should be masonry, concrete, or cement fiberboard. Gypsum sheathing has been a contributing factor in the failure of many applications. When water enters the system for whatever reason, it is absorbed by the sheathing, and when gypsum sheathing is kept moist (20% or more water by weight), the paper facing delaminates from the gypsum core, debonding the system. At approximately 30% moisture, the gypsum core deteriorates and wood studs can rot. These problems can occur with relatively small amounts of water penetration, minor cracking, and no water leakage into the building interior.

One alternative is Georgia Pacific's Dens Glass (ASTM C1177). This product is significantly more water resistant than standard gypsum sheathing, although more testing and field experience are necessary to determine its long-term durability.

- The expanded polystyrene (EPS) insulation board must have good bead fusion to resist the passage of water when the surface is damaged. You can check for bead fusion by snapping a piece of board. At least 50% of the beads should break in two, rather than pull apart and remain whole.

- EPS board joints must not align with door and window openings and must be offset from sheathing joints (see illustration). Board joints aligned with openings are a

INSULATION BOARD LAYOUT AROUND WINDOWS

8" x 16" mesh at all corners

Double mesh for 4" minimum

4" minimum between board joint and aesthetic joint

6" minimum

Cut corners out of single rigid foam board

Minimum 12" board width

Cut sill to proper slope

Insulation board joints aligned with door and window openings are a common cause of cracks. To prevent problems, joints must be offset from the openings and the corners reinforced with diagonal mesh. In addition, decorative joints should not align with board joints or openings; board joints should not align with sheathing joints; and laps in the mesh should be offset from the edges of openings, grooves, and corners.

HUD's desire to improve the quality standards for EIFS materials and application.

Common Problems

The most common deficiencies found were caused by poor workmanship and were evident on the majority of projects reviewed.

Thin base coat. Applications with base coats thinner than the manufacturer's required thickness were very common.

Exposed mesh. Many jobs had exposed mesh at joint edges and at terminations (Figure 27). We observed mesh on the surface of the base coat on some jobs under construction, and we could see mesh patterns through the finish coat on a few jobs. These are signs of thin base coats and mesh that is not adequately embedded in the base coat.

Mesh that's not fully embedded is exposed to moisture and won't provide good impact resistance. Moisture alone can reduce the tensile strength of reinforcing mesh, and it is well known that moisture combined with alkalinity (from the cement) speeds the strength reduction of the mesh.

Sealant failure. The majority of projects, including some less than six months old, had some sealant failure. Failures at EIFS field joints were more common than at perimeter joints (Figure 28). The typical failure was a *cohesive* failure of the finish coat. This means that the sealant didn't pull away from the finish coat; rather, the finish coat itself pulled apart. This is because some acrylic finish coats

---

common cause of cracks. When V-grooves align with board joints at openings, cracking is very common.

- Decorative grooves must not align with EPS board joints or openings, and their use should be held to a minimum. Rounded grooves are preferable to V-grooves.
- The base coat should have no more than 33% cement by weight. Many U.S. products currently use 50% cement. The main problem is that the high alkalinity of the cementitious base coats weakens the fiberglass reinforcing mesh. Although mesh has an alkali-resistant coating, the quality and quantity of the coating is inconsistent, and the amount of coating on U.S. mesh is substantially less than on European mesh. In addition, base coats with higher amounts of cement are less flexible and can become brittle with age.
- The base coat should be applied in two layers with at least 24 hours between applications. This has several distinct advantages over a single application. In this system, the mesh is troweled onto the surface of the first layer, and the second application then fully covers the mesh. No mesh or mesh pattern is visible.

Because the polymer-modified base material is more "sticky" than traditional cement stucco, it is difficult to apply in thick layers. With a double-layer application, however, the typical installer can get adequate thickness and fully cover the mesh.

- The minimum base-coat thickness should be $3/32$ inch. This is the actual minimum allowed at any location, not an average or nominal thickness. Thinner base coats do not adequately protect the mesh from moisture and have inadequate impact resistance.
- No mesh or mesh pattern should be visible at any surface, including corners and joints. Corners and surfaces that will receive sealant are especially critical because thin base coats provide a weak substrate for sealants, and exposed mesh will wick moisture into the system. A third application of base material is often necessary to touch up corners and joints.
- Cementitious base coats must be primed before the finish is applied. The acrylic primers improve the water resistance of the base coat and provide a surface with uniform suction to receive the finish. Some newer non-cementitious base coats are being developed that may not require primer.
- Failed elastomeric sealant joints are a major cause of water entry in EIF systems. To prevent these failures, the sealant must be applied to the primed base coat, not to the finish coat, which can soften when wet. And because EIFS is a relatively weak substrate

for elastomeric sealants, you must choose a *low-modulus* sealant that maintains its low-modulus over the life of the sealant. (When a low-modulus sealant stretches, it exerts less stress on a joint.)

Ideally, the sealant should last as long as the system, because it is difficult to remove and replace sealant without damaging the thin layers. In general, silicone sealants are less affected by aging and cold temperatures than urethane sealants. Dow 790 Silicone Sealant is the recommended sealant for most EIFS applications, although its appearance may be an issue with some designers.

- Window sills, parapet tops, and similar sloped surfaces should be protected with metal flashing. EIFS is not an acceptable roofing material, even for very small "roofs." The manufacturers' requirements for a 1:2 pitch is not adequate to shed snow and prevent lengthy wetting. A minimum 1:1 (45-degree) pitch is preferred when it is not possible to properly flash the surface.

The only PB EIF systems currently marketed in the U.S. that meet all these criteria are Premium Cementitious System 3 and Premium Full Synthetic System 3 by Parex Inc. (Redan, Ga.). We have successfully used other systems, however, when they have been modified to meet our criteria. — *R. P. & R. K.*

Figure 29. V-grooves, added for decorative effect, should never line up with window or door openings. This one cracked, was recoated with the manufacturer's elastomeric coating, and cracked again within a year.

Figure 30. Gaps between EPS insulation boards are a common cause of cracks. To prevent problems, fill any cracks with insulation slivers.

soften when kept damp and therefore do not generally provide a durable surface for elastomeric sealants. Nevertheless, most EIFS and sealant manufacturers still either require or recommend sealants to be applied to the finish.

Cracking in V-grooves. V-grooves are sometimes added for decorative effects. Approximately one half of all projects with V-grooves had some cracking in the grooves sufficient to allow water penetration. Cracking is most common when the V-groove falls on an insulation board joint beneath (Figure 29).

Cracking at openings. Approximately one third of all projects had some cracking at the corners of windows and similar openings. These cracks are caused by stresses at the

reentrant (inside) corners. Almost all projects with vertical V-grooves extending from window to window, in line with the jambs, had some cracks in these grooves, and many cracks were continuous the full height of the V-groove.

Cracking at board joints. More than 10% of all projects had some cracking not associated with openings or joints. These cracks mostly occur over the gaps between insulation boards (Figure 30) and grow worse as the reinforcing mesh loses tensile strength from exposure to moisture and alkalinity.

Workmanship Falls Short

We observed three projects while the EIFS was being applied. In one of these, mediocre workmanship

resulted in gaps between insulation boards and poorly embedded mesh at sealant joints. A few V-grooves had already cracked before the job was completed.

On the second project, workmanship was poor, resulting in large gaps between boards, exposed mesh at joints, and a thin base coat. The third project showed very poor workmanship, resulting in a thin, brittle base coat, large areas of exposed mesh, inadequate board adhesion, and other serious violations of the manufacturer's standards.

On three other projects, prefabricated panels were adhesively applied to either precast concrete or gypsum sheathing. Two of these buildings had been occupied for less than six months and one for 18 months. The latter project had many failed sealant joints, V-groove cracking, exposed mesh at joints, a thin base coat, and water weeping out of the system in a few locations. The first two projects showed failed sealant joints, exposed mesh, a thin base coat, and V-groove cracking. Several panels had blown off the most recently completed project.

In summary, less than half of the buildings more than seven years old were in good condition, and none over two years old were without visible deficiencies.

This survey suggests that the high rate of EIFS failure on HUD-funded buildings is primarily due to improper application. It also suggests that improved standards for materials and application are critical if PB EIF systems are to provide a reasonable service life without extensive maintenance and early repair.

Gypsum Sheathing Vulnerable

Most of the cracks and sealant failures we saw in the survey were sufficient to allow water to enter the EIF system. From our earlier investigations of several hundred EIFS buildings, we know that such leaks can lead to water damage of the gypsum sheathing underneath (Figure 31). When wet, the sheathing is prone to deterioration and delamination. Water also tends to collect at horizontal terminations and joints that are "back-wrapped" with mesh. The water often collects well below the point of entry, and it can cause the gypsum sheathing to delaminate and the sealant joints to fail.

Because EIFS — as typically applied — often cracks and allows water penetration, we believe that EIFS should not be adhesively applied to gypsum sheathing (ASTM C79). The fact that the current systems continue to be adhesively applied to gypsum sheathing on high-rise buildings in locations exposed to high winds and heavy rains is hard to understand or justify. Projects with masonry, concrete, or cement fiberboard substrates are less vulnerable to water penetration.

Application

For EIF systems to last, quality workmanship is critical. Good materials and details, alone, will not guarantee a durable finish. The work must be inspected during installation by those knowledgeable about EIFS. Unfortunately, such knowledge is not commonplace in the architectural and construction industry today, which results in a large number of EIFS applications failing to meet the manufacturers' minimum requirements. The major concerns during installation are:

- *Board application.* Provide good adhesion between the insulation board and substrate. Offset board joints from sheathing joints and door and window openings. Also, offset them from any decorative V-grooves. Fill any gaps larger than 1/16 inch between boards with insulation. Rasp all insulation surfaces to rough them up and remove weathered material before applying the finish.

Figure 31. Moderate wetting will cause the facing of gypsum sheathing to delaminate. With increased wetting, the core will deteriorate, as seen in this cut-away section.

Figure 32. Areas near walkways face greater wear and tear. Use high-impact mesh in these locations.

- *Base coat.* Make the base coat at least 3/32 inch thick, and apply it in two layers. Use primer on all cementitious base coat surfaces.
- *Mesh.* Offset any laps in the mesh from edges of openings, grooves, and corners. Use diagonal mesh for reinforcing at door or window (reentrant) corners. Use a double layer of mesh, lapped at least 4 inches, at all outside and inside corners. Fully embed the mesh, leaving no mesh ends or mesh pattern visible. Use high-impact (heavyweight) mesh at all surfaces near grade or near balconies or walkways, where they will face additional wear and tear (Figure 32).
- *Sealant joints.* Provide smooth, straight, sound surfaces to receive sealants, with no mesh or mesh pattern visible. Allow adequate joint width for the expected movement. Use primer on all surfaces to receive sealant. Apply sealant to the base coat only, never to the finish coat, and tool all sealant joints.

Properly detailed and applied, PB EIFS can provide durable, cost-effective exterior walls with a service life of 20 to 30 years. Improperly designed and applied systems, on the other hand, will have a greatly reduced useful life, and many will require extensive repairs or early replacement.

By Richard Piper and Russell Kenney, of R.J. Kenney Assoc. Inc. in Plainville, Mass. Piper and Kenney consult on building exteriors and have conducted extensive research on the performance of EIF systems.

SOURCES OF SUPPLY

Caulking Guns and Tools

Albion Engineering Co.
Moorestown, NJ
856-235-6688
www.albioneng.com

Joint Sealants

Dow Corning Corp.
Midland, MI
989/496-7881
www.dowcorning.com

GE Silicones
Wilton, CT
866/275-4372
www.gesilicones.com

Sika Chemical Corp.
Lindhurst, NJ
800/933-7452
www.sikausa.com

Tremco Inc.
Beechwood, OH
800/321-7906
www.tremcosealants.com

Joint Sealants and Water Repellents

Chemrex Inc.
Sonneborn Building Products
Shakopee, MN
800/433-9517
www.chemrex.com

Pecora Corp.
Harleysville, PA
800/523-6688
www.pecora.com

CHAPTER 5

ROOFING

- Asphalt Shingle Failures

- Shallow Roof Details

- Restoring Wood Shakes and Shingles

- Preventing Ice Dams

- Slate Roof Repairs

- Tricky Flashing Details

ASPHALT SHINGLE FAILURES

The most common residential roofing material applied in the U.S. today is fiberglass asphalt shingles. Since they were introduced in the late 1970s, fiberglass shingles have come to dominate the market, accounting for nearly 90% of all shingles installed today. In fact, the original "organic felt" shingles are now hard to find in many areas.

Evaluating the quality of organic shingles has always been pretty straightforward: In general, the heavier the shingle, the longer it will last on the roof. Fiberglass shingles, on the other hand, have a different composition and cannot be easily evaluated based on weight. This has made it more complicated for builders to choose a shingle. And recent reports of some fiberglass shingles failing prematurely have made the choice even tougher.

Anatomy of a Shingle

All asphalt shingles consist of a fiber mat coated with asphalt (Figure 1). The fiber mat, which gives the shingle most of its strength, is made either from an organic cellulose material (derived from wood or recycled paper) or from the newer and more popular fiberglass. The organic mats, sometimes called "felt" mats, are similar to ordinary roofing felt. They are saturated with a soft, pure asphalt to form a sturdy, pliable base. Fiberglass mats are much thinner, and are not saturated with asphalt.

Both types of mat are surface-coated on both sides with a layer of hard asphalt that has been "stabilized" with inexpensive mineral fillers, such as finely ground limestone or slate. The filler adds bulk and helps to make the shingles more

fire resistant. The top coating of asphalt also holds a layer of small granules of rock, usually colored with a ceramic coating, that protect the asphalt from damaging sunlight. The back surface of the shingle is covered with a fine mineral dust, such as talc, sand, or mica, to keep the shingles from sticking together and from staining each other in the package.

Worth Its Weight?

All of these components add to the weight of a shingle, but only some add strength and durability. Heavier stone, for example, can add weight without increasing shingle life. Similarly, in a high-profile "architectural" shingle, the added weight of the extra layer of stabilized asphalt contributes little to shingle strength unless it's applied to a thicker mat.

Despite this, the quality of organic asphalt shingles can still be reliably judged from their weight — when comparing shingles of the same brand and type. This is because the additional weight of the heavier shingle is mostly accounted for by a thicker mat with more soft asphalt saturant — factors that add strength and durability as well as weight. The pure asphalt typically adds 25 or 30 pounds per square.

But weight is generally not a good basis for comparison of fiberglass shingles. The additional weight of a heavier fiberglass shingle is accounted for primarily by additional hard, stabilized asphalt — a component that adds weight but not necessarily strength or durability. In fact, if too much mineral filler is used in the hard coating asphalt, it can make the shingle brittle and more likely to crack, despite the added weight.

As for the fiberglass mat, a better mat will make a stronger shingle. But it is the type of binder, strand

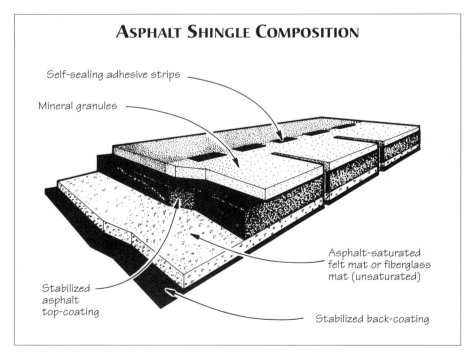

ASPHALT SHINGLE COMPOSITION

Self-sealing adhesive strips

Mineral granules

Stabilized asphalt top-coating

Asphalt-saturated felt mat or fiberglass mat (unsaturated)

Stabilized back-coating

Figure 1. All asphalt shingles are built around a mat of either organic felt or fiberglass. The organic mats are thicker and are saturated with soft, pliable asphalt. Both types of shingles have a top layer of harder, stabilized asphalt topped with colored stone to protect against UV light. On the bottom, all shingles have a thin coating of asphalt coated with talc, sand, or mica to keep the shingles from sticking together in the package.

orientation, and other components of the base material that make a better fiberglass mat, not necessarily the thickness or weight. Also, a heavier fiberglass mat adds only a pound or two per square, so it barely registers anyway.

Warranty Woes

Since you can't use shingle weight as a standard for choosing fiberglass shingles, a lot of roofers look at the manufacturer's warranty to gauge quality. This has traditionally worked for organic shingles, since the heavier, longer-lasting shingles usually carry a longer warranty. But the warranty periods of fiberglass shingles — typically expressed as 20-year, 25-year, and 30-year — do not necessarily correspond with shingle quality. In some cases you are simply paying more for a longer warranty.

The warranties differ from company to company, but none gives the installer full coverage. According to the terms of most warranties, for example, the manufacturer agrees to pay only the depreciated cost of the roofing material, and none of the labor to install it or the cost to dispose of the old shingles, which are two of the biggest expenses for roofers. Also, most shingle warranties aren't transferable when the home is sold. Since the average American homeowner sells after about six years, shingle companies are not liable even if their product doesn't perform as advertised. The builder's reputation, however, is still at risk if the roof fails, no matter who owns the house.

Even though warranties don't necessarily predict shingle life, it's still worth comparing coverage among the different roof manufacturers. Some warranties, like CertainTeed's, include payment of labor costs and provide 100% coverage for the first five years. BPCO, a Canadian manufacturer of organic shingles, provides similar "up front" coverage in a warranty that is transferable to subsequent owners of the home.

Another key to warranty protection is installation: If you want to ensure coverage, you have to install the roofing properly. And for warranty purposes, the "right" way is the way the package says to do it. Bear in mind, also, that no matter how the shingles are installed, the warranty could be voided if the roof framing, sheathing, or ventilation is determined by the manufacturer to be substandard.

Shingle Failure

In past years, warranties weren't much of a concern because the organic felt shingles usually lasted longer than the 15 or 20 years for which they were guaranteed. Some organic shingles on roofs today have seen 30 years and are still hanging on.

Many roofs with fiberglass shingles, however, aren't faring as well. Several roofing contractor associations have heard complaints from their members that some fiberglass shingles are failing within ten years — and sometimes as early as six months — into the warranty period.

When fiberglass shingles were first introduced, their biggest problem was with blow-offs. Manufacturers responded by improving the adhesive in the shingle sealant strip. The more recent failures usually involve cracking, which can occur vertically up the roof over many courses of shingles, horizontally across tabs, or diagonally (Figure 2). No one has fully documented how common the problems are, but industry experts feel they are fairly widespread.

The causes are also difficult to pin down, but appear to involve a combination of weak fiberglass mats, thin and inflexible asphalt, and the effects of thermal expansion and contraction. Some shingles crack because they can't adjust to movement in the roof substructure. More commonly, however, cracks are caused by dimensional changes in the shingles themselves as they respond to temperature changes. Shingles expand in the heat and contract in the cold, but because they're pinned to the roof by nails and stuck

Figure 2. Fiberglass shingles that fail early usually crack, either vertically up the roof over many courses of shingles, or horizontally and diagonally across tabs.

to each other by their own adhesive strips, the shingles rip themselves apart. Ironically, manufacturers' efforts to solve the blow-off problem by improving seal strip adhesion may have made the cracking problems worse.

Aging is also a factor in early failure. Over time, the volatile elements in the asphalt cook off, reducing the tensile strength and flexibility of the shingles. So roofs that get a lot of sun or are not well ventilated may fail sooner.

According to Don Berg, of the National Roofing Contractors Association's (NRCA) technical department, the cracking is "not limited to one or two brands, or one or two types or qualities of shingle. It has occurred in the commodity-grade and the architect-grade shingles." Berg has received reports of the problem "from generally around the country" but says NRCA "doesn't really have a handle on how widespread it is."

The Midwest Roofing Contractors Association (MRCA), another trade organization, has also received reports from their members of early failure of fiberglass shingles. And the president of Western States Roofing Contractors Association (WSRCA), Don Bosnick of Bosnick Roofing in Tacoma, Wash., says his organization has looked at samples of failed shingles "from Connecticut to California," mostly in the 20-year three-tab type.

The Asphalt Roofing Manufacturers Association (ARMA) is also aware of the problem, and responding in part to WSRCA test results, has recently formed a task force to study it and find solutions. According to Joe Jones, a retired senior technical executive at Owens Corning, who heads the ARMA task force, "The cracking problem occurs in a number of different types of shingles, from a number of different manufacturers, in many parts of the country." Jones emphasizes, however, that the number of homes reporting cracking problem "is miniscule compared with the number of shingles sold."

Tear Strength

There is growing evidence that a shingle's tear strength is a good indicator of its resistance to cracking. The American Society of Testing and Materials (ASTM) has a minimum standard for tear strength, included in ASTM D3462. The standard establishes that, using an Elmendorf tear tester, it should take at least 1,700 grams ($3^3/_4$ pounds) of force to tear a shingle that already has a notch in it. Although the tear test does not directly relate to cracking of shingles, high test results indicate a strong fiber mat. This standard was adopted in 1976 when fiberglass shingles were first introduced, and was based on the lightest organic shingle known to have performed acceptably. Most organic felt shingles still available today have tear strengths of over 2,250 grams, and some as high as 3,500 grams.

Compliance with ASTM D3462 is voluntary, and ASTM does not check whether manufacturers who claim their shingles meet the standard actually comply. In fact, many don't. In tear strength tests conducted in early 1992 by two independent laboratories at the request of WSRCA, 22 of 24 fiberglass shingle samples (two each from 12 manufacturers) tested below the 1,700-gram standard.

Underwriters Laboratories recently announced that it would independently check tear test results, so you can start looking for UL certification of ASTM D3462 in a special box on the shingle wrapper. So far, only CertainTeed has received such certification, but a spokesman for UL says several other companies are expected to receive certification soon.

Manufacturers Respond

According to Jones, head of the ARMA task force, most manufacturers have already taken steps to eliminate the cracking. Some have gone to a heavier fiberglass mat; others have changed their asphalt formulation.

San Francisco-based WSRCA is also continuing to work on the problem. WSRCA's Bosnick says the association is looking at several different characteristics of new fiberglass shingles, including tensile strength, flexibility or pliability, and response to thermal shock. In February 1992, WSRCA started a comprehensive testing program on actual shingle samples from failed roofs, hoping to determine exactly why the shingles have cracked.

An ASTM subcommittee, which includes representatives from industry and the trades as well as consultants, architects, and academics, has

---

SHINGLE INSTALLER'S DISCLAIMER

The roofing contractor and materials supplier have no control over the production quality of shingles or the length of time the manufacturer claims they will last. The manufacturer has the sole liability for these properties of the shingle.

In your case, the name of the manufacturer of the product being applied is _____ and the type of shingle is _____.

Contractor's sole liability is limited to the warranty in the contract. This is in lieu of all other warranties, express or implied.

Figure 3. WSRCA has distributed this disclaimer to its members so they don't unintentionally warrant the roofing materials they install. Roofers give the disclaimer to homeowners along with the roofing manufacturer's warranty.

also been trying to develop a new standard. But since ASTM subcommittees make decisions by consensus, new ASTM standards may be slow in coming.

Choosing A Shingle

Until new standards are set and enforced, contractors need to be careful when choosing a shingle. One option is to avoid fiberglass and use organic felt shingles, which have not shown any premature cracking problems. Some organic shingles have been reported to "blister" and "curl," but the problem is not as widespread as the cracking of fiberglass shingles, and rarely

results in leaks or blow-offs. Organic shingles have higher tear strength, good flexibility, and a high resistance to nail pull-through. They usually cost more than fiberglass shingles, primarily because their heavier weight makes them more expensive to ship.

If you use fiberglass shingles, consider stepping up to a longer warranty period. This may reduce the chances of a roofing failure, because the cracking problem seems to occur mostly among the 20-year fiberglass shingles. But you still can't be sure, because 25-year and 30-year fiberglass shingles have failed prematurely, too.

Also be careful how you guarantee your work. WSRCA has distributed a standard disclaimer to their members to be given to customers along with a copy of the manufacturer's warranty (see Figure 3). The disclaimer states that the contractor guarantees his workmanship, not the shingles; the shingles are covered only by the manufacturer's warranty. If you say something vague to the customer like "this is a 20-year roof" or "these shingles will last 25 years," you may be held to that promise even though the shingle warranty doesn't really say that.

By Ted Cushman, an associate editor with The Journal of Light Construction.

SHALLOW ROOF DETAILS

Asphalt shingles, clay and cement tiles, and wood shingles and shakes work well on steep slopes, where rain and melting snow drain rapidly. On shallow slopes, however, wind-driven rain and ice dams at the eaves can cause water to back up under the roofing and find its way into the house. That's why single-ply roofing materials, such as EPDM and modified bitumen, are a better choice for shallow slopes.

But in many cases, putting a single-ply material on a shallow roof — a porch or a shed dormer, for example — clashes with the shingles used on steeper roof planes on the same house. Builders who want to use shingles on a shallow roof, need to take extra precautions against leaks.

How Low Can You Go?

Building codes are not much help when it comes to shallow slopes. CABO's *One and Two Family Dwelling Code*, for example, sets a minimum slope of 3-in-12 for tiles, 2-in-12 for asphalt shingles, and 3-in-12 for wood shakes and shingles. Roofs below these minimums are

not permitted without approval of the building inspector.

There are two problems with these code minimums. First, porch roofs and shed dormers are often shallower than code minimums, but the code leaves it up to the builder to devise a roofing application that will

meet approval. Second, depending on what part of the country you work in, the code recommendations for underlayment may not provide sufficient protection, even at permitted minimum slopes.

Underlayment. The most important factor in devising a watertight

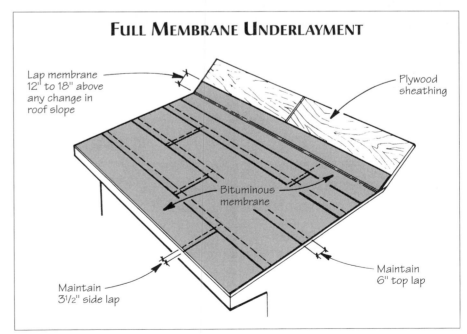

FULL MEMBRANE UNDERLAYMENT

Lap membrane 12" to 18" above any change in roof slope

Plywood sheathing

Bituminous membrane

Maintain 6" top lap

Maintain 3½" side lap

Figure 4. On shallow slopes, lay a bituminous membrane from the eaves to the ridge, or from the eaves to a point 12 to 18 inches above any change in slope.

roof at shallow slopes is the type of underlayment you use. An underlayment is a backup watershed installed beneath the shingles that prevents water from reaching the sheathing. On a shallow roof, it's wise to lavish some extra care on this part of the job.

The most current (1989) edition of the *Steep Roof Manual*, published by the NRCA (National Roofing Contractors Association, 10255 W. Higgins Rd., Suite 600, Rosemont, IL 60018; 847/299-9070) recommends two layers of 15-pound, asphalt-saturated felt glued together with plastic asphalt cement. To keep water from seeping between the layers, the cement must be spread uniformly with a comb trowel, at a rate of two gallons per 100 square feet, so that the two layers of felt don't touch at any point.

This method, however, is messy and time-consuming, and the final quality depends heavily on workmanship. And because the two layers of felt are glued to each other but not to the roof sheathing, any water that does get beneath the membrane can travel to other parts of the roof.

All of the roofers I've spoken with agree that the best underlayment is a self-adhering bituminous membrane, like Grace's Ice and Water Shield — a 4-mil polyethylene film backed by a 36-mil layer of rubberized asphalt adhesive. At about 60¢ to 80¢ per square foot installed, bituminous membranes are fast becoming standard fare for lining valleys and eaves, but they're also good for shallow roofs.

Compared to felt-based systems, membranes are easier to install and are relatively foolproof. They're also self-healing in that they automatically seal nail penetrations. And because membranes are fully adhered, water can't travel beneath them, so any leaks remain localized.

In fact, NRCA Deputy Director of Research and Technology Mark Graham says that a revised manual due out later this year will add bituminous membranes as a second underlayment option. (By the way, the association won't be recommending single-ply roofing membranes, like EPDM rubber, for roof underlayment. Those membranes are cumbersome to work with — if you want them fully adhered, you have to use messy adhesives — and they're not self-healing.)

Roofers who start using bituminous membranes are easily hooked. "We cover the entire roof with Ice and Water Shield whenever the slope is 5-in-12 or below," notes Joe Cazeault, a Weymouth, Mass., roofing contractor with 30 years in the

Figure 5. Workers place self-adhering bituminous membrane at the edge of a shallow-pitched roof. The membrane is installed by unrolling it across the roof while peeling off the backing paper. The job requires at least two sets of hands — one to hold the roll and another to smooth out the wrinkles.

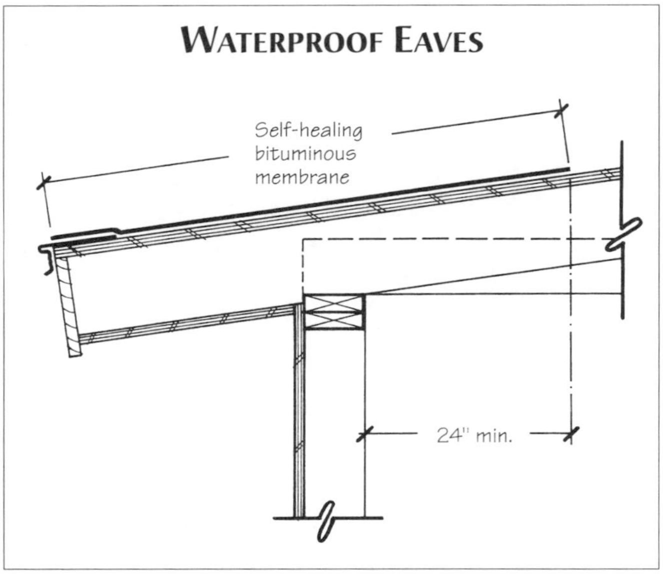

WATERPROOF EAVES

Self-healing bituminous membrane

24" min.

Figure 6. To prevent water backed up behind an ice dam from entering the building, place a self-adhering bituminous membrane from the edge of the roof to a point 24 inches inside the living space. Install metal dripedge on top of the membrane.

business. It may not be required by code, he says, but there's just too much chance that snow will back up under the shingles. Cazeault recommends laying the membrane from the edge of the roof to the ridge or to a point 12 to 18 inches above a change to a steeper pitch (Figure 4).

Membrane Tips

Properly installing self-adhering membranes takes practice. First, roll the membrane out and cut it into 10-foot to 15-foot lengths, then reroll it. Sweep the roof clean and apply the membrane by peeling off the paper while unrolling the membrane across the roof. This takes at least two sets of hands: one to work the roll, and a second to smooth the membrane onto the roof (Figure 5). The membrane should be applied with a 6-inch top lap (the amount of each course that's covered by the succeeding course) and a 3½-inch side lap (the amount adjacent sheets overlap at the ends). Peel-and-stick membranes are slippery, so they're more dangerous to walk on than felt systems. Rubber-soled shoes are a good idea.

Wrinkles. A big problem with membranes installed by inexperienced workers is excessive wrinkling. "It's like putting up wallpaper for the first time," says Larry Shapiro, a product manager at Grace. The membrane sticks to the sheathing on contact, so there's little room for error. A nail driven through a wrinkle won't seal properly and may leak. Wrinkles can be repaired by cutting them away with a utility knife, then patching them with a small piece of membrane.

Temperature. Shapiro stresses the need to follow the manufacturer's application instructions, especially the minimum installation temperatures. Membranes don't stick well below 40°F, making them more vulnerable to leaks. Some products may also have upper temperature limits, above which the adhesive tends to

melt. In the worst cases, says Shapiro, a gooey mess can seep out from beneath the membrane at the eaves. To prevent seepage during peak summer temperatures, make sure the product you choose is rated for at least 180°F.

UV damage. Membranes are also subject to damage from the sun's ultraviolet rays. While short-term exposure to the sun — up to several months, depending on the product — doesn't harm them, long exposure can cause the polyethylene film to become brittle and crack. Some brands of membrane last longer in the sun than others, but none is designed as a finish roof material. Of course, a membrane used as an underlayment is protected by the finish roof.

Nailing. The self-healing properties of bituminous membranes effectively seal smooth-shank roofing nails, but you'll need to be more careful with other types of fasteners. Ring-shank nails, for example, may tear the membrane instead of slicing cleanly through it. The result is a slew of isolated leaks.

Ventilation. Membrane manufacturers also caution that their products should be installed over a well-ventilated roof deck. On inadequately ventilated roofs, a membrane acts as a cold-side vapor barrier, making it more apt to trap heat and moisture. In the worst cases, this results in damage to the roof sheathing and framing.

Shallow Slope Roof Details

Whether you use felt paper or a bituminous membrane, shallow slope roofs require special care.

Asphalt shingles. CABO sets the minimum slope for asphalt shingles at 2-in-12, and requires that any roof below 4-in-12 be covered first with a double layer of building paper. The eaves must also be protected with underlayment, whether lapped-and-glued felt or a bituminous membrane.

Although codes allow a double layer of cemented saturated felt at the eaves, bituminous membranes offer the best eaves protection. Manufacturers recommend placing the membrane from the edge of the sheathing to a point at least 24 inches, measured horizontally, inside the living space (Figure 6). Where metal dripedge is used, place it on top of the membrane.

Wood shingles and shakes. CABO sets a minimum slope of 3-in-12 for wood shingles and shakes. At those slopes, however, you'll have to reduce the weather exposure according to the length of the shake or shingle (Figure 7). And remember that decreasing exposure increases the number of shingles needed to cover a square of roof area.

For slopes below these minimums, NRCA and the Cedar Shake and Shingle Bureau (P.O. Box 1178, Sumas, WA 98295; 604/820-7700; www.cedarbureau.org) recommend installing wood roofing on a lattice-like framework of strapping over a

MAXIMUM EXPOSURES FOR WOOD ROOFS

Length of Shingles/Shakes	Shingles (3:12 min. slope)	Shakes (4:12 min. slope)
16"	3 ¾"	—
18"	4 ¼"	7 ½"
24"	5 ¾"	10 "

Figure 7. These exposures will work at slopes below 3:12 for wood shingles and 4:12 for shakes, but only in conjunction with a watertight subroof and a double-strapping system.

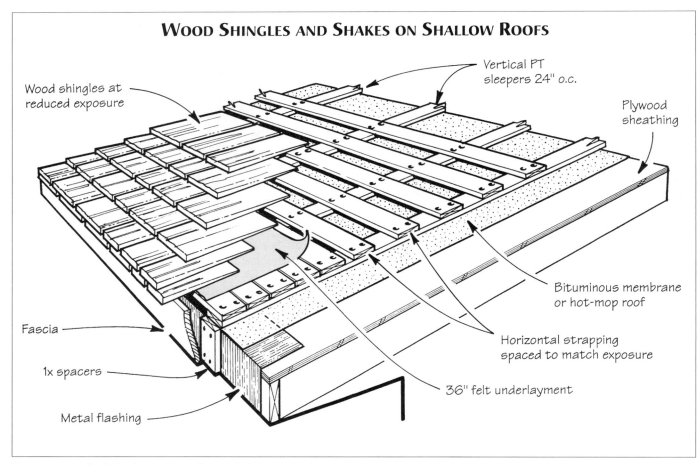

WOOD SHINGLES AND SHAKES ON SHALLOW ROOFS

Wood shingles at reduced exposure

Vertical PT sleepers 24" o.c.

Plywood sheathing

Bituminous membrane or hot-mop roof

Horizontal strapping spaced to match exposure

Fascia

1x spacers

Metal flashing

36" felt underlayment

Figure 8. On shallow slopes, install wood shingles and shakes over a watertight subroof and a framework of pressure-treated strapping. The fascia is spaced out from the metal flashing at the eaves to allow any water that gets under the roofing to drain from the subroof.

watertight membrane (Figure 8). First, install the membrane over solid sheathing, making sure that water will drain freely over the drip edge. Next, lay 1x2 pressure-treated strapping from the eaves to the ridge, spaced at 24 inches on-center. Over this, install a layer of horizontal strapping, spaced to ensure proper shingle exposure. The wood roof does most of the water-shedding and protects the membrane from UV degradation. The double strapping provides air circulation and permits free drainage of any water that does get beneath the shingles.

Slate, clay, and concrete tile. The minimum slope CABO allows for flat concrete, slate, and clay tile is 3-in-12, but in snow country, some manufacturers won't guarantee their tiles below 4-in-12.

As a general rule for shallow slopes, install the tiles with a minimum 4-inch top lap on the same type of double strapping and waterproof membrane system used for wood roofs. The tiles function like shingles and shakes, shedding most, if not all, of the water and protecting the membrane from damage.

In coastal regions and other windy areas, you'll need to nail all the tiles, and you may need to place hurricane clips along the eaves. In most other parts of the country, the first three tiles or courses should be nailed at eaves, rakes, valleys, and hips. On the rest of the roof, the tile's head lug grabs the batten to keep the tile from sliding down the roof, while the weight of the tiles themselves hold them down. Details should be available from the tile manufacturer.

Flashings

Whatever the roofing surface, remember that flashings are a weak link, especially on shallow roofs. A good flashing job takes time, so you can expect to pay your roofing sub a little extra for this part of the job.

For a watertight subroof, the flashing should be installed before the roofing goes down, and the joints should be soldered. Use at least 28-gauge galvanized steel or an equivalent noncorrosive, nonstaining material, such as lead or aluminum. Copper is an excellent flashing material, but water runoff from copper can leave stains on the house siding. Lead-coated copper has the advantages of copper, but doesn't cause stains.

By Charles Wardell, a contractor and freelance writer from Edgartown, Mass.

RESTORING WOOD SHAKES AND SHINGLES

Cedar shakes and shingles offer strength, durability, insulation, and beauty to our homes. A wood roof imparts a look of quality that few other roof coverings can match. Only a few years of exposure to the weather, however, can drastically change this "quality" roofing. Sunlight and rain can cause cedar shakes and shingles to lose virtually all their natural preservatives in as short a time as five years. Around this age, most cedar roofs begin to show signs of cupping, curling, splitting, and decay.

Unlike most roofing materials, however, cedar shingles and shakes can be restored and maintained through proper care and treatment, often doubling or tripling their remaining service life (Figure 9).

Why Wood Roofs Weather

Western red cedar is an extremely durable material even under adverse conditions, but its useful life depends upon the environment. If left unprotected it can suffer photodegradation from ultraviolet light (sunlight), leaching, hydrolysis, shrinking and swelling from water exposure, and discoloration and degradation from decay microorganisms.

Photodegradation by sunlight. Solar radiation is the most damaging component of the outdoor environment. Photodegradation due to sunlight occurs fairly rapidly on the exposed shingle surface. The initial color change from the golden, orange-brown color to gray is related to the decomposition of lignin in the surface wood cells. (Lignin is Mother Nature's way of holding wood cells together.) The wood cells at the shingle surface lose their strength and eventually are washed away by rainwater. In addition, microscopic cracks and checks develop, allowing deeper water penetration.

Degradation by moisture. Accompanying this loss of wood fiber at the shingle surface are the shrinking and swelling stresses set up by fluctuations in moisture content. These stresses cause deeper checks and splits to develop. The result: shakes and shingles begin to cup, curl, split, and check at an accelerated rate.

Degradation by wood-destroying fungi. The natural decay resistance of western red cedar is due to its heartwood extractive, including the *thujaplicins* and a variety of *phenolic compounds.* The thujaplicins contribute to the decay resistance of red cedar while the phenolic compounds and resins give cedar its ability to repel water and its *lubricity* (slippery surface).

Since the natural preservatives in cedar are somewhat water soluble, they can be depleted in service. In roof exposure, extractives may leach out in a relatively short time and allow colonization by wood-inhabiting fungi. Aided by favorable climatic conditions, these in turn allow the growth of wood destroying fungi, which ultimately cause the early failure of a roof (Figure 10). The wood becomes soft and spongy, stringy, pitted, and cracked or crumbly. This usually occurs first at the butt region of the shingles where they overlap.

An added factor is that more shakes and shingles are being manufactured today from younger, less decay-resistant cedar since old, high-thujaplicin-content logs are no longer readily available. This shortens the roof's life expectancy even more.

How fast a wood roof weathers is a function of slope, direction, and shading. The more shallow a roof is, the more likely it is to suffer decay from fungi. South-facing slopes suffer because they experience the greatest swings in temperature and humidity — leading to more splits and other degradation. Shade is also a concern. Wood roofs shaded by trees are more likely to develop mold, mildew, and decay than unshaded roofs.

Shake and Shingle Quality

In the past, Grade No. 1 (Blue Label) shingles and shakes were cut from 100% clear, vertical-grain heartwood. However, grading stan-

Figure 9. After power washing and repairing this red-cedar roof, a worker applies a wood preservative, which will keep it free of mold, lichen, and decay for up to five years.

dards have been relaxed over the years allowing more flat-grain and defects. These shakes and shingles are particularly susceptible to cupping, curling, and splitting. Improper nailing, nailing too high or too far in from the edge, only worsens the problem.

To Repair or Not

The older the roof, the more difficult it is to repair satisfactorily (see "Repair Procedures"). Although you can salvage a roof that requires as many as 30 repairs per square, it may not be cost-effective. A good rule of thumb is that shingle roofs older than 20 years, and shake roofs older than 25 years, will be extremely diffi-

cult, if not impossible, to repair satisfactorily (Figure 11). In some geographic areas such as the Gulf States, repairs on shingle roofs over 10 years old and shake roofs over 15 years old should not be attempted. Foot traffic on these roofs will cause considerable breakage and dislodging of shingles.

The final decision to repair, clean, and treat with preservatives a wood roof is going to be a subjective one. There are no iron-clad rules. But don't go ahead with restoration if the benefits are questionable.

Cleaning With Bleach

Depending on the condition of the wood roof, there are two methods of cleaning prior to treatment:

chemical cleaning (bleaching) and power washing. In many areas of the country, wood roofs are discolored primarily by sunlight and surface mildews or algae. These roofs can be cleaned quite easily and effectively with bleaching agents such as sodium hypochlorite (household bleach) or calcium hypochlorite (swimming-pool chlorine) mixed in tapwater. These chlorine solutions quickly remove the oxidized wood fibers on the shingle surface as well as kill surface mildews and algae. The roof is transformed from its initial dirty gray color to a "buff" or buckskin tan color.

To use liquid chlorine (Purex, Chlorox, etc.), mix one gallon of liquid bleach (5% sodium hypochlorite) with one gallon of water to remove mold, mildew, and the gray color. Higher concentrations of bleach (12% to 15% sodium hypochlorite) are available through commercial cleaning-supply companies. They can be diluted with water or used up to "full strength" if necessary to remove discoloration.

Stronger, more cost-effective chlorine solutions can be formulated using granular chlorine (calcium hypochlorite) mixed at a ratio of 2 to 4 ounces per gallon of water. The type found at swimming pool supply companies (65% available chlorine) does a very good job of removing mildew and discoloration due to weathering. Bleach solutions are not effective, however, in removing dirt, rust stains, extractive stains, heavy moss, or lichen growth.

Whichever type of chlorine you use, you can apply the solution of chlorine and water to the roof using a typical garden-pump sprayer. Scrubbing or brushing is not necessary. Let the chemical do the work. The recommended coverage is 1 to $1\frac{1}{2}$ gallons per 100 square feet of roof area. Leave the solution on the roof for 15 to 30 minutes, then rinse thoroughly with a high-pressure power washer or a garden hose. The

Figure 10. These 14-year-old untreated shingles (top) in the humid Houston area show severe decay, splitting, and heavy accumulations of moss and lichen. Organic debris left on the roof (above) traps moisture and hastens decay.

high-pressure rinsing gives more dramatic results and aids in removing the oxidized roof fibers, plant organisms, and leaf debris from the roof.

Take care not to spray vegetation. If this does happen, rinse the plants thoroughly with water. Also, chlorine solutions are corrosive and should be applied using commercial spray equipment with stainless-steel or plastic internal parts. Pump-up garden sprayers work fine for small roofs but are too slow and cumbersome for large jobs or commercial applications. High-pressure spray rigs or airless sprayers are not necessary to effectively bleach the wood. Pressures of 100 to 125 psi are adequate with flow rates of a half gallon to 1 gallon per minute. To minimize any possible damage to shrubbery

Figure 11. Any wood roof that requires more than 30 repairs per square, such as this one, is probably not worth restoring. Shingle roofs over 20 years old and shake roofs over 30 may be too far gone.

REPAIR PROCEDURES

One common way to spot-repair damaged or decayed shingles is merely to replace them with new ones. All you need are a roofing hammer, metal hacksaw blade or heavy wire cutters, a wood block, nail set, shingle nails (hot-dipped galvanized), and new No. 1 grade shingles or shakes.

The replacement of a shingle or shake can be completed in seven easy steps:

1. Split the old shingle using the blade end of the roofing hammer, in line with the original attachment nails.
2. Then remove the broken shingle with the serrated head of the roofing hammer.
3. Saw or clip off the nail heads left just under the butt of the overlapping shingle.
4. Then drive a new shingle into the void until the butt is within approximately 1 inch of the butt line of the adjacent shingles.
5. At this point, toenail two nails (which should be about 1/2 inch longer than the original nails) through the shingle up under the overlapping shingle at a 45-degree angle.

6. Finish driving the nails, using the nailset to avoid damaging the shingles.
7. After setting the nails, drive the shingle in by striking the wood block held against the butt of the shingle, until the butt of the new shingle is even with the shingle course line.

The entire process generally takes about five minutes to complete. *Under no circumstances should new shingles be "face nailed" leaving the nailheads exposed.* When face nailing, the nails tend to extrude and the shingles tend to crack through fastener holes in the weathered surface.

Repeated wetting of shingles causes them to swell, grabbing the nails and raising them. As the shingles dry, the wood shrinks, leaving the nails elevated. Over time, this can cause loose shingles and lost nails. In addition, as the wood ages, it tends to shrink, causing holes to enlarge, and leaving the nails loose in the nail holes.

One problem with removing damaged or decayed shingles is

that surrounding shingles can be loosened or broken.

Undershimming. Another method of spot repair, especially on older and more weathered roofs, is "undershimming." Undershimming involves placing a waterproof shim under the damaged shingle. Recommended shimming materials are heavy 45-pound roofing felt, aluminum, or galvanized sheet metal.

Undershimming is easily accomplished. With a claw hammer, the shingle is raised, and a 4x8-inch shim is slipped in under the shingle. Friction between the wood and the asphalt-impregnated felt is sufficient to hold the shim in place. Metal shims have either a rough burr on the surface, or the lower corners can be bent down to bite into the wood to hold the shim in place. The shim should not be visible after installation. Obviously this technique is only suitable when the shingles or shakes are split and not decayed or loose. This technique is faster and less expensive than replacing individual shingles and it doesn't disturb surrounding shingles. — *B.B.*

and grass, the area should be sprayed with water thoroughly before, during, and after bleaching. This eliminates the need to cover the shrubbery with plastic tarps.

Power Washing

Because certain forms of algae, moss, and lichen are unaffected by chlorine solutions, they must be mechanically removed using a high-pressure washer, similar to those used to clean automobiles. Power washing of wood roofs works quite well and is used extensively on the West Coast (Figure 12). Power washing essentially removes the top layer of wood fibers from the shingles much the same way sandblasters remove rust from metal. Take care not to damage the shingles by using too high a pressure. Pressures of 1,000 to 1,500 psi are generally adequate to clean the roof quickly and efficiently. Although power washing is slow and dirty work, the results are truly remarkable with the roof returning to its original cedar-brown color.

Power washers can be rented through local equipment rental companies or paint stores such as Sherwin Williams for $50 to $75 per day. If you purchase a power washer, you should choose a gasoline or diesel-powered unit with 1,500 to 3,000 pounds of pressure, and a flow rate of 4 to 6 gallons per minute.

Power washing roofs is fairly straightforward. Always work from the top of the roof down, keeping your feet on the dry portion of the roof. Keep the spray wand moving a distance of 8 to 12 feet from the shingle surface. Use cold fresh water. Hot water washing or the use of strong soaps or cleaners is unnecessary. Experiment with various tip sizes to get the best results. A 15-degree spray fan is recommended.

Figure 12. Power washing with water (top), popular in California, restores cedar roofs to their original brown color (above), even if they are covered with bleach-resistant lichen and algae. Power washers can be rented at many paint stores. Roofs that are merely discolored can be bleached instead, which is easier on the wood.

Preservative Treatments

Until recently, it made little sense to preservative-treat an existing wood roof because of the low cost to replace. But as replacement costs have increased, the economics of preservative treatment look much better. One roofer's advertisement reads, "Why worry about a dirty roof? Because a clean and preserved roof looks a lot better than a re-roofer's bill!"

The high replacement costs of wood roofs and the development of new preservative finishes that are cheaper, less toxic, and more durable has made treating wood roofs feasible and desirable.

In 1975 the Texas Forest Service (Forest Products Laboratory) began evaluating preservative treatments for wood shakes and shingles.

Results from both accelerated and long-term outdoor exposure tests indicate that a number of both water-borne and oil-borne treatments are quite effective in controlling the effects of weathering and decay for up to five years. The most effective products are those that contain one or more of the following:

- Copper octoate (1% metal content)
- Copper naphthenate (1% metal content)
- Zinc naphthenate (3% to 4% zinc metal content)
- Busan 1009 or Busan 1025 (2% to 5% TCMTB)
- Polyphase (.5% to 1% 3-iodo-2-propynyl butyl carbamate)

The following is a more detailed examination of these preservatives, their cost, availability, and use. They are ranked in order of overall performance. This ranking is based upon actual long-term outdoor exposure tests on wood roofing in East Texas.

Water-Borne Preservatives

For maximum mildew and decay resistance in a water-borne treatment, *Cunapsol 5* is recommended. Cunapsol 5 (cut 1:4 with water) is quite popular with roof applicators in northern California and the Pacific Northwest because of its low cost and effectiveness in controlling moss and lichen growth. Because Cunapsol contains copper naphthenate, it imparts an initial green color to the wood. If allowed to weather naturally, the color changes to a pleasing cedar brown. To hide the initial bright green color, you can pigment the Cunapsol solution with Presco Cedar Brown Pigment or Millbrite 582 Pigment. Cunapsol 5 and the pigments are available from ISK Biocides (Memphis, TN; 901/344-5350). Cunapsol 5 provides excellent mold, mildew, and decay resistance for up to five years or longer (Figure 13). But like other water-borne preservatives, it has *little effect* on cupping, curling, or

splitting of the wood. The cost per gallon of a pigmented, ready-to-use solution is approximately $2.50 to $3.50. Cunapsol is available in both concentrate and ready-to-use form in 5- and 55-gallon quantities.

Busan 1009 (TCMTB) is a liquid microbicide which, when mixed with water at a 2% to 5% concentration, provides effective mold and mildew control for up to three years. Outdoor exposure tests now in progress show Busan 1009 superior to zinc naphthenate in controlling surface discoloration due to molds and mildew. How well the Busan 1009 formulations will do over a five-year period remains to be seen. Current results lead me to recommend Busan 1009 at a 5% to 9% concentration as a suitable alternative to zinc.

Busan 1009 is available in concentrate form from Buckman Laboratories (1256 N. McLean Blvd., Memphis, TN 38108; 901/278-0330). A 5% concentration of Busan 1009 in water will cost approximately $2 to $2.50 per gallon.

Oil-Borne Preservatives

One of the main drawbacks of waterborne treatments is they do very little to control the drying effects of the sun and subsequent

cupping, curling, splitting, and surface checking. A durable oil-borne preservative containing a suitable naphthenic or paraffinic oil will replenish the wood with oils that have been lost by sun and rainfall (Figure 14). Both naphthenic and paraffinic oils (when applicable) are resistant to oxidation by sunlight, do not contribute to the flammability of the treated wood, and are reasonable in price. Care should be taken to choose only those oils *not* restricted by OSHA's Standard 29 CFR Part 1910.1200, which became effective in 1985. In essence, it states that certain oils manufactured today have been tested and concluded to be carcinogenic. As of 1985 these oils and any products that contain them require special labeling. Please check with the oil supplier for clarification on this. Examples of good naphthenic oils are Chevron's Shingle and Floor Oil and Sun Oil Company's Sunthene 410.

Copper octoate has shown great promise not only in controlling mildew and decay, but also in giving "life" back to aged wood when combined with a suitable naphthenic oil. A 10% concentrate of copper octoate must be diluted 1:9 with

Figure 13. In a side-by-side test, cedar shingles treated with Cunapsol when new (at right) outshine untreated shingles (at left) after four years of exposure in the humid Gulf Coast region.

Figure 14. These 12-year-old shingles from an arid climate suffer more from sunlight than wood decay: the UV breaks down the wood, leading to cupping, curling, and splitting. Oil-borne treatments are needed to fight these drying stresses.

Figure 15. Small commercial applicators can purchase spray equipment for bleach or preservatives from lawncare or golf course suppliers. This unit is the Suburban Sprayer from Weatherguard Systems, Inc., in Marshall, Texas.

naphthenic oil. Like Cunapsol, the preservative is green in color and therefore must be pigmented to provide natural-looking finishes for wood roofs. It's available in 55-gallon drums only. The cost per gallon of a ready-to-use solution (with pigment) is $5 to $6.

Oil-soluble copper naphthenates are an alternative to copper octoate and are available from many suppliers, including OMG America (Cleveland, OH; 800/519-0083; www.omgi.com) and Continental Products (Euclid, OH; 800/305-5869; www.continentalprod.com). Pound for pound, copper naphthenate and copper octoate are equal in performance. However, the copper octoate is available in higher concentrations than copper naphthenate so it's more cost-effective to large-volume users. In addition, there is less odor with the copper octoate. Prices for 1% copper naphthenate solutions can vary from $3 to $6 a gallon. Copper naphthenate solutions will be green in color but can be pigmented.

Zinc naphthenates in oil are readily available and in use in many areas of the country, but I cannot recommend them at concentrations lower than 3% to 4%. In mildew-prone areas, particularly in the South, 1% to 2% zinc naphthenate solutions are poor performers over time (they have some merit in areas not prone to mildew and decay). Price per gallon of 3% zinc naphthenate solutions will vary from $4 to $7 per gallon. Zinc naphthenate is available from manufacturers such as OMG America (MGARD S-150).

Because many of the preservative suppliers cannot or will not sell their products in small quantities (less than 5 gallons), the applicator should consider the following ready-to-use treatments because of their availability, price, and performance:

- Natural Seal X-100 (American Building Restoration Products, Inc., Franklin, WI; 800/346-7532; www.abrp.com)
- Seal Treat II (W.M. Barr, Co., Memphis, TN; 800/398-3892; www.wmbarr.com)
- TWP Roof and Deck Coat (800/297-7325; www.wood-sealants.com)

The Texas Forest Products Laboratory is continually searching for new and effective finishes for wood roofing. The recommendations given in this report are based solely upon tests performed here in East Texas. The opinions given here are just that — opinions — and by no means should be interpreted as an official endorsement by the Texas Forest Service.

Equipment Needed for Roof Restoration

There are as many different designs for spray equipment as there are people who sell it. Because of its low cost and availability, the common garden sprayer is an easy and effective way of applying bleach solutions, water-borne preservatives, and preservatives in light solvent. It is not suited, however, for the naphthenate-oil treatments. Also note that this is a slow and cumbersome way to apply chemicals to the roof.

Many commercial applicators choose an airless sprayer such as those manufactured by Graco, Binks, or Hero. These are excellent choices but are quite expensive and "overqualified" for roof restoration work.

A much cheaper and more reliable sprayer can be made with a diaphragm pump (Figure 15). Twin diaphragm pumps, such as those available from Hypro Company, are an excellent choice for wood restoration work. They are economical, dependable, long-lived, and highly adaptable. They are capable of delivering oil- or water-borne chemicals to the roof with plenty of pressure and volume. Diaphragm pumps are superior to gear and piston pumps in handling the abrasiveness of preservative solutions, particularly those containing pigments or mildewcides.

For information on quality diaphragm sprayers, contact manufacturers that supply the lawn, turf, and pest control industry, such as the Broyhill Company or Oldham Chemicals Company. Both provide complete sprayer packages including diaphragm pumps, storage tanks, hose reels, and spray guns. Most complete spray packages sell for under $2,000.

Sprayers can be truck-mounted or totally portable depending on personal preference. Truck-mounted units eliminate the need to continually move the sprayer around the job site. Everything is self-contained on the truck bed. Usually 300 feet of hose is adequate to reach most roofs. Manual or electric hose reels are advisable when using over 100 feet of hose. Pumps are usually driven by gasoline or diesel engines.

Spray guns can be purchased from companies such as Spraying Systems. They should be the high-pressure type (800 to 3,000 psi capacity) with spray tips of .015 to .040 orifice and a 15- to 65-degree fan. Attaching a 10-inch extension wand to the gun makes the coating process less tiring. Longer wands up to 64 inches can provide greater reach but can be heavy. They are very useful where foot traffic on the roof is limited or dangerous.

By Brian Buchanan, a forest products researcher and consultant in Lufkin, Texas and former wood technologist for the Forest Products Laboratory.

PREVENTING ICE DAMS

Ice dams are not peculiar to northern regions: They can and do occur in any area of the U.S. with a total mean snowfall of 6 or more inches annually — which is nearly three-fourths of the continental United States, according to U.S. Weather Bureau data.

Most of us are familiar with how ice dams form, and the damage they can cause. But few of us seem to know how to prevent them or even how to limit their damage.

Ice Dam Basics

For those unschooled in the mechanics of ice dams, a quick review may be helpful. On the roof of an *unheated* building, snow will melt gradually from the perimeter first, while slowly sinking over the entire blanket. On a *heated* building, the snow will melt in the same pattern if the roof is properly designed and built. On a roof with ice-dam problems, however, the snow will soon take the shape of a wedge. It is paper-thin at the top where it melts faster from warmed attic air that has risen to the peak, and thickest at the eaves, where it ends in a ridge of ice. In old houses that have little or no attic insulation, the roof above the attic will soon be bare but snow and ice will cling to the overhangs.

Most roofs, unfortunately, have too little insulation for the climate or insulation that was installed sloppily. In addition, few roofs have adequate ventilation, and many have none at all.

Heat from the living quarters works its way through the ceiling insulation or convects into the attic (or rafter spaces in a cathedral ceiling) through unsealed openings around chimneys, bathroom fans, recessed light fixtures, plumbing vents, electrical wires, or attic hatches. This warms the attic air and the roof sheathing to temperatures above the freezing point. The snow blanket begins to melt and the melted water runs down the roof where it freezes as it reaches the end of the insulating snow blanket or a cold eaves. Ice begins to build up and can get as thick as a foot or more. Once this happens, run-off from the melting snow begins to pond behind the ice curb and finds its way under the roof shingles and into the building.

In houses with overhangs and steep roofs, water penetration may end there. In shallower roofs or during winters of heavy snowfall, however, water may penetrate the attic and walls and even the inside finishes, particularly at door and window heads where the leakage is often first noticed.

Regardless of the type of construction of a house, ice dams and the water damage they cause can be avoided. What are the solutions?

Shoveling all the snow off the roof or building the roof so that it will shed its snow cover after each snowfall are two very effective ways to prevent ice dams. However, the former is not too practical, hard on the roof covering, and dangerous to life and limb.

Removing the snow partially from the bottom of the roof by means of a snow rake, while standing on the ground or on a ladder, only results in a secondary ice dam forming higher up the roof at the bottom of the snow blanket. All that this accomplishes is to shift the water leakage higher where it can create more havoc with the ceiling insulation and finish.

Every fall, hardware stores heavily advertise electric roof cables as a sure means of solving the ice dam problem. Instructions recommend their installation in a zigzag pattern at the eaves of the roof and in valleys, gutters, and downspouts. Secondary ice dams form just out of reach of the tape and the situation is further aggravated by the fact that you now have "V"s of ice catching the water.

Metal ice belts are very commonly used in heavy snow areas and many contractors swear by them. They are certainly more effective at eliminating leakage than the previously mentioned methods, but are no panacea.

Secondary ice dams form at the upper edge of the metal band after it has shed the ice that formed on it. And do you really want a roof with a 3-foot (or wider) metal edge if you can avoid it? Why do so many contractors still install these unsightly devices when far better means are available?

W.R. Grace, the pioneer of the now widely used bitumen membrane, came out several years ago with its Bituthene Ice and Water Shield. There are now several competitors on the market. The material comes in a 3-foot-wide roll and is self-adhering to clean roof sheathing. It is applied at the eaves, in valleys, and around skylights — wherever the possibility of water ponding behind

ice dams exists. In houses with wide overhangs and shallow roofs, it may be advisable to use more than one strip at the eaves in order to obtain at least 2 feet of coverage above the line of the wall plate.

The roof covering is simply nailed right through the membrane, which seals around the nails much like a puncture-proof tire does.

But as effective as this underlaid membrane is, you should use it only where you can't *design in* the best solution: a combination of adequate insulation and ventilation.

Design Solutions

With what we know today, ice dams are inexcusable in new houses.

ICE DAMS BELOW SKYLIGHTS

Heat loss around a skylight is usually greater than on other parts of a roof, causing melting and subsequent ice buildup below the skylight — even on a well-ventilated roof. In extremely cold temperatures, melted water from around the skylight can get trapped between the cold, vented roof and the snowpack on the roof, freezing almost immediately. A thick sheet of ice can form between the skylight and the eaves causing water to back up into the building.

Since there is no way to prevent the melting altogether, I recommend the following procedure, even on cold roofs.

After the skylight is installed, but before the counterflashing is in place, cover the area around and below the skylight with a self-adhering bituminous membrane, such as Ice and Water Shield (W.R. Grace Construction Products, 62 Whittemore Ave., Cambridge, MA 02140; 617/876-1400). Begin at the eaves, and lay the membrane so that it extends 3 feet above the skylight as well. To prevent water from leaking into the skylight, roll strips of membrane up the sides of the curb, lapping the main

membrane by 6 inches. Finally, apply the skylight counterflashing and roofing in the normal manner.

While you may not need this kind of protection every year, the

extra cost of the protective membrane layer is a small price to pay for peace of mind. And it's a lot easier than standing at the top of a ladder, chipping away at an ice dam. — *H.D.*

PROTECTING SKYLIGHT WITH MEMBRANE

Plywood roof sheathing

3'-0"

3'-0"

3'-0"

6"

Adhere membrane to sides of skylight curb

6" overlap typ.

When ice dams can't be prevented, protect against leaks with a continuous bituminous membrane applied before the skylight counterflashing. Extend the membrane 3 feet on all sides of the skylight, and run it all the way down to the eaves.

First, the designer should avoid roof details that make good ventilation difficult or impossible.

Valleys are one of the worst offenders. If dormers are necessary, use shed dormers instead of "A" roofs, which converge the snow into the valleys. Avoid secondary gables as decorations over front doors or half circle windows. Get rid of valleys and you are well on the way to preventing the problem, if you follow it up with the right combination of insulation and ventilation.

The goals are to:
• reduce heat loss to the attic by using ample insulation that's properly installed
• carefully seal all ceiling air leaks mentioned earlier by means of foaming urethane, packed mineral wool, caulking, weatherstripping, or sheet metal, as appropriate
• install an effective air-vapor retarder on the winter-warm side of the ceiling and walls
• provide ample and effective attic ventilation to quickly remove from the attic whatever heat gets through the insulation before it has a chance to warm the sheathing

Particularly vulnerable areas are the wall platelines. Standard construction generally leaves very little space for insulation over the top plate. And often, insulation over the plate blocks any air passage from soffits to attic space. In new construction, however, it's easy to allow space for both the full thickness of insulation and adequate ventilation at the plates.

Raised Heels

If you're using trusses, order them with an elevated seat (Figure 16). Otherwise, set a secondary 2x4 plate on top of the ceiling joists at the eaves and set the rafters on top of it instead of next to the joists (Figure 17). Use metal fasteners to tie rafter ends to the plate and

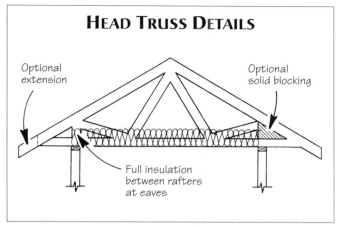

HEAD TRUSS DETAILS

Optional extension

Optional solid blocking

Full insulation between rafters at eaves

Figure 16. If you use trusses, order them with an elevated seat to accommodate a full thickness of insulation at the eaves. Note the vertical support at the bearing point.

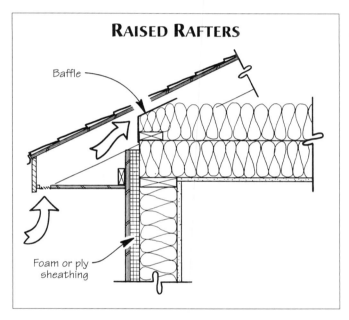

RAISED RAFTERS

Baffle

Foam or ply sheathing

Figure 17. To get extra room for insulation with conventional rafters, you can set a second top plate above the ceiling joists. You may want to tie rafter to joist with metal connectors.

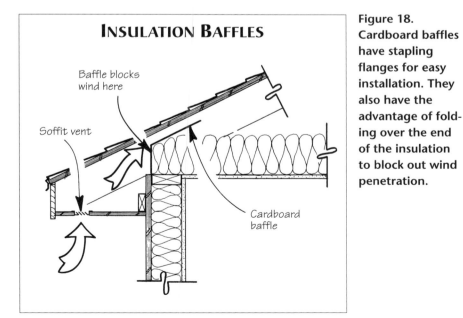

INSULATION BAFFLES

Baffle blocks wind here

Soffit vent

Cardboard baffle

Figure 18. Cardboard baffles have stapling flanges for easy installation. They also have the advantage of folding over the end of the insulation to block out wind penetration.

joists if you need stronger anchoring here.

In order to ensure that the air channels at the eaves remain unblocked as the insulation fluffs up, use insulation baffles. Molded-polystyrene baffles do not cover the vulnerable lower ends of the insulation batt, have rather shallow air slots, and do not ventilate the entire width of the rafter bay. Condensation can occur in the remaining unventilated area.

Cardboard baffles are preferable since they can be easily altered to fit any insulation thickness (Figure 18). The cardboard baffles have the advantage of providing a pocket that seals the lower end of the insulation, preventing soffit air from washing through and reducing its R-factor. Another strategy with elevated rafter seats is to carry the foam or plywood sheathing all the way to the rafters thus sealing the ends of the insulation as shown in Figure 17. For retrofits, you can use a site-built plywood baffle with extended arms for slipping it into place (Figure 19).

The depth of the air space generally recommended is 1 1/2 inches.

Provide more wherever possible, as cold winter air is very heavy and sluggish. The insulation thickness at the eaves should be at least R-38 for northern regions.

Adequate Ventilation

HUD's minimum property standards offer guidance on how much ventilation to have. The standards call for 1 square foot of net-free (unobstructed) vent area for every 150 square feet of attic floor area, or for every 300 square feet if the ceiling has a vapor barrier. But I have seen problem-free roofs with far less than the recommended ventilation levels, while others that appeared to meet the standards have had horrendous ice problems. Therefore, be guided by the commonsense rule that says there is no such thing as too much ventilation in an attic.

We still find many technical writers advocating the use of gable vents. However, anyone who has studied the subject should know that no ventilation system, except for continuous soffit and ridge vents, does a complete job of venting an attic.

Gable louvers function only when the wind is blowing against them, and then they ventilate only partially. Combined with soffit vents, their performance is not much better.

Other types of vents, such as cupolas, roof vents and fans, turbines, or soffit vents alone, do not do a thorough job. There are always large areas of the sheathing that do not get ventilated.

On the other hand, a balanced combination of soffit and ridge vents encourages a continuous air wash of every square inch of sheathing where condensation is most likely to occur.

All Vents Not Equal

But not all ridge vents are created equal. The only type that should be used is a *baffled* ridge

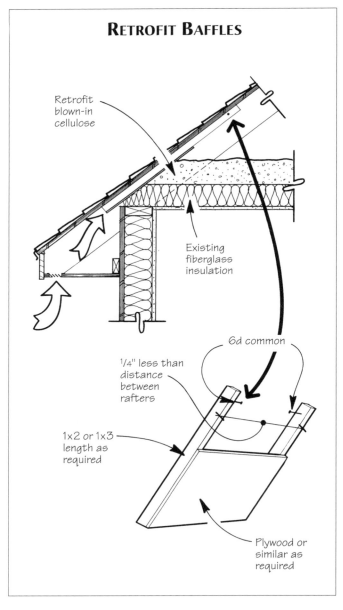

RETROFIT BAFFLES

Retrofit blown-in cellulose

Existing fiberglass insulation

6d common

1/4" less than distance between rafters

1x2 or 1x3 length as required

Plywood or similar as required

Figure 19. For retrofits, you can fashion baffles from strapping and thin plywood. The strapping extensions form handles to slip the baffle in place, and provide a convenient place to nail.

vent. The baffle deflects wind blowing up on the roof. This both increases the airflow from the attic (due to the *venturi* effect), and prevents the penetration of water and snow. Conversely, ridge vents without baffles can admit water and snow in large quantities, wetting insulation and ruining ceilings.

The better ridge vents are made of metal and have an integral metal baffle. (Do not accept accessory plastic wind baffles.) In heavy snow regions, however, even the best aluminum ridge vents can collapse from the weight of a deep, wet dump. To prevent this, order enough joint blocks so that you can insert one

every 24 inches maximum into the ridge-vent sections before installation.

Most metal ridge vents available commercially are manufactured for shallow to medium-pitch roofs. When used on steeper roofs, they must be bent to fit the pitch. This closes their throats and reduces the air flow, while also exposing the lou-

CATHEDRAL CEILING RETROFIT

The roof panels of this pre-cut house in northern Vermont were panelized and built of 2x4s, 16 inches on-center, with a plastic vapor retarder towards the inside, R-11 fiberglass batts, and plywood glued and nailed to both faces. This formed a cathedral roof that was covered with cedar shakes with felt strips interlaid. The ice-dam problem was very serious and eventually the eaves rotted.

The roof was retrofitted by the addition of 1-inch extruded polystyrene over the old sheathing. Two-by-three sleepers were fastened on edge over the rigid insulation from eaves to ridge but extending 3 inches past the old fascia. New sheathing was nailed over the sleepers and covered with new fiberglass shingles. Continuous soffit venting was installed under the projection of the sleepers as was a new fascia. Ridge venting was also installed. In the last four winters not a sign of ice damming was seen. This same system can be used to retrofit uninsulated cathedral ceilings with exposed wood decking (see illustration).

With cathedral ceilings, it is important to pay close attention to design and workmanship. You must take great care to seal all possible paths of convection of moist, heated air from the living spaces into the rafter spaces and to provide the best possible air-vapor retarder. Recessed lights are out.

The amount of insulation is limited by the depth of the rafters and the ventilation space. The pre-

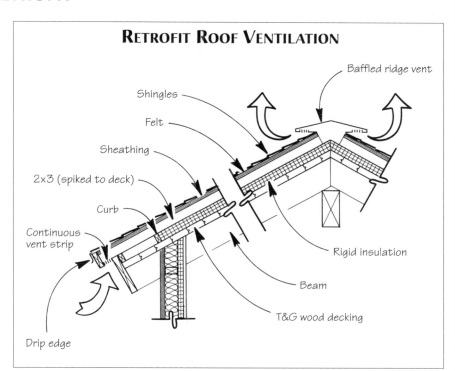

RETROFIT ROOF VENTILATION

Baffled ridge vent

Shingles

Felt

Sheathing

2x3 (spiked to deck)

Curb

Continuous vent strip

Drip edge

Rigid insulation

Beam

T&G wood decking

To retrofit insulation into a cathedral ceiling with exposed wood decking (common on log homes and vacation homes), insulation and ventilation must go on top.

ferred system, in my opinion, is to allow a 2-inch minimum air space under the sheathing, fill the rest of the rafter spaces with fiberglass insulation, and fasten rigid insulation below the rafters.

Now, what will assure that the 2-inch air space will not be restricted by the fiberglass insulation, which might fluff up? Instead of the molded polystyrene vents discussed above, I would suggest tightly stapling nylon cord in a zigzag pattern to the sides of the rafters no less than 2 inches below the sheathing. Preferably use two

staples at each point and drive them in with a follow-up blow if necessary.

Wherever the levels of insulation and ventilation can be improved enough to reach this goal, that is what should be done. But where this is not possible, the next best alternative is to install a product such as W.R. Grace's Ice & Water Shield at the eaves and at all other leak-prone points of the roof.

No other procedure, except building a metal roof steep enough to shed snow, is truly safe or foolproof. — *H.D.*

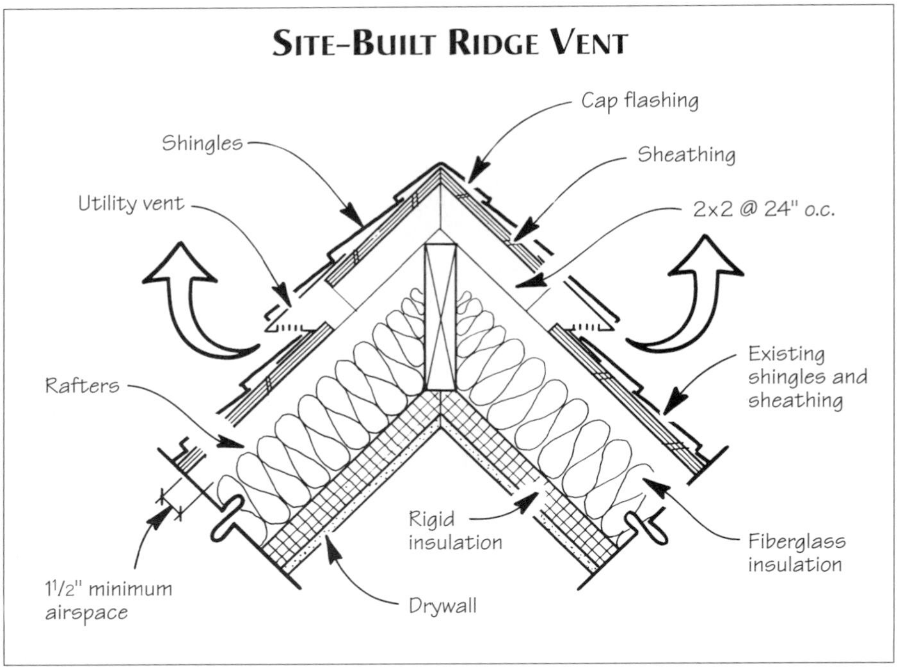

SITE-BUILT RIDGE VENT

Cap flashing

Shingles

Sheathing

Utility vent

2x2 @ 24" o.c.

Rafters

Existing shingles and sheathing

Rigid insulation

Fiberglass insulation

1 1/2" minimum airspace

Drywall

Figure 20. A standard baffle won't work well on steep pitches. A simple site-built vent with two half vents (such as Air Vent's Utility Vent) does the trick.

vered sections to wind-driven snow and rain (since the louvers are now above the baffle). Ridge vents should not be used when they need to be deformed to fit.

Some manufacturers make a version of their standard ridge vent for steeper roofs, or recommend installing a wedge under the base of the vent to reduce the pitch of the roof. Neither of these suggestions work as well as a site-built vent that makes use of a product called the Utility Vent (Air Vent, Inc., Peoria, IL; 800/247-8368; www.airvent.com). The utility vent is nothing more than a half ridge vent (see Figure 20 for installation procedure).

By Henri deMarne, a home inspector and nationally syndicated columnist from Waitsfield, Vt.

SLATE ROOF REPAIRS

SIZING REPLACEMENT SLATE

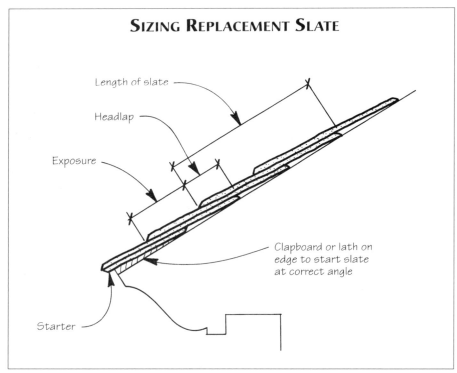

Length of slate

Headlap

Exposure

Clapboard or lath on edge to start slate at correct angle

Starter

Figure 21. To find the size of the replacement slate, multiply the exposure by two, and add 3 inches for the headlap. Then round up to 12, 14, or 16 inches — the standard sizes of slates.

Slate is a very desirable roofing material. Once the hard, dense stone is properly laid, it will require little maintenance to keep it in prime condition. And as a product of nature, a slate roof will permanently add to the appearance and character of a building.

Houses are sometimes enlarged or remodeled, however, requiring slates to be removed and replaced. Or slates are sometimes broken by various causes (including careless workers). When replacing a slate, it's absolutely essential that you use the right size and that you match the existing roof in both shade and texture.

The Right Size

The width of the replacement slates should be obvious. But be observant. Some slates may be wider than the rest, such as along the rake or gable edge, or for use in the valleys. The roof may also have random-width slate with as many as five or six different widths.

To find the proper length, it may be possible to measure the slate along a gable end or some other place where the underside of the slate is exposed. If this is not possible, you can calculate the length from the amount of the slate exposed to the weather (Figure 21).

Measure the exposure, then multiply by two, and add 3 inches for the *headlap* — the area covered by three shingle layers. Bear in mind two factors: Slate comes in even lengths only — 12, 14, 16 inches and so on — so you may have to round up. Also, steeper roofs such as mansards, or improperly laid roofs, may have only 2 inches of headlap.

Matching Color

Slate color depends on chemical and mineral makeup, and can vary drastically from quarry to quarry. The grey and black slate quarried in Pennsylvania is very common in some areas. Many times it can be identified by obvious streaks or ribbons. A higher quality slate from Virginia is blue-grey to black in color. This is a very tough and durable slate. An equally durable slate is that quarried along the Vermont-New York border. It comes in a wide variety of colors including grey, green, purple, and red.

Color is further qualified as either unfading (permanent) or weathering. The former will not change in color over the years, whereas the weathering type may change to a brown, rust, or grey. This change occurs for the most part only on the exposed surface, so by looking at the underside or the inside of the broken slate you can ascertain the original color. If you are still in doubt as to the color or origin of the slate, send a sample to one of the slate companies listed at the end of this chapter.

Rippers and Hooks

First, all remnants of the original slates need to be removed along

Figure 22. To remove the damaged slate, first hook the ripper (top) on one of the two nails holding the slate. Then hammer downward on the ripper (middle) to cut or pull the nail. Next drive in a slate hook (above) to hold the replacement slate.

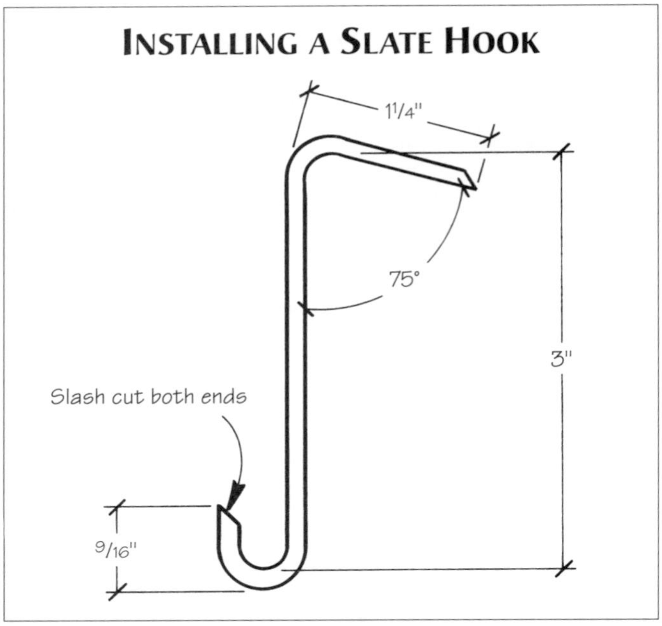

INSTALLING A SLATE HOOK

1 1/4"

75°

3"

Slash cut both ends

9/16"

Figure 23. A slate hook is driven into the sheathing in the joint under the replacement slate. Use copper or stainless steel for a permanent repair.

with the nails that held them in. This first step is done with a tool called a ripper (Figure 22). Use the ripper carefully. It's very important that when you slide it under a slate, you exert very little upward pressure on the slate above the broken one. Since slates will break very easily, you could end up with two slates to replace.

By sliding the ripper under the slate that is to be removed you can hook the ripper on one of the two nails that hold it. Then hammer downward on the ripper — you will either cut or pull the nail out. (You may wish to use a rubber mallet so your ripper will last longer.) Repeat this procedure on the other nail.

The broken slate will now slide out. (Note: Some larger slates such as 24x14-inch and larger have four nails holding them.) After all of the slates are removed, install a *slate hook* (Figure 23). The slate hook is installed in the joint underneath the slate that is being replaced. Drive the 3-inch shaft of the hook into the roof above the headlap of the slate below it. Then simply slide the replacement slate up into the area once occupied by the broken slate. The slate is pushed up past the hook

— then pulled down (usually with the ripper).

Slate hooks are available at some lumberyards, but these are usually galvanized. These will start to rust after only a couple of years and can fail completely after 40 to 50 years. For a more permanent installation, you can buy copper or stainless-steel hooks through the slate quarries in Vermont and New York (see "Sources of Supply" at end of this chapter).

Stagings

How do you get out onto the field of a slate roof to repair a slate or two? Many people work off a rope. This is economical, but in the end may cost you more, since you can easily break more slates than you set out to fix. To spread your weight around, you can pad the area where you are working with rigid foam insulation or plywood.

If practical, you can set up standard triangular roof brackets, but only after removing a slate where the bracket is to be nailed. Broken or missing slates offer good spots to place brackets.

The method we prefer in most cases is to work off a ladder with a ladder hook attached. As with plywood, this puts the pressure on a

large portion of the roof rather than in one spot. But each case should be examined individually, and a bit of ingenuity is often required.

Larger Repairs

If a larger area has to be removed — whether for an addition, dormer, or skylight — the same principles can be applied. Starting at the uppermost spot to be stripped, you can remove these slates using the ripper. From that point on, many of the slates can be taken off simply by pulling the nails with a hammer, with some help from the ripper.

When it's time to reinstall the slates, two preliminary steps are necessary: You must cut the slates to size and make nail holes.

There are two ways to cut slate. The old-fashioned, but still acceptable way, is with a slater's stake and slate hammer. A somewhat easier method for a novice would be to use a slate cutter. These tools are available through most slate quarries.

To make nail holes, you can either punch them with a slate hammer (one end of the slate hammer comes to a point that is designed for this very use), or use a drill. A 3/16-inch masonry drill does very nicely. Punch or drill the holes, one-quarter to one-third the length of the slate from the upper end, and approximately 2 inches from the edge. On slates larger than 14x24 inches, a second course of nails is recommended 2 inches above the regular holes.

As you reinstall the slates, work them back into the areas that remain open, cutting them to fit where necessary. The joints in each course should be well broken with those below. They should never be any closer than 3 inches from the joint above or below.

Nail the slates so the nail heads just touch the slate. Do not drive them home or draw the slate into the roof. Rather, the slate should just hang on the nails. For a better quality job, you may want to use copper or stainless-steel slating nails instead of galvanized.

If the new slate roofing comes up to a vertical wall or a skylight, you'll have to use step flashing. If only half of the upper portion of a slate is exposed for nailing, you can either use a slate hook or use two nails on that side of the slate. Space the two nails as far apart as you can along the edge of the slate in the upper half, and these two nails will hold the slate firmly in place.

By Les Gove, owner of Middlebury Slate Company located in Montgomery Center, Vt. Gove specializes in the repair and restoration of slate roofs.

TRICKY FLASHING DETAILS

Flashing often gets too little attention in the design process, particularly in residential work. Blueprints end up vague on the flashing details, and contractors end up doing a make-shift job with roll stock and roofing cement.

But that's asking for trouble. You can do beautiful work on the big expanses of siding or roofing, but water is going to get in where things intersect. And the designs today aren't short on intersecting planes.

The only way to make sure the structure is weathertight, and will remain that way, is to take the time to review tricky flashing situations on a job-by-job basis. Here are four tough areas we see often, and the way we flash them.

Garage/House Corner

Where the roof on a one-story attached garage butts into a two-story

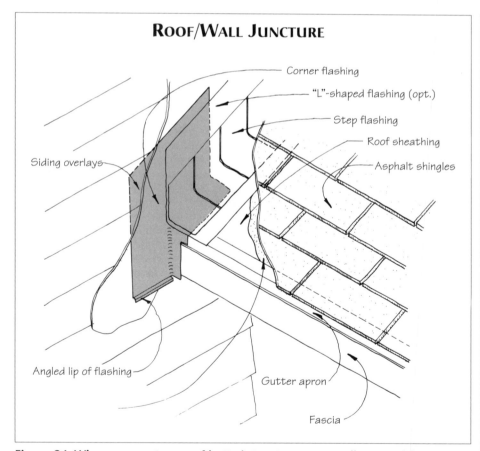

ROOF/WALL JUNCTURE

Corner flashing
"L"-shaped flashing (opt.)
Step flashing
Roof sheathing
Asphalt shingles
Siding overlays
Angled lip of flashing
Gutter apron
Fascia

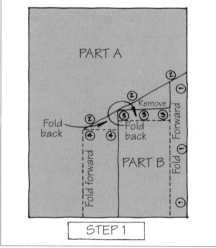

PART A
Remove
Fold back
Fold back
Fold forward
Fold Forward
PART B
STEP 1

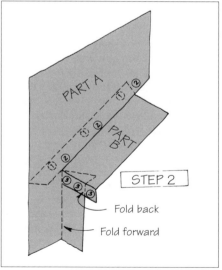

PART A
PART B
STEP 2
Fold back
Fold forward

Figure 24. **Where a one-story roof butts into a two-story wall, start with a custom-fabricated corner flashing (above). Then add L-shaped pieces up the slope, and step flash the rest as usual. The corner flashing can be made out of a square piece of heavy-gauge metal, cut into two pieces — Part A and Part B (at right). Cut along solid lines and bend along dotted lines on a metal brake. Solder parts A and B at the overlapping flaps.**

wall, you'll need more than a straight flashing running from the garage's eaves to ridge. Where water running down the garage roof spills off the edge, it damages the siding and saturates the wall behind it. Even gutters don't always intercept the flow, particularly if the gutter is clogged.

The best solution is to have a sheet-metal or roofing contractor make up a flashing to fit this corner, or if you own a sheet-metal brake, you can try it yourself (Figure 24). Use a heavy gauge metal, such as 16-ounce copper or baked-enamel galvanized sheet metal.

The corner flashing, which is the piece you install first, is cut from a square piece of metal as shown in Figure 24. The square is cut into two pieces which you solder together to form the flashing.

At the job site, make one change from your standard procedure. Use a simple gutter apron, rather than a style-D drip edge. Place the corner flashing on top of your gutter apron and black paper. Make sure you're using nails compatible with your flashing. Galvanized nails will corrode copper flashing, though they are fine if you're using galvanized flashing. Also, get your step flashing in the same metal as the back-up flashing. Flashing is always going to be damp or wet, and electrolytic action between different metals will create pin holes in no time.

You can install the corner flashing behind the fascia, or the corner flashing can overlap the fascia if it's already in place. Overlapping the fascia, as shown in Figure 24, looks best if you use a baked-enamel galvanized flashing because you can match the paint color.

Let the bottom edge of the corner flashing run long until you see where your siding falls, then trim the bottom edge, and create a narrow, angled lip with a hand brake. Place the flashing over the lower piece of siding, then install the siding over it. This routes any water that gets into this area to the outside.

If you want a little extra protection behind your step shingles (which you might, if you use an off-the-shelf step shingle), put in pieces of L-shaped back-up flashing that are 8 to 10 inches high. Each length of L-flashing should overlap the preceding piece by 8 to 10 inches. The L-flashing is formed on a metal brake.

Now you're ready for step flashing. I prefer a 5-inch-high by 4-inch-out shingle for the extra protection it gives, and you could leave out the L-shaped flashing if you use these larger step shingles.

FLASHING MATERIAL OPTIONS

Flashing should last at least as long as the roof covering, preferably longer. In the long run, it doesn't pay to skimp on quality materials. Upgrading from lead to copper, for example, will only add $50 to the cost of the average chimney, but the flashing will last as long as the building. And on a big job like a chimney pan, most of the cost is for labor anyway.

Before putting different types of metals together (say, aluminum and copper or lead), make sure you understand the galvanic series, which classifies metals by how chemically active they are (see illustration, facing page). The gist of it is that when two dissimilar metals come into contact in the presence of moisture, the more active metal corrodes by transferring ions to the more passive; the more passive metal remains unharmed. The farther apart the metals are on the list, the faster the ion exchange, and the greater the corrosion. (This same process is used to advantage to pro-

tect steel by galvanizing: The zinc coating on a piece of galvanized steel corrodes instead of the underlying steel.) The best way to prevent galvanic corrosion is to not use dissimilar metals in the same place; if that's impossible, combine only those metals that are close together on the list. Painting the metal surfaces with a primer may help, but I typically separate dissimilar metals with a piece of eaves membrane.

Here is a rundown of the main choices for flashing materials:

Galvanized steel is probably the least expensive flashing material, but I rarely use it because it will eventually rust. If you've ever seen a metal roof on an old shed, you know that once the protective zinc coating corrodes, the underlying steel is left bare to the elements. The rust stains will then run down the siding.

Zinc is also common in my area. I never use zinc, however, because it becomes pitted when exposed to salt or acid. This includes acid rain

and chimney exhaust from an oil burner or wood stove.

Aluminum is widely used for step flashings, which are generally covered by roofing and siding. But I don't recommend aluminum in other areas. For one thing, it can't be soldered by normal means. For another, it tends to pit and oxidize, especially in salty or polluted air. If you must use aluminum in these environments, the .032-inch thickness will last substantially longer. Anodized or painted aluminum is less prone to oxidation, but remember that a cut edge will eventually deteriorate.

Aluminum is also inappropriate around masonry, because the lime and acids in the masonry will eat the aluminum. If you must put aluminum flashing against masonry, either paint the flashing or separate the flashing from the masonry with a membrane.

Copper flashings can be fabricated from either cold-rolled or soft copper. Soft copper is easily

Metal Valleys

Contractors often call asking for "valley aluminum." This is very lightweight roll aluminum, about .015 inch thick, but it is much too thin to last in a valley. Lightweight aluminum will wrinkle. If it does wrinkle it will break from thermal expansion and contraction. Leaks start wherever kinks or buckles occur.

If we do a job with metal valleys, we use .032- or .040-inch aluminum and cut it to 8- or 10-foot lengths (the thicker aluminum comes in a sheet, not a roll). Or we use 16-ounce copper or .015-inch stainless steel.

Depending on the slope, we overlap the valley sections 8 to 12 inches, with less overlap on steeper slopes (Figure 25). On steeper slopes we don't seal the overlap to allow expansion and contraction of the metal, but on lower slopes (5/12 or

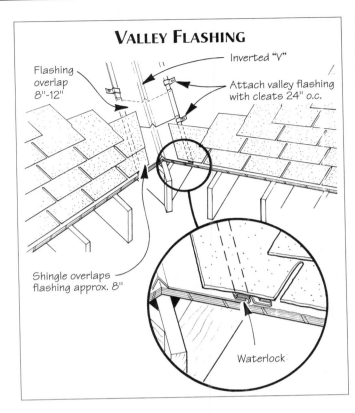

VALLEY FLASHING

Inverted "V"

Flashing overlap 8"-12"

Attach valley flashing with cleats 24" o.c.

Shingle overlaps flashing approx. 8"

Waterlock

Figure 25. An inverted "V" in the middle of the valley makes the flashing stronger and keeps water from rushing up the opposite slope. Fastening with cleats allows for expansion and contraction and keeps the flashing free of nail holes. On shake, tile, or slate, you'll also need a waterlock at the edges (inset).

worked, making it useful for decorative jobs, as well as for complicated shapes like the tops of valleys, where malleability is a real asset. Cold-rolled copper is harder to work with, but it's far stronger.

The green patina that eventually appears on copper can stain trim and shingles when rain runs off it. Even new copper isn't immune, as its surface is etched by acid. The main symptoms are bright red streaks on the roof and green stains on the siding.

Lead is durable and malleable, making it a favorite for cap flashing. It's also very common at the tops of valleys or at the bases of dormers and chimneys. Lead won't stain and is paintable. Before painting lead, let it weather for a bit, then scrub it with a good household cleaner to remove any oily film. Lead is a good choice for use in industrial environments.

The main problem with lead is the very softness that makes it popular. Lead tears easily, making it a poor choice for places where workers might walk at some point. Lead

GALVANIC SCALE

Active

Zinc
Aluminum
Steel
Cast Iron
Lead
Tin
Copper

Passive

When two dissimilar metals come together in the presence of moisture, the more "active" metal will corrode — a process called galvanic corrosion. The farther apart the metals are on the galvanic series, the greater the corrosion. To prevent galvanic corrosion, don't put dissimilar metals together, or — if you must — separate them with building paper or a bituminous membrane.

is also more durable if left hanging fairly free, as on a apron; when fastened on all sides, it will fatigue from movement.

Lead-coated copper is my first choice for most jobs, since it combines copper's durability with lead's resistance to staining. It consists of a sheet of 6-ounce cold-rolled copper with a coating of lead on each side. It has the same working properties as cold-rolled copper.

For added insurance, I install metal flashing over a self-adhering bituminous membrane, which serves as a backup watershed if the flashing develops any leaks. Membranes are easy to install and are relatively foolproof. They're also self-healing, which means that they automatically seal nail penetrations and the laps between sheets. And they're fully adhered, so water can't travel beneath them. Any leaks will remain localized. This prevents any water that gets under the roofing from reaching the sheathing.

By Joseph Cazeault, a roofer and metalworker from Edgartown, Mass.

INTERSECTION DETAILS

Valleys meeting at top. One place to avoid a soldered joint is where two valleys meet at the peak of a roof. Some builders cap the valleys with the same metal they use in the valley, and solder the valleys to the cap. But expansion and contraction of the valley will eventually break the soldered joint. The solu- tion is to lap the cap over the valley as much as possible. I use lead flashing for this application (Figure A). If the overlap is sufficient, it will keep out windblown water without soldering. Six inches overlay is usually sufficient on a valley.

Shed dormers. Another problem area is where the sidewall of a shed dormer dies into the main roof, since snow can pile up at the intersection and water can blow up under the dormer's eaves. The cheek of the dormer is generally lined with step flashings, so the solution is to install taller step flashings along the top few feet of the dormer, and to fold these over the top of the roof sheathing (Figure B). The intersection where the dormer roof and sidewall meet the main roof is then covered with a continuous sheet of lead (which can be molded to fit the intersection) and isolated from the step flashings with a bituminous membrane. This takes some extra planning on the part of the builder, since the tall step flashing must be installed before the rake boards on the dormer. But it can save a callback down the road.

Cross gables. Where a pair of cross gables meet at an outside corner, drainage can be a headache. Since there's no place to put a gutter here, water is usually left to dump on the ground. But this invites water to puddle up against the foundation, and can soak the siding. The traditional way to drain these trouble spots was with a conductor head — a cylindrical catch basin poised at the top of a downspout. But if the downspout gets clogged, the conductor head can fill up with water and freeze. This can break it apart at the seams and cause water to back up under the roof.

A better solution is to use a cone-shaped scupper (Figure C). If the downspout stops up, the scupper's cone shape lets excess water spill over the sides instead of backing up under the roof; if it freezes, the ice will push itself up out of the cone, rather than pushing the cone apart.

Recessed windows. A tough flashing job which I occasionally

Figure A. A soldered joint at the top of a valley will break when the valley expands and contracts. Instead, the author laps a lead cap over the top of the valley flashing.

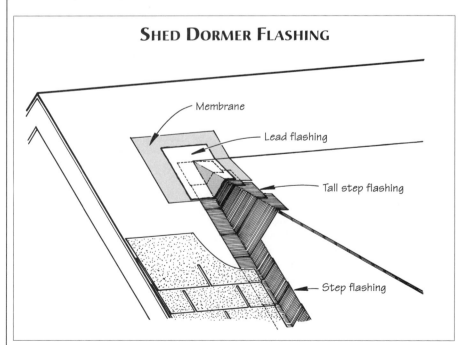

SHED DORMER FLASHING

Membrane

Lead flashing

Tall step flashing

Step flashing

Figure B. Using taller step flashings along the top few feet of a shed dormer will keep melting snow and windblown water out of the intersection.

Figure C. The author catches water at the junction of two cross gables with a soldered, cone-shaped scupper. Besides being attractive, the cone lets excess water spill over rather than backing up beneath the roof.

encounter is second-story windows recessed into a sloped roof — an application where sloppy flashings could spell disaster. Framing is important in these windows. I've seen recessed windows that sit right on the floor of the recess — a mistake that practically begs melting snow to seep under the sill. To prevent this, I typically ask the framer to step the rough sill at least 4 inches up from the recess. It's also good practice to slope the recess away from the window and toward the edge of the roof; the more slope, the better.

After lining the opening with a membrane, I solder together a lead-coated copper pan that covers the rough sill and the floor of the recess, as well as bending about 8 inches onto the shed roof (Figure D). The asphalt roof shingles later tuck beneath this bend. I then set the pan in place and carefully solder on a series of counterflashing pieces, making the flashing along the sides of the recess wide enough to extend a few inches beneath the roofing. The pan is left free-floating so that expansion and contraction doesn't break the solder joint. To keep out drafts and windblown rain, I set the window in a thick bead of caulk, holding the bead 1 1/2 inches back from the sides of the opening to allow for drainage.

Crickets. Chimneys aren't the only places that need crickets. You need a cricket anywhere a roof slope runs into a vertical surface — such as the small towers that commonly break the roof line in Victorian houses (Figure E). A cricket should be a single piece of metal, whether bent in the shop or soldered together on site. The cricket needs firm support underneath, usually a base made of plywood.

Since a cricket is typically a large sheet of metal, it shouldn't be locked in place with nails, which will restrict expansion and contraction. Instead, it should be held with cleats like a valley flashing.

By Joseph Cazeault, a roofer and metalworker from Edgartown, Mass.

Figure D. To protect recessed windows, the author first covers the sloping shelf with bituminous eaves membrane, then covers the membrane with a one-piece soldered pan. Counterflashings are soldered on as needed.

Figure E. A cricket should be a single piece of metal, whether shop-fabricated or soldered together on site (left). To permit expansion and contraction, attach a cricket with cleats (below).

CRICKET CONSTRUCTION

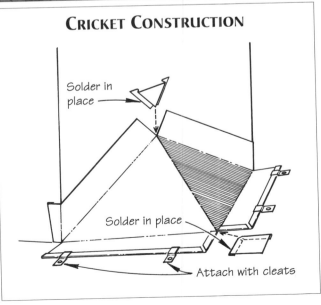

Solder in place

Solder in place

Attach with cleats

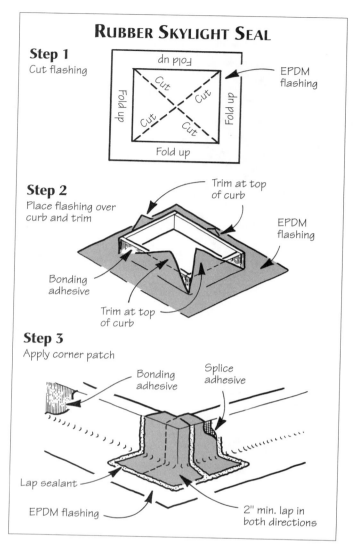

RUBBER SKYLIGHT SEAL

Step 1
Cut flashing

Fold up
Fold up
Fold up
Fold up
Cut
Cut
Cut
Cut
EPDM flashing

Step 2
Place flashing over curb and trim

Trim at top of curb
EPDM flashing
Bonding adhesive
Trim at top of curb

Step 3
Apply corner patch

Bonding adhesive
Splice adhesive
Lap sealant
EPDM flashing
2" min. lap in both directions

Figure 26. Cut a square of EPDM flashing to fit around the skylight. Trim the triangular flaps flush with the top of the curb. Bonding adhesive holds the EPDM rubber to the curb. The material is flexible enough to patch the corners as shown. Use splice adhesive where pieces of EPDM overlap.

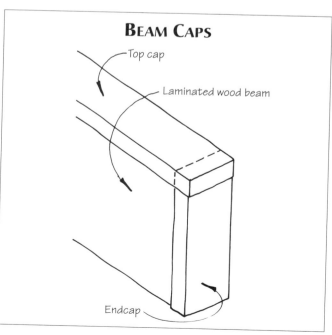

BEAM CAPS

Top cap
Laminated wood beam
Endcap

Figure 27. Cover the ends and tops of laminated beams with flashing to prevent delamination.

less) we use a silicone sealant to keep blowing rain or snow out.

How far we extend the flashing under the shingles has a lot to do with the slope of the roof, but in general, we shoot for 24-inch-wide flashing. This gives us 12 inches up each slope. At the top of the valley, the shingles overlap the flashing 10 inches on each side, leaving 4 inches of valley flashing exposed. We plan our valleys so more of the valley is exposed as we get closer to the eaves. We need more exposure near the eaves because the valley carries more water lower on the roof. Besides, a slightly tapered valley looks better.

To give a valley greater strength and to keep water from rushing down one slope and up the other, we often form an inverted "V" in the center of the flashing. You can have a sheet metal shop form this "V" on a brake. This knocks about an inch off the flashing width, so you have to start with wider flashing. You always want shingles to overlap the flashing by about 8 inches.

On a slate, tile, wood shake, or concrete-tile roof, you should always use the "V." You also have to use flashing with a *water lock* — the edge on each side of the valley is folded back to stop the water. Also, cleats slip over the water-lock edges, and your nails go through the cleats, not the flashing. This makes your valley a trough to contain any water flowing into it.

Skylights

Flashing skylights can be a big headache, particularly if the skylight is attached to a curb. The traditional way to flash skylights is to use a metal flashing, but lately I've been using a synthetic rubber (EPDM) flashing, and I've found it a lot less expensive and more reliable.

I think an EPDM flashing beats metal for reliability, and it costs less too. For flashing, you'll want to use *uncured* EPDM, which is material intended to take a shape. Cured EPDM sheets lay flat and are used for large, flat roofs. If you go to a local roofing company and ask for a scrap piece of uncured EPDM flashing and a small quantity of the bonding adhesives, you'll be in business. The four major manufacturers of EPDM roofing market under many trade names, but if you use the generic name "uncured EPDM flashing," you should be able to buy what you need. The EPDM carries a 20-year warranty, and the material costs less than copper flashing.

Synthetic rubber is very simple to work with. You can take a large square of rubber, your shears, and adhesive (bonding adhesive, splice adhesive, and lap sealant) and carry them up to the roof. Sitting on the roof, you cut the rubber into pieces, brush on the bonding adhesive, and make up a fully waterproof skylight flashing. With metal, I have to measure the job, go back to the shop to make up the flashing, then go back and install it.

Use bonding adhesive to stick the EPDM to a 3½- or 7½-inch-high wood curb, but don't glue it down to the roof deck. Run the EPDM flashing 12 inches out under the shingles, on top of your black paper. At the corners, where you're bonding EPDM to itself, use splice adhesive (Figure 26). It's as easy as patching an inner tube, and if you make a mistake, you can always repair it. When you're done, run a bead of lap sealant along all the patched seams.

Nail shanks from the roofing nails can go through EPDM without causing leaks. I favor rubber for wood shingle or shake roofs because they're hard to flash with metal. You can't use EPDM over skip sheathing, but many shake, shingle, and tile roofs are installed over solid sheathing.

Projections

Any wood member that projects from the house should be flashed. Cornice returns, glulam beams, and balconies should be protected with flashing.

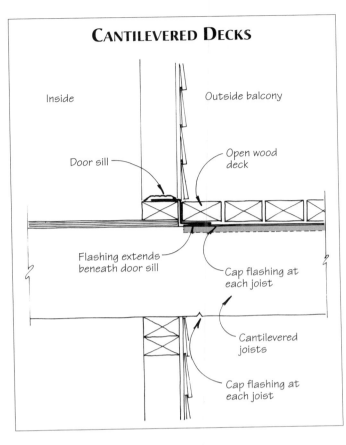

CANTILEVERED DECKS

Inside

Outside balcony

Door sill

Open wood deck

Flashing extends beneath door sill

Cap flashing at each joist

Cantilevered joists

Cap flashing at each joist

Figure 28. Flash cantilevered balcony joists and where the deck meets the wall. Run the flashing underneath the door sill and up the walls on either side of the door. A saw cut or bead of caulk on the underside of the joists about 2 inches from the siding will make water drip off the beam rather than run into the building.

Glulam or heavy timber beams projecting from the peak or eaves should be capped with metal. Turn down the metal an inch around the sides. You need flashing over the ends of glulam beams to keep the laminations from separating (Figure 27).

Balconies aren't immune to water damage, even when you build with pressure-treated wood. Water can run back into the house and damage untreated wood. Also, pressure-treated wood eventually decays. We're seeing many relatively new apartment buildings with cantilevered balconies that are rotting off. You can always replace a deck if it decays, but replacing the cantilevered joists is an expensive proposition.

You need to handle balcony flashing carefully because water or snow can pile up on the balcony and creep in under the sill of a sliding door. Water can also run back into the house from dripping balcony joists.

Bring your flashing under the door

sill, and if the door is on the same level as the balcony, caulk between the sill and the flashing (Figure 28). You should also flash the wall where the balcony deck joins the house. Use the same flashing detail where the deck meets the wall, only run your flashing up under the siding.

It's also a good idea to top off your balcony joists with a 2½-inch-wide piece of metal flashing running the length of the joist. Make it U-shaped so it slips down half an inch on both sides.

To keep water from running off the bottom of the joists, we make a saw mark across the bottom of the joists a couple of inches from the house, or we run a bead of caulk an inch from the wall if the client objects to the saw mark. This break causes water to drip off and keeps it from crawling inside.

By Lloyd Hitchins, president of Hitchins Roofing in Urbana, Ill., and a roofer of 45 years.

SOURCES OF SUPPLY

Slate Suppliers

Buckingham Virginia Slate Corp.
Arvonia, VA
434/581-1131
www.bvslate.com

Evergreen Slate Company
Granville, NY
800/872-7528
www.evergreenslate.com

Structural Slate Company
Pen Argyl, PA
800/677-5283
www.structuralslate.com

Vermont Structural Slate Company, Inc.
Fair Haven, VT
800/343-1900
www.vermontstructuralslate.com

Organic Felt Asphalt Shingles

BPCO Inc. - a division of Emco Building Products Corp.
Lasalle, Quebec, Canada
800/567-2726

Organic Felt Asphalt & Fiberglass Asphalt Shingles

CertainTeed Corp.
Roofing Products Group
Valley Forge, PA
800/233-8990
www.certainteed.com

GAF Materials Corp.
Residential Roofing Products
Wayne, NJ
973/628-3000
www.gaf.com

Georgia-Pacific Corp.
Atlanta, GA
404/652-4000
www.gp.com

IKO
Chicago, IL
888/456-7663
www.ikogroup.com

TAMKO Building Products Inc.
Joplin, MO
800/641-4691
www.tamko.com

Bituminous Membranes

CertainTeed Corp.
Valley Forge, PA
800/233-8990
www.certainteed.com
Winter Guard

GAF Building Materials Corp.
Wayne, NJ
973/628-3000
www.gaf.com
Weather Watch

Protecto Wrap Co.
Denver, CO
800/759-9727
www.protectowrap.com
Ice and Water Guard

W.R. Grace & Co.
Cambridge, MA
800/354-5414
www.na.graceconstruction.com
Ice and Water Shield

CHAPTER 6

PAINTS AND COATINGS

- Painting Failures: Case Studies

- The New Water-Based Paints

- Clear Finishes for Wood Siding

- Problem-Free Floor Finishes

- Remodelers and Lead Paint

PAINTING FAILURES: CASE STUDIES

Case One: Yellowing Enamel

Project: White oil enamel on the interior trim in high-end condos in southern California.

The problem. The building interiors were specced out in straight white, both walls and trim. The plan called for a good oil enamel on the baseboards and a lot of other interior trim that normally doesn't get a gloss finish. The walls were flat latex. And within six months, the trim in some of those houses was almost a mustard color next to the white walls. The enamel had yellowed, but the flat latex remained white.

The builder tired to correct the problem by painting again with another batch of white oil enamel, but it yellowed too.

What the painting contractor Mark Robson had run into was a two-fold problem: a regional decorating trend calling for straight white enamels on trim surfaces; and new environmental regulations that have compromised the fade resistance of those same oil-based enamels.

All oil-alkyd resin materials yellow. But they yellow more now than in the past because of the higher resin content in the low-VOC

paints. The yellowing effects can be dramatic in as little as three months. And it's especially noticeable with extremely light colors like pure whites and near whites.

Robson found that the degree of yellowing varied with exposure to sunlight. Surfaces that got little or no sunlight yellowed faster than those that were well-lit. Sunny living rooms might not have a noticeable problem, while a closet or the interior of a cabinet would have mustard-colored trim.

The fix. One option is to use latex. But latex has its own problems. It doesn't stand up to abrasion and

THE IMPORTANCE OF PREP WORK

Applying a top coat on bare wood without first brushing the dust off and priming is a frequent source of early peeling on new houses. Experienced painters carry a dust brush in their overalls pocket and brush all areas to be painted.

On already-painted buildings, paint failure can be caused by:
• Applying a new coat over chalky, dusty, oily, or dirty paint.
• Painting over mildew.

Backed-up water from ice dams can wreck both interior and exterior finishes — including paint on the soffit, fascia, and siding.

No primer was used here and the result was poor adhesion and wholesale peeling to bare wood. One telltale sign was the absence of any white pigment on the wood or the back of the paint chips.

• Painting over shiny paint.
• Applying oil-based paint on a surface not thoroughly dry.

Some of the remedies should be self-evident, but others aren't. How should a surface be prepared to ensure a longlasting job?

Bare wood should first be brushed dry and then be primed with an oil-based primer; it has a greater penetration of the wood-fiber surface than latex.

It's best to brush the bare wood as you go along and prime only an area you can handle in a day. Try to do only one side of the house or stop at logical spots where picking up later will not show. Then, applying a finish coat over the day's primer coat within 48 hours, if possible. The longer you wait the weaker the bond is going to be, since the surface of the primer is increasingly compromised by dust and weather.

Previously painted surfaces should also be brushed clean and even washed if dirt, chalk, mildew, or other impurities are present. Rub your hand on the wood to determine chalkiness, a self-cleaning feature of many oil paints. Wash a small test area with detergent

washing as well as oil does, and it doesn't stick to previously painted surfaces as well unless you really prep the surface. It can freeze windows shut and stick other surfaces together, though latexes are better about that than they used to be. Sometimes it doesn't cover as well as oil material would, on both old and new work. But mostly, you just cannot get the appearance, feel, and hard durability of oil from a latex enamel.

Another option is to change the color of off-whites — since these tend to be yellow-gray to begin with — so the discoloration will be less noticeable. Use something as dark as a Navajo White and you're probably not going to have problems with the homeowner. Lighter than that, though, and you're taking chances if you're using oil.

Case Two: Slippery Stucco

Project: Exterior woodwork on a 40-house subdivision in southern California. The siding material was spray-on stucco, a plaster material.

Where painting contractor Mark Robson paints, in southern California, spray-on stucco — actually a plaster material — is a popular exterior treatment. But Robson has found that the prep work done by stucco subs can foul things up for the painters.

The problem. Robson's crew painted the woodwork on an entire 40-house subdivision. It looked fine when they finished, but the paint on the exterior of the window frames peeled off in less than three or four months. It was the worst nearest the glass, but it peeled away from the glass as well.

With a little detective work Robson discovered that the plasterers, who sprayed the stucco over the outside walls, had sprayed an oily solution over all the windows. Like greasing a frying pan, this lets any stucco that hits the glass come off easily. Unfortunately, this solution hit the frames as well as the windows, causing the paint to peel.

In the end, Robson had to go back to the site, scrape all the peeling paint off the window frames to expose bare wood, wash the wood with solvent,

(trisodium phosphate works best) and water to determine if the blotchy look is caused by dirt, mildew, or both. Dirt will come off but mildew spores will not be affected.

Mildew, however, will respond immediately to the bleach test; put a small amount of fresh bleach in a glass container, add the same amount of water, and rub the suspected spots with a white cloth dipped in the mixture. Rubber gloves and eye protection are advised as well as old clothing. If the spots yellow and disappear before your eyes, mildew is the culprit and must be entirely removed before painting (or staining, for that matter).

A good way to clean a chalky, oily, or dirty surface while killing mildew spores is to wash it with a mixture of one cup of trisodium phosphate (TSP), one quart fresh bleach, and three quarts of warm water (do not mix any products containing ammonia with bleach as the resulting gas is deadly). Use a scrub brush. Rinse thoroughly with fresh water.

If mildew is a severe problem, follow the above treatment by scrubbing with a solution of 50 percent fresh bleach and 50 percent water but, this time, do not rinse. Let dry and follow immediately

Make sure you prep and paint the butt edges and butt joints to prevent this type of water penetration and peeling. Also avoid painting when the wood is swollen with moisture lest it shrink and crack the paint at joints — especially if you're using oil-based paint, which is less flexible than latex.

with painting before airborne spores of mildew are deposited again. (Water-based paints can be applied while the surface is damp but not wet.)

Mildew, however, is likely to recur. The spores are everywhere in the air and will take hold and develop wherever the conditions are propitious: warmth, humidity, and lack of sun. A mildewcide added to the paint should delay new growth for a while.

Before repainting, remove all peeling paint, feather the edges of any paint still adhering, prime the bare wood, and apply a new coat over all. A word of caution here: If the remaining coats of paint are thick, adding another on top may create more problems. It would be better to only spot-paint the bare, primed areas — even though the house may look like it has a rash or jaundice — unless you want to sand down or remove the areas of thick paint.

The only reason to paint over an existing coat in good shape is to change color. If the paint is still shiny, it will have to be roughed up with sandpaper and brushed clean to form a good bond with the new coat.

By Henri deMarne, a consultant, home inspector, and nationally syndicated columnist from Waitsfield, Vt.

and reprime and repaint. (The builder paid for it all.) But even with these steps, the longevity of the finish coat will be compromised.

To avoid this problem, have the plasterers mask the windows; leave the window casings off until after the plasterers are gone; or have the painters come out ahead of the plasterers and prime the windows. Of these, priming is the least effective, since the oil will still stick to the primer, which will require cleaning afterward. Keeping the oily solution from ever hitting the window frames in the first place is the best prevention and keeps painting costs down.

Case Three: Mildew on New Home Siding

Project: White oil-based paint on the wood siding of a custom home in Illinois.

The problem. This was a large new house built in 1989 for a retiree. The owner wanted oil paint, so the contractor Margaret Clifton specced top-of-the-line oil. The owner also insisted that the painter use up a few gallons of 8- to 10-year-old Sears oil paint he had in the basement.

A year later, the owner asked Clifton to stop by and showed her that the expensive oil-based paint had turned gray on every side of the house with mildew (Figure 1). However, the old Sears paint, which they had used on the garage, remained sparkling white.

The rep from the paint company came to the site and confirmed that it was mildew caused, in part, by the cool, damp spring.

But why did the porch with the old Sears paint look so good? As it turns out, the older paint had mercury in it as a mildewcide, while the newer paint didn't. The company had removed mercury from all its formulations because of the impending ban on mercury. The new mildewcides, the rep said, are not as effective, and furthermore, mildew feeds on the oil in oil-based paints.

The fix. The rep's suggestion was to wash the house with a mixture of one part chlorine bleach to three parts water and one part trisodium phosphate. That, he said, would remove the mildew but it wouldn't prevent the mildew from coming back.

For that, they would need to repaint the house with latex — after sanding the entire house to rough up the nice glossy finish of the oil paint.

Case Four: Cool, Wet Weather Peels Paint

Project: A repaint of a large 150-year-old colonial in northern Vermont.

The problem. In Vermont, where painting contractor Jay Bowen is based, the painting season is short, and summertime brings heavy use of the second homes and resort sites that make up much of his work. So Bowen must often paint exteriors in early spring or late fall, when cold evening temperatures can bring heavy dew. Under some conditions,

Figure 1. Mildew appeared on this house (top) in Momence, Ill., within a year of repainting. The contractor traced the problem to new blends of oil-based paint that don't contain mercury mildewcides. Where a ten-year-old Sears paint was used on a porch (above), the walls were still gleaming white.

dew can take new paint off the same day it's applied.

In this case, the house needed major prep work: scraping and sanding right down to the wood. Then Bowen's crew applied an oil primer and two coats of white latex finish on both the clapboards and trim. This was in late September.

They finished brushing the second coat on a nice fall day with the temperatures in the 60s. They worked until late in the afternoon, and as they were putting away their brushes it got cooler and damp. It didn't start raining, but a mist developed as it got dark. It stayed foggy all night. Most of the paint had tacked up nicely before they left.

When they went back the next day to hang the shutters, they found the paint on two sides of the house was completely wet — as if they'd just brushed it on.

The fix. Because the paint was still so wet, they were able to brush out what was on there, using a can of paint to keep the brushes wet. Had the paint been oil, a skin would have formed, and the water from the dew would have discolored everything. Then they would have had to let it dry, sand it, and repaint. With the latex, there was no skin and they could pick up where they left off.

They were also fortunate that they

PAINT PROBLEMS

Cross-grain cracking and alligatoring are frequently found on older houses that have been painted many times over the years, and often before a new coat of paint was due. These problems occur because the paint becomes too thick to flex with the seasonal movement of the wood.

The paint principally cracks perpendicular to the brush strokes, which generally follow the grain of the wood. Hence the term "cross-grain cracking." The phenomenon is also known as "alligatoring" because the cracking paint mimics the pattern of the skin of that amphibian.

If this is the paint condition, all paint should be removed down to bare wood by scraping, sanding, or heat gun (never a torch). Painting over alligatoring is a waste of energy and money.

Blistering can also occur when a second coat of oil-based paint is applied before the first one is thoroughly dry. In this case, paint thinner instead of water vaporizes under the influence of the sun and causes the paint to blister.

Bleed-through can be caused by certain natural wood products. Redwood and cedar contain a pigment which is dissolved by moisture and leaches out onto painted surfaces through cracks in the paint surface. Resolving the moisture problem, whether it is through leaks from the outside or from internal moisture pressure, then letting the wood dry

over several months of summer and fall, is the solution.

The remaining stains can be washed off with a mixture of 50% denatured alcohol and 50% water after the failed paint has been removed. The edges of the sound paint should be feathered and the wood primed.

Hardboard siding has similar problems. Bleed-through is caused by some of the products used in its manufacture — including wax. The treatment is similar to that for redwood and cedar; the composition siding must be allowed to dry and the reason for its wetness removed. Hardboard siding is more prone to problems caused by internal moisture pressure because it does not have the moisture storage ability that wood has.

Some species of wood exude resin at knots. This may be a tricky problem to resolve. The excess resin should be removed with a sharp knife or chisel and the knot treated with a stain killer such as B.I.N. This treatment may not be successful at first. It may have to be repeated until most of the resin has oozed out.

Nailhead staining is caused by rusting nails. (Using hot-dipped galvanized nails in new construction will prevent this.) Where encountered, the rust should be removed by sanding, wirebrushing, or the application of a liquid rust remover. The coated nail should be slightly countersunk and primed. The hole should be filled

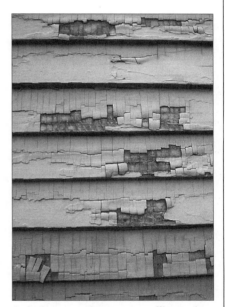

Painting too often causes alligatoring and cross-grain cracking. These problems are most common on areas sheltered from the weather where the paint is put on but never wears off. Painting every 5 to 10 years is best.

with caulk which can be painted when dry.

Obtaining a successful and lasting paint job requires proper preparation of the surface, good application procedures, and quality products. Where failures occurred in the past, you'll need to find and resolve the underlying problems if you want the new coat to last.

By Henri deMarne, a consultant, home inspector, and nationally syndicated columnist from Waitsfield, Vt.

arrived on the job early in the day, because if they had waited until afternoon, the drips would have hardened, and they would have had to scrape or sand. It also happened to be a good sunny day, so by the afternoon the backbrushing work had set up nicely. Six years later the paint job still looks great.

The moral of this story, says Bowen, is that with a high dew point (high relative humidity and cooler night-time temperatures) and a short day, you can get into trouble. In fall and spring he now pays atten-tion to weather forecasts to find out whether the overnight low is expected to dip below the dew point. Then he keeps an eye on the after-noon weather so he can leave the paint sufficient time to dry. If there's any chance that they might get a big enough drop in temperature to cross the dew point, says Bowen, they knock off with a couple of hours of daylight left.

Case Five: Two Coats in One Day

Project: Solid oil-based stain on new cedar siding in Vermont.

The problem. Painter Jay Bowen was called in to diagnose and cor-rect a problem on a new house in Vermont that had been sided in cedar and stained just four months earlier. Two coats of oil-based solid stain had been applied and both coats were bubbling right off the surface. This was on two or three areas of the house — the back, and two areas on one side. So Bowen suspected an application problem rather than a problem with the wood or stain.

The factory rep from the stain manufacturer was called in to take a look, and his best guess was that the first coat hadn't been allowed to fully cure before the second coat was put on. At that point the owner recalled that the shaded front of the house — which was the side in best shape — had been first-coated one afternoon and top-coated the next. The prob-lem sides, on the other hand, got two coats in one day, and got a lot of midday sun.

This is actually a fairly easy mis-take to make with solid stains, says Bowen, because they can appear dry on the surface but still be damp underneath. If you put on a second coat at that point, the solvent in the first coat won't be able to evaporate, and it'll bubble the stain. In this case, the sides in question were exposed to the sun, so after a first coat in the morning, the painters probably checked it at lunch and found it dry to the touch. But underneath, the first coat hadn't cured.

The same thing can happen with an oil-based paint, since oil-based coatings can't breathe. It's less dan-gerous with a latex.

The fix. For this reason, Bowen likes to let all oil-based coatings cure for at least 24 hours before recoat-ing, while he'll recoat latexes after only 12 hours.

As for the bubbled stain job, Bowen had to scrape the problem areas off and repaint. That was most of the material on those two walls

Figure 2. No vapor barrier and high indoor humidity caused the paint to peel on this building (top). The painting contractor found that driving small wedges (above) under every sixth row of siding, 3 or 4 feet apart, allowed the moisture to escape and solved the problem.

which came off with one pass of a sharp scraper.

After scraping he left the surface bare for two or three days to let it dry, then resealed it with another linseed-oil-based solid stain. He let that dry for another three days, then put on the second coat. The house didn't have any more problems.

Case Six: Missing Vapor Barrier

Project: A large wood-frame commercial building in Vermont with wood siding that needed frequent repainting.

The problem. One of the most common causes of paint failure is moisture being pushed through the siding from behind, due to high indoor humidity and the lack of a good air and vapor barrier. The ideal solution for this problem is to install vapor barriers indoors, ventilate bathrooms and kitchens, and back-prime the siding. A house wrap can also help by keeping moist interior air from getting to the back of the siding. But owners may balk at the expense of these retrofitting measures. Painter Jay Bowen found an innovative way to increase paint longevity on a building he was repainting every two years.

It was a big clapboard building near a river, with shops downstairs and apartments upstairs. It was about 150 years old. Every year the whole thing would peel, despite the fact that they would do a high-quality job — scraping it down to the wood, putting on an oil-based primer and two coats of good latex.

The side that peeled the most faced the river, but it also got a lot of sun in the afternoon. So it tended to pick up moisture at night and dry in the day. But the main problem was from within. The worst peeling came from exactly where the bathrooms and kitchens were.

The fix. Since Bowen couldn't keep the moisture inside, he decided to let it get out easier so it wouldn't peel the paint. His solution was to tap wedges under every sixth row or so of clapboards, spaced about 3 or 4 feet apart (Figure 2). The tiny wedges were just big enough to leave a fingernail-sized gap. He also put a few round, 1-inch vents into the walls, and primed the whole building with Zinsser's Bull's-Eye (William Zinsser & Co. Inc., Somerset, NJ; 732/469-8100; www.zinsser.com), which is designed to prevent cedar and knot bleed, and followed that with two coats of latex.

There were no further serious problems. There were still small areas that would peel every few years, but these were easy to repair.

David Dobbs is a freelance writer from Montpelier, Vt.

THE NEW WATER-BASED PAINTS

The paint industry is changing fast these days. As coatings manufacturers reformulate their products to adhere to stricter air pollution standards, they are altering the way paints and other finishes behave, both on the brush and on the finished surface.

The move to water-based paints (often generically called "latex" paints, though latex is no longer an ingredient) is being driven by a growing body of state and city regulations that limit the amount of VOCs — volatile organic compounds — allowed in paints. When VOCs are released into the air, they react with other elements and with sunlight to form ozone. Ozone is desirable in the upper atmosphere, where it filters sunlight; at ground level, though, it's a harmful pollutant and the main ingredient in smog.

Because traditional oil-based paints contain very high levels of VOCs (about 5 to 10 times higher than water-based coatings), manufacturers have had to radically change their formulations. This has reduced the workability of oil-based paints, radically lengthened drying time, and produced enamels that lose their gloss or discolor within months of application. The problems have proved so difficult to solve that most paint professionals believe that oil-based paints are on their way out, except for specialized uses.

Because I share this opinion, I've made a conscious effort to move gradually toward the use of water-based paints in almost all applications.

Water-Based Advantages

Today's best water-based paints have several advantages over reformulated oil-based finishes, and manufacturers are rapidly solving the remaining deficiencies.

Water-based coatings generally apply more easily and retain both color and sheen better than the new oil-based paints do. Dark colors fade less, whites stay white longer, clears are clearer. Water-based paints, which use acrylic or vinyl-acrylic binders, flex and stretch more readily, allowing them to withstand wood movement. They dry faster, too, which can sometimes cause problems but usually proves an asset because it speeds the job.

Water-based paints present fewer problems in humid or damp weather; you can even paint over slightly damp surfaces, because the more open chemical structure of water-based paint lets moisture out. Water-based paints resist mildew better than oil-based paints do. And of course, water-based paints are less messy to apply, easier to clean up, and don't smell as strong as oil-based paints.

Application Tips

With water-based coatings, attention to quality products and good technique are more important than ever.

Buy the good stuff. Most contractors already know that the best latex paints are the "all acrylics" — those in which the binders are 100% acrylic, which is more durable than the vinyl used in early latex paints and in some bargain paints today.

I use different brands of paints for different applications, but if I have a favorite overall brand, it's Miracle Adhesives (Pratt & Lambert Specialty Products, Buffalo, NY; 800/289-7728; www.prattandlambert.com). Pratt & Lambert offers

good quality across its entire product line, and their technical assistance has been excellent. Benjamin Moore (Montvale, NJ; 800/344-0400; www.benjaminmoore.com) is another brand with high quality across its entire line. I also like Sherwin-Williams (Cleveland, OH; 800/321-8194; www.sherwin-williams.com) because they have such a wide selection, particularly in speciality products like sign paint and primers for metal surfaces.

Whatever brand you choose, buy at or near the top of the line. It's also important to read the label directions and any supplementary literature the manufacturer offers. And don't be shy about calling the company's technical staff with specific questions. These people often possess recently acquired information that has not yet found its way onto

the paint can.

For instance, I once called Sikkens (AKZO Nobel Coatings, Inc., Troy, MI; 800/833-7288; www.akzo.com) because I was having problems getting a semi-transparent finish to adhere to some cedar benches and decks. The Sikkens people told me that the "mill glaze" on the new lumber was probably repelling the stain and suggested I wash the wood before finishing it. I did, and the stain adhered beautifully. This was a few years ago, at a time when mill glaze was a new problem, and the tech people were just learning how to deal with it. Such current information is particularly helpful today, when product manufacturers are in the middle of a learning curve themselves.

Be prepared. Water-based finishes require more thorough surface preparation, cleaning, and careful application than oil-based finishes. Remove any loose paint, and clean any dirty or oily surfaces. For most surfaces, I use Spic-and-Span powder; on a very oily surface, I use painter's naptha.

Put it on right. Applying water-based paints is different from applying oil-based paints. Spraying water-based paints, for instance, often produces an orange-peel texture. Sometimes you can solve this problem by adding thinner — water in the case of water-based paints — though too much thinner degrades the paint film. You might also try using larger or smaller spray tips. As a last resort, have a second person brush or roll right behind the sprayer. Paint manufacturers are making progress on this problem, but brands vary, so it pays to experiment a bit.

Also take care not to spray too thick a coat, because water-based paints have a greater tendency to run and sag. To prevent this, don't linger with the nozzle and avoid lapping passes, both on flat surfaces and in corners. And stay alert: Because

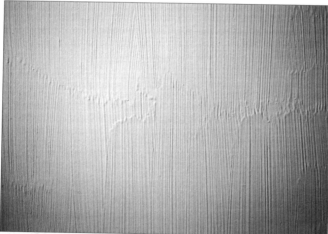

Figure 3. Because water-based paints dry quickly, it's easy to over-brush — leaving visible brush marks in the finished surface (left). Likewise, with latex stains, lapping marks result when a second coat is applied over partially dried stain (below). Avoid laps by brushing or spraying small areas at a time and keeping a wet edge.

water-based paints dry so quickly, you have only a few minutes — often less than 20 — to go back and brush or roll out any sags or runs. Brushing requires similar cautions. It's a good idea, whether brushing, rolling, or spraying, to keep a wet edge. This may mean painting smaller areas at a time (Figure 3).

Interior latex enamels are even more demanding. The best new interior acrylic enamels level fairly well with a high-quality paintbrush — but you should brush less than you would with oil-based paints. It takes practice not to leave fine brush marks in high-gloss latex paints. Use long, fairly rapid strokes, taking care not to abruptly dive in or pull off with the brush at the beginning or end of a stroke. Use as few strokes as required to produce an even coat, then leave it alone — you'll leave a brush mark if you try to touch up when the paint is half-dry.

Finally, use the best brush you can buy. This should be standard practice by now, but I'm still surprised at how many contractors try to save money on paintbrushes. I like brushes made by Purdy, which are widely available.

Inside Jobs

Here's how I handle the peculiarities and limitations of water-based finishes in different interior situations.

Walls. Since most people already use latex interior wall paint, I'll limit myself here to a summary of the different finishes and their uses. Different paint makers use varying nomenclatures, but most make three wall finishes: flat; eggshell (slight sheen); and semi-gloss, or satin. I use flat for most walls, though I often use eggshell in closets, because glare is not a problem and the sheen makes the wall more cleanable. I use eggshell or satin for bathrooms or kitchen walls that will receive some splash or dirt (Figure 4).

For priming walls before wallpapering, oil-base primers have long

been standard, and many wall covering manufacturers still specify it. However, I successfully use Zinsser's Shieldz (William Zinsser & Co., Somerset, NJ; 732/469-8100; www.zinsser.com).

Trim: the last frontier. By "trim" I mean doors, door and window casings, baseboards and other moldings, and cabinet work. The finish on these areas will receive close scrutiny, so you want an attractive and smooth, easy-to-clean surface. Trim paint must be durable, for it will be touched, bumped, banged, and brushed against. The paint surface will have to stand up to chemicals (oils from hands on door jambs, chemical cleaners mopped up against baseboards) and abrasion.

At present, oil-based enamels still

excel in providing most of these qualities — particularly the smooth, lustrous sheen — and trim is thus one of the few areas where I still routinely use oil-based paints. (Where I live, you can still buy the older formulas.) I've already used a latex enamel, however — Sherwin-Williams Super Paint — on a couple of small jobs, and it's worked pretty well. I had difficulty preventing sags and runs when spraying, though I worked that out, and the paint lacked the luster that oil paints have when they dry. But the owner was pleased and the job is holding up well.

Water-based enamels are catching up with oil-based, and I expect to switch over within a few years.

Primers for trim. I may be slower to switch to water-based interior

Figure 4. The author uses water-based paints for interior walls and ceilings (left), though he prefers oil-based paints, which are glossier, for interior trim (below).

primers for trim — this seems to be an area where water-based products still lag significantly. To produce a really smooth surface for enamel finishes on trim, I often extensively sand the primer (which itself needs to lay on smoothly), but the water-based primers I've tried so far don't sand well. Their "gummy" nature clogs the paper, and the rubberlike surface often stretches and tears rather than powdering. What's worse, the water in water-based primers can raise the wood's grain, thus requiring even more sanding. Between the raised grain and the difficulty with sanding — and the severe degree to which these problems compromise the final finish — I find it better to stick to oil-based primers for now.

Even here, though, there are signs of promise. For instance, the Hydrocote Co. (Somerset, NJ;

800/229-4937; www.hydrocote.com) makes a water-based sanding sealer, a protective clear coat you put on wood — cabinets, for instance — before painting, and it sands beautifully. I would never have dreamed a water-based finish could sand so well. I don't know how this quality is achieved, but it bodes well for the sandability of future paints and primers.

Interior stains. With the old oil-based stains I once used, I could put a beginner on a job and end up with a good finish. With water-based stains I've used, any place you overlap or brush twice — such as at a corner — will be twice as dark as the places you brush just once. And the quick drying time leaves little opportunity to go back and level out thick spots. The stains perform well, however, if you spread them evenly, don't overlap, and make sure you produce a uniform thickness. In other words,

use an extra measure of the same good technique that all water-based products require.

Interior clear finishes. I started using Hydrocote for floors and other interior clear finishes about six years ago, and I have stuck with it. Most of the major brands make similar products now. These new products behave differently from their oil-based cousins, and you have to get the hang of using them. For instance, the labels on Hydrocote products warn of a temporary purplish cast on the drying finish, but on those first couple of jobs, I still got nervous waiting for that loud purple sheen to clear up. The color disappeared, however, and the finishes have held up well.

On the Outside

Outdoors, I use water-based paints for almost everything except priming tricky spots or tannin-heavy wood species.

Walls. Latex paints are more flexible, breathable, weather-durable, and mildew-resistant than oil-based paints are — all the qualities we look for in an exterior paint. The only place an oil-based topcoat might hold a marginal advantage is for frequently handled surfaces such as doors or handrails.

For routine outdoor priming, including priming the backs and ends of new siding (a must with today's finicky lumber), I use latex primers; they apply easily, hold up well, and their quick drying time lets me get to the topcoats more quickly. There are two exterior conditions, however, in which I still prefer oil.

Priming those iffy spots. I don't do too many exterior repaint jobs, but when I do, I still use oil primers where the paint is chalky, oily, or poorly adhered (Figure 5). Ideally, such areas should be sanded to bare wood before priming; but where budget restrictions prevent such preparation, an oil-based primer will provide the most secure base for the finish coat. Some of the new water-based acrylic

Figure 5. For exterior jobs, the author uses an oil-based primer on woods that are prone to staining, such as redwood and cedar, and on any previously painted surfaces where the paint has failed. Examples include cross-grain cracking, which results from excessive paint buildup (above), and intercoat peeling, which is caused by poor surface preparation (left).

primers, such as Zinsser's 1-2-3, are closing this gap. This is an area in which I'm experimenting, but for now I tend to go with oil-based primers.

Priming tannin-heavy woods. The other place most water-based primers presently fall short is in blocking the tannin stains characteristic of cedar and redwood. Some of the new "stain killing" water-based primers may do the job, but they usually require two coats. If I just need to seal a few knot-holes, that's okay. But if I need to block tannin stains in an entire siding job, as with redwood or cedar, priming twice costs too much — I'd lose the bid. So I still use oil-based primers for priming redwood or cedar; then I follow with a topcoat of high-quality acrylic.

Exterior stains and clears. Outside, I still use oil-based stains and clear finishes, usually Sikkens or Penofin (Performance Coatings, P.O. Box 1569, Ukiah, CA 95482; 800/736-6346). These look great, though they require washing and recoating every year or two. I haven't found any exterior stain or clear finish, either oil- or water-based, that will hold up longer than that. For a clear finish on cedar siding, you might also consider Flood's CWF — a petroleum-distillate-based product that usually costs less than many oil-based formulas (The Flood Co., P.O. Box 2535, Hudson, OH 44236; 800/321-3444).

As far as water-based stains go, the ones I've used so far don't penetrate well and look kind of muddy. If you use a water-based exterior stain, take care to apply a consistent coat and minimize overlaps so as not to produce uneven color.

Adapting to Change

When change is unavoidable, as it is now with paints, smart painters and contractors will embrace it slowly rather than all at once. You can't just bring in a whole new line of paints on a big job and expect to dodge major trouble. It's better to change proven methods and products gradually, experimenting when time permits, working out the bugs one at a time. That way, you will avoid major disruptions in your schedule and maintain the quality of work you are known for.

By Byron Papa, a custom builder and remodeler in Durham, N.C.

CLEAR FINISHES FOR WOOD SIDING

In siding, the "natural" look is in vogue these days, with many customers wanting to preserve the color of new redwood or cedar siding without painting or staining. However, keeping the natural look requires unnatural finishes to block the action of moisture and sun.

Wood siding turns gray because of two factors: the degradation by sun and water of the outermost layer of wood cells, which turn gray as their natural oils dry out; and the growth of tiny mildew spores on the wood's surface. Preventing this graying while retaining a natural look is the job of the current generation of clear and natural-tone tinted finishes. These coatings are formulated to protect the wood from graying with a combination of replenishing oils (which are essentially the same as in any other oil-based stain) and what the industry calls "UV blockers."

Clear Vs. Tinted

Clear finishes, having no pigment, attempt to block the sun's effect solely with UV blockers. These come in two basic types, either or both of which might be present in a given clear finish. (Manufacturers are fairly secretive about their formulas.) One type is an inorganic "reflector," made of transparent iron-oxide pigments that let visible light through, but which block UV light. The other type is the "absorber," composed of organic chemicals that protect the wood by absorbing UV rays.

These UV blockers are similar to skin sunscreens: They block and/or absorb the sun's UV rays, but only for a while. Given exposure to sun and water, they eventually wear off (in the case of the "reflecting" clear pigments) or wear out (in the case of UV absorbers). This usually happens within a year or two. At that point, they must be replenished if the skin of the building is to remain protected. If they're not, the siding gets its version of sunburn — it turns gray.

A *tinted* finish — that is, one lightly pigmented to a wood tone such as cedar or redwood — is often a better choice than a clean finish when a client or builder wants to preserve and enhance the natural tones of new cedar or redwood siding; that is, they want the siding to retain its original honey or reddish tone and not turn gray. While a tinted finish won't substantially change the appearance of the wood (other than heightening the grain and deepening the tones), its pigments will protect the wood longer than a clear finish will — perhaps for three to five years instead of one to two years.

However, there are cases where a clear finish is called for: When the client wants already-weathered siding to retain its gray or pewter tones or when an owner has new siding treated to turn the wood gray, for a weathered appearance. In some cases, the siding will have taken on some other color tone, either through age or previous stain, that the owner likes and wants to preserve.

In these cases, a clear finish can preserve the wood's appearance while helping to protect it from further weathering or degradation. But it will need to be reapplied every year or two to remain effective.

Finding a Good Product

Whether you want clear or tinted, you'll find many finishes to choose from. Over the last 20 years, I've used many of the available products. I've found quite a few clear finishes that would protect siding for a year or so, and many tinted finishes that would work for two to three years. But over the years I've settled on two products that roughly double these figures and outperform anything else I've tried: Amteco's Total Wood Preservative (TWP), and Flood's Clear Wood Finish, or CWF.

These products have several important similarities and a few differences. They are both oil-based products with paraffin added for water protection. Both come in clear and wood-tone tinted versions. In both cases, the clear finishes will turn wood slightly darker on application; but that will lighten up in a few days or weeks to return to the original new-wood tone. In the tinted versions, the pigments add depth and color to the grain of the wood, and they may even out variations in the natural wood's tone. But they won't change the wood's basic color.

Amteco

Amteco's clear and tinted products are known in the trade as TWP — the clear finishes as TWP 100, the tinted versions (redwood and cedar) as TWP 101 (Amteco Inc., P.O. Box 9, Pacific, MO 63069; 800/969-4811). TWP stands for different things in the older, non-VOC-compliant and newer, compliant versions. The non-compliant version — still available in places without VOC regulations — is known as Total Wood Preservative. The compliant version, available mainly in regulated areas, is called Total Wood Protectant.

I've used the older, non-VOC-compliant formulas for 12 years. In the past few years, I've switched mainly to the new compliant versions. These have a higher solids content than the older formula (about 90%) and so take longer to

MAKING OLD WOOD LOOK NEW

There are three common types of siding restoration jobs:

- a homeowner wants his old, gray siding to have that "new-wood" look (which he'll then preserve with a clear or tinted finish)
- the older, weathered siding on an existing home needs to be restored so it can match the new siding on an addition or section of replaced siding
- clear-finished siding has been left to weather too long between coats, and needs to be reconditioned before refinishing

In any of these cases, the task is the same: restore the weathered siding to an even, "new-wood" appearance so that it can then be protected with a clear or tinted finish. This involves cleaning the mildew, algae, fungus, and dirt off the siding. You might also need to replace a few pieces of far-gone siding or trim here and there.

Match the Cure to the Disease

In most cases, the best way to clean mildew and dirt from siding is with a solution of sodium hypochlorite (bleach) in water. Some sources recommend equal parts bleach, water, and trisodium phosphate, but I never found that TSP added anything.

Before: Unfinished siding exposed to sun and rain eventually darkens as the surface degrades, turning gray and providing a habitat for mildew.

Because I use large quantities, I buy my sodium hypochlorite in commercial tubs and dilute it in my sprayer tanks. But for smaller jobs, household bleach works fine. (We used to use it, until we found ourselves cleaning out stores' entire stocks — several grocery carts full of bleach.) Depending on the job, you might use anywhere from 1 part bleach to 8 parts water (2 cups for every gallon) to 1 part bleach to 1 part water. Occasionally you might need to use straight bleach, which is about a 4% sodium hypochlorite solution.

How concentrated a solution you need will depend on how much mildew you're dealing with. This, in turn, will depend on how much sun and (especially) moisture the siding has been exposed to, and for how long. I've had to hit ten-year-old, exposed, untreated wood in Baton Rouge, La., with three coats of straight bleach, while in Chicago I usually find a 1:2 solution handles the toughest jobs.

To find out what's necessary on a given job, experiment with a few different concentrations. One

dry. But since they soak into the wood, this doesn't pose a serious problem; if anything, it gives you a little more leeway when trying to get a wet-on-wet application.

It's too soon to tell if the new versions will last as long as the old versions — up to two years for the clear finishes, four to five for the tinted. But I've used a similar Amteco product — Shake and Shingle Sealant — in a VOC-compliant version for about four years, and it has performed quite well.

Amteco's clear TWP 100 lasts as long as any clear finish I've used. With a single coat on most surfaces and a double coat on southern or southwestern surfaces, it can last up to two years before graying starts. (Amteco's basic recommendation is for one coat; but with all these products, we've found a second coat increases longevity.) After that, exposed wood will begin to gray, turning completely gray by the end of the third year. Like other Amteco products, TWP 100 applies easily and doesn't tend to "lap" — that is, reasonable variations in spraying thickness don't produce uneven tones.

Amteco's tinted products are also highly durable. Generally, TWP 101 applied at 150 square feet per gallon (one coat on most surfaces, two on southern exposures) will last about 36 to 40 months; sometime in the fourth year, the wood will begin to turn brownish. At this point, a cleaning with a bleach solution (see "Making Old Wood Look New") will remove mildew and dirt, and another coat of TWP will reestablish that new-wood look for another three to four years. (TWP's tinted products can also be used for roof and deck surfaces, on which they will generally last for about two to three years.)

Flood's

Flood's CWF (P.O. Box 2535, Hudson, OH 44236; 800/321-3444) also comes in both VOC-compliant and non-VOC-compliant versions; the compliant version, out for about a year and a half now, is labeled CWF/UV. I've found that CWF's tinted finishes wear out about a year earlier than Amteco's — lasting about three to four years. But they, too, are easy to recoat, requiring little

---

coat will do its work in 10 to 15 minutes, after which you can see whether you need a stronger solution or another coat. For environmental and health reasons, I like to use the lowest concentration possible.

Use plastic containers for mixing the solution, since sodium hypochlorite corrodes metal. And always wear gloves, long sleeves, goggles, and masks when spraying bleach solution.

If the wood has algae along with mildew, we've found a 10% solution of calcium hypochlorite works better than sodium hypochlorite. Sodium hypochlorite remains active for only about 10 minutes, whereas calcium hypochlorite works for 24 hours. Calcium hypochlorite, commonly known as HTH, is a 70% granular chlorine available at most pool chemical companies.

Applying The Cleaner

Rate of delivery isn't as crucial with cleaner as with finishes, so you can spray with anything from a pump-up garden sprayer to a gas-driven pump. Smaller sprayers with aluminum parts, however, will be destroyed by the bleach. Don't spray at over 1,500 psi, or you may gouge the wood.

Start at the gables or fascia, and let the water cascade down the siding as you work your way down. The solution itself should kill and clean the mildew. If a second application doesn't wash the mildew and dirt off, you may want to hit it with a long-handled scrub brush while the solution is still fresh.

Watch Those Plants

You'll need to protect any plants below your work. To do so, saturate the ground around the roots and soak all the leaves with water. Then cover the plants with woven poly tarps; these will shed the bleach solution, but let the plants "breathe" more than ordinary plastic will. You should also cover any brass, copper, or aluminum fixtures so they're not corroded by the bleach, and any stained or painted wood, such as window frames, casing, or other trim, that you don't want to bleach.

When you're done, rinse everything (including the windows and woodwork) thoroughly with water, and uncover the plants so they don't overheat under the tarps. Replace any rotten or damaged siding with fresh stock, let everything dry a couple of days, and you're ready to apply the clear finish. — *A.R.*

After: Cleaning with a bleach solution, however, can remove the mildew and brighten the wood to close to its original tone. It can then be protected with a clear or tinted finish.

prep as long as the client doesn't wait too long. You can tell it's time to recoat when the siding shows the usual graying. With Flood's you might also see some light flakes on the surface that can easily be rubbed off with your hand.

You can clean the siding of both mildew and the CWF flakes by spraying with a bleach solution. At that point you can repeat your original application, except that, as mentioned above, you probably need only one coat (at 150 sq.ft./gal) rather than the two coats Flood's recommends for a first application. You would, however, need to apply two coats if the siding has turned completely gray.

If you're applying only one coat of CWF, you must take care to produce an even coating; if you lap the brush or spray strokes too heavily, you can produce the uneven tone called "lapping." If this happens, however, a second coat will usually make it disappear.

Application Fundamentals

Most general contractors sub out their finishes. But for those who do their own, or who do the occasional small job, a few application basics will help the job go smoothly — or help you keep tabs on the sub.

Open the grain. Any penetrating finish works best if it's applied to wood that is relatively free of moisture and excess oils and extractives, so that the finish can soak in. Old wood is almost always this way, but new wood often needs help. One approach is to let new wood siding age in the sun and rain. But that degrades the wood's outer layer and grays it.

A quicker way, and one that doesn't degrade the wood, is to spray the new siding with a solution of household bleach — one cup to a gallon of water — and then power rinse. The bleach removes any surface oil, extractives, and mill glaze, and the wetting and drying helps to open the wood's grain. Make sure you wait at least two days after rinsing (or any rain) before

applying the finish so the wood can dry. Sun or wind, of course, can accelerate this schedule a bit.

No discussion of opening grain would be complete without a reference to the perennial question of whether the siding should be rough-side out or smooth-side out. Like any penetrating finish, a clear or tinted finish works best if applied to the rough side of siding. The more open grain of the rough side absorbs more of the finish, giving the siding more protection. Smooth sides should be reserved for paint jobs.

What to spray it with. The easiest way to apply these finishes is with sprayers (Figure 6). I use sprayers from the Wagner 8000 to 8500 series (Wagner Spray Tech, Minneapolis, MN; 800/686-8525; www.wagner-spraytech.com). These are gas-powered, airless, diaphragm-type sprayers capable of delivering constant pressure up to 2,500 pounds per square inch. We tend to spray around 800 psi, which delivers at a good rate but prevents overspraying.

These Wagner sprayers can pump from $1/2$ to $1 1/2$ gallons per minute, supplying up to three hoses. We generally leave the pump on a trailer pulling either a 200-gallon or 500-gallon tank, and run long hoses from there. We use about 200 feet of hose per gun. Each gun has a Graco Reverse-A-Clean IV 517 nozzle, which has a .017-inch opening and a 10-inch fan to spread the finish.

This, of course, is expensive equipment, appropriate only for big operations like ours. Wagner (and other companies) also sell smaller, electric airless units, complete with guns and one- to five-gallon hoppers, for under $500. You might consider buying or renting one. (Bleach will destroy these pumps, however, so on a small job just use a garden-type pump sprayer for bleach.)

How many times to spray? On most jobs, I apply one coat on the whole house and add a second coat to southern and southwestern exposures.

Figure 6. High-volume painting contractors require sprayers with a large tank and a heavy-duty airless pump. For smaller operations, rented pumps and small buckets or tanks will suffice.

We generally let any side we're going to recoat soak up the first coat for an hour or two before hitting it with the second. My feeling is that you might get a little extra wear if you waited until the next day for the second coat. But those extra few months aren't worth the considerable cost of setting up and taking down everything a second time.

Sometimes more coats are appropriate. For instance, in sun-intensive places, where wood takes an extra beating, a second coat all over, and a third on the most exposed areas, can significantly increase the value of the job, particularly if you can do them all in one day, as is often possible.

How to spray. For the first coat, we generally spray clear and tinted finishes at a rate of 150 square feet per gallon. On the second coat, we go slightly lighter, at 200 square feet per gallon. If a budget is extra tight, we might make our second southern-exposure coat just a mist coat to save materials.

Start spraying at the top of the wall, and work your way down in long side-to-side sweeps. Spray just enough to saturate the wall — enough, in other words, so that the preservative slightly runs down the wall, or "curtains," as the trade calls it.

You can also pace yourself if you know the delivery rate of your sprayer and the area of the walls you're covering: If you're spraying a gallon a minute, for instance, you'll want to take about one minute to cover a 15-foot stretch of 10-foot-high wall.

In general, you want to spray from about a foot away, making horizontal passes with the tip turned vertically to the siding. A 3-foot pole is the best general-use extension pole; it will keep you out of the spray but still reach the eaves. Some pros use a 6-foot pole, which can be a little unwieldy and takes some practice.

By Al Rubin, a finishing contractor from St. Louis, Mo.

PROBLEM-FREE FLOOR FINISHES

The performance demanded of finishes for wood flooring makes this the most critical coating application in the entire house. But as we all know, typical job-site conditions are much less stable than finishing-room conditions. Good floor finishers have learned how to make the best of these less-than-ideal conditions, but there's generally plenty that a GC can do to improve the situation. It helps to understand how temperature and humidity affect finishes, and to learn how to prepare for the finishing process.

Drying Vs. Curing

The question a flooring contractor hears most often is "When will the floor be dry enough to walk on?" The question betrays the common misconception that once a coating is dry, it is ready to be put into full service. Following the application of the floor finish, there is usually a flurry of activity at the job site. Punch lists, final inspections, walk-throughs — the list goes on. If everything is in order, the owner is backing trailers up to the door and unloading furnishings or the real estate agent is

tying balloons to a sign in the yard that invites the free world inside to buy the house of their dreams.

Unfortunately, the fact that the finish is dry to the touch simply means that it's no longer tacky and will not stick to your hand or shoe. But only when the coating is fully *cured* will it reach maximum hardness. Until then, the finish is susceptible to scratching, abrasion, and chemical damage.

The curing of a floor finish is like the curing of concrete: It's a chemical process that continues for days after the floor finish is dry, until the finish

Figure 7. To ensure proper curing of oil- or water-based finishes, keep the site warm, dry, and traffic-free.

Figure 8. Hidden source of moisture. Think twice before setting up a portable combustion heater to warm the site for floor finishing. For every 28,000 Btus such heaters produce, they release 1¹/₂ pints of water as a byproduct of combustion. Use them only in conjunction with a dehumidifier.

is as hard as it's going to get. With concrete, moisture drives the process; with flooring finishes, oxygen is typically the crucial ingredient.

Until the curing process is complete, all activity on the surface should be minimal (Figure 7). Depending on the product, *drying time* can vary from two to eight hours. However, *curing* can take from five to thirty days, depending on the product. And these figures are for ideal conditions — the type seldom found at the job site. As the conditions become less than ideal, the curing times will be extended.

Effects of Excessive Humidity

There are two basic variables that can extend the drying and curing time of finishes and coatings. One is *moisture*, which includes the relative humidity in the air and the moisture content of the wood being finished. The second is *temperature*, which includes the temperature of both the air and the wood being finished.

Excessive humidity on a job site slows down the drying and curing of coatings; this is the single greatest threat to proper finishing. As floor coatings dry, the solvents escape and fill up microscopic voids in the sur-

rounding air. As humidity increases, the air becomes "crowded" with particles of water and will not allow the solvents to evaporate, or "flash off." Solvent that does not flash off the coating just sits there.

Since drying occurs from the top down, any solvents left in the product are released at a much slower rate. Combine this with the fact that you are usually applying more than one coat and you begin to see how excess humidity can prolong drying.

Theoretically, as the coating cures, all the solvents should percolate through the various layers and eventually make their way out of the coating and into the air. The key word here is "eventually." When the curing process is delayed from too much humidity, the coating will remain soft for a much longer time.

If humidity levels exceed 75%, the curing time can easily be doubled. The real danger with extended curing times is the damage that can — and will — occur to the soft finish if normal construction activities are allowed to take place. (In fact, according to a staff chemist at one of the finish manufacturers, if curing is extended over too long a time, the finish may *never* reach its maximum hardness.)

Thick vs. thin coats. There are a number of application devices that allow a finisher to apply a thicker coat of finish. The desired final thickness can be achieved in fewer applications, saving time for the finisher. But if curing is slowed by excessive humidity, thicker coats of finish will produce greater amounts of solvent that will take even longer to flash off. This approach saves time for the finisher but increases drying and curing time.

Watch out for stains. Stains applied before the final finish are also affected by excessive humidity. Even under ideal conditions, many popular brands of stains actually have longer drying times than the coatings applied on top of them.

Also, if the solvent base of the finish and the stain are the same (oil-based, for example), you are walking on thin ice if you apply finish to stain that has not dried. In areas where the stain has not dried completely, the finish coat will not bond properly to the flooring. But if the solvent bases are different (water-borne finish over oil-based stain, for example), you're going right through that thin ice and will most likely see a complete failure of the coating to adhere to the stain. The irony is that the failure is usually blamed on the products, when the real problem is the failure to provide the right conditions for drying and curing.

Recognizing Sources of Moisture

With the emphasis on building tighter homes, controlling humidity at the job site has become a much more important issue. In older, drafty homes, humidity introduced by job-site activities is quickly reduced by rapid air exchanges. In tighter homes, however, this humidity will remain. Before you can hope to control humidity at the job site, you must first learn to recognize the sources of moisture that will raise humidity levels.

There are two main moisture sources: activity-induced and site-induced. Site-induced moisture could come from a damp basement, lack of gutters, or poor grading and drainage. These sources tend to be more of a problem during periods of high rainfall.

Activity-induced moisture most often comes from trade activities that take place before and, in some cases, during the floor finishing process. The most common sources are drywall mud and latex paints. Water-based replacements for petroleum-based adhesives and mastics are another source of job-site moisture. Recently completed tile and masonry work — a tile floor over a mud bed or a recently poured base-

EDGE-BONDING: YOU HAVE TO SEE IT TO BELIEVE IT

Water-based floor finishes have a number of advantages over oil-based finishes: They dry quickly, release less toxic vapors as they dry, and form a stronger bond to the wood flooring. But as with many new products, unpleasant side effects are often discovered as they are used more extensively in the field.

Last year, I agreed to install 350 square feet of ash flooring in a 100-year-old home. Since the house was occupied during the installation, I made every effort to keep the dust down and arranged to have the flooring presanded. My floor finishing contractor and I both agreed to finish the floor with a water-based product, since it would produce less objectionable fumes.

The floor turned out beautifully, the customer was satisfied, and I went on my way. About eight months later, though, I received a call from the customer, complaining that cracks were appearing in the flooring, so I stopped by to take a look. What I found was not a pretty picture.

The joint between every sixth or seventh course of flooring had opened up, in some cases as much as 5/16 inch. In certain places, the actual ash board had split, creating large, unsightly cracks (see photo).

After a few days of phone calls, I found out that this floor was a victim of edge-bonding. When edge-bonding occurs, the floor finish acts like an adhesive, effectively gluing the boards together. In December, well into the heating season, the humidity in the house had dropped significantly, and the flooring was adjusting to this change by shrinking. Typically, each individual floor board would shrink between 1/32 and 1/16 of an inch. In this case, however, the entire floor was behaving like a glued-up panel and was trying to absorb more than 3 inches of combined shrinkage. As the staples resisted this movement, the flooring broke into smaller "panels" of six or seven courses.

My floor finisher had used this

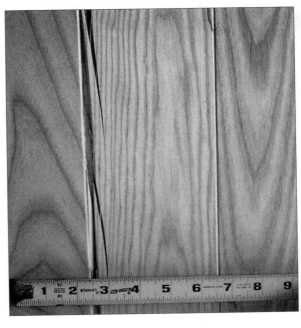

The edges of these ash floor boards were effectively glued together by the flooring finish. As the floor shrank in the winter, large gaps and splits occurred every six to seven courses.

product on more than a hundred floors and never encountered the problem. So what caused edge-bonding to occur in this situation?

The only reference material I found on the subject was from the National Oak Flooring Manufacturers Association (NOFMA), which prefaced its explanation of edge-bonding by stating that the phenomenon is not fully understood. When I questioned a technical representative at NOFMA, he explained that a "latex filler" should be troweled into the joints of the flooring to prevent edge-bonding. (There was no mention of this procedure, or edge-bonding in general, on the instructions found on the finish container.)

After reviewing what little available information there was and describing the event to product representatives and other tradespeople, I concluded that three circumstances contributed to the edge-bonding.

Presanded flooring. Because the flooring was presanded, the sanding fines that would normally sift between floor boards and discourage the finish from bonding to the edge of the boards were absent.

Eased edging. The flooring was machined with an eased edge. The resulting small V-groove probably had a funneling effect, directing additional finish into the joint.

Ambient humidity. The flooring was installed in late spring, when humidity levels were high, so the moisture content of the flooring increased after it was installed. The slight swelling caused by the increase in moisture content produced a clamping effect that forced the floor boards together immediately after the finish was applied.

The outcome? The NOFMA reference offered some hope. It mentioned that with time, many floors affected by edge-bonding tend to release at the joints, thus spreading the effect of shrinkage more evenly among more joints. In some cases, the finish will release its grip as the flooring expands and contracts through the annual heating and cooling cycle. At this point, the clients and I are waiting to see what happens; with any luck, I may have to replace only a few boards.

By Carl Hagstrom, an associate editor with The Journal of Light Construction.

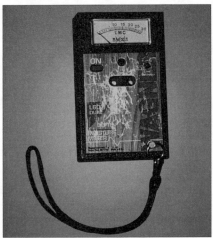

Figure 9. Tools of the finisher's trade. The author uses two diagnostic tools on every job: a combination thermometer/hygrometer (top) and a moisture meter (above) to measure the wood flooring's moisture content. If conditions are not within the proper range, the finish may fail.

ment slab — will also release large amounts of moisture as they cure. The moisture generated by these products means there is less "room" in the air for the floor finish to dry.

You Can't Beat Heat

Lack of heat has similar consequences for drying and curing: The lower the temperature, the longer it takes for an application of finish to dry. This tends to be less of a problem than excessive humidity, since job sites are usually kept at a reasonable temperature range for the comfort of the workers. But when temperatures fall below 60°F, drying time increases significantly. I remember a project where temperatures fell below 50°F during the evenings, and I had to wait *four days* for each coat of finish to dry.

As temperatures decrease, air density increases, and the solvents escaping from the floor finish have fewer places to go. When what little air space there is becomes filled, all drying and curing of the finish stops.

Beware combustion heaters. When the temperature drops, many builders bring out a kerosene "torpedo" heater or a propane "salamander" heater. This seems like a good idea, except that a typical 150,000-Btu kerosene or liquid propane heater produces about a gallon of water per hour as a byproduct of combustion (Figure 8). So instead of improving drying conditions, these heaters can actually make matters worse by significantly raising the relative humidity at the site! If you must use this type of heater, use it only in conjunction with a dehumidifier. A better choice is to use an electric heater, which adds no humidity to the air.

Air conditioning. In summer, when outside temperatures and humidity are high, crank up the A/C if possible. That will dry the air and keep the temperature in a workable range. High temperatures (above 85°F) cause the finish to dry so quickly that it doesn't flow and level as well. If there's no air conditioner, apply finish early in the morning when the temperatures are lower.

Simple Precautions

As complicated as this may sound, there are some simple steps you can take to ensure proper conditions for floor finishing.

• The surest approach is to have all hvac systems operational and running three to four weeks before any finishing work begins. This will help keep excessive humidity in check and prevent unfinished wood from absorbing any moisture from the surrounding air.

• Many contractors and homeowners object to the use of the heating system during construction out of fear that the duct system will become contaminated with dust. If a forced-air heating system is being used, place prefilters on all air return vents, and change the furnace filters regularly during sanding and screening operations. I use a paper towel over the air return vents and I have never stressed a heating system yet.

• If your only source of heat is a torpedo heater, be sure you have a simple dehumidifier on the project to remove the moisture that the heater introduces. The dehumidifier should be in place when the flooring is installed. Unfinished wood flooring acts like a sponge;, it will absorb any excess moisture when humidity levels are high.

• Purchase a good moisture meter and use it (Figure 9). Mine goes with me everywhere; I am constantly taking readings. If the cost seems high ($200 to $300), just think how much you'll lose going back to correct mistakes. A moisture meter is worth every penny.

• Monitor the temperature and humidity levels. You'll need a hygrometer to measure the relative humidity. The ideal range for drying and curing coatings is between 45% and 75% RH at 65°F to 85°F.

Controlling job-site conditions will always be a challenge. But the next time your flooring finisher makes some special demands, don't just assume he's a whining pain-in-the-neck. Remember, it's your product and your reputation he's protecting.

By Michael Purser, a second-generation wood flooring contractor in Atlanta, Ga. Purser owns and operates the Rosebud Company.

REMODELERS AND LEAD PAINT

Lead paint has garnered lots of media attention in recent years, and there are valid reasons for the concern. Not only can lead poison children, but it can also poison adults — namely, your crew and your clients. Common symptoms of lead poisoning include loss of appetite, stomach cramps, nausea, constipation, decreased sex drive, difficulty sleeping, moodiness, headache, joint and muscle aches, even anemia.

How Big a Hazard?

Lead used to be added to paint to make the pigments brighter and more durable. By 1978, dangerous lead levels were banned from paints, furniture, and toys by the Consumer Product Safety Commission. (This ban specifies concentrations of .06% of lead by weight or higher, so paint, toys, and furniture aren't always completely lead free.) But because vendors were allowed to sell existing paint inventories, any work performed on houses built prior to 1980 has the potential for exposing workers to lead. In fact, 75% of the housing built before 1980 still contains some lead-based paint, and the older a house is, the more likely it is to have lead: 80% of the housing built between 1940 and 1959 contains lead paint, and 90% of housing built before 1940 contains lead paint. Older homes are also more likely to have been remodeled, and to continue to need remodeling. This all adds up to a significant risk for remodeling contractors, their crews, and the homeowners.

The two major routes of exposure to lead are inhalation and ingestion. Exposure by inhalation can be caused by any activity that creates dust and fumes — scraping and sanding, for example, or using a heat gun to soften paint. Exposure to fumes can be caused by operations such as torch cutting, burning paint, even smoking.

Unlike children, who are often attracted to the sweet taste of lead paint, adults rarely ingest lead on purpose. Still, it is not uncommon for dust or chips to make their way into food, beverages, and cigarettes, or for workers to forget to wash their hands before eating, drinking, or smoking.

Abatement Vs. Remodeling

To control lead hazards, the federal and state governments have instituted several regulations, some of which apply to residential remodelers (see "Contractors and the Law," page 153). But many remodelers think that lead paint regulations don't apply unless they're purposefully removing lead paint. Remodelers also wrongly assume that only "lead abatement" contractors need to be concerned about lead paint hazards.

However, renovators and remodelers perform many of the same activities that lead abatement contractors perform: removing paint; removing and demolishing painted plaster, concrete, and wood surfaces; and

Figure 10. Chemically stripping painted woodwork (left) is a safer alternative than sanding. If you must sand, wet the woodwork to keep dust levels down (below), then repaint with a high-quality oil/alkyd for maximum protection.

WILLIAMSPORT PRESERVATION TRAINING CENTER, NPS

NEIL SANDLER/NIBS

Figure 11. Using a stripper with a paper cover, remodelers safely strip lead paint. The lead-laden residue adheres to the paper after the stripper has softened the paint.

Figure 12. When sanding or water blasting a house exterior, shroud the scaffolding with plastic or tarps to contain dust and over-spray.

covering over, encapsulating, or otherwise enclosing painted materials. In fact, any activity that disturbs painted surfaces in older homes can create hazardous conditions that might cause lead poisoning. The only real difference between an abatement contractor and a remodeler is the purpose each one has for doing the work. Remodelers need to approach their work just as responsibly as abatement contractors do to prevent exposing those around them to lead hazards on site.

Plan Your Work

At the beginning of every remodeling job, it is imperative that you first find out if lead-based paint is present on site (see "Testing for Lead," page 155). If any lead-based paint is found, then you must take certain steps to protect your crew and your customers.

Keep in mind that the quickest way to spread a lead hazard is to disturb lead-painted surfaces by creating a lot of dust or fumes. Dust and fumes are much harder to contain than large pieces of painted material. When evaluating the scope of the work, consider the options you have to reduce dust and fumes. Rather than sanding down a piece of existing woodwork, for example, you might consider removing or replacing it.

Of course, a contractor doesn't always have absolute control over how a job will be done. If a homeowner has strong preferences or a constrained budget that you'll have to work around, explore alternatives. If the customer wants to keep the woodwork, consider chemical stripping on site (see "Sources of Supply" at end of chapter). Another alternative is to have the components dip-stripped off site. Yet another option is to wet scrape and sand (Figure 10).

A fourth alternative is to remove the woodwork and scrape or sand it outside where there is more ventilation. When working outdoors, however, take precautions against contaminating the yard, especially if children play in or around the area. Lay down 6-mil poly to collect the dust and chips and to prevent them from spreading through the grass and into neighboring yards. When you pick up the plastic, make a concerted effort to contain the paint chips. Some dust will inevitably escape, either tracked away from the work area or blown into the air. But use common sense: Avoid working if there's a stiff breeze. And don't leave piles of paint chips in the grass, where they will draw kids' attention after you have left the job.

Similarly, if you are removing lead-based paint from the outside of a building by scraping, water blasting, or stripping (Figure 11), it's important that you not let stray dust and particles contaminate the ground around the house and neighboring homes. Precautions include covering the ground, and shrouding scaffolding with plastic or tarps to contain the dust and overspray (Figure 12).

Engineering Controls

You may hear lead abatement professionals talk about "engineering controls." This is a fancy way of describing tools and equipment used to control dust and fumes. For example, if the homeowner insists on sanding, use a tool-mounted dust shroud connected to a high-efficiency particulate air (HEPA) vacuum to capture the dust. A HEPA vacuum filter will capture micron-sized particles that contain lead.

One of the most important steps in any renovation job is to seal off the work area to restrict entry and to prevent contamination throughout the entire house. During work operations, the work area should be off-limits to nonessential workers and to visitors, especially children and pregnant women. To segregate the area, use 6-mil poly taped on all edges.

Don't forget to seal hot-air registers, air conditioners, and baseboard

CONTRACTORS AND THE LAW

Title X, Residential Lead-Based Paint Hazard Reduction Act of 1992, pertains to virtually every type of construction, including residential remodeling. Several government agencies — the Environmental Protection Agency (EPA), Housing and Urban Development (HUD), Health and Human Services (HHS), Occupational Safety and Health Administration (OSHA), and others — are responsible for gathering information and enforcing the provisions of Title X.

OSHA requirements. Section 1031 of Title X directs OSHA to issue safety standards to address lead hazards for construction. OSHA's rule, published in May 1993, sets requirements for contractors to assess exposures to lead, provide respiratory protection and protective work clothes, install work-site facilities for cleanup and clothes changing, provide safety training, and pay for periodic blood testing. For a copy of the OSHA standard, *Lead in Construction,* contact the Government Printing Office (866/512-1800) or your local OSHA office.

Occupant awareness. Title X also requires remodeling contractors to provide the owner and occupant with printed information about lead paint before starting work on any house or apartment built prior to 1978. The EPA, HUD, and HHS shared the responsibility for writing and distributing a pamphlet, which includes information about the health risks of exposure to lead, the risks of renovation, methods to evaluate and reduce lead-based paint hazards, and a discussion about the effectiveness of these methods. You can obtain a copy of this pamphlet and a copy of the proposed rule by contacting the National Lead Information Clearinghouse (800/424-5323).

Disclosure. One of the provisions of Title X includes mandatory disclosure in all real estate transactions. If you know about any lead hazard on the premises, you will be required to disclose this knowledge before selling, leasing, or renting the property. If you do not know, you must allow the buyer time to find out before closing the deal. While no requirements to correct a problem will be placed upon the property owner, this is a hotly contested law, pitting the real estate industry against lending institutions that handle mortgages. For more information on this rule, contact the National Lead Information Clearinghouse at the phone number printed above.

Certification. Another seriously debated issue concerns contractor certification. Under Title X, the EPA will issue a federal certification program that will go into effect in 1997, except where a state has instituted its own program. Anyone *abating* lead from a building will have to be certified under the program; at this point, the EPA is still leaning towards exempting anyone *remodeling* buildings.

But there is mounting evidence that remodeling activities have a greater effect on children in terms of lead poisonings than was previously assumed. In New York state, for example, recent data have revealed that almost 10% of children with elevated blood lead levels were poisoned by some type of remodeling work. In some cases the work was performed by homeowners; in others, by professional contractors.

Such data underscore the fact that everyone must take precautions during any remodeling project to avoid contaminating the environment. — *E.F.*

convectors. After the work is complete and these hvac systems are put back in service, any lead-laden dust that settled in them could be spewed into the air, poisoning the homeowners and their children.

Before starting a job, remove furniture, carpeting, food, clothing, and toys from the area. If these items can't be removed, cover them with 6-mil poly to keep lead dust from settling on them. Cover floors with poly, taped continuously to the perimeter baseboards or walls. Then lay down hardboard or thin plywood to protect the poly and create a less slippery work surface. Taping the sheets together will prevent this surface from shifting over the poly as you work on it.

Also, provide additional ventilation, such as a window fan blowing outward, to depressurize the work area. This will help keep dust from getting blown through the plastic barriers into other parts of the house. The idea here is to get air moving out of the work area; you're not trying to suck up clouds of dust and push them outside.

Clean Up Daily

Give the work area a good cleaning at the end of each day to assure that no dust or paint chips are left behind. Perform another thorough cleaning at the end of the job.

To clean up properly, use a lead-specific cleaning product (Figure 13) and a HEPA vacuum (a vacuum that does not have a HEPA filter may actually put lead dust *into* the air through the exhaust port). Lead-specific cleaners contain phosphates or EDTA (ethylenediaminetetraacetic acid), both of which bind with lead, so they clean up the hazard better than other cleaners. If the label doesn't list EDTA or phosphates, consult the Material Safety Data Sheet (MSDS), which lists the active contents. (Manufacturers are required to provide an MSDS, and OSHA requires contractors to keep an MSDS for all materials used on site.) TSP (trisodium phosphate) is a widely available cleaner, although it is banned in some states. Many automatic dishwasher detergents also contain phosphates, and can be used if no other cleaning products with phosphates or EDTA are available.

Disposal. All debris should be disposed of properly at the end of a job. Most states have specific guidelines for disposing of lead-laden debris; check with the public health department. Don't just take the lead hazard from inside the job and move it to the outside of the building. If lead-coated materials or dust and debris are left on the curb for pickup, children could play in and around the area and become poisoned. All lead-covered components — such as painted trim, flooring, and old plas-

ter and lath — should be wrapped in 6-mil poly to keep them from contaminating the area.

Respirators

In addition to working responsibly to protect clients and their neighborhood, you need to take measures to protect yourself and your crew. Again, substituting a less hazardous method or using engineering controls should be the first alternatives you consider. But workers who are continually exposed to the hazard inside the work area need additional protection.

A respirator is the most important personal protective device a worker can wear — but it must be the right respirator. If a worker wears the wrong type of respirator or one that does not fit properly, it is actually worse than not wearing one at all because workers may take unnecessary chances, thinking they are well protected.

HEPA filters. The minimum level of respiratory protection is a half- or full-face HEPA-filtered respirator. As levels of dust and fumes increase, other protective measures, such as air-purifying or continuous-flow respirators, may be needed. Regardless of the manufacturer, you can always recognize HEPA filters by the bright pink cartridges or the bright pink label.

Proper sizing. Before passing out respirators, make sure your workers are examined by a physician to assure that they are capable of wearing a respirator safely. Also insist on buying respirators that are sized to fit each worker.

Every time a worker puts on a respirator, he or she must perform a "fit check." A fit check involves covering the exhalation valve and breathing out, then covering the cartridges and breathing in. In both cases, no air should leak in or out from any part of the respirator.

Also remember that if the respirator is taken off for lunch or break

Figure 13. Job-site cleanup includes washing down walls and woodwork with a phosphate solution, such as TSP, or a detergent containing EDTA.

TESTING FOR LEAD

Before making any decisions about the costs, scheduling, and scope of a remodeling job, a contractor must find out if there's any lead paint on site. There are three test methods available: X-ray fluorescence, laboratory analysis, and chemical spot tests.

XRF. A portable X-ray fluorescence (XRF) analyzer measures a concentration of lead on a painted surface (in milligrams per square centimeter). These instruments give instant results, so a large number of surfaces can be sampled in a short time. Also, XRF machines read through many layers of paint without marring or discoloring the surface.

Unfortunately, XRF can't tell you which layer of paint contains lead, and the instruments often give inaccurate readings on samples that contain low levels of lead. Dense substrates such as concrete and metal may affect the accuracy of measurements as well. Also, the instrument must be held against a flat surface — readings taken from curved, molded, or textured surfaces may be too high or too low, depending on the material and the shape of the surface.

Finally, XRF is expensive. The instruments themselves cost from $4,000 to $40,000. The cost to hire someone to test the house for you is a few hundred dollars, depending on where you live.

AAS. Laboratory analysis — technically known as Atomic Absorption Spectrophotometry (AAS) — is widely regarded as the most accurate test method for lead. AAS results are given as a percentage of lead by weight, and are very precise (anything at 0.5% or higher is considered a hazard).

The accuracy of AAS depends on how well the sample is taken. For a testable sample, you need about a teaspoonful of flakes, or several large chips, from one area. The object is to get all the layers of paint in each chip but none of the underlying substrate. This requires a steady hand with a sharp chisel or

utility knife. Put the flakes in a resealable plastic bag labeled with the location of the sample surface (for example, "upper bedroom, north windowsill"), and your name, address, and phone number.

It's important to take a sample from each surface that will be disturbed in the course of work. In the case of a gut remodel, for instance, you would need to take a sample from the floor, baseboards, wall, windowsills, casing, crown molding, and ceiling of each affected room. And don't assume the paint is the same in every room — different-colored paints may have differ-

This test swab contains rhodizonate, a chemical that reacts with lead and turns pink if the paint contains around 0.5% or more lead by weight.

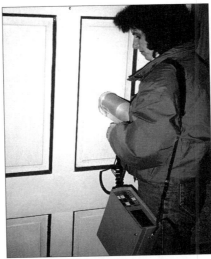

The author uses an XRF machine to test the paint on a door for lead paint. XRF gives instant results and will read through all layers of paint without marring the surface.

ent quantities of lead in them.

Test labs (call the Public Health Department or consult the Yellow Pages under "Laboratories — Testing") typically charge between $20 and $30 per sample. A standard turnaround time is usually a week to 10 days. If you want faster results, you may have to pay more. A 48-hour turnaround can cost double the standard fee; 24-hour turnaround may be four times the original fee.

Spot testing. A third type of test for lead uses chemical test kits, which are available from local paint or hardware stores. These typically include a swab or dropper that allows you to apply a chemical reagent that reacts to lead and changes color if the paint contains approximately 0.5% or more lead by weight. One of two reagents is used — rhodizonate turns pink, sodium sulfide turns gray or black.

Chemical spot tests give instant results, but the reagent only reacts with lead on the surface. So it's important to cut, scrape, or sand the paint to expose all layers.

Spot tests are inexpensive — 14¢ to $6 per test — and the kits have a long shelf life, so you can keep them on hand to use as needed.

Combine tests. You can use chemical test swabs to scope out a job. But if the results show up positive for lead, send the samples to a lab to get accurate, quantitative AAS results before deciding on the level of precaution you should take. Make sure to double check any negative spot-test results to be sure there are no dangerous levels of lead.

If you have room in the budget and need to take many samples over a wide area, or if you are especially concerned about not marring surfaces, use XRF. But if the surfaces you are testing are uneven, or the substrate is questionable, follow the XRF with AAS analysis to accurately nail down the extent of the hazard and the exact layer of paint where the lead is found.

— Eileen Franko and Kevin Sheehan

and left lying around, there is a good chance lead dust will settle inside the mask. When the worker puts it back on and breathes in, he or she may inhale dust from inside the respirator. Respirators should be stored in plastic bags, cleaned regularly (use nonalcohol cleaning wipes available from safety supply houses), and checked for broken or damaged parts.

Habits Count

Next time you have a morning cup of coffee with your crew on site, notice how the plastic lids are neatly folded back to allow dust and chips in the coffee. This is one of the most common ways workers accidentally ingest lead dust and chips. The same holds true for food that is stored or eaten in the work area. Anything that falls onto the food or is on the worker's hands can end up being ingested. Cigarettes can easily become contaminated with lead dust, either from a worker's hands or when stored filter up in a worker's chest pocket.

The best way to prevent these exposures from ingestion and inhalation is to not eat, drink, smoke, or store any of these items in the work area. Keep them in the truck, prefer-

ably in a covered lunch box or cooler. And always wash your hands prior to eating, drinking, or smoking.

Work clothing. Improper handling or laundering of work clothing can expose you and your family to high levels of lead. Change your clothing and shoes before you head home from work, especially if you have young children. Any lead dust on clothes and shoes can come off as you walk in the house. A child crawling on the floor may get this dust on her hands, then put them into her mouth, ingesting the lead.

Launder all work clothing contaminated with lead separately from the rest of the family's laundry. Never shake the clothing prior to washing; this will only create a cloud of dust. You might consider disposable clothing, such as a Tyvek suit, for working on site. If you do use these, be sure to replace them anytime they rip or start to fall apart.

Clean truck policy. It's also important not to take any of the lead home with you in your work vehicle. If you have a dedicated work vehicle, do not give your children rides in this vehicle or let them play in it or with any of your tools. If you do not have a dedicated work vehi-

cle, make sure you change your clothes and shoes prior to getting into your vehicle. At a minimum, wash your hands and face and never let your children play with any of your work equipment.

Employee Blood Tests

Any worker who is exposed to lead should have periodic blood tests to assure that engineering controls and personal protective equipment used on the job are sufficient to keep their exposure to lead at acceptable levels.

OSHA's *Lead in Construction* standard requires blood tests every two months for the first six months of a job involving lead, then every six months thereafter until the end of the job. Based on the varied exposures remodeling contractors and their crews face, it's important to get blood tests as frequently as possible. Use the OSHA requirements as a minimum so that elevated blood lead levels do not go undetected.

By Eileen M. Franko, M.S., a research scientist and industrial hygienist at the New York State Bureau of Commercial Sanitation and Food Protection, in Albany, N.Y.

SOURCES OF SUPPLY

Lead Paint Test Kits

Hybrivet Systems Inc.
Hybrivet Systems Inc.
Natick, MA
800/262-5323
www.leadcheck.com

The Lead Detective
Innovative Synthesis Corp.
Newton, MA
617/965-5653
www.theleaddetective.com

Chemical Strippers

Dumond Chemicals Inc.
New York, NY
212/869-6350
www.dumondchemicals.com

Fiberlock Technologies Inc.
Andover, MA
800/342-3755
www.fiberlock.com

CHAPTER 7

INSULATION & AIR SEALING

- Hidden Heat Leaks

- Air-Sealing One-and-a-Half Story Homes

- Problem-Free Cathedral Ceilings

HIDDEN HEAT LEAKS

For ten years researchers at Princeton University looked at where and how most buildings lose energy. Studying hundreds of buildings under real-life conditions, the researchers found many ways that heat escapes by *bypassing* the usual weatherization measures of weatherstripping and caulking (see "Common Thermal Bypasses," page 160). These thermal bypasses can greatly compromise a home's comfort, contribute to moisture problems, and add significantly to energy bills.

The benefits of fixing these bypasses vary greatly from building to building; Princeton researchers found a 15% to 20% average annual energy savings. In some buildings the problem areas are inaccessible or just too difficult to identify. However, many problems can be found and corrected with simple measures, reaping significant energy savings, clearing up moisture problems, and — perhaps the biggest benefit to consumers — increasing comfort.

In existing houses, these gaps are usually hidden behind walls and can be hard to see and get to — thus the fancy diagnostic equipment. In new construction, however, they are easy to see and fix. Either way, they are

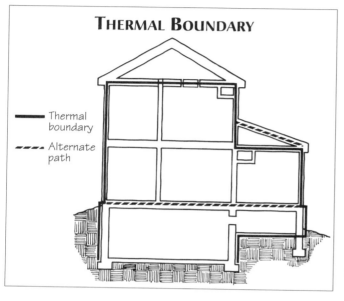

THERMAL BOUNDARY

—— Thermal boundary

- - - - Alternate path

Figure 1. The thermal boundary divides conditioned indoor space from unconditioned space. The boundary needs to be continuous and should follow the shortest, most compact route. Heating equipment and other utilities should lie inside the thermal boundary.

PLUGGING THE GAP: A CASE STUDY

Imagine an apartment conversion of a 1920s three-story brick school building, with a corridor down the middle and high-ceilinged classrooms on each side. The contractor blew insulation into the exterior walls and installed new windows and mechanical systems; it was a quality project. All in all, everyone did their jobs competently, but the thermal boundary got lost because no one was in charge of thinking about it. This scenario often happens.

In this case, each apartment had two zones. Zone 1 was living room and bedrooms, which had the existing high ceilings. Zone 2 had dropped ceilings over entry, kitchen, bath, and mechanical rooms — several different ceiling heights, some made of drywall, some of dropped-in tile. Open-backed walls framed with steel studs joined the staggered ceilings. Through these and other chases ran the wires, plumbing lines and vents, AC ducts, refrigerant lines, and kitchen and bath exhausts, with lots of fiberglass laid over the ceilings and tucked down along the adjoining walls for insulation.

Now try to imagine the thermal boundary in this building. It's difficult, right? That's because there wasn't any. A three-dimensional maze of air passages had been created from the building's top to bottom. In places, it would have been possible to raise a ceiling tile and release a bird that could then find its way to the open attic without encountering any barrier.

Plenty of cold air could travel the same path downward. This would have caused a disaster from burst water lines alone, but fortunately it was October and not January when the owner, on a hunch, called the house doctors. It took two crews (six of us) about three weeks to set things right.

Zone 1 was fine because the insulation had been laid over the existing plaster, as in any house attic. In Zone 2, we didn't even try to follow and fix every zig and zag. Instead, we established a new boundary by putting a simple cap over the whole thing. We removed all the batts, constructed an auxiliary 2x6 frame at a higher level, laid polyethylene over this, carefully stapling seams and edges, and then laid the insulation on top of that. The only other item was the stairs to the attic, which we covered with an insulated flap. — *T. B.*

easier to find and fix if you know where to look, which is where a knowledge of common problem spots comes into play.

A Few Fundamentals

Knowledge of a few crucial concepts can help builders and remodelers diagnose or prevent most thermal leaks.

The thermal boundary. This is the boundary between the cold and windy outside and the inside, which we want to keep warm and draft-free (Figure 1). This seems obvious. However, many buildings have compromised thermal boundaries where cold air gets in the spaces and hollows behind finishes and in floors, walls, and ceilings. If buildings were made of solid concrete, the only problems would be cracks and imperfect joints. But as we know, most buildings in North America are assembled out of thousands of little sticks and layers of sheet material laced with holes for pipes, wires, and mechanicals.

Infiltration. Infiltration occurs when outside air enters the building envelope; an equal amount exits elsewhere (Figure 2). This often occurs at doors and windows, but other places are often more important to examine for leaks.

Convective loops. A convective loop begins when warm interior air loses heat to a cold surface, such as a cold attic hatch or an open-block party wall (Figure 3). As the air loses heat, it drops, making room for more warm air to move into place, thus setting up a circular pattern of movement. With a convective loop, the home's interior air temperature drops, even though air isn't penetrating the thermal boundary — only heat is passing through.

Gaps between insulation and air seal. Insulation suppresses heat flow not with the insulation material, but with the air it traps. If air is moving through the material, it

doesn't insulate. (Fiberglass, for instance, is often used as a filter material.) So unless the insulation is up against the air seal — typically the poly vapor barrier — it doesn't do its job well. Rigid board insulations do, of course, form their own air seal when properly sealed at the edges.

Air seals on the inside. Buildings should be sealed at the inside finish surface (that is, on the warm side of

the insulation), and there should be no gaps between the insulation and the air seal. The more snugly the insulation fits against this barrier the better, because air movement is discouraged. On the outside of the insulation layer there needs to be an escape for any moisture that does penetrate the finish. Thus it is useless, and can even be detrimental, to deal with infiltration through a frame wall by caulking the exterior,

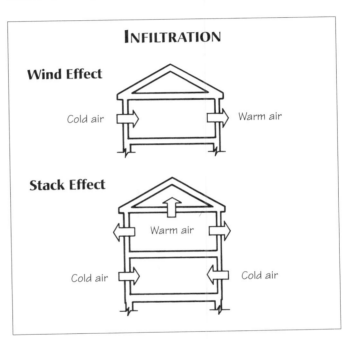

Figure 2. Infiltration occurs when outside air enters the building through an opening in the thermal boundary. An equal amount of inside air will always exit elsewhere. Infiltration occurs because of wind (at top) and the stack effect (at bottom).

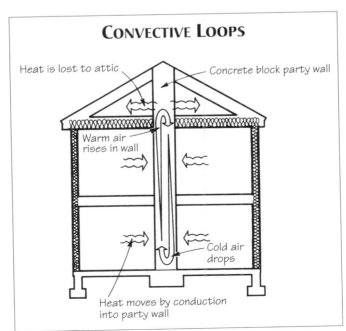

Figure 3. Convective loops occur when warm inside air loses heat to a cold surface, such as a party wall that bleeds heat into an unheated attic. No air exchange takes place; only the heat leaves the building.

which should be done only for the purpose of keeping rain out.

Stopping the Gaps

The illustrations in the box below show some good examples of thermal bypasses. In a building under construction, you can watch out for these bypasses and fix them while it's easy, before the drywall goes up.

Search for the symptoms. In an existing building, however, you'll most often find thermal bypasses by identifying their symptoms. A cold corner at a partition wall or wall-ceiling intersection, for instance, may reveal itself through mildew that has formed on its cold surface. A draft from an outlet might suggest that the wall is serving as a conduit for cold air coming all the way down from the attic. Cold floorboards on the second floor of a garrison might suggest air is leaking in through unblocked cantilevered framing. And a blast of cold air from the cabinet under the sink might suggest that cold air from the soffit is entering the stud space.

Without a knowledge of where bypasses occur, these symptoms are just mysteries. But if you know enough to make an educated guess as to where the cold air is coming from, you can often track down the cause.

In all cases, it is a matter of thinking about how air moves. Air, being a

COMMON THERMAL BYPASSES

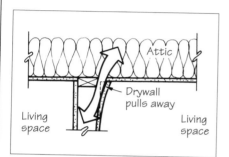

Leaks at wall-ceiling intersection. If the top plate shrinks and pulls away from the drywall, cold air will enter the partition and then the living space through openings such as electrical boxes. Prevent this by caulking the top plate or laying poly beneath the insulation batts in the ceiling. The same problem can also occur where a partition wall joins an exterior wall.

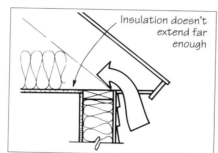

Cold wall-ceiling intersection at eaves; may have mildew from condensation. This occurs when insulation doesn't extend deeply enough into the eaves. Fix by extending batt far enough to completely cover the living space, but make sure to leave ventilation space below the roof sheathing.

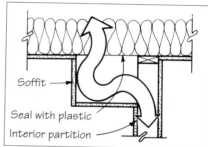

Unsealed kitchen or bath soffit. This happens all the time. A soffit is hung from the framing with no wallboard at ceiling level to seal the insulation. Cold air filters down through the insulation and into the partition wall. Seal with plastic under the ceiling insulation. This may be hard to retrofit, but it's a major problem.

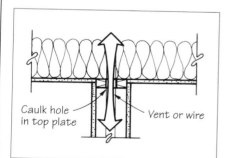

Leaks around plumbing vents and wiring. This is one of the most frequent problems. Fix by caulking or foaming around openings in the top plate or using rubber boots that slip around pipes or chases.

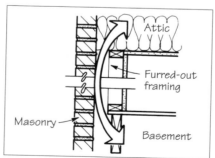

Furred-out masonry. Cold air winds its way between masonry wall and stud wall, resulting in both convective loss and infiltration. Seal the top of the space with caulked rigid foam.

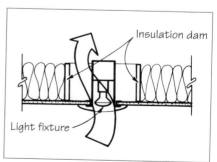

Recessed ceiling lights. These are tough to deal with, though some models now offer good air sealing. Reduce use of recessed cans as much as possible.

gas, obeys the laws of physics, moving in response to differences in pressure and temperature; humidity plays a role, too. But I find it helps to think of cold air as smart and resourceful — assume it will find a house's weak spots and get in. The stack effect — cold air entering the basement, moving up through the house, and out the attic — spurs much of the leakage. This makes the attic the most important place to look for leaks. The basement is second in importance, but don't tighten the basement so much that the heating unit can't draw enough combustion air.

House doctoring on a budget. If you want to get into professional house doctoring, you can spend quite a bit of money. A late-model Agema hand-held infrared scanner that can detect even slight temperature differences behind walls can cost about $25,000. A blower door with accessories is a bit more rea- sonable at around $2,000, but that's still more than most builders/ remodelers want to pay for use on the occasional house-doctoring day. But you can diagnose many of the problems illustrated here by digging around and spotting the signs of infiltration already men- tioned, such as moisture. This is something akin to the family doctor diagnosing ills by poking, prodding, and asking questions, rather than by putting the patient

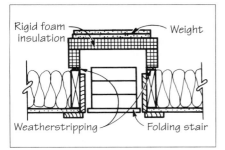

No seal or insulation over folding attic stair. The best solution is a box made of rigid foam with a little weight on top (wallboard works well), with weatherstripping to seal it.

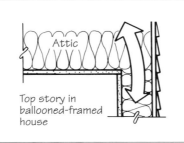

Unblocked stud bay in balloon framing. Whether in partitions or outside walls, the stud bay needs a cap at attic level even if the wall is insulated. Use rigid foam and caulk.

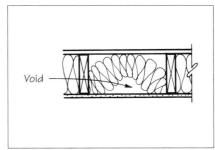

Insulation installed with voids allows small convective loops to form, lowering the insulation's R- value. Prevent or fix by cutting and installing insulation accurately.

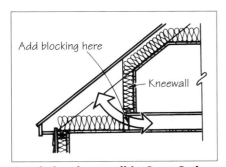

Gap below kneewall in Cape Cod second story. Unless the joist space is blocked below the kneewall, cold air enters the joist space. Block with rigid foam sealed with caulk.

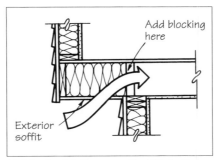

Unblocked joist space behind over- hang. In garrison and other can- tilevered designs, soffits are almost never well sealed. To fix, block the joist space just over the plate with rigid foam sealed with caulk.

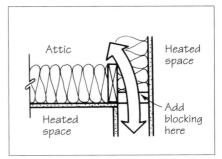

Unblocked stud bay to attic in split-levels. Similar to the problem in balloon framing, this happens where stud bays continue past ceil- ing joists to the attic. Block with rigid foam.

through a battery of high-tech tests. In most cases, it will work.

Actually fixing the thermal breaks once you find them requires relatively inexpensive materials and tools — mostly insulation scraps, poly, and caulk and sealants. Blockers and hatch covers can be made from ³/4- or 1-inch foil-faced rigid insulation. The type of foil-faced duct board used to fabricate insulated ducts works, too. By joining the duct board into a box with foil-faced tape, you can make a nice hatch over folding stair units; flat doors over stairs need an insulated

door made of hardboard, rigid foam, and 1x framing.

For blocking stud cavities, use waxed cardboard (such as that used for eaves ventilation chutes), duct board, or scraps of rigid foam cut to fit. Seal cracks with acrylic-latex or siliconized acrylic caulk. (Use acrylic-latex for any surfaces to be painted, as siliconized caulks won't take paint.)

Another good material for cracks is the foam backer rod used to back caulk joints in masonry. Backer rod comes in various diameters. Another option for such cracks, or

for the spaces around window or door frames, is the foam insulation that comes in pressurized cans; the cans come in various sizes with hoses and nozzles. Get the nonexpanding kind if possible, as the expanding type can get out of control and sometimes bulge window or door frames. It takes some practice to be able to dispense neatly — be careful what you get it on, as it never comes off. (Gloves and coveralls are definitely required; I've ruined lots of clothes with that stuff.)

Despite the low cost of these materials, fixing thermal gaps can be expensive in existing homes if you have to tear away and replace existing finishes — walls and ceilings, most commonly — to get to the trouble spots. But often enough there is a way. In new homes, it's simply a matter of sealing the area in question before the wallboard goes up.

Don't Forget the Basics

When combing a house for cracks, crevices, unblocked stud and joist spaces, and other thermal bypasses, don't neglect the more fundamental issues of temperature and air control. Doors and windows should close well and have good weatherstripping. Hvac systems should be well-tuned and in good working condition, with any ductwork sealed and checked. The house should have high-quality, properly vented bathroom and kitchen exhaust fans to expel moisture. Eaves and ridge vents should be properly sized and clear of obstruction. Any dirt crawlspaces or basement floors should be covered with 6-mil poly to prevent moisture infiltration.

By Thomas Blandy, an architect in Troy, N.Y. Blandy operated a house doctoring company in the early 1980s and currently specializes in the adaptive reuse of older buildings.

MECHANICAL SYSTEM
Problems and Solutions

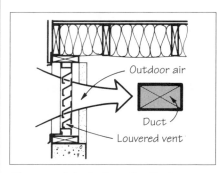

Pipes and ducts in unheated spaces. Either insulate them or include them in the thermal boundary by insulating the basement or crawlspace.

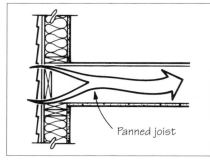

Return air plenum pulls outside air. This occurs when a joist bay is used as a return air plenum. Block and caulk at the inside of the band joist.

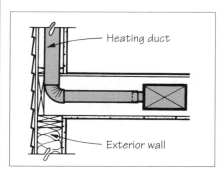

Ducts in outside walls lose heat, both by radiant loss and by leaks through untaped seams. This is a tough one to solve; the options include using insulated duct, moving the duct, or adding exterior rigid foam.

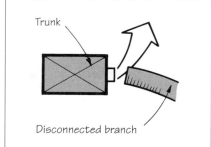

Are ducts connected? If the hot-air furnace isn't blowing well or warmly enough, perhaps the ducts aren't well-connected. Check all connections and tape any seams.

AIR-SEALING ONE-AND-A-HALF STORY HOMES

One of the toughest styles of houses to insulate and seal is, surprisingly, one that is visually very simple — the cape. The architectural details that make cape homes popular and attractive — the cozy upstairs rooms with knee walls, the affordable "expansion" shed dormers — can also make them big energy losers. Another style that creates problems is the Colonial with an overhanging upper story.

Using blower doors, infrared imaging cameras, and pressure gauges, weatherizers have identified the main structural areas in wood-frame homes that cause heat to bleed away. We call these critical framing points the "key junctures" in a house. Over the years, we've learned to cut energy losses in existing homes by attacking these key junctures in order of importance. The bulk of energy savings is often achieved by plugging a few big leaks.

Unfortunately, however, the big leaks aren't always accessible. That's why it's most cost-effective to seal up a frame house while you're building it, rather than coming back later to crawl around under the eaves plugging leaks.

The Five Key Junctures

Five main framing details cause most of the energy problems in wood-frame houses (Figure 4):

- floor-knee wall transitions
- eyebrow roofs
- cantilevered floors
- balloon-framed gable ends
- balloon-framed shed dormers

Unless these five areas are carefully sealed and insulated, the building will have one of two problems, and probably both. In the simplest cases, heated air will escape from the house completely, with cold makeup air finding its way in somewhere else. But often, even when house air

can't actually leave the building, convection currents will move air around or through insulation, so that either cold air contacts a warm surface or warm air contacts a cold surface. The result is often not only heat loss, but condensation on roof or wall sheathing, which can lead to mildew and rot.

Floor-Knee Wall Transitions

Knee walls can cause big energy losses, even in a tight house. Usually, the problem is that the insulation (thermal boundary) and the air barrier (sometimes called the "pressure boundary") are not located in the same place. The key to insulating this area successfully is to make sure that there is a continuous thermal boundary and a continuous air barrier, and that both are in the same place.

There are two common ways to insulate the knee wall area. Some builders install fiberglass batts in the crawlspace floor, in the knee wall, and in the ceiling rafter bays. This creates a thermal boundary in the floor and the wall. Others simply install batts between the rafters all the way down to the exterior wall top plates. In the latter case, the thermal boundary follows the roof.

But either way you do it, you must make sure that the air barrier will follow the insulation (Figure 5). If you install the insulation in the floor and the knee wall, you must also install a continuous poly air barrier on the inside face of the knee wall, and on the ceiling below the insulation. In addition, you have to block air movement through the joist bays by installing solid wood blocking,

LEAKAGE TROUBLE SPOTS

Figure 4. Five "key junctures" account for most of the energy leaks in wood-frame houses. Taking the trouble to seal and insulate each of these spots will pay off in lower energy bills and improved comfort for your customers.

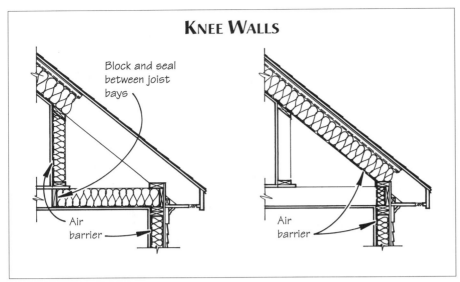

KNEE WALLS

Block and seal between joist bays

Air barrier

Air barrier

Figure 5. When building knee walls, make sure that you place an effective air barrier on the warm side of the insulation. When the thermal boundary follows the knee wall — a trickier detail to get right — it's especially important to install an air block between the joists directly below the knee wall (at left). The author prefers to insulate between the rafters all the way to the outside walls, then install a continuous air barrier on the inside face of the rafters (at right).

Figure 6. In existing structures, foil-faced foam provides an effective air barrier behind knee walls. Here, spray foam seals the gaps left where the foam board has been installed over unfaced batts between the rafters.

Figure 7. In new construction, rigid foam can easily provide an air block below an upper-story knee wall. Gaps are sealed with spray foam and the ceiling air/vapor barrier is taped to the foil face of the foam board.

waxed cardboard, or rigid foam, then caulking or foaming the joints.

If you choose to install your insulation in the rafter bays, you need to put the air barrier on the bottom side of the rafters, facing the heated space. A continuous poly barrier is fine, but it should be sealed to the framing at the bottom with tape. In retrofits, we usually attach 4x8-foot sheets of rigid foil-faced foam insulation to the rafters, sealing the edges and joints with expanding foam (Figure 6).

Often, builders staple Kraft-faced fiberglass batts up to the rafters inside the knee wall crawlspace. If you then cover the insulation with drywall and seal the edges, that can make an effective air barrier. But Kraft-faced insulation by itself, with nothing covering it, is ineffective as an air barrier. I recall one particularly bad case of a cape with Kraft-faced insulation between the rafters. The occupants were extremely uncomfortable because the air was always very dry in the winter, despite a humidifier that ran constantly. The humidified air easily bypassed the insulation batts in the knee wall area, and the moisture condensed on the underside of the roof sheathing. That house was very expensive to heat, very uncomfortable, and the roof sheathing was a fungal jungle. But curiously, it had a pretty low blower-door reading because it was a reasonably tight house. The problem was that the effective air barrier formed by the roof sheathing was on the cold side of the insulation. To prevent condensation and heat loss, the air barrier has to be continuous and be on the warm face of the insulation.

The most common mistake builders make is not providing an air barrier between the joists below a knee wall. Fiberglass batts between the joists, by themselves, will not stop air movement. Without an air barrier, warm air in the joist bays between the first and second stories will flow through the fiberglass into the cold crawlspace, contacting the roof sheathing or even making its way into the attic and outside. If the first-floor ceilings are strapped for drywall, which they often are, the strapping provides a further channel for airflow, and effectively connects just about every framing void in the building to the attic.

Figure 7 shows an effective air barrier and insulation combination for the knee wall-floor area in a new cape. The poly air barrier on the outside walls continues up onto the ceiling of the first floor. The plastic is taped to rigid foil-faced foam insulation installed between the floor joists. The joist cavities are insulated with R-30 fiberglass batts. When insulation and a poly air barrier are installed in the knee wall directly above, there will be a continuous pressure and thermal boundary between the heated space and the cold space, ensuring a snug house.

Eyebrow Roofs

Depending on how they are framed, these small decorative roofs, usually attached to shed dormers, can cause significant problems. In retrofits, we've often found that sealing up the floor-knee wall transition on one side of the house has no effect until major leaks in the eyebrow roof area are plugged.

I often see eyebrow roofs that have no insulation at all — I suppose because the builders don't think they're important. But if air from the house can get into the small eaves area, it is often able to move along to the end of the building and flow up the gable-end rafter cavities into the attic. That kind of large leak is quite costly.

In retrofits, we try to find a way to pack the whole eyebrow roof space with dense-blown cellulose. (To provide an air barrier, cellulose has to be installed at a density of 3.5 pounds per cubic foot. This requires a powerful blower in good working order.)

How we gain access to the space depends upon the framing details. Usually we have to drill a hole for the blower hose through either the soffit or the roof sheathing, then patch and seal the hole.

In new construction, it's important to concentrate on stopping the airflow. It helps to sheathe the wall before you frame the eyebrow roof, attaching the small rafters to a ledger board nailed over the sheathing (Figure 8). If you frame the eyebrow roof by nailing small rafter-tail pieces onto the sides of second-floor wall studs, it will be hard to seal and insulate the area — you'll create a lot of small, irregular voids.

Cantilevered Floors

Many Colonial-style houses have a section of second floor cantilevered over the first-story wall. Without proper attention, this area can lose a lot of heat.

Typically, builders jam a fiberglass batt into the space between the joists where it extends past the wall (that is, if they insulate it at all). Often it's an R-19 batt that doesn't completely fill the space, so that air movement is not impeded at all. Even if it's a bigger batt and it's carefully installed, fiberglass is still not a good air barrier, and convection currents will bring warm air from between the floors in contact with the building's skin.

To compound the problem, baseboard heating units in second-floor rooms are often directly above this cold between-floor space. We can observe the continuous energy loss from a setup like that from either inside or outside the house with an infrared scanner.

During construction, you can treat cantilevered floors like the floor-knee wall transition, but the vapor barrier goes on the subfloor of the second floor rather than on the ceiling of the first floor (Figure 9). Where the poly air barrier on the wall meets the floor, tape the

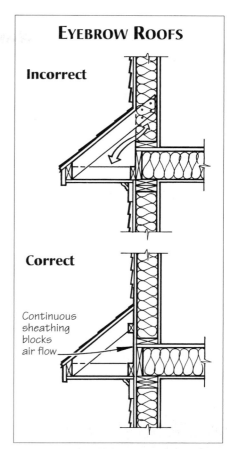

Figure 8. Eyebrow roofs, if built wrong (at top), allow cold air to penetrate exterior walls and leak out the ends of the building. To build one correctly, sheathe the exterior wall first, then attach the rafter tails to a ledger (above).

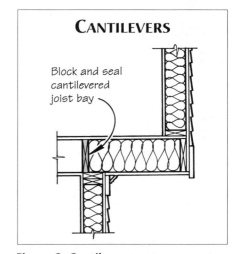

Figure 9. Cantilevers can cause convective heat loss unless an air block is added in the joist bay above the first-story top plate.

BALLOON-FRAMED GABLES

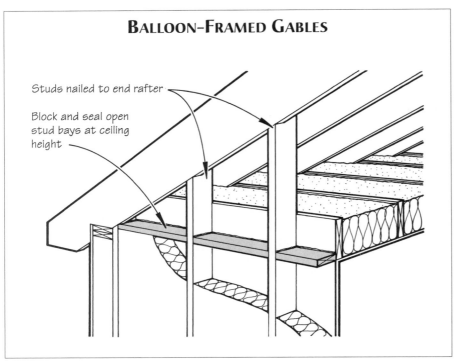

Studs nailed to end rafter

Block and seal open stud bays at ceiling height

Figure 10. Balloon-framed walls should always be blocked to prevent convective air movement into the attic.

Figure 11. It's much easier to seal balloon-framed stud bays during framing than to have to do it later. Here, a weatherization worker foams a cardboard baffle into place where a gable-end stud bay passes into the attic.

Sometimes heated air enters the wall through a penetration, like an electrical outlet or even a crack around the baseboard and drywall at the bottom of the wall. The warm air rises in the stud cavity like smoke in a chimney, escaping into the cold attic and exiting through the roof vents. But even where there is no penetration in the wall, cold air from the attic will drop into the stud cavity, where it is warmed by the wall and rises back into the attic. This kind of convection loop carries heat out of the house.

Fiberglass insulation works well as long as the stud cavities are sealed. In retrofits, we crawl into the attic and seal the top of stud bays with waxed cardboard, stapled in place and sealed with a bead of expanding foam (Figure 11).

In new construction, you should block off the top of open stud bays at ceiling height with cardboard, rigid foam, 2-by blocking, or spray foam. Seal the blocking with caulk or expanding foam. Another option is to insulate the wall with dense-blown cellulose.

Balloon-Framed Shed Dormers

Shed dormers on many capes are framed like the gable ends, with the sidewall studs attached directly to the rafters, so that open stud bays run past the ceiling, and air can pass freely into the attic. These walls lose heat the same way the gable walls do: Either hot air enters wall penetrations and escapes into the attic, or convection currents carry heat away. The solution is the same as in the gable ends: Close off the tops of the stud cavities, or use an insulating material that is also an air barrier, such as dense-blown cellulose. The simplest option, of course, is to frame dormer side-walls with top plates in the first place.

By David Legg, an energy-efficiency consultant from Auburn, Mass.

plastic to the plywood. Then seal all the seams in the plywood subfloor with tape or caulk — that way, the plywood will function as an effective air barrier on the warm side of the insulation. Between the cantilevered floor joists, fill the voids completely with fiberglass or cellulose insulation, then install rigid foil-faced foam insulation in the bays where the joists bear on the first-floor wall and seal the edges where the foam meets the framing with caulk or foam. Tape the joint

where the poly on the first-floor wall face meets the foam between the joists.

Balloon-Framed Gable Ends

Often, builders frame gable ends by nailing end-wall studs directly to the end rafter, or to a plate attached to that rafter (Figure 10). The end ceiling joist is then nailed to the gable-wall studs. This means that there is no top plate at ceiling height, and air can move freely between the stud cavity and the attic space.

PROBLEM-FREE CATHEDRAL CEILINGS

For a cathedral ceiling to perform well and not collect moisture, the rest of the house must also work to keep dampness out. No ceiling ventilation scheme can compensate for big influxes of moisture. Adequate gutters, good site drainage, and foundation drain tile will keep water away from the house, while sealed poly, rigid foam, and pea gravel under and around the basement floor and foundation walls will keep the house from sucking up moisture from the ground. Without such control of moisture sources, no cathedral ceiling will perform well. With proper control and a good air barrier, such ceilings can work beautifully even when unventilated.

Sealing the Interior

The tighter you build a house, the higher the indoor moisture levels typically are. In an airtight home, you can maintain this high moisture level without doing damage to the structure. But if moist indoor air finds a leak in the air barrier — even of a few square inches — you can expect to find damp insulation in the attic and condensation stains on the ceiling. A larger leak may cause it to "rain" inside. This is one reason I use an exhaust-only ventilation system in most of my houses; the slight negative pressure it creates inside the house tends to reverse the air flow through any small leaks in the building shell, reducing the likelihood that excessive moisture will be forced into the ceiling.

For the same reason, I try to seal the inside surfaces of the house as tightly as possible. To achieve this, we use the Airtight Drywall Approach (ADA), taping all drywall carefully, sealing switch and outlet openings, and installing rubber gaskets around the top plates to make the drywall system airtight (Figure 12). Other alternatives for airtight walls include sealed layers of rigid foam or sealed sheets of polyethylene.

Any of these air-barrier systems, if applied diligently, can keep moisture out of ceilings and walls. Roof ventilation then becomes unimportant. In fact, I have so much confidence in my airtight drywall system that in many cathedral ceilings, I use no ventilation at all.

Tape, gaskets, and blocking. In our airtight drywall system, we seal the tops of the drywall to the edge of the top plate with 3/8 x 3/8-inch saturated urethane "Sure-Seal" gaskets from Denarco Inc. (301 Industrial Drive, Constantine, MI 49042; 269/435-8404). EPDM rubber gaskets from Resource Conservation Technology (2633 N. Calvert Street, Baltimore, MD 21218; 800/477-7724) also work

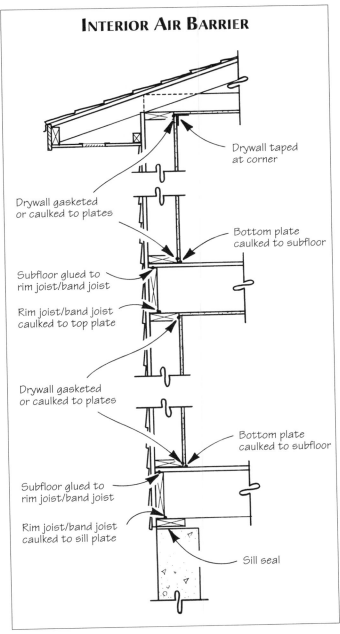

INTERIOR AIR BARRIER

Drywall taped at corner

Drywall gasketed or caulked to plates

Bottom plate caulked to subfloor

Subfloor glued to rim joist/band joist

Rim joist/band joist caulked to top plate

Drywall gasketed or caulked to plates

Bottom plate caulked to subfloor

Subfloor glued to rim joist/band joist

Rim joist/band joist caulked to sill plate

Sill seal

Figure 12. Cathedral ceiling moisture problems are caused when moist indoor air leaks through walls and ceilings into roof cavities. To prevent problems, tightly seal all interior surfaces using the Airtight Drywall approach, shown here, or with polyethylene.

well. Such gaskets cost 10¢ to 15¢ per lineal foot. We apply them around the perimeter of the ceiling on the top plate or on the drywall backing, then lay the wallboard over them so that it compresses them; this ensures a tight seal between the wallboard and the top plate, preventing any moisture within the wall cavity from finding its way to the ceiling space.

As for interior walls that meet the cathedral ceiling, we always install and seal the ceiling before building those walls so there's no internal connection.

We also carefully seal all penetrations in the outside wall top plates. Foam sealants work best for larger gaps around pipes or wires, while flexible caulks or acoustic sealants work for smaller cracks. For larger pipes you can also use rubber boots like the ones used on roofs for plumbing vents.

Sealing light fixtures. Recessed lights in cathedral ceilings also present problems. Standard units are very leaky and are responsible for a number of moisture problems. However some of the new units rated for insulation contact (IC) are well sealed. We use the X18 Series made by Scientific Component Systems (1514 N. Susan St. #C, Santa Ana, CA; 714/554-3960; www.scsix18.com).

Another option is the recessed compact fluorescent, by Scientific Components Systems. It has a low wattage (two 7-watt bulbs), low operating temperature, and high lumen output, yet it costs about the same as a standard recessed fixture, and it is airtight. Its only drawback is that you can't use a dimmer switch with it, and trim choices are limited.

Standard light openings are relatively easy to seal. Bring the light wire through a solid 2x4 block, seal the wire with a foam sealant, and then use a shallow, surface-mounted metal rough-in box after the drywall is hung. Another way is to use a poly pan rough-in box (from Lessco, W1330 Happy Hollow Rd., Campbellsport, WI 53010; 920/533-8690) and seal the poly air barrier to it. Yet another method uses a special ceiling box made by NuTek Plastics, a Canadian company, and available from Thomas & Betts (8155 T&B Blvd., Memphis, TN 38125; 901/252-5000; www.tnb.com). NuTek's product has a recessed flange that makes it easy to seal the drywall barrier or poly air barrier to it. The poly pans cost about $2 to $2.50 each, and the Nutek boxes cost about $4.

Dealing with skylights. To reduce condensation potential and save energy, I use the highest R-value skylight my budget allows — at minimum, a double-glazed, low-E, R-3 model. I carefully gasket between the

Figure 13. Foam blocks at the bottom of a rafter-framed cathedral ceiling will prevent cold air intrusion into the insulation near the eaves. The blocks should be caulked in place to ensure a good seal.

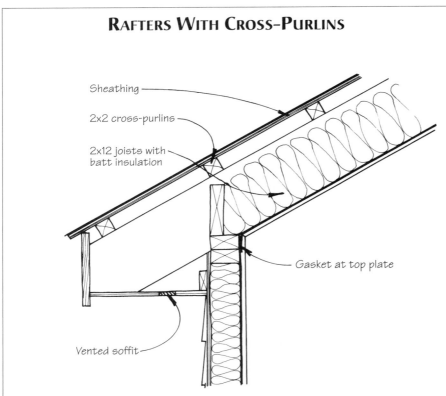

RAFTERS WITH CROSS-PURLINS

Sheathing

2x2 cross-purlins

2x12 joists with batt insulation

Gasket at top plate

Vented soffit

Figure 14. On a rafter-framed cathedral ceiling, cross-purlins provide good air movement under the sheathing, even where there are obstructions such as skylights.

skylight's jams and the framing to prevent air leaks around its frame. To provide ventilation in the rafter space below and above the unit, I either notch the top edges of the rafter below and above the skylight or install cross-purlins over the rafters to provide lateral flow (more on that later).

Framing and Insulating

We have two basic ways of framing and insulating vaulted ceilings. Where budgets are tight, we go with a 12-inch-thick, R-38 rafter system insulated with fiberglass batts. When we can spend more, we use 16- to 18-inch parallel-chord trusses with blown or batt insulation and end up with an R-55 system.

Ventilation an option. For both systems, we consider ceiling ventilation optional for most jobs. As explained earlier, that's one of the beauties of creating a tight air barrier — it does more than just keep the house warm, it can actually eliminate the need for ventilation.

Nevertheless, I've included ventilation details in this section for those times when sealing problems, code requirements, client insistence, or other factors make ventilation necessary.

Shallow systems. For the 12-inch system, we use ordinary 2x12 rafters and insulate with fiberglass batts. To keep the batts from sliding into the soffit space and to prevent undue airflow through the batts, we install scraps of foam or wood blocking vertically at the bottom of the rafter spaces, leaving a 1¹/₂- to 2-inch space above the blocking if we want to ventilate (Figure 13). This is a good place to use up your scrap pieces of foam sheathing. You can cut them snug between the trusses and caulk them in place, or you can leave your exterior wall sheathing one inch short of the top of the wall and nail the infiltration stops in when the soffit is installed. After the blocking is in and as the ceiling goes up, we lay in the batts (either one 12-inch layer or two

6-inch layers), taking care that we don't leave any gaps or spaces.

When I want to ventilate a rafter system, I add a 2x2 nailer along the top edge of each rafter (to allow an air space above 12 inches of insulation), then nail 2x2 cross-purlins perpendicular to those. This arrangement allows air to flow freely over the entire roof system regardless of obstructions such as skylights (Figure 14).

We prefer standard continuous soffit vents and a ridge vent when ventilating. I prefer vents made by Air Vent (Peoria, IL; 800/247-8368; www.airvent.com).

Finally, to prevent the batts from piling or fluffing up to block the vent opening over the eaves blocking described earlier, I first attach a plastic air chute made by ADO Products (Rogers, MN; 866/240-4933; www.adoproducts.com) to the sheathing just above the eaves. The

chute is about 4 feet long and slides down to the space over the blocking and then staples to the sheathing to make sure the ventilation path doesn't get clogged by insulation. We've found these plastic chutes much more durable than similar cardboard and foam chutes.

Bigger budget, deeper ceilings. For our deeper ceilings we usually use parallel-chord trusses 16 to 18 inches deep. Parallel-chord trusses can either sit atop the exterior wall or butt against it. In either case, the top chord extends out to form an overhang (Figure 15). If you set the truss atop the plate, you will need to seal at the eaves with foam or wood blocks as shown in Figures 13 and 14.

If a truss roof has a fairly shallow pitch — 6/12 or less — we blow in loose fill insulation, leaving enough space (1¹/₂ to 2 inches) above the fill to provide air flow along the sheathing. Steeper pitched roofs will

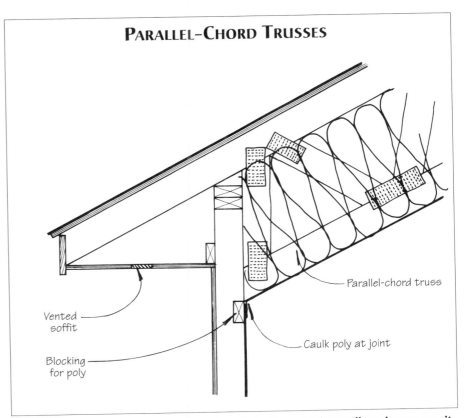

PARALLEL-CHORD TRUSSES

Vented soffit

Blocking for poly

Parallel-chord truss

Caulk poly at joint

Figure 15. Parallel-chord trusses can butt into the exterior wall as shown, or sit atop the top plate. In either case, the top chord extends outward, providing an overhang.

encourage the loose fill to collect down toward the eaves, however, so for those roofs we go with batt insulation, choosing thicknesses that will bring the insulation to within a couple of inches of the sheathing. Whenever possible we get batts as wide as the on-center truss spacings — for instance, a full 24 inches instead of 22 inches for trusses 24 inches on-center — so that the batts will expand sideways to fill the spaces between the webs.

Ventilating a truss roof system is fairly simple: you adjust the thickness of insulation to leave a space ($1\frac{1}{2}$ to 2 inches) on the sheathing's underside, and provide for air intake and outflow by installing continuous soffit and ridge vents.

Worth the Headaches

Building a cathedral ceiling that works requires constant attention to detail — one or two oversights and you can run into some serious problems down the line. But it's worth the trouble. The visual excitement and sense of space a cathedral ceiling generates make the client's home a greater asset almost instantly. And that, in turn, translates into the builder's greatest asset, which is another satisfied client.

By Bill Eich, a builder and the owner of Bill Eich Construction Company in Spirit Lake, Iowa.

CHAPTER 8

HVAC SYSTEMS

- Heating System Tuneups & Upgrades

- High-Efficiency HVAC

- Mechanical Cooling Systems

- Water Heaters

- Simple Ventilation for Tight Houses

- Flue and Chimney Safety

- Backdrafting Causes and Cures

HEATING SYSTEM TUNEUPS & UPGRADES

Heating systems more than three to five years old can usually be improved through add-ons, modifications, or improved maintenance. Most combustion units are oversized, for instance — particularly if the house has had insulation added since the unit was installed — and most have unsophisticated control systems. In addition, heat distribution systems can usually be improved through adjustment, new products, or in the case of air systems, tightening of the ductwork.

The options presented here are among the most promising and practical, and should apply to the 65% of our nation's homes that are heated by forced hot air and the 10% heated by forced hot water. Remodeling contractors who educate themselves about these options have an opportunity to give clients a valuable service. These modifications may well result in fuel savings that will help pay for more remodeling work; in many cases, an upgrade will give you the extra heating capacity you need to heat any space you add.

All Systems

We'll consider forced-air and hydronic systems separately, but there are some steps you can take that apply to both types of heating systems.

Cleaning and tuneups. Routine maintenance is the homeowner's job, but it won't hurt for you to point out the importance of regular tuneups (yearly for oil-fired systems, every two years for gas). These should include combustion and flame checks, draining hot water systems of sediment and bleeding them of air, checking air ducts for leaks, and so on. Table A lists routine maintenance for forced hot air and forced hot water or steam systems; these steps alone will promote better performance and longer life in nine out of ten systems.

Upgrade thermostats. Another way to quickly improve virtually any hvac system is to upgrade its brain — the thermostat. Compared with "clock" thermostats first introduced in the 1970s, today's microprocessor-controlled setback thermostats are more sophisticated but easier to install and use (Figure 1). An investment of $30 to $100 will buy a computerized thermostat that can improve system efficiency from 7% to 10%.

Some setback thermostats have two cycles, one for weekdays and one for the weekend; the better ones have

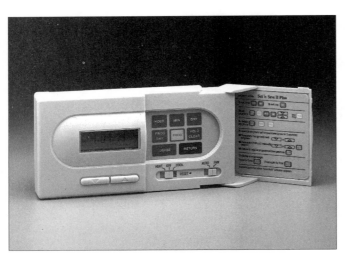

Figure 1. A programmable thermostat, such as the Set 'n Save II Plus (Hunter Fan Co., Memphis, TN; 888/830-1326; www.hunter-fan.com), saves on fuel by automatically lowering the temperature setting when the house is unoccupied.

C. BATES

Figure 2. Nearly 11% of all heat loss in forced-air systems comes from leaky ducts. Replace duct tape at joints and seams with a high-quality mastic.

Figure 3. Pay close attention to sealing cracks where ductwork penetrates unconditioned spaces such as attics or basements.

seven-day cycles, for people who want to be able to program each day of the week individually. Almost any unit allows a user to temporarily override the programmed settings. If you avoid the bottom of the line, you'll usually get a unit that's easier to program. I've found that the more buttons a thermostat has, the simpler it is to use, since you don't have to figure out how to make buttons serve multiple tasks.

Hot Air Systems

These modifications apply primarily to forced hot air systems — those with a fan that drives the air through the house. But many (particularly those concerning ductwork) also apply to passive, or "gravity-fed," hot air systems.

Focus first on flow. Assuming the basic layout of the air distribution system is sound, you need to check the condition of the ductwork itself. Unfortunately, loose ductwork is the rule: One study found that the average home with forced hot air heat lost 11% of its heat through leaky ductwork. The cost of fixing these leaks can run anywhere from the price of a few hours of labor and some mastic to hundreds of dollars for a ductwork overhaul. But any repairs *should* bring immediate returns in comfort, and most will provide a payback of no more than two to five years.

The three most common leak sites are in the return air plenum, at joints between branch ducts and the main trunk line, and where ducts attach to room outlets (see "Mechanical Cooling Systems," Figure 12, page 182). Ideally, you should seal all seams and joints that appear loose or that are sealed with duct tape, which will degrade within a few years. Tear off the duct tape (even the stuff that looks okay) and seal the seams and cracks with mesh tape and a high-quality mastic (Figure 2), such as Uni-Mastic or Seal-N-Save (United McGill Corp., P.O. Box 820, Columbus, OH 43216; 800/624-5535). Use a flexible caulk to seal penetrations where the ductwork passes through to the exterior or to unconditioned spaces such as attics or basements (Figure 3). Make sure ducts are clean near their terminal ends and that the registers aren't covered or blocked by furniture or rugs and such. Finally, insulate any ductwork running through unconditioned spaces with R-11 fiberglass blankets.

Do the balancing act. One potential drawback of forced-air systems is that they can cause pressure differences throughout a house. If the system isn't properly designed or if someone messes with the control dampers, some rooms will be pressurized and some depressurized, leading to unwanted temperature discrepancies within zones. Pressurized rooms are poorly heated because new air can't get in. In depressurized areas, infiltration of outside air causes drafts and dryness, and raises fuel consumption. This is more than an occasional problem: The Electric Power Research Institute found that,

---

TABLE A.
RECOMMENDED MAINTENANCE FOR GAS AND OIL-FIRED SYSTEMS

All Furnaces and Boilers
- Clean burner and combustion chamber.
- Run combustion test to check furnace or boiler efficiency and preclude any danger of backdraft.
- Check for fuel-line leaks.
- Check and calibrate thermostat.
- Change oil filter.*

Forced-Air Systems
- Test airflow.
- Check for duct leaks and make needed repairs.
- Check fan belts for snugness and wear.
- Clean or replace air filter.
- Clean fan.
- Lubricate fan motors.
- Adjust fan switch.
- Make sure registers are properly oriented and free of obstructions.
- Vacuum ducts.
- Check, repair, and improve duct insulation.
- Clean humidifier (if present).

Hot Water or Steam Systems
- Clean or replace fuel nozzle.
- Insulate pipes with compressed fiberglass.
- Keep radiators clean and free of obstructions.
- Manually adjust aquastat.
- Bleed air out of system.
- Lubricate motor and pumps.
- Drain expansion tank.
- Drain sediment from boiler.
- Clean or replace clogged radiator vents.**
- Replace bad steam trap.***
- Check system for proper amount of water.

* Oil-fired systems only.
** One-pipe steam system only.
*** Two-pipe steam system only.

Note: The maintenance steps listed here should be performed yearly for oil-fired systems and every two years for gas systems.

on average, household infiltration rates are 15% to 36% higher in forced hot air homes than in others.

The way to avoid pressure differentials — to "balance" the system — is to match supply and return air capacity and, just as important, to provide low-resistance return air paths between every room and the return air register or registers. Giving every room its own ducted

return register solves this challenge but is expensive. Instead, most homes have one or two centrally located return registers to which return air must flow. The problem comes when something — usually a closed door — blocks the free flow of air to this central return register from individual rooms.

It takes a sharp hvac contractor with a blower-door test kit to eval-

uate and fix a system where the supply and return capacities are badly out of balance. But there are some simple things a GC can do to improve return airflow. You can undercut the doors to bedrooms and other isolated rooms 1½ to 2 inches, or you can install transom grilles. Unfortunately, both of these easy solutions badly compromise privacy. A more discreet solution is

TABLE B. EFFICIENCY UPGRADE

Upgrade	Cost	Estimated Fuel Savings	Comments
Forced-Air Furnace			
Replace fuel nozzle with a smaller one	Up to $60	2% to 10%	More expensive with gas furnaces; may be free with oil furnace tuneup.
Flame-retention head oil burner	$250-$600	10% to 25%	Oil furnaces only; may require downsizing the combustion chamber.
Replace pilot light with electric ignition	$150-$300	5% to 10%	Gas furnaces only.
Install automatic vent damper	$250-$400	3% to 15%	Closes flue to reduce standby heat loss up chimney. Savings usually greater with oil furnace than with gas.
Install a setback thermostat	$40-$280	7% to 10%	Lowers the temperature setting automatically while occupants are sleeping or away from home.
Install power burner	$400-$600	10% to 20%	Converts old oil and coal systems to gas.
Boiler			
Install thermostatic radiator valve (TRV)	$200 per unit	10% to 15%	Do-it-yourself project on one-pipe steam system will cost $35 to $75 per radiator.
Weather-responsive control (outdoor reset control)	$300-$1,000	5% to 25%	Hot water boilers only. Adjusts boiler water temperature according to outdoor temperature. Savings highest when used with setback thermostat and TRVs.
Replace fuel nozzle with a smaller one	Up to $60	2% to 10%	Hot water systems only. More expensive with gas boilers; may be free with oil boiler tuneups.
Flame-retention head oil burner	$250-$600	10% to 25%	Oil-fired boilers only. A better but more expensive option than downsizing the nozzle.
Replace pilot light with electric ignition	$150-$300	5% to 10%	Gas boilers only.
Install automatic vent damper	$250-$400	3% to 15%	Closes flue to reduce standby heat loss up chimney. Savings usually greater with oil than with gas.
Install setback thermostat	$40-$280	10% to 20%	Lowers temperature setting automatically while occupants are sleeping or away from home.
Install gas power burner	$400-$600	10% to 20%	Converts old oil and coal systems to gas.
Radiator reflectors	$10-$100	Varies	Galvanized sheet metal, aluminum foil, foil-faced insulation, or metalized film mounted to the walls behind radiators reduce heat loss through walls.

Note: Most furnaces five years old or older will benefit from one or more of these upgrades. Estimated savings are not cumulative, however. On older furnaces, consult with your hvac sub or energy auditor about the cost effectiveness of modifying the furnace versus installing a new one.

to install "transfer" grilles high on one side of a stud bay and low on the other side, connecting an airway to rooms on both sides of the wall. For yet more privacy, create a "jumper duct" by putting a ceiling grille in the isolated room and connecting it via a short run of duct to the open space nearest the main return register.

Keep in mind, however, that you shouldn't make these modifications unless you have good reason (such as a blower-door test) to believe you've got blocked return air paths.

Consider adding zones. In houses so badly out of balance or so spread out that the above steps won't work, extra ductwork may be required to balance the system. If that's the case, consider having an hvac contractor create some zones in the existing system. This usually involves installing a thermostat for each new zone, new ductwork or modifications to existing ductwork to create the new zones, and a few tweaks and add-ons to the furnace (a good control electrician or manufacturer's tech consultant can help here). A new zone can often be created by putting in "variable air volume" or "flow control" dampers in existing duct runs. These dampers, which include some innovative products such as pneumatically-controlled dampers, respond to the thermostat setting by automatically opening or closing to allow more or less treated air into the zone.

It can run from $1,200 to $1,500 to add a second zone to a one-zone system; installing a variable air volume system could cost twice that. Again, this should be done only by hvac contractors with lots of experience in FHA design and with training from the system's designers, because it's easy to mess up. But if it's done right, zoning will deliver a huge increase in the flexibility, comfort, and efficiency you can get out of an existing forced hot air system.

Tweak the furnace. Table B lists several modifications you can make to forced hot air furnaces. All bring real savings quickly, and most pay for themselves in one or two heating seasons. While these changes won't get a standard five- to ten-year-old system up into the 85% efficiency range of today's new units, they can take a furnace that is running at about 55% or 60% efficiency and bring it up to 70% or 75%.

One furnace modification not listed in the table is a variable speed blower, which kicks on and off gradually to reduce noise and also varies its speed depending on the heating or cooling load. These blowers are a nice improvement found in many new systems, and in theory they should make a sensible retrofit. But putting one into an existing furnace and blower unit is tricky and likely to lead to problems and expense, so I don't recommend them as a retrofit option.

Hydronic Systems

I like hydronic systems because they're less finicky than forced hot air systems and because they offer many options for increasing control of where, when, and how much heat is delivered. Many of the patches and modifications I will mention have been developed in just the last few years, offering new opportunities to improve even old steam radiator systems. And most of these modifications are fairly easy to make.

Table A shows the routine maintenance every hydronic system needs; as with forced hot air systems, these should be the first line of attack in any evaluation or overhaul. Table B shows options for upgrading or modifying hydronic systems, with rough estimates for both costs and benefits of each upgrade.

Most of these options are straightforward, but a few, particularly the newer ones, are worth describing in some detail.

TRVs. Thermostatic radiator valves (TRVs) have been used for decades in Europe, but have become more readily available in the U.S. over the past ten years or so. TRVs mounted on individual steam or hot-water radiators control the flow of hot water (or venting air in steam radiators), acting as thermostats for those individual radiators. TRVs allow the occupant to tailor the amount of heat delivered to different radiators within a single zone. On a second floor, for instance, an infant's bedroom can be kept at a toasty 70°F degrees all night, the parents' at 60°F, and the spare bedroom at 55°F. Depending on the household,

Figure 4. Weather-responsive boiler controls like this one from Tekmar adjust the temperature of boiler water to match changes in outdoor temperature. This increases system efficiency because the boiler never heats the water more than is necessary to keep the house at the desired temperature.

the increased convenience and comfort comes with considerable energy savings.

Weather-responsive controls. A fairly recent development for hot water (but not steam) systems is the weather-responsive boiler control (also known as "modulating aquastats," or "reset controls"). A weather-responsive boiler control works by constantly sensing the outdoor temperature and adjusting the boiler water temperature accordingly via the aquastat (Figure 4). Thus, when it's 0°F out, the boiler will heat the water to maximum temperature (usually around 180°F); if it's around 30°F out-

side, the boiler might heat the hot water to only 135°F. The system never heats the water any more than necessary to keep the house at the desired temperature. For every 3°F that you can lower the boiler water temperature and still heat the building, you save 1% in fuel. This increased efficiency can cut a home's heating bill by 15% to 25%. Good models include those from Honeywell (Morristown, NJ; 800/328-5111; www.honeywell.com), Viega (Wichita, KS; 877/843-4262; www.viega.com), and Tekmar Control (Vernon, BC, Canada; 250/545-7749; www.tekmarcontrols.com).

Weather-responsive controls aren't cheap — the control itself runs about $300 and takes an hvac contractor a half day or so to install. These controls also can't be used with a tankless boiler system unless you install a four-way mixing valve, which gets a bit more complicated and pricey. These aren't reasons to avoid weather-responsive controls; they're simply factors that an experienced hvac or plumbing-heating contractor should evaluate before going ahead.

By Richard Trethewey, an hvac contractor and consultant from Dedham, Mass.

High-Efficiency HVAC

Some residential hvac appliances have enjoyed a relatively trouble-free evolution to higher efficiencies. Heat pumps and air conditioners, for example, have not been radically modified to increase efficiency. No new major components have been added and the newest units are not generally more complex or more difficult to install than older, lower-efficiency models.

Gas furnaces, on the other hand, have had a long and bumpy journey to high efficiency. Several new major components have been added, including secondary heat exchang-

ers, draft inducers, and electric ignition (Figure 5). Some of the mechanical components in early models were poorly designed and failed regularly. A few models, such as the Amana Energy Command and Lennox Pulse used totally new technology with almost no resemblance to "conventional" furnaces.

The Amana unit, which used water and glycol heat transfer fluid, is one of only two furnaces that can heat domestic water (the other is Glowcore). However, it ran into a string of problems, including glycol leakage in early units. In 1990,

Amana brought out a new and less expensive condensing gas furnace using more conventional technology.

The Lennox unit pioneered "pulse combustion," and after early problems with noise, turned out to be one of the biggest success stories in high-efficiency hvac (Figure 6). The first ten years of development, from 1980 to 1990, were fraught with factory recalls, contractor callbacks, and dissatisfied consumers who complained of nuisance shutdowns, noise problems, and poor comfort. Some homeowners even (unfairly) blamed their high-efficiency furnaces for moisture and indoor air quality problems.

Things got so bad that in 1985 a group of contractors at the Air Conditioning Contractors of America annual meeting offered a resolution stating that they had suffered "unacceptable loss of time, money, and reputation due to multiple failures of new high-efficiency equipment."

The good news is that after a number of years of trial and error combined with applied research, most of the design problems appear to be fixed. But there is still one

Avoiding Corrosion Problems

To minimize corrosion problems with high-efficiency furnaces and boilers, follow these recommendations:
- Use only outdoor air for combustion.
- Locate air intake away from potential outdoor chloride sources such as swimming pools and dryer exhaust vents. If necessary, run the air intake through the roof rather than a sidewall.

- Make sure the furnace is installed level. If not, condensate may collect in the heat exchanger, increasing the potential for corrosion.
- Never use an installed high efficiency furnace as a construction heater. Not only is this likely to contaminate the furnace and duct system with construction dust (true for any type of furnace), but sealers and adhesives can quickly damage the heat exchanger surfaces.

catch. Unlike automobiles, which are fully preassembled and ready to drive, hvac must be properly installed. High-efficiency equipment, particularly condensing furnaces and boilers, is generally less forgiving of installation error than older equipment. A few basic guidelines and specifications must be followed to ensure good performance and trouble-free, long-lasting service.

Corrosion in Condensing Gas Furnaces

The Arkla Recuperative Plus gas furnace was introduced in 1982 and recalled in 1984 after more than 2,000 reported claims of heat exchanger corrosion and carbon monoxide problems. The same furnace was also sold under different names by GE, Trane, and SnyderGeneral. This was the beginning of the worst problem to plague high-efficiency gas furnaces. The next five years saw recalls of Heil, Whirlpool, and Coleman condensing gas furnaces — all for heat exchanger corrosion.

The situation has been vastly improved, but not completely fixed. After extensive research at Battelle Laboratory and the American Gas Association Laboratories, manufacturers now use corrosion-resistant materials for heat exchangers and other components. Most use a special stainless-steel alloy called AL29-4C for the secondary heat exchanger (Figure 7), although some have tried different approaches with varying success. For example, Heil tried a ceramic-lined heat exchanger that had to be recalled due to scaling problems, while Carrier uses a plastic-lined heat exchanger, which seems to be working well.

Chloride a problem. Regardless of the type of heat exchanger, high-efficiency furnaces can and do still rust badly if the combustion air contains high levels of chlorides. The chloride combines with water vapor in the flue gases to form a corrosive condensate that attacks metal parts in the heat

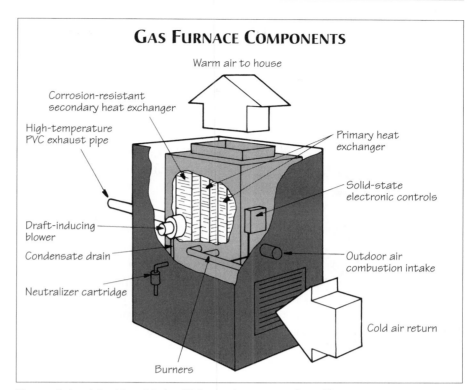

Figure 5. Look inside a high-efficiency furnace and you'll see components not found in low- and mid-efficiency models. The draft-inducing blower plays a key role, drawing air into the combustion chamber for more efficient controlled combustion, then forcing the hot air through the primary and secondary heat exchangers for maximum heat transfer. As the combustion air passes through the secondary heat exchanger, it cools to the point where moisture condenses, releasing another burst of heat.

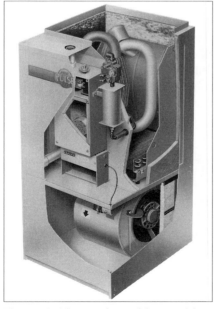

Figure 6. After early problems with noise, the Lennox Pulse turned out to be one of the biggest success stories in high-efficiency hvac.

Figure 7. The Yukon oil furnace, one of only two condensing oil furnaces on the market, uses highly resistant (and very expensive) AL29-4C stainless steel for the secondary heat exchanger and 301 stainless steel for the primary.

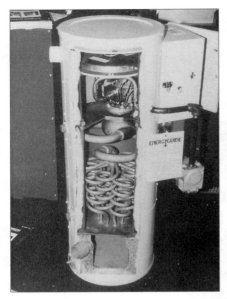

Figure 8. The Hydropulse is the first and only residential pulse boiler. Like its furnace cousin, the Lennox Pulse, it has enjoyed a relatively trouble-free history.

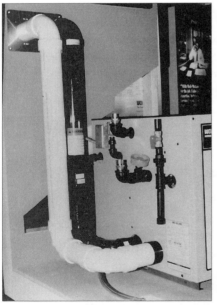

Figure 9. To prevent corrosion in a high-efficiency boiler, such as the Weil McLain GV model shown here, the venting system must be Ultravent or Plexvent high-temperature plastic vent pipe (the black pipe). Made of GE Ultem plastic, these vent systems can withstand temperatures up to 480°F. The white pipe is the fresh air intake, which is made of ordinary Schedule 40 PVC.

exchanger and exhaust system. Bard Manufacturing Company voids its lifetime warranty if a heat exchanger in one of its gas furnaces is corroded from "contaminated air."

Unfortunately, indoor air often contains large amounts of chloride compounds, especially in basements and near laundry rooms. It comes from chlorinated tap water, chlorine bleaches, and a host of other household products such as paint, paint stripper, and adhesives. The results of an extensive testing of 572 houses conducted by Battelle Laboratory indicated that 1 in 10 homes has indoor air chloride concentrations high enough to produce corrosive flue-gas condensate.

Even outdoor air sometimes contains high chloride levels, particularly near swimming pools, hot tubs, and clothes dryer exhausts. One horror story is told by David Hahn, a training specialist at Wisconsin Natural Gas who has inspected hundreds of failed systems.

Hahn was called in to inspect a Lennox Pulse furnace with corrosion problems. The house was located near a road-salt storage depot and the road was usually covered with spilled salt. The chloride concentration in the outdoor air was so high that the furnace rusted out completely in only eight months! The solution, according to Hahn, was to install a new furnace with the combustion air intake at the back side of the house, away from the road.

Venting Problems

Venting high-efficiency condensing furnaces (those in the 83% to 97% AFUE, or *annual fuel utilization efficiency*, range) is actually easier and less problematic than venting mid-efficiency furnaces (78% to 83% AFUE). But despite their apparent simplicity, these vent systems have had problems.

Nuisance shutdowns. A 600-house Canadian study of high-efficiency gas furnaces found that 16%

of the installations suffered frequent shutdown due to improper vent installation. These "nuisance shutdowns" are most likely to occur if the vent system is too long or improperly sloped. Some building codes prohibit venting a furnace in the direction of neighboring houses. To comply with this restriction, contractors sometimes install long horizontal runs to reach the back or front of the house. The long pipe creates high static pressure. A wind against the termination may then be all that is needed to raise the back pressure above the setpoint of the safety pressure switch, which then shuts down the system. (This typically occurs around midnight on Christmas eve.)

Annoying fumes. Flue gases from condensing furnaces are not terribly toxic, but they do contain slightly acidic vapors, considerable moisture, and trace amounts of pollutants. They are also accompanied by noise. Improperly positioned exhaust vents can kill bushes, steam up windows, and annoy neighbors. In one installation in Madison, Wis., a contractor put the exhaust vent directly over the outdoor air conditioner unit. Dripping condensate corroded the air conditioner casing and eventually penetrated into the outdoor coil, causing the air conditioner to fail.

In another installation, a dripping roof vent termination rusted out the metal rain gutters. And one disgruntled homeowner in Arlington, Mass., had her contractor move the vent termination for her Glowcore furnace because of the unsightly "steam" visible through the living room picture window.

Noise. High-efficiency gas furnaces are generally noisier than low-efficiency units because the main blowers are bigger and because they have an additional draft-inducing blower that is not used in low-efficiency furnaces. The original Lennox Pulse furnace was terribly noisy, especially when not installed properly. (Lots of jokes were made about small outboard motors in the basement.)

The best news regarding noise is the development of variable-speed furnaces by Carrier and Trane, both of which are so quiet that it is hard to tell they are operating when standing 2 feet away. And Lennox has significantly reduced sound levels from the Pulse furnace.

Boilers

Despite some radical departures from conventional design, high-efficiency boilers have been relatively trouble free (Figure 8). One nagging

problem that plagued the first high-efficiency systems was condensate formation in the heat exchangers and flue pipes.

To protect the heat exchangers, all high-efficiency boilers now have thermostatic bypass valves which shunt supply water back to the heat exchanger to prevent flue gas condensation. Unfortunately, nothing is foolproof. In one case, a contractor in Springfield, Mass., neglected to install the bypass valve on a Heatmaker boiler. With no temperature control, the boiler ran too cool, resulting in serious condensate damage to the heat exchanger.

To eliminate flue corrosion, liter-

ally every manufacturer now recommends high-temperature plastic flue pipe made of GE "Ultem" resin (Figure 9). Some manufacturers also allow Type 301 stainless steel, which is almost as resistant to corrosion, but much more difficult to work with.

One problem with mid-efficiency (83% to 88% AFUE) boilers has to do with condensation in masonry chimneys, particularly with chimneys located on outside walls. The corrosive condensate can attack mortar joints in unlined chimneys and can even cause damage in chimneys with clay liners. If possible, mid-efficiency boilers should be

VENTING GUIDELINES

- Keep vent runs as short as possible. Never exceed manufacturers' guidelines (typically 30 to 40 feet with two elbows).
- On horizontal runs, the vent pipe must slope toward the furnace, allowing condensate to drain back into the furnace.
- Keep the exhaust termination 10 inches from the wall to reduce icing on the wall and to prevent paint damage. If the vent faces prevailing winds, install a protective plate around the termination to protect the wall.
- Maintain about a 2-foot clearance from shrubbery.
- Never use a "U" termination on a roof vent. Dripping condensate can damage roofing and gutters. The roof vent should be a straight vertical pipe. Rain will not be a problem since it will drain through the condensate drain.
- Insulate any section of vent pipe that passes through unheated spaces or extends more than 3 feet outdoors. The vent pipe should also be insulated if an exterior masonry chimney is used as a chase.
- Do not install exhaust vents over anything that cannot tolerate dripping condensate. This

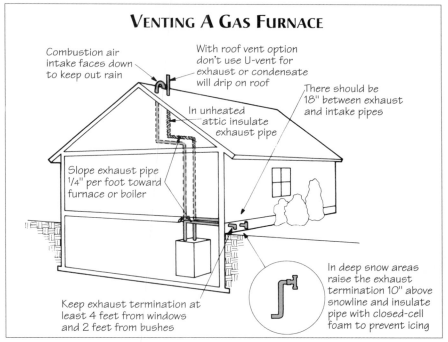

By following a few basic guidelines, most of the annoying problems associated with venting high-efficiency furnaces and boilers can be eliminated.

includes walkways, windows, air conditioners, gas meters, etc.
- Do not install the exhaust vent near any air intakes or under windows. Aside from the obvious hazard of drawing exhaust gases into the house, rising water vapor will be visible through win-

dows and can even condense moisture on the glass surface.
- Locate the vent terminal so that the noise will be directed toward open space or through the roof rather than toward a neighboring house which could echo the sound (and annoy the neighbor).

Figure 10. The new Copeland Compliant Scroll compressor is more efficient and reliable than conventional piston compressors. Most major heat pump manufacturers now sell models equipped with scroll compressors.

side-vented using stainless-steel or high-temperature plastic vent pipe.

Air Conditioners and Heat Pumps

High-efficiency air conditioners and heat pumps have not suffered any notable problems other than those normally associated with compressor technology. If anything, the new high-efficiency air conditioners and heat pumps are more reliable than older equipment.

The most noteworthy development was the scroll compressor (Figure 10), which was first introduced by Lennox in 1987 in its HP-20 heat pump. Most of the other major equipment manufacturers quickly followed. Using far fewer parts than conventional piston-type compressors, scroll compressors are not only more efficient, they also are quieter and more durable.

One problem with high-efficiency cooling equipment is its generally lower dehumidification capacity. During very humid weather, these units sometimes reduce indoor temperature without removing sufficient humidity — the so-called "cool but clammy" effect.

Manufacturers have effectively addressed this problem with variable-speed (Carrier and Trane) and two-speed (Lennox) equipment that has variable dehumidification capacity. Contractors can also help the problem by not installing oversized equipment, which naturally tends to cycle more frequently. Since dehumidification is lowest during startup, frequent cycling causes poor dehumidification.

Federal Regs

High-efficiency heating and cooling equipment has captured a significant share of the residential market since the new federal minimum efficiency standards took effect in 1992.

These federal regulations completely eliminated low-efficiency furnaces, boilers, and air conditioners from the marketplace. Given the relatively small price differential between the remaining mid- and high-efficiency models, the buying public tends to skip to top-of-the line models. So it makes sense to familiarize yourself with the new technology.

Training available. When Weil McLain introduced its new GV series boiler, it also produced an excellent training video and workbook that explains exactly how and why the system works and then shows detailed step-by-step installation procedures. Carrier, Trane, and Lennox all produce comprehensive training materials and seminars. In addition, the installation manuals that accompany all appliances usually (but unfortunately not always) include most of the recommendations and guidelines given here, along with all the necessary details for proper installation and startup.

By J.D. Ned Nisson, president of Energy Design Associates Inc., a New York City-based building systems consulting firm, and editor of Energy Design Update.

MECHANICAL COOLING SYSTEMS

Field studies across the nation indicate that residential air conditioners are running far below their rated efficiencies because of poor installation. One extensive study found that duct leakage alone raised the average cooling load in new homes by about 23%. Duct leakage is the largest loss, followed by improper charge, air flow problems, and oversizing.

The time to fix these problems is during design and construction, when small improvements will yield big payoffs in efficiency. Retrofitting at a later date, however, when many of the problems are buried behind drywall and finished floors means less gain for more money. In addition to saving the homeowner a lot of money, a better job up front means fewer callbacks for the contractor — for the electric bill that's "twice as high as my neighbor's" or the unit that won't stop running but still leaves the owners uncomfortable.

Duct Leakage

Because of standard installation practices, duct leakage plagues almost all forced-air heating and cooling systems. While only 10% to 15% of the total air leakage in a home is located in the duct system, duct leaks are under pressures 10 to 20 times higher than other building leaks whenever the air handler runs. The result is that when the air handler is running, duct leaks can double or triple the total air leakage in a home. And this typically happens when you least want it — at the hottest or coldest times of the year.

So where do the leaks occur? Disconnected ducts and framing cavities are the most common leakage sites (Figure 11). It is not unusual to find ducts that have either been accidentally disconnected by another trade or that were never connected in the first place. The take-offs and collars where branch lines exit the trunk are notoriously leaky (Figure 12). Basically, there are leaks wherever there is a joint or a seam in the system (one exception is the snap-lock joints along the length of a straight section of duct). Even the cabinets that house the units are leaky.

Another big problem is the widespread use of framing cavities as part of the air supply and return system. This includes platform plenums, and panned joist and stud cavities (Figure 13). Typically, the hvac contractor says it's the contractor's, drywaller's, or framer's responsibility to seal up framing cavities; whereas the contractor points the finger at the hvac sub. Even if the contractor does a thorough job of sealing these cavities, they may not survive the work of plumbers and electricians. Regardless, most framing lumber shrinks as it dries and new cracks will appear. Our conclusion is that the building industry must get away from using building cavities as part of the air distribution system.

If you are skeptical, we suggest you examine one of your duct systems as it is being installed. Pop off a return grille on a panned joist return and scrutinize all the seams. Examine where supply lines branch from trunk lines. If you have the opportunity, look down a trunk line while it is being installed. You will most likely see light coming in every 48 inches where the sections connect. A flashlight and an inspection mirror are handy for this.

Sealing the ducts. Fortunately, duct leakage is simple to eliminate during

Figure 11. Prime leakage sites include: connections where flex ducts join junction boxes (top), disconnected ductwork (center), and poorly installed boots at grilles and registers (bottom). Leaky ductwork can spoil the performance of an otherwise tight, well-insulated home.

new construction if you know where to look for leaks and how to seal them. Depending on the complexity of the system, sealing can cost from $150 to $350. Research has shown that the payback period on this added cost ranges from less than a year to about three years. And there are important health and safety benefits as well.

The product of choice for duct sealing is water-based mastic accompanied by a fiberglass mesh on larger holes. Two good duct mastics are Glencoat (Thrifty Supply, Sacramento, CA; 916/381-1800) and

RCD #6 (RCD, Eustis, FL; 800/854-7494; www.rcdcorp.com). These mastics have the consistency of mashed potatoes and can be easily spread over joints in the ductwork with an inexpensive paint brush or one's gloved hand. On cracks and gaps wider than $1/4$ inch, place a section of 2-inch-wide fiberglass mesh tape in the bed of mastic to reinforce the seal. The beauty of water-based mastic is that it provides a long-term durable seal and cleans up with water.

The traditional duct tape approach doesn't work. Because of

the extreme temperature conditions that ducts are subjected to, the tape eventually fails. Mastic is actually less labor intensive than a "good" taping job (Figure 14).

The last step in the sealing procedure is to test to make sure your hvac contractor got it right. You can use either a blower door and flow hood or the newest arrival — the Duct Blaster (The Energy Conservatory, Minneapolis, MN; 612/827-1117; www.energyconservatory.com). With proper training, these diagnostic tools are fairly simple to use (Figure 15). The goal is to have no more than 25 cfm of leakage at .10 inches of water column in smaller homes and no more than 50 cfm leakage in larger homes. This is achievable, but it takes a lot more attention to detail than most hvac contractors are accustomed to.

The testing has several benefits. First, when an hvac contractor knows his work will be tested, he's more likely to get it right the first time. Second, diagnostic tools turn up leaks that are virtually undetectable by visual inspection. And third, the test teaches the participants where to seal better next time, as well as making believers out of skeptics.

Improper Charge

The second most important problem with mechanical cooling systems involves the refrigerant charge. Over half the homes we evaluated in one study had the wrong charge. For the most common systems (capillary tube), a 10% overcharge results in a 10% loss in efficiency. When undercharged by 20%, the same system loses 16% of its designed efficiency. Incorrect charge also reduces capacity and may shorten compressor life.

An undercharge causes the compressor to run longer and hotter, while an overcharge causes the compressor to work harder and can lead to compressor failure. In the case of an undercharge, less heat is removed from the indoor air as it passes through the coil, so the unit has to run longer.

Technicians typically use guesswork to determine if the charge is correct. One common but unreliable technique is to feel the suction line. If the temperature to the compressor "feels right," then the charge is assumed to be correct. The accurate way to check the charge is straightforward for a trained person and takes less than an hour. The process involves first checking the air flow and then either the *superheat* or *subcooling*, depending on system design.

Low Air Flow

The third major problem with mechanical cooling is low air flow over the indoor coil. The indoor coil, or evaporator, is where heat and moisture are removed from warm indoor air. Most manufacturers recommend that air flow across the coil should be 400 cfm per ton. When the air flow drops below 350 cfm, the unit's efficiency drops off.

In simple terms, lower air flow means less heat is transferred to the refrigerant, so the unit has to run longer to remove the same amount of heat. Another effect of low air flow is that the coil may begin to freeze,

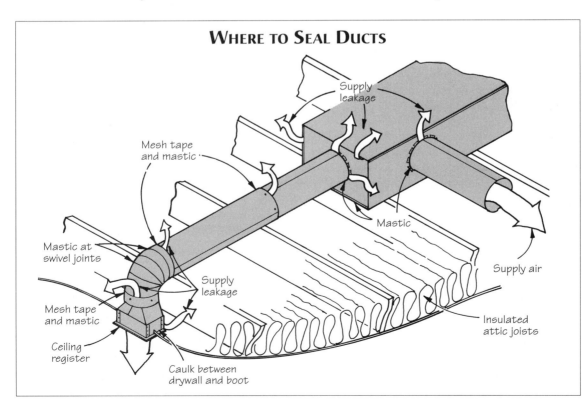

WHERE TO SEAL DUCTS

Supply leakage

Mesh tape and mastic

Mastic

Mastic at swivel joints

Supply leakage

Supply air

Mesh tape and mastic

Ceiling register

Caulk between drywall and boot

Insulated attic joists

Figure 12. To control metal duct leaks in attics and other unconditioned spaces, seal all joints with mastic except lengthwise snap-lock joints, which are relatively tight. With flex duct, seal the inside liner to the metal collar with a plastic tie, then apply mastic and fibermesh.

which further reduces efficiency and can cause the compressor to fail.

A study we conducted of 175 newer homes revealed that 24% of the homes had air flow of 350 cfm per ton or less, some as low as 196 cfm per ton. The average efficiency loss was 8%.

Reduced air flow has many causes. The most common cause is poor duct design and installation (Figure 16). Closed registers also reduce the air flow. If the air distribution system relies on a filter grille at the return, return leaks can suck dust and insulation into the duct system, which accumulates on the coils and reduces air flow. A dirty air filter has a similar effect. Even without duct problems, it is important to inspect both the indoor coil and air filter on a regular basis.

Unfortunately, the indoor coil is often installed in an inaccessible location. If the supply plenum has to be dismantled to gain access to the coil, chances are it will never be inspected. If, on the other hand, an access panel is incorporated into the supply riser and only a handful of sheet metal screws have to be backed out, the service technician can make a visual inspection as part of the annual service.

The best way to measure air flow is with the Duct Blaster, described above. For efficient performance, the flow should be within 5% of manufacturer's specs.

Oversizing

The majority of air conditioners are oversized by 25% or more. When duct leakage, low air flow, and improper charge have been addressed, this oversizing becomes apparent. An oversized unit is more expensive to run, compromises comfort, and can be a source of callbacks. Once again, the penalty for this problem involves more than just a higher utility bill.

An oversized system will "short cycle," meaning the unit cycles on and off rapidly instead of running steadily. A capillary tube system takes over five minutes to reach 95% of its operating capacity. Short cycles never allow the equipment to perform to its designed capacity.

Oversizing can also degrade comfort in hot, humid climates, because the unit's ability to dehumidify (latent cooling) is reduced. The unit cools the air so quickly that it kicks off before the indoor coil removes an

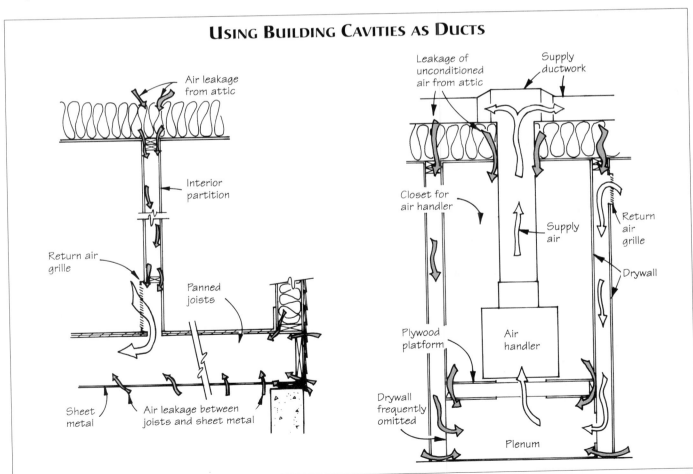

USING BUILDING CAVITIES AS DUCTS

Figure 13. Stud and joist bays make handy return ducts, but are a major source of leakage (left). Air handlers set on raised platforms (right) suffer from similar leaks. The author's recommendation: Use ductwork instead of building cavities.

Figure 14. Throw away your duct tape and smear on water-based mastic instead, if you want a long-lasting seal against duct leakage. Duct mastic has the consistency of mashed potatoes and is applied by hand or with a cheap paint brush.

Figure 15. Measuring duct leakage takes under half an hour using the Duct Blaster, a portable calibrated fan. Used as a powered flow hood, it can also accurately measure air flow through the duct system.

Figure 16. Too many twists and turns in the duct runs create excess resistance to flow. This lowers system performance and can freeze up the evaporator coil.

companion manual, Manual D, is for sizing duct work. The manuals cost $45 each from the Air Conditioner Contractors of America, (Arlington, VA; 703/575-4477; www.acca.org). Both procedures are also available on computer software called Right-J and Right-D (WrightSoft Corp., Lexington, MA; 800/225-8697; www.wrightsoft.com). With the software, an experienced estimator can do a run on a simple 1,800-square-foot home in about an hour — compared to about three hours manually.

The time it takes to correctly size a cooling system is well spent. A properly sized unit will often reduce the initial cost of the system, run more efficiently, last longer, and enhance the comfort level in the home. If your hvac contractor isn't already sizing systems correctly, encourage him to learn how to use Manual J and Manual D.

Summary

It's safe to say that over 95% of new air-conditioned homes being built today will suffer from one or more of the problems discussed here: duct leakage, low air flow, improper refrigerant charge, and oversizing. To correct these problems, builders and designers need to start using detailed specifications that require quality installations. The payback period for eliminating these problems is typically less than three years, not counting the benefits of better comfort and indoor air quality, as well as fewer callbacks.

For More Information

Professional training in duct doctoring is offered by the Florida Solar Energy Center (Cocoa, FL; 321/638-1000; www.fsec.ucf.edu).

By Michael Uniacke, a building science educator and consultant in Prescott Valley, Ariz. And by John Proctor, P.E., of Proctor Engineering Group in Corte Madera, Calif., a consultant and researcher on hvac and building shell efficiency.

adequate amount of moisture. The indoor humidity remains high, preventing a person's body from keeping cool through natural evaporation from the skin.

The result is that the air ends up cool and clammy, and occupants respond by turning down the thermostat further, driving up energy use. For example, turning the thermostat down from 75°F to 70°F can easily increase the cooling load by 25%.

Ask your hvac contractor how he sizes equipment. Most rely on rules of thumb based on the square footage of the house. Window orientation, levels of conservation, and occupant load are often not taken into consideration.

The solution is Manual J, which is a simple method for sizing heating and cooling loads. Manual J becomes fairly easy to navigate once you've waded through it a couple of times. A

WATER HEATERS

Many times, the failure to recognize a small, easy-to-repair problem leads to an expensive — and unnecessary — replacement. Recently, for instance, a client who wasn't getting enough hot water "solved" the problem by purchasing a bigger water heater. When he called us in to hook it up, we found that his cold water dip tube had broken off, so cold water had been entering at the top, diluting the hot water. A little troubleshooting could have solved this problem with a $5 replacement part.

Maintenance is the best way to avoid problems (see "Maintaining Water Heaters," next page). When troubles do arise (short of a leaking tank), it helps to be familiar with a heater's parts (Figure 17). Good troubleshooting may prevent the need for heater replacement.

Before you start. Always turn off the power before troubleshooting an electric water heater (assuming you've determined that the problem isn't electrical). For gas heaters, it's usually sufficient to turn the control valve down to the "pilot" setting.

Next, shut off the water supply to the water heater; you can turn it back on later if you need to perform a test. Most installers provide a shut-off at the cold water supply inlet; otherwise, use the main house shut-off. To remove any pressure buildup in the tank, open a hot water faucet at any fixture in the house. Finally, hook up a hose to the drain valve on the bottom. (When it's time to refill the tank, leave the house faucet open until all of the air is out of the system.)

Now you're ready to explore the symptoms of trouble.

No Hot Water

Only two things cause no hot water: Either the energy supply has

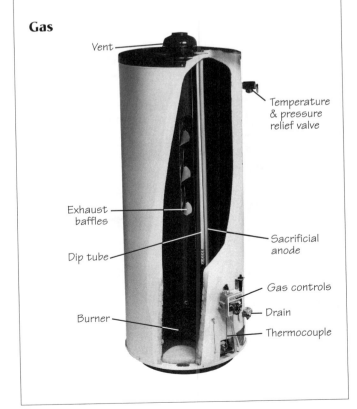

INSIDE A WATER HEATER

Electric

Dip tube
Sacrificial anode
Heating elements
Thermostats

Gas

Vent
Temperature & pressure relief valve
Exhaust baffles
Sacrificial anode
Dip tube
Gas controls
Drain
Burner
Thermocouple

Figure 17. Electric heaters (left) have one or two immersed electric elements and thermostats; in gas models (below), the water is heated from the bottom and by flue gases traveling through the baffled center vent. In both types of heaters, a supply connection on top delivers cold water to the bottom of the tank through a plastic dip tube; a sacrificial metal anode prevents rust.

been interrupted, or there's a control problem.

Electric heaters. If an electric heater has no hot water, look first at the upper thermostat (Figure 18). Use a volt-ohm meter or a "pigtail" tester to check for power at the top two screw connections. If you find no power at these screws, there's no power getting to the heater: The problem is somewhere between the water heater and the main panel.

If you do have power at these two screws, but not at the two screws just below the red reset button, then the

high-limit switch has turned the power off. If the red button clicks when you press it, power will be restored.

A tripped high-limit switch, however, is a symptom of very high temperatures, and unless the culprit is found, the problem will recur. One possible cause is fusing of the contacts in either the upper or lower thermostat. This prevents the heating elements from shutting off and leads to overheating. Also, a thermostat that is not mounted firmly against the tank wall, or one that is

missing its insulation cover, may not read temperature correctly.

If there is no hot water in a dual element heater, the upper element may be burned out, preventing power from being switched to the lower element (which does most of the heating). With the power off and one wire disconnected, use a volt-ohm meter to check for continuity in the suspect element. Replacing the bad element will restore hot water.

Gas heaters. In gas heaters, the problem is usually either a worn-

---

MAINTAINING WATER HEATERS

Like all heavily used appliances, water heaters need maintenance. You can often spot early signs of trouble simply by looking at the tank. A great ooze of calcium and other scale debris piling up on top of the heater (Figure A) usually signals leaky connections in the plumbing overhead.

Some maintenance items, however, are less obvious. Here's a list of simple checks to encourage homeowners to become involved with.

Check the Anode

All glass-lined tanks come with a sacrificial anode rod which is usu-

ally screwed into a separate port at the top of the heater (Figure B). The anode is about 3/4 inch in diameter and formed around a steel wire that extends down nearly to the tank's bottom. Other tanks do not have separate anodes but combine their anode with the hot outlet. If the original anode cannot be found or unscrewed, you can add an anode by screwing a combination-type anode into the hot water outlet port. Where overhead clearance is restricted, flexible-link anodes can be bent and "snaked in." The lower rod in Figure B is a link-type combination anode.

The magnesium or aluminum anode rods are meant to corrode

slowly as part of an electrochemical reaction that prevents rusting in the tank, and which in turn prevents leaks. We prefer to use magnesium anodes, especially until aluminum is proven innocent of contributing to Alzheimer's Disease. (You can tell these metals apart by bending the anode: Aluminum is soft, while magnesium is somewhat springy.)

Anode replacement. You need the right tool to get the anode out. Usually, a 12-point socket on a breaker bar will do; other times you'll need a 6-point socket and a torque multiplier to free stubborn anodes.

It's best to find a source for replacement anodes before open-

Figure A. Leaking at unions in the overhead plumbing caused this scale to accumulate on top of the water heater. Because the leaks went unnoticed for several years, the heater rusted through from the outside in and had to be replaced.

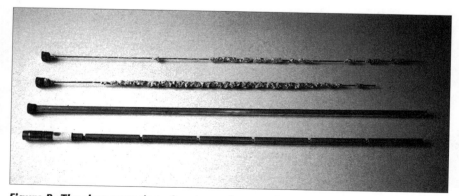

Figure B. The slow corrosion of a magnesium or aluminum anode rod protects glass-lined tanks from rust. Check the anode every few years and replace it if 6 inches or more of the steel core wire is exposed, or if the rod is coated over with a brittle scale. Use a flexible-link rod where overhead clearance is restricted.

out thermocouple or a faulty gas control (Figure 19). First, look to see if the pilot flame actually touches the end of the thermocouple, as it's supposed to. Then check to see that the thermocouple is firmly screwed into the control. If you have doubts about this connection, unscrew the thermocouple, use extra-fine sandpaper or a knife to polish the contact point, and re-install. Special thermocouple testers are also available, but it may be easier (and cheaper) to replace the thermocouple and see if that

revives the heater. (A thermocouple costs about $15 and takes ten minutes to replace.)

If the heater was supplying very hot water before there was no hot water, the energy cutoff switch, which is built into the gas control, was probably activated. With modern heaters, once this has tripped, the control valve must be replaced (about $80 plus installation).

Insufficient Hot Water

When there's not enough hot water, first check to see if the heater

is correctly sized for its demand. A heater should deliver about 75% of its volume as hot water. You can measure flow at fixtures such as the showerhead to determine how much the tank is capable of delivering. (Empty five-gallon drywall buckets work well for this test: Count the number of buckets you can fill with hot water, then compare the result with the tank's capacity.)

Cross connections. If the tank is not overtaxed, check for cross connections. Turn off the water supply

---

ing up your tank. While hardware stores seldom stock anodes, plumbing supply houses have them for $18 to $45.

It's time for anode replacement when 6 inches of the steel core wire is exposed, or if the rod is coated over with a brittle scale. Check anodes every three to four years (more often if you have hard, softened, or acidic water).

Control Sediment

Sediment is the curse of water heaters. Accumulated sediment slows heat transfer in gas heaters, and the elevated temperatures weaken the steel and dissolve the glass lining. Sediment also provides a breeding ground for bacteria. In gas heaters, sediment can cause annoying noise, and in electric heaters it can cause the lower element to burn out.

Getting rid of sediment. You can remove sediment by dissolving, vacuuming, or flushing it out of the tank. If you decide to try dissolving, do not use compounds containing lye. It's very dangerous. Instead, use a citric acid product such as Mag-Erad. The process takes several hours and may need to be repeated if not initially effective.

We like to vacuum sediment using a tool we developed called the Muck-Vac, which pulls water and sediment off the bottom and returns filtered water to the tank

(Figure C). In electric heaters, you can pull out the bulk of the sediment using a wet/dry shop vac with a piece of $3/4$-inch pipe for a nozzle. Go in through the element port after draining the tank.

The third method, flushing, is effective only if water pressure and flow are good, and the sediment buildup is not too heavy. For flushing to work, a heater must have a ball-valve drain and a dip tube with a curve on the end. Some heaters come from the factory with curved dip tubes already installed; if not, you can replace a straight tube with a curved one on standard tanks.

To flush the tank, attach a hose to the drain, open the ball valve, and let water run out full force for three to five minutes. The curved dip tube creates a swirling action in the tank that stirs up sediment and rinses it out the drain.

Prevent sediment buildup. Softening the water helps to reduce sediment accumulation, as does lowering the water pressure; high pressure tends to cause more sediment. If you can adjust the gas pressure to the main burner of your gas heater, turn it down: The smaller flame will slow sediment buildup.

Inspect Relief Valves

The temperature and pressure (T&P) relief valve kicks in at temperatures over 210°F and pressures of more than about 150 psi. If the valve

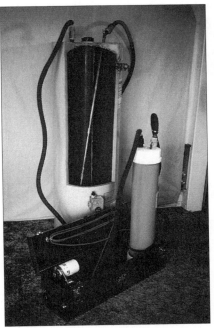

Figure C. The authors designed the Muck-Vac to pull sediment off the bottom of the tank, filter it, and return clean water to the heater.

is blocked with scale or rust, neither water nor steam will be able to escape, and you'll have a very dangerous problem. The valve should be checked every six months.

Checking the T&P operation is easy. Lift the lever on the valve. Be sure there is good water flow and that it shuts off when you let the lever flip back down. If it drips or doesn't reseat, replace it.

— L.W. & S.W.

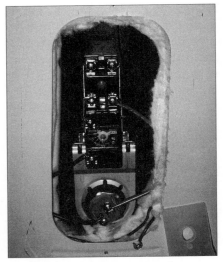

Figure 18. Lack of hot water from an electric water heater is often caused by a failed upper element. Use a volt-ohm meter or pigtail tester to check for power at the two pairs of screws above and below the red reset button.

to the heater and turn on any hot tap. If you continue to get a flow of water, there is a cross-connection somewhere between the hot and cold plumbing. Cross connections can be found in clothes washers, tempering valves, and many single-handle faucets and shower valves.

Sometimes hot and cold lines are inadvertently switched at the water heater when it is hooked up. This delivers cold water to the top of the tank and causes warm water to be drawn through the dip tube from the bottom.

Faulty dip tube. Split, broken, or missing dip tubes may allow cold incoming water to mix with hot water at the top of the tank. To check the condition of the dip tube, undo the cold inlet and remove the pipe nipple from the tank. Insert a straight pliers handle or a wooden

dowel into the dip tube and, using a circular motion, pull up and "walk" the dip tube up high enough to grasp. Pull it out to check for damage. Replace it, if needed, with another plastic dip tube (a copper tube will increase corrosion).

Gas supply and controls. Gas heaters may not produce enough hot water because of gas supply or control problems. Start your diagnosis by watching the main burner in operation. Is the flame sooty or too small? Poor draft, inadequate combustion, or low gas pressure may be at fault. If the temperature of the water leaving the tank varies widely, the on and off set points in the control may have drifted; a new control may be needed. Another possibility is that heavy sediment buildup in the tank is covering the control's probe and slowing response time.

TROUBLESHOOTING CHECKLIST

No Hot Water

Cause: Faulty electric thermostat; faulty electric heating element

Remedy: Check power to thermostat; if okay, trace power back to panel. Replace thermostat or element.

Cause: Inoperative gas thermocouple; failed gas control valve

Remedy: Reposition, tighten, or replace thermocouple. Replace controls.

Rumbling or Popping Noise (gas heaters)

Cause: Sediment buildup
Remedy: Remove sediment.

"Singing" (electric heaters)

Cause: Scale buildup on elements
Remedy: Clean scale from tank and elements; install low-watt density element.

Not Enough Hot Water

Cause: Damaged dip tube
Remedy: Replace dip tube.

Cause: Incorrect plumbing
Remedy: Eliminate cross connections at faucets and water heater. Check operation of tempering valve.

Cause: Check-valve on recirculating line is missing or stuck open
Remedy: Repair or replace check valve (use a spring-loaded valve on pumped systems).

Rusty Water

Cause: Glass lining is failing
Remedy: Replace sacrificial anode; test water for iron content.

Sulfur Oder

Cause: Bacteria, which thrives in sediment
Remedy: Flush sediment; treat tank and water lines with hydrogen peroxide solution; use zinc-alloy anode.

Water on Floor Near Heater

Cause: T&P valve leak due to excessive pressure
Remedy: Install T&P on house side of pressure reducer (set to release at 20 pounds higher than pressure reducer). Install expansion tank.

Cause: T&P valve leak due to overheating
Remedy: Adjust or replace thermostat. Lower thermostat setting to prevent overheating from frequent small draws.

Cause: T&P valve leak due to stuck valve
Remedy: Operate valve to flush debris. Replace valve if leak persists.

Cause: T&P valve leak due to surge from washing machine or dishwasher
Remedy: Install water hammer arrestor.

Heating element and thermostat. Not enough hot water in electric heaters is usually caused by problems with the lower element or either thermostat. Use a volt-ohm meter or pigtail to check for power at the element. If there's power, then check for continuity. A burned-out lower element was probably buried in sediment and overheated. Remove the sediment before installing a new element. Consider using a low-watt density element in hard-water areas to slow sediment buildup.

If the element is good, check the upper thermostat as described earlier. If it tests okay, lower the setting until it's below the water temperature (about 130°F). At that point, the thermostat should switch power to the lower thermostat. If it doesn't, the upper thermostat is bad and needs to be replaced. If power does switch but the lower element still isn't getting juice, replace the lower thermostat.

Subtle Symptoms

Some water heater problems are less obvious, but can cause everything from mild annoyance to panic when they are finally discovered.

Water on the floor. This symptom may be reason for panic, but only after ruling out several simple problems. With a gas heater, the water you see on the floor may only be condensation. Water is one of the main byproducts of combustion, and it will condense out of the flue gases if the tank is cold, especially after a heavy hot water demand.

If there's always a puddle, check for leaks in the line running from the temperature and pressure (T&P) relief valve. A faulty valve may be constantly dripping water that then runs down the pipe alongside the tank, creating the puddle.

If neither of these is the problem, look at every threaded fitting on the tank, especially the plastic drain valve. Don't rule out overhead

plumbing: Flex-line connections and packing nuts on gate valves are notorious seepers. (If you tighten up flex-line unions when they are about six months old, you'll head off trouble.) In electric tanks, check for leaks where the elements attach to the tank wall.

If you still haven't uncovered a problem, go ahead and panic. With a little contortion and a dental-type mirror, you can look up through the combustion chamber to the bottom of the tank and the base of the flue. If you see any water marking or heavy rusting, or if you find water inside the combustion chamber, start shopping for a new tank. If the combustion chamber is dry, it has to be a fitting or tank leak. Recheck those fittings.

Sulfur odor. The rotten egg odor that some heaters develop occurs when hydrogen gas generated by the action of the anode feeds anaerobic bacteria in the tank. The bacteria take up residence in the sediment, where the warmth of the water encourages growth. Both aggressive and artificially softened water will speed anode consumption and generate even more hydrogen. Things get really bad when the tank sits unused for any length of time.

The cure lies in making the tank less hospitable for the bacteria. First, flush out any sediment to remove the breeding ground. Then oxygenate the water with hydrogen peroxide (one or two pints of 3% peroxide per 40 gallons of water) to kill off the remaining bacteria in the tank. Also, run some of the treated water into the plumbing to clean the pipes. Allow the hydrogen peroxide solution to sit for at least one hour in both the tank and the pipes. This treatment is nontoxic and does not require rinsing the way bleach does.

If the odor returns, replace the anode with one that contains a small percentage of zinc. Turning the heat down or off when the tank is unused

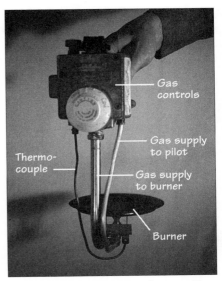

Figure 19. In a gas water heater, the burner will not operate unless the pilot flame is touching the thermocouple. To operate properly, the thermocouple must also be firmly screwed into the gas control.

will also help. Should the problem persist after all this, then a plastic-lined tank (which has no anode) or an instantaneous heater are the only options.

Bothersome noises. A rumbling or popping noise can occur in gas heaters when sediment builds up on the bottom. This sediment slows heat transfer from flame to water, causing overheating of the bottom. Overheating causes boiling and the noise you hear. Every time hot water is used, water pressure is lowered; this allows boiling to occur more readily, and the noise begins to sound like a bowling alley. Getting rid of the sediment is the key.

For many of us, water heaters are memorable for all the wrong reasons, but it doesn't have to be that way. Given a little attention from time to time, water heaters will give dependable service without complaint for decades.

By Larry and Suzanne Weingarten, partners in Elemental Enterprises, a Monterey, Calif., company that services conventional and solar water heaters.

SIMPLE VENTILATION FOR TIGHT HOUSES

Today's builders, seeking to save energy, are building homes significantly tighter than those built 20 or even 10 years ago. This is admirable. But too often neither builder nor owner recognizes that these tight homes need controlled ventilation.

Historically, natural air leakage (infiltration) has ventilated our homes and controlled moisture levels, odors, and indoor air pollutants. The tradeoff has been that we've had to accept cold drafts and excessive heat loss. To get the best of both worlds, we need tight houses that have *controlled* ventilation systems, so that we, and not the weather, determine where, when, and how much ventilation occurs.

How Much Ventilation Is Enough?

ASHRAE publishes ventilation standards based on house volume, but requiring no less than 15 cfm air change per hour per person. But because sizing by house volume can lead to overventilation in a large home and underventilation in a small home, I prefer to design my ventilation systems based on number of bedrooms. This keeps the ventilation needs in line with the number of occupants the house is likely to hold, rather than square footage.

I also slightly oversize the system, and I provide a speed control that lets the occupants turn the system down below maximum capacity. Oversizing accomplishes several things: It provides extra capacity in case ductwork or other calculations aren't perfect; it may provide enough capacity for more ductwork if the house is expanded; and since the oversized fan will usually be run at less than peak capacity, the system runs quietly. The extra cost for the added capacity is usually quite small, adding less than 5% to the system's cost.

So how much is enough? A good rule of thumb is to provide exhaust capacity of 100 cubic feet per minute (cfm) in a two-bedroom unit and 150 cfm in a three-bedroom unit. The fan control should be either two-speed or, preferably, variable speed so that these peak capacities can be reduced when occupants are few or moisture levels are low. If a house is bigger than 2,500 square feet and four or five bedrooms, I usually go to a 200 cfm fan, which is large enough for all but the biggest abodes.

Ventilation Basics

A ventilation system needs both an exhaust system and a fresh air supply. Stale air should be exhausted from rooms likely to have high moisture or odor content, such as the kitchen, bathrooms, laundry, or special-use rooms such as darkrooms. Fresh air should be supplied to the bedrooms and living areas where people spend most of their time. The goal in locating inlets and exhaust grilles is to create airflow paths from inlet to exhaust that will ensure good distribution of fresh air throughout the habitable areas of the home (Figure 20).

You can do this with an air-to-air heat exchanger (with both intake and exhaust fans). That can be a good choice when the budget allows it and heating fuel cost is high. But buying a heat exchanger is an economic decision, rather than one of occupant health or building durability. You can effectively ventilate a tight house with a modest amount of heat loss with any of several whole-house ventilation systems that use exhaust fans only. This article describes how to create such a system and what the options are for fresh air intake and stale air exhaust.

Breathing In

In exhaust-only systems, fresh air supply is passive, meaning that it is provided by adjustable holes through which air is drawn as the fan-driven exhaust system removes stale air from the home. There are at least three variations of this method.

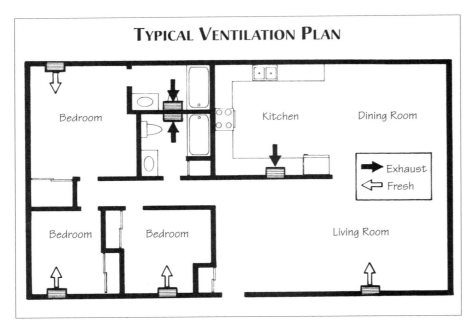

TYPICAL VENTILATION PLAN

Bedroom

Kitchen   Dining Room

➡ Exhaust
⬅ Fresh

Bedroom   Bedroom   Living Room

Figure 20. Fan-driven exhaust vents pull moisture, pollutants, and odors from kitchens and baths, while passive inlets in bedrooms and living room provide fresh air.

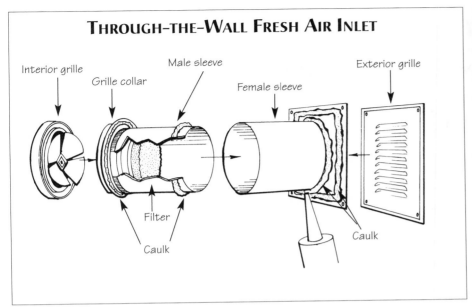

Figure 21. What looks like a closet light is actually a through-the-wall fresh air inlet. The pull cord opens and closes the vent as needed for intake control. Other models offer adjustable intakes operated either manually or by humidity sensors.

Through-the-wall vents — sold by American Aldes (Sarasota, FL; 941/351-3441; www.american-aldes.com) and Therma-Stor LLC (Madison, WI; 800/533-7533; www.thermastor.com) — offer the simplest, lowest-cost solution. These have adjustable openings designed to admit from 5 to 20 cfm quietly and without drafts. Some have humidity sensors that increase the airflow opening as indoor humidity rises. In most cases, through-the-wall vents offer the most cost-effective fresh air intake.

A second option is a ducted system with a single inlet from outdoors supplying ductwork that carries fresh air to selected rooms. These ducts carry cold air, and therefore should have insulation and an exterior vapor barrier to keep moisture from condensing on the outside of the ductwork. This method costs more than the through-the-wall vents, but provides the future option of converting the entire ventilation system to a balanced heat recovery system with an air-to-air heat exchanger.

Houses with a forced-hot-air heating system present a third option: duct the fresh air from a single dampered outdoor inlet to the heating system's return duct. This is a tricky system to spec correctly, however.

In most cases, I recommend through-the-wall vents, unless the owner is serious about later adding a heat exchanger. But whichever fresh air supply method I choose, I site the inlet point(s) away from outdoor pollution sources such as garages, chimneys, and plumbing vents. In addition, even though incoming air mixes with room air quickly, I site the intake points to minimize drafts — preferably high on a wall and at least 4 feet from any seating areas. Bedroom closets (Figure 21) make ideal sites as long as any solid doors are undercut at least $^3/_4$ inch.

Exhausting Possibilities

The exhaust side of the ventilation system is powered by a fan. There are three approaches you may take, depending on house size, budget, and how important you find the convenience of a packaged system: upgraded range hoods or bath fans; an in-line fan system you put together yourself; or a multiport system that comes complete from the manufacturer.

Upgrading the Range or Bath Fan

This least-cost approach works best in homes of not more than 1,500 square feet. In many homes, range and/or bath fans already exist to provide spot ventilation, so all that's needed to create a whole-house fan is to upgrade to a fan of higher capacity and lower noise level.

Such fans must be rated for continuous service — this means high-quality bearings with permanent lubrication. Sound level ratings should be no more than 5.5 sones for the range hood, 2.5 sones for the bath fan.

Range hoods. A range hood serving as a whole-house fan should have a capacity of 200 to 350 cfm and a solid-state, infinitely variable speed control so it can be turned down to barely audible ventilation flowrate levels of 50 to 100 cfm. Both Sears and Broan Mfg. Co., Inc., (Hartford, WI; 800/558-1711) make this type of range hood, which costs

DUCTWORK AND FAN INSTALLATION

Multiport systems come with full sets of ductwork, hanging hardware, and instructions. In a single-port in-line system, however, you need to put the pieces together yourself. Installation is mainly a matter of hanging ductwork and fans from framing members and installing grilles in walls — pretty basic hvac procedures. Following a few rules of thumb can make the installation go smoother and help you maximize the system's performance.

Installing ductwork and fans. Maximize airflow by making ductwork runs as short and straight as you can, with as few elbows and fit-

tings as possible. To keep the ductwork simple, I like to make the plumbing wall 2x8, stack the baths, and serve both baths with one 6-inch thinwall sewer and drain PVC duct run up through the plumbing wall. I usually use PVC instead of galvanized duct because it goes in quickly, seals easily with PVC cement, and won't rust if bathroom moisture condenses inside. The PVC hangs easily from joists or other framing with metal straps placed at roughly 10-foot intervals. Some installers may prefer to use regular galvanized hvac ductwork for its familiarity. (If you do this, make sure to tape all

seams, transverse and longitudinal, with tape meeting UL 181A-P requirements; I like Nashua 324A, available from Grainger.) I often use both rectangular and round duct, joining them with transitional galvanized boots readily available at hvac suppliers. The schematic drawing (Figure A) shows such a system.

I recently came across a product that looks promising: galvanized oval ductwork made by Southwark Metal (1600 Washington Ave., Philadelphia, PA 19146; 800/523-1052). It comes in what the company calls 5-inch, 6-inch, and 7-inch sizes; these are basically what you'd

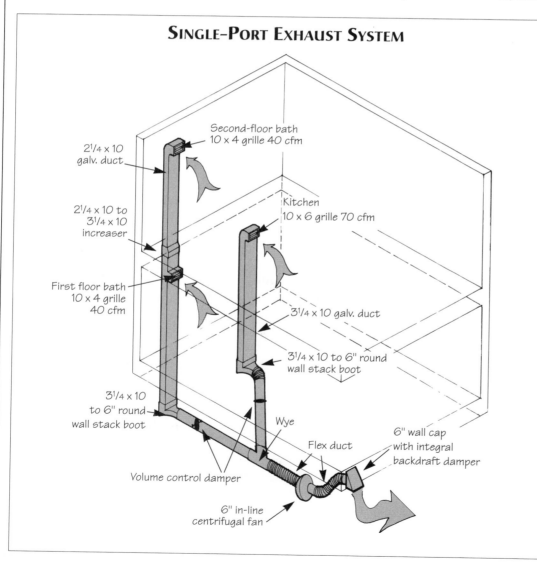

SINGLE-PORT EXHAUST SYSTEM

Second-floor bath
10 x 4 grille 40 cfm

2¼ x 10
galv. duct

2¼ x 10 to
3¼ x 10
increaser

Kitchen
10 x 6 grille 70 cfm

First floor bath
10 x 4 grille
40 cfm

3¼ x 10 galv. duct

3¼ x 10 to 6" round
wall stack boot

3¼ x 10
to 6" round
wall stack boot

Wye

6" wall cap
with integral
backdraft damper

Flex duct

Volume control damper

6" in-line
centrifugal fan

Figure A. In a single-port ducted exhaust system, a single rectangular duct exhausts the stacked baths; a boot at the bottom of its vertical run makes the transition from rectangular to 6-inch round duct. A separate, larger duct exhausts the kitchen. Both runs of duct have volume control dampers for fine-tuning the system after installation.

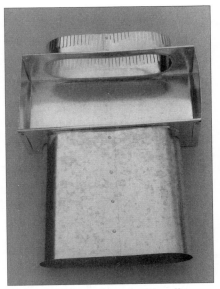

Figure B. This stackhead with collar, made by Southwark, allows you to vent stacked baths with a single duct run.

Figure C. Putting four to six feet of flexible duct on either side of the in-line fan minimizes fan noise and can help reduce sharp bends in the exhaust line.

get if you slightly flattened round ductwork of those same dimensions to fit them into a 2x4 wall. This flattening somewhat reduces the cross section and flow capacity.

The company also makes fittings that make putting a ductwork system together easier. Their No. 150 stackhead with collar, for instance, enables you to easily vent two stacked baths with one riser (Figure B). For faster assembly, the ductwork comes in 100-inch lengths (as opposed to the 30-inch lengths common in rectangular ductwork).

There are two basic options to mounting the fan: You can attach it to plywood lagged to a concrete wall; or you can suspend it from framing, with ductwork runs on either side (Figure C). I usually do the latter. The important thing is to isolate the fan's vibration from the building's structure and the ductwork.

Rubber boots help reduce vibration and noise when attaching PVC pipe to fan housings. They are available from major suppliers, and come in sizes that let you step up or down from one duct diameter to another. They attach with standard hose clamps.

Transmitted fan noise can be a problem in very short duct runs. In these situations I like to use 4 to 6 feet of insulated flexible duct — called "flex duct" — on either side of the fan. This really quiets a system down. Be careful to hang flex duct so that it doesn't have any kinks, which drastically reduce airflow.

If you use flex duct, you might want to opt for a fan that has hanging brackets attached; this will make it easier to hang the fan. But you can still use one of the round, in-line centrifugal fans (such as a Rosenberg or Fantech), attaching the fan to the joists with plastic or rubber straps.

Sizing ductwork. Size the ductwork according to the airflow it will carry. The table at left shows my rules of thumb for ductwork as well as for stale air grilles.

If you have trouble deciding between two sizes, use the larger one, as it will permit higher airflow. If your duct runs are long (over 40 feet or so), have more than two turns in them, or number more than three, it might be worthwhile to hire an engineer or systems designer to make sure everything is sized correctly. — M.R.

SIZING DUCTS AND GRILLES

Expected Airflow	Less than 50 cfm	50-100 cfm	100-150 cfm
Duct Type			
Round PVC or metal	4-5 in.	6 in.	7 in.
Round flex duct	5 in.	6-7 in.	8 in.
Rectangular metal	$2^{1}/_4$ x 10 in.	$3^{1}/_4$ x 10 in.	$3^{1}/_4$ x 14 in.
Southwark oval	5 in.	7 in.	N/A
Grille Type			
Rectangular	10 x 4 in.	10 x 6 in.	14 x 6 in.
Round	6 in.	6 in.	8 in.

about $225. Using the range hood as the whole-house ventilator has the advantage that the kitchen is the best location to use if only one exhaust pickup is provided. You should still have a bath fan in the bathroom for spot ventilation.

If you use an upgraded bath fan for the whole-house fan, use one that has the capacity you need (100 to 200 cfm, at 0.3 inch of water, depending on house size). Typical upgraded bath fans, costing about $80 to $100, are the Nutone QT series (NuTone Inc., Cincinnati, OH; 888/336-3948; www.nutone.com), the Broan Lo-

Sone fans, and the Penn Zephyr series (PennBarry; Richardson, TX; 972-497-0417; www.pennbarry.com). To ventilate the whole house, the bathroom door must be undercut by at least one inch to allow the fan to draw air from the rest of the house. If there is more than one bath, put the whole-house fan in the one nearest the kitchen.

Single-Port, In-Line Systems

The next step up in cost and performance is a central, single-port, in-line centrifugal fan. This will cost about $125 for the fan and another $150 to $400 for the ductwork and grilles. This is my preferred choice in the typical three-bedroom, two-bath home. Such a system can effectively ventilate houses up to around 3,500 square feet, provided the ductwork runs aren't too long or convoluted (see "Ductwork and Fan Installation," previous page). The housings of these centrifugal fans, which are manufactured by companies including Kanalflakt (Sarasota, FL; 888/359-3267; www.kanalflakt-us.com) and Fantech (Sarasota, FL; 800/747-1762; www.fantech.net) mount easily in line with round ducts (typically 6-inch-diameter, although sizes are available to fit duct diameters from 4 to 16 inches).

In these systems, the single fan is hung from joists in the basement (Figure 22), crawlspace, or (as a last resort) attic. The fan is fed by a single duct into which are channeled stale air ducts from the kitchen, all baths, the laundry, and any other odor or moisture producing rooms. The fan pulls exhaust air from these rooms and ejects it through a wall terminal equipped with a backdraft damper. I avoid attic locations whenever possible, because the chimney effect sends warm house air up the ducts, and also because frost may form in the frigid attic ductwork.

This single remote fan replaces any individual bath fans, but does not replace the kitchen range hood, which is still needed. Its principal advantage over the range hood or upgraded bath fan is that the remote mounting results in a quieter system, and one fan can serve multiple bathrooms. If the fan is adequately oversized, it can also handle a bath or laundry added later. The only additional cost would be for ductwork and a grille.

These systems, along with through-the-wall vents or other fresh-air intake, can provide integrated, controlled whole-house ventilation for moderately sized houses — say, 1,500 to 3,500 square feet. They require

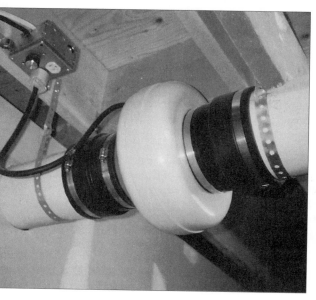

Figure 22. This single-port in-line fan, made by Fantech, is quiet, fairly inexpensive, and powerful enough to exhaust most three-bedroom, two-bathroom houses. The rubber boots on either side dampen the fan noise; the fan is light enough that simple metal straps easily support it from the joists.

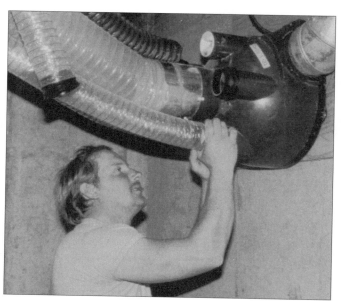

Figure 23. This Aldes multiport fan is lagged to concrete. Large flexible ducting completes the kitchen run; the smaller ones come from baths. The galvanized duct is the exhaust to outdoors. Such systems, which can exhaust several rooms, can also be suspended by wire in either attic or basement installations.

sound planning and some running around to collect materials and components. But since the materials are fairly inexpensive as long as the ductwork is not too complex, the installed cost is usually lower than the third option, a multiport exhaust fan package complete from the manufacturer.

Central, Multiport Systems

These fan systems can be mounted in the basement, crawlspace, or attic. The multiple stale air connections typically include a 6-inch connection for the kitchen and 3-inch or 4-inch ones for the baths and laundry (Figure 23). Most have two-speed fans and integrally mounted controls. Often the low speed is continuous or timer-controlled, and the high speed is an occupant-selected boost to clear the kitchen or bath. American Aldes, Fantech, and Therma-Stor Products all sell complete systems, including fans, controls, some ductwork, grilles, and wall jacks.

The fans alone are $200 to $300; complete systems start at around $500 (materials only). You pay more for one of these systems, but if you want to save the time of rounding up separate components, want to have the assurance of manufacturer support, or need to vent more than three or four spaces, it may be your best option.

Maintaining Control

A ventilation system's controls should be readily accessible and easily understood. Multiport systems come with their own controls, some with on-demand switches as well as 24-hour or even seven-day timers, so that occupants can coordinate ventilation rates with the house's use.

For range, bath, and single-port ducted systems, I usually recommend, at minimum, variable speed controls with manual on-off switches. Range fans can have these on the unit, since the kitchen is centrally located, but bath or remote ducted fans should have controls mounted in a central location. For added flexibility, you can wire any of these controls to a 24-hour or seven-day automatic timer. The timer will provide regular intervals of venting which can be overridden by the manual on-off switch.

Finally, you should provide each bathroom with a 15- or 30-minute crank timer or time delay switch. This timer should be wired in parallel to the central control so the bathroom's occupant can select ventilation as needed.

Most of these control devices, as well as many of the fans and accessories, can be obtained from W.W. Grainger (Portland, OR; 888/361-8649; www.grainger.com).

You can also control ventilation systems automatically with a dehumidistat (instead of a timer). In theory, this is an excellent way to control ventilation, except in very dry regions, where the ventilation will seldom come on. But dehumidistats have fallen somewhat into disfavor because field results show that few people understand how to use a dehumidistat or what a desirable humidity level is (usually around 40%), and so use them incorrectly.

Finally, I like to label all controls clearly and provide for the owner a "user's manual" that explains the operation of the system and the function and importance of the various components.

Operating Costs

Operating costs for these systems consist of fan operating costs of about $7 to $20 per year, plus the cost of heating the fresh air intake. The added heating load (compared to an unventilated tight house) is surprisingly low, about $20 to $100 per year for a 1,500- to 2,500-square-foot house, depending on fuel costs.

A Note on Backdrafting

Powerful exhaust-only ventilation systems can reverse the flow of combustion gases in chimneys, creating a potentially lethal hazard. For this reason, I insist that any fuel-burning appliances be sealed combustion models, which have their own air intake and exhaust systems. This completely decouples the combustion process from the house air pressure levels and prevents backdrafting.

By Marc Rosenbaum, P.E., a designer and engineer of solar and low-energy-use homes in Meriden, N.H.

FLUE AND CHIMNEY SAFETY

Every remodeler will eventually be asked, "Can we use this chimney?" Obviously, if the exterior masonry is cracked, bricks are loose, and mortar is falling from the joints, you have to assess the integrity of the chimney structure. But usually evaluating an old chimney comes down to evaluating the flue, and matching a new liner with the combustion appliances you will hook up to it. The following information will help you make the right choices.

Avoid Tile Liners

If an old chimney has a liner, it will most likely be clay tile. Most codes allow tile liners for use with virtually all appliances. But code assumes proper installation, and in my experience, that's a bad assumption. In the thousands of chimneys I have inspected or taken apart, I have never found a chimney (not one!) in which the tile liner was properly installed.

The biggest problem is that masons always cement the tiles into

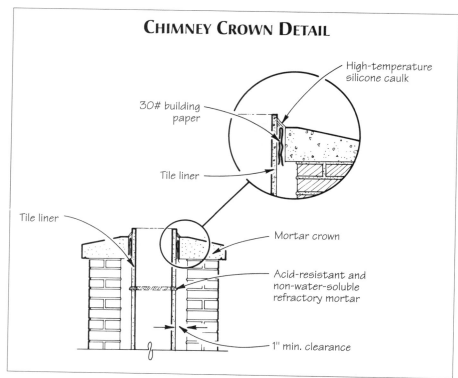

CHIMNEY CROWN DETAIL

High-temperature silicone caulk

30# building paper

Tile liner

Tile liner

Mortar crown

Acid-resistant and non-water-soluble refractory mortar

1" min. clearance

Figure 24. A proper crown installation requires a bond-breaker such as 30# felt between the tile and the crown. After the mortar crown has set up, cut back the building paper just below the surface of the concrete and apply a bead of high-temperature silicone caulk. This creates a slip joint, which allows the chimney to expand upward when it is hot.

place, usually by grouting around them at the bottom and top of the chimney. Sometimes the space around the entire length of the liner is filled with mortar. This prevents the liner from moving freely as it expands and contracts with normal use.

Tile expansion. Tile expands a lot when it gets hot. I have seen tile liners that have expanded 4 to 5 inches upward when heated by a chimney fire. An inch or two is not unusual under normal conditions. This movement is particularly noticeable at the crown, which cracks almost as soon as it is installed because the liner pushes up when it gets hot. A chimney crown must have a bond-breaker between the flue and mortar (Figure 24).

Corrosion. Even when installed correctly, there's ample evidence that tile does not perform well. Tile is very susceptible to corrosion from moisture and other compounds in flue gases. If the chimney gets cool enough, the vapor

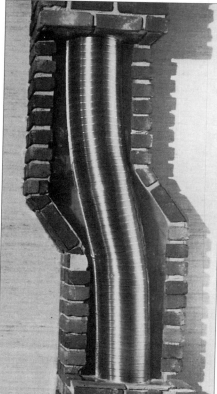

Figure 25. Flexible stainless-steel pipe is a good choice for lining an old masonry chimney (far left). It comes in several alloys to match different fuel types, and it easily installs in any chimney configuration, even one with an offset (left).

Z-Flex

condenses on the inside of the chimney as a very acidic solution. Consequently, most codes require acid- and water-resistant refractory cement in tile joints. Yet this is rarely done in new chimneys, and was never done in older chimneys. The acidic water rapidly eats away the tile joints, exposing the unglazed ends of the clay tile and the masonry of the chimney, which will then rapidly degrade.

If there is enough moisture, it will be absorbed into the masonry. At excess levels, it can cause water staining and paint blistering inside the house. When this problem begins to show up, most people think they have a roof leak, but no amount of tar slapped over the chimney flashing will cure the problem.

More typically, the moisture absorbed by the tile and masonry freezes, causing the tile to break up and collapse inside the chimney. Sometimes the masonry of the outer chimney will also crack. If freezing occurs only rarely, it can take years for problems to appear. In northern climates, however, problems can surface very quickly.

Code exception. To meet code, every lining material *except clay tile* must have a UL 1777 listing. Tile has been grandfathered in, even though it failed heat shock resistance and heat transfer tests conducted by the National Bureau of Standards in 1949. In tests similar to those required for the UL standards, 21 masonry chimneys were subjected to 200 test procedures using coal, wood, and gas fuels. After the fires, examination showed that all the tiles were cracked, a few were badly broken, but all remained in place. Also, all the chimney walls were cracked, and in 24 cases, the wooden test structure caught fire. I have found no evidence to show that clay tiles are any better now than they were then.

Hopefully, you get the idea that tile is not a good choice for a chim-ney liner. But if you must use tile liner, try to limit its use to fireplaces or oil-burning appliances. Gas causes too much corrosion (see "Match the Liner to the Appliance," next page). Make sure the chimney is inspected by a chimney expert before installing the appliance. To find one, look in the yellow pages under "Chimneys, Cleaning and Repair." In most parts of the country you will find someone who offers *Chim-Scan* inspections. A Chim-Scan is a video camera that can be moved up and down inside the chimney, plus a monitor to view what the camera sees. With this instrument, an inspector can literally see if the chimney is safe to use. If the tile liner is not safe, it should be removed and a new, better liner installed.

Stainless-Steel Liners

Stainless-steel pipe is a much better choice than tile for a chimney liner. Stainless-steel liner is available in almost any size or shape, and in either flexible (Figure 25) or rigid form. Stainless steel is made in many types, depending on the alloys used, and the type must be matched with the intended use (see table, below).

All stainless-steel liners require insulation, which reduces creosote buildup and condensation by keeping flue gases warm (Figure 26). In addition, every liner, regardless of the material, requires a cap to meet code. The cap keeps out rain and snow, and reduces the chance of downdrafts from wind and low pressure, which can block the draft. However, many installers do not include a cap in their bids. Do not accept a bid without one.

Insulation critical. The most common installation problems I have found with stainless-steel liners relate to insulation systems. The type of insulation and how it should be applied is specified in each liner manufacturer's manual. Most liner insulation comes in foil-faced sleeves that are secured by a stainless-steel mesh. Using an insulation system approved by one manufacturer with liner pipe produced by another violates the UL listing and may be unsafe. And under no circumstances should a loose insulation be poured into the chimney around the liner pipe. I have found vermiculite, perlite, fiberglass, and even cellulose. None of these is approved for use by any manufacturer, and all can create a dangerous chimney.

All masonry absorbs water when it rains or snows. If loose-fill insulation fills the cavity between the chimney and flue, water is transferred through the insulation from the masonry to the hot flue pipe, creating steam. I have seen chimneys literally hopping up and down on the roof, "burping" steam with each

STAINLESS-STEEL LINER TYPES

Combustion Appliance	Stainless-Steel Liner
Wood	Type 304
Pellet	Type 304
Coal	Type 316 or 321
Oil (noncondensing)	Type 304
Mid-efficiency gas (noncondensing)	Al 29-4C

Note: Do not use stainless-steel liners with any condensing gas appliance. Use only high-temperature plastic vent.

MATCH THE LINER TO THE APPLIANCE

Different residential appliances have varying flue requirements, both in size and material. Here's a look at the common types, starting with fireplaces.

Fireplaces

A properly-sized fireplace flue will go a long way towards assuring that the new fireplace will draw well and not leak smoke into the home. The size (cross-sectional area) of the flue and its height above the damper determine the size of the fireplace opening. For a conventional style fireplace (one in which the opening is wider than it is high), follow the sizing rules shown in the chart below. If you are considering a Rumford fireplace, the flue size should be even larger, as shown.

Gas Appliances

Gas-burning appliances vary widely in their venting needs, depending on how efficiently they produce heat. Old-style furnaces (less than 78% AFUE) send so much heat up the flue that there is rarely a problem, because the exhaust gases stay hot until they are safely past the flue cap. But as furnaces have improved, more heat goes into the house and less goes up the flue. If the flue gases cool below about 130°F before they leave the flue, the water vapor that is a natural product of combustion will condense in the flue.

High-efficiency furnaces. These run at 83% to 97% AFUE and always condense. They should never be hooked up to a conventional chimney. Instead they must be direct-vented through plastic pipe. These vents must have a drain line to carry the acidic condensate to a floor drain.

Mid-efficiency furnaces. Like most of the high-efficiency models, any mid-efficiency (78% to 83% AFUE) boiler or furnace must have a fan-induced draft to drive the cooler combustion gases up the vent. These also have a tendency to condense and may require high-temperature plastic vents. Follow the manufacturer's recommendations closely.

This is not to say that furnaces designated "noncondensing" can't cause condensation in the chimney. In fact, damage from condensation is the most common problem I see in chimneys with mid-efficiency furnaces connected to them. If you add a new gas furnace to an existing tile flue, you're likely to see flue damage within a couple of years.

Proper vent sizing is the most important way to ensure that combustion gases stay warm. If the vent is too big, the combustion gases won't be able to warm the large column of cold air in the flue and will condense immediately. Familiarize yourself with the new sizing tables in the National Fuel Gas Code (available for $42 from the American Gas Association, Washington, DC; 202/824-7000; www.aga.org, or the National Fire Protection Association, Quincy, MA; 617/770-3000; www.nfpa.org). This code, which is referenced as NFPA 54 ANSI Z223.1, includes new vent

FLUE SIZING FOR FIREPLACES

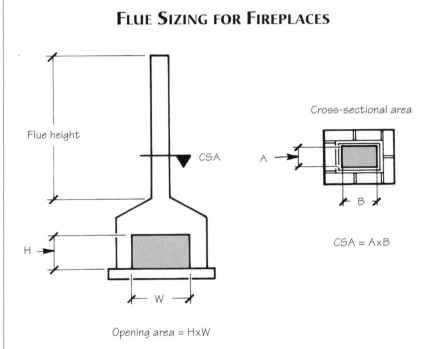

	Flue height		
	11 to 15 ft.	**15 to 25 ft.**	**25 ft. or more**
Conventional fireplace	CSA = $1/10$ opening area	CSA = $1/12$ opening area	CSA = $1/14$ opening area
Rumford fireplace	CSA = $1/8$ opening area	CSA = $1/10$ opening area	CSA = $1/12$ opening area

In determining the size of a fireplace flue, the cross-sectional area (CSA) of the flue must be proportional to the area of the fireplace opening. The proportion varies with flue height. Note that the proportions differ for Rumford fireplaces.

sizing tables. To make sense of these in "real world" vent configurations, get a copy of Simpson DuraVent's Sizing Handbook (see "Sources of Supply" at the end of this chapter).

If your client has an outside chimney, lives in a very cold climate, or heats the house only intermittently, the chances are high that the gases from a natural-draft appliance will condense. Where the possibility of condensation exists, use Al 20-4C stainless steel or one of the cementitious liners. Be aware, however, that recent evidence indicates that even A1 20-4C may not resist corrosion well if the furnace draws chlorine vapor in its combustion air (as may occur if the laundry area is near the furnace). The chlorine and water vapor produce hydrochloric acid, so even the slightest wetting of the flue liner leads quickly to corrosion.

Oil Appliances

In general, oil-fired appliances have fewer flue problems, because flue temperatures are higher and the exhaust gases contain less water vapor. Type 304 stainless steel is suitable for noncondensing oil-fired appliances. Nevertheless, the safest liner choice is A1 20-4C stainless steel or one of the cementitious liners. Oil soot contains sulfur, which combines with water to make highly corrosive sulfuric acid. To avoid this, do not vent a gas water heater into the same flue with an oil-fired furnace. Also have the chimney cleaned before hooking up a new gas appliance to a flue that used to vent an oil-fired appliance. Even if you stick with oil, the chimney should be inspected and cleaned yearly.

Solid-Fuel Appliances

Solid-fuel appliances include wood, coal, and pellet-burning stoves and furnaces.

Wood. Any cementitious liner or Type 304 stainless steel is suitable for use with wood or pellet fuels. However, the flue must be cleaned regularly.

Most wood furnaces regulate heat output by damping down the fire. This causes inefficient combustion, which creates a lot of creosote in the chimney flue, particularly if the flue is too large. A heavy creosote accumulation in a flue is a significant fire hazard. The chimney should be cleaned to remove this creosote whenever the deposits inside the flue reach 1/4 inch in thickness. Since this amount can form in a few weeks (or sometimes in a few days), any homeowner planning to use a wood furnace should be prepared to inspect and clean the chimney often. If the chimney is not cleaned, the accumulating creosote will eventually cause a chimney fire.

Wood stove flue requirements are similar to those for wood furnaces. Wood stoves are the most common type of heating appliance I see in my area and they have the most problems, chiefly because the draft required for combustion is directly regulated by the owner.

In general, wood should always be burned in a flaming fire, not a smoldering fire. If more than a few wisps of smoke are visible coming out of the chimney, wood heat is being wasted. If less heat is required, the owner should put less wood in the stove instead of reducing the draft.

Pellet. In some areas, pellets are the cheapest fuel available on a heat output basis. Pellet fuels look like feed-grain pellets and are produced with similar equipment. They are made from various organic materials, usually considered waste, that are high in cellulose. These materials include lumber mill trimmings and sawdust, used cardboard, corn cobs, and shells from pecans and walnuts. Pellet furnaces require a small flue, usually 4 to 6 inches in diameter. Combustion residue in the flue consists of a fine noncombustible ash, which accumulates quite slowly.

Coal. Unless you go with a cementitious liner, Type 316 or 321 stainless steel is required for coal. Coal combustion produces considerable ash and some of it collects inside the flue. This ash has a lot of sulfur in it and is hydroscopic, drawing moisture out of the air when the furnace is not operating. This cre-

ates sulfuric acid, which attacks the mortar joints between flue tiles and will rapidly destroy the vent pipe on a furnace as it sits idle for the summer in a damp basement.

Coal stoves, in common with coal furnaces, require very precise draft regulation to operate properly. But stoves tend to have more draft problems because they are usually not installed by professionals. Coal stoves require a barometric damper in the vent pipe; this damper must be adjusted with a draft gauge when the stove is operating. In my experience this is usually not done, and creates incomplete combustion with its attendant problems.

Combining Appliances

The National Fuel Gas Code prohibits mixing the combustion gases from any solid-fuel appliance with any gas appliance. If a client wants to hook up a wood stove to a chimney that vents a gas furnace, for example, each appliance should have its own properly-sized flue. If you need two flues, say for a wood stove and a gas furnace, and the existing chimney is not large enough for both, the safest choice may be to replace the furnace with a direct-vented model. Then line the chimney to accommodate the wood stove.

The code does allow mixing gases from oil and gas appliances in the same flue, provided the flue is sized and connected properly. But while this practice is legal, I don't think it's wise. By introducing the "wet" gases from a gas-burning water heater into a flue that vents an oil furnace, for example, you are increasing the risk of creating a highly-acidic condensation that will degrade a chimney rapidly.

In general, I don't recommend combining the combustion gases from two different fuels in one flue. However, if you must, mixing oil and wood is the least likely to cause problems. And, of course, it's all right to vent the gases from like fuels — a gas water heater and a gas furnace, for example — provided the flue is big enough to handle both appliances. — *P.S.*

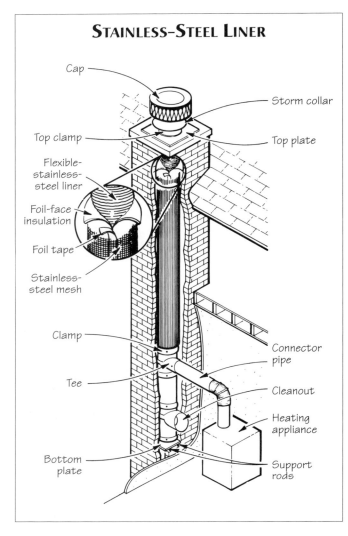

STAINLESS-STEEL LINER

Cap
Storm collar
Top clamp
Top plate
Flexible-stainless-steel liner
Foil-face insulation
Foil tape
Stainless-steel mesh
Clamp
Tee
Bottom plate
Connector pipe
Cleanout
Heating appliance
Support rods

Figure 26. All stainless-steel chimney liners must have insulation to meet UL standards. The insulation jacket prevents flue gases from condensing inside the flue. Also, every liner, regardless of the material it is made from, must have a cap to meet code. The cap keeps out rain and snow and reduces the chance of downdrafts that can block the draft.

Figure 27. A Class A chimney is suitable for all fuel types, but it works better as a free-standing chimney than as a liner for an existing masonry chimney. The sections can be installed only in a straight chimney, and are extremely heavy, requiring a power winch and cable to lower them into place.

hop, during normal operation of a wood stove. If a chimney fire occurs in this situation, the release of steam can be explosive.

If properly installed, however, a tested and listed liner can usually contain a chimney fire. But after the fire the liner must be replaced, even if it looks undamaged. Most fire codes require this, and for good reasons. When stainless steel is overheated (generally above 800°F to 900°F), it loses its corrosion-resistance, and can develop holes after only a few months of continued use. Overheated liner pipe can also become very brittle. I have seen pieces of 24-gauge stainless steel that you could snap as easily as a potato chip.

Class A and B Chimneys

Aluminum and galvanized-steel liners — sometimes referred to as factory-built chimneys — are sometimes used as liners, but are more appropriate for free-standing chimneys or vents inside a wooden chase.

Class A chimneys — often referred to in the field by the trade-name *Metalbestos* — can be used with all fuels (Figure 27). These are made in two types: solid-pack-insulated double-wall pipe and air-insulated triple-wall pipe. The chief problem in using factory-built chimney sections as liners is that the old chimney is usually not large enough to allow for their installation. Also, you can use these sections only in a straight chimney, and they are extremely heavy — you'll need a power winch and cable to lower one into a chimney. For this reason, the installed cost of a retrofit job is often much higher than that of an insulated stainless-steel liner.

Class B (double-wall air-insulated) chimneys — commonly called *B-vent* — are designed for venting noncondensing gas appliances only. Typically, these have an aluminum liner inside a galvanized steel sleeve. Although usually installed inside a wooden chase, this type of vent can be installed as a liner in a masonry chimney if space allows. B-vent is much lighter than a Class A chimney, and so is much easier to install.

No factory-built chimney has a zero-clearance listing, so all Class A and Class B chimneys must be installed with the clearances specified by the manufacturer. Most of the builder installations I see violate these clearances.

Cast Liners

From my experience, cementitious, cast-in-place liners are the best choice for all fuels. In general, the insulation properties and moisture resistance of these lining systems are superior. This means they are more resistant to heat shock and condensation problems and therefore offer the longest expected lifetimes. They are often the most expensive option, but not by a lot. Material costs vary by the amount of cement required. An 8x8 chimney with a 6-inch flue, for example, doesn't require a lot of cement, and so can be a less expensive option than an insulated stainless-steel liner, depending on conditions.

The most common brand names are Ahrens, Golden/Flue, National Supaflu, and Solid/Flue (see "Sources of Supply" at the end of the chapter). All of these products, except Ahrens, are installed in a similar manner (Figure 28). A rubber "tube form" is inserted and centered in the chimney, then inflated to the diameter of the flue required by the appliance being installed. A "gate form" is positioned in the thimble opening (where the vent pipe connects), then the liner material is mixed and pumped into the chimney. In general, these liner materials should not be bucketed and dumped in the chimney. Bucketing is slow and can cause

cold joints in the concrete and consequent damage to the liner.

Ahrens uses a different installation method. A vibrating steel bell of the correct flue size is suspended in the chimney. Then a very stiff liner mix is dumped into the chimney while the bell is winched to the top. This vibrating bell compacts the mix and forms the flue opening.

Look for UL rating. Most cast liners are tested and UL-listed. The exception is Insulcrete. If you run across someone who installs this brand, be warned that this product is not tested and listed.

To pass the test for a UL 1777 listing, a liner must survive a series of

high-temperature burns (with flue gas temperatures ranging from 1,000°F to 2,100°F). The test procedures monitor the liner for resistance to *heat shock damage* and *resistance to heat transfer* (see "Common Chimney Terms," next page) to make sure that liners can withstand even the worst chimney fire without causing a fire in the building. All listed products have passed these tests with a 1-inch air space around the chimney. However, chimney liner installers wanted the products to be tested to zero-clearance standards, since few chimneys outside the laboratory have an air space around them. UL devised an

CAST LINER INSTALLATION

Figure 28. Starting with an unlined chimney (A), a rubber tube form is inflated with air, then centered between the chimney walls. Next, the liner material is mixed and pumped into the chimney (B). After the mix sets up, the tube is deflated and removed, creating a flue (C). Depending on the fuel to be burned by the appliance, the flue may have to be sealed.

optional, second series of tests, but only Solid/Flue passed the original tests for a zero-clearance listing. Manufacturers then lobbied UL to reduce the burn times. Now all the cast liners have a zero-clearance listing.

Conflicting requirements. To pass the tests, cast liners must have a low coefficient of expansion (to prevent heat shock that will crack the material when heated). But they must also insulate well (to prevent heat transfer to the structure) and be lightweight (so the wet mix will not push the chimney outward when it's installed). These requirements call for a low-density cement with a lightweight, insulating aggregate. But

resistance to abrasion, high strength, and low water-absorption are also required, and for these you really need a heavy, dense cement.

Different manufacturers solve these conflicting requirements in different ways. To meet the heat transfer requirements, different brands require various minimum thicknesses. For the 1-inch clearance requirement, Solid/Flue requires only 3/4 inch of material. The other brands require 1 inch to meet the revised UL 1777 zero-clearance standard. Because of the testing expense, Ahrens and Solid/Flue have not been tested to the new standard and still require 1 1/2 inches for a zero-clearance listing.

These differences in thickness may seem small, but they can be very important. Suppose the furnace you need to connect has a 7-inch-diameter outlet pipe. The lined flue in this case would need to be 7 inches in diameter, too. If the existing brick chimney has a typical interior dimension of 8 1/2 x 12 1/2 inches, only Solid/Flue could line this chimney and meet code. (Ahrens could do it too, if an oval bell 5 1/2 x 9 1/2 inches were available, but to my knowledge the smallest oval bell is larger than that.)

To pass the strength requirements, manufacturers vary the compressive strengths of the concrete mixes. Compressive strengths range from a

COMMON CHIMNEY TERMS

Chimney and flue: The terms "chimney" and "flue" are often used interchangeably, but this is incorrect. A *flue* is a shaft designed to vent the products of combustion from a stove, furnace, or water heater to the outside air. The *chimney* surrounds and supports the flue. Many chimneys have just one flue. But a chimney can have more than one flue, such as a colonial center chimney with flues for several fireplaces, or a wooden condo chimney with several metal chimney flues inside.

Draft, buoyancy, and flue sizing: The tendency of hot air to rise is called the *buoyancy* of air. In a flue, hot air venting from the furnace is confined by the flue and "floats" upward, allowing the surrounding air to flow into the furnace. This is what we know as *draft*.

From this you can see the importance of proper *flue sizing*. If a small amount of hot gas venting from a furnace mixes with a large amount of cool air in an oversized flue, the gas will cool rapidly and reduce the draft. If the flue gas cools to the temperature of the surrounding air, the draft stops altogether.

Heat shock: This occurs when a cold liner undergoes a rapid change in temperature. When outside temperatures are below freezing, any part of the chimney not enclosed by the house will be frozen, too. So just building a rip-roaring fire in the fireplace can crack a liner. Tile, which is not UL listed for resistance to heat shock, is particularly susceptible.

Heat transfer: This is simply the insulation value of the liner material, and is important since virtually all old houses, and some new ones, have framing that touches the chimney. Therefore it is very important that the liner you choose has passed the UL zero-clearance test, and even more important that the liner is installed according to the manufacturer's instructions.

Liner: This term is often used interchangeably with "flue." This is okay, though the term *liner*, when correctly used, refers to the material that the flue is made of, while "flue" denotes the space inside the liner. An *unlined chimney* is a chimney without a flue, which is not

suitable for any use. Using an unlined chimney to vent any type of combustion appliance is a violation of all fire codes. But just because a chimney has a liner does not automatically make it suitable for all uses.

Pyrolization: During a chimney fire, temperatures inside a flue can exceed 2,000°F. This will heat the outside of the chimney to extremely high temperatures, causing combustibles such as framing or lath that touch the chimney to catch fire. Wood normally combusts at just over 400°F. But if chimney fires have occurred in the past, the combustion point of the surrounding wood can be much lower. Repeatedly heating wood to temperatures near its combustion point causes a chemical change called *pyrolization*. This change can cause the wood to combust at temperatures below 200°F.

Vent: The term *vent* is commonly used to refer to a flue of any type, but in the official language of building codes, it specifically refers to a flue for a gas-burning appliance. — *P.S.*

low of 693 psi for National Supaflu to a high of 2,090 psi for Solid/Flue. A high-strength mix allows you to save an old chimney made with soft bricks and weak mortar joints. A chimney like this may require temporary support while it is being lined, but once lined, the liner material in effect supports the chimney.

Finally, cementitious materials must have good resistance to water absorption. Ahrens requires coating the inside of the cast liner with a sealer before using the flue for any type of fuel. Some of the other brands require a coating only when using gas-burning appliances. All of these coatings must be redone periodically to maintain the service life of the flue — except Solid/Flue, which does not require a coating for any fuel.

New Liners

There are also a few brands of tile liner, usually imported, that are very different from common clay tile. For example, Ahrens produces a ceramic liner called Ceramu-Flue, which can be lowered into a chimney in sections. It seems equivalent in durability to the best of the cast-in-place liners, but can be used only in a straight chimney without any offsets.

Solid/Flue has a similar product on the drawing boards. In general, these products promise to handle much like tile liners, but without all of their attendant problems.

By Peter Scripture, a builder who has specialized in building, repairing, lining, and cleaning chimneys for the last 16 years.

BACKDRAFTING CAUSES AND CURES

If there were universal laws to describe ventilation, the first might be: *Air out equals air in.* This means that all of the air exhausted from fans and chimneys in a house is immediately replaced — somehow. Either it is forced into the house by a fan, or the indoor air pressures drop until outdoor pressures are strong enough to push replacement air through leaks and holes in the structure.

This works fine up to a point. But when indoor negative pressures overcome the natural buoyancy of warm gas in chimney or furnace flues, they can reverse the upward flow of combustion gases and draw them back down into the house. When this happens, you have *backdrafting*: the pressure-induced spillage of exhaust gases into the house's living space.

Backdrafting is a health, safety, and comfort concern. To prevent it you must either build a house without a chimney, or balance all the ventilation systems to prevent indoor-outdoor pressure differentials. In short, houses need to inhale as easily as they exhale.

Tighter Houses
Part of the Problem

Backdrafting has always been a problem. But several recent trends in construction have narrowed the margin of safety for houses with unbalanced ventilation systems.

Tight houses. We're building tighter houses than ever. Tight houses are more prone to backdrafting problems because you can't rely on air leaks to balance sudden surges in "exhalation" from a powerful stovetop, bathroom, or dryer fan. As the shift to tight housing continues, builders will have to counter the backdrafting potential created by airtight construction.

More powerful exhaust fans. Today's more numerous and powerful local exhaust fans also contribute to backdrafting. Downdraft cooktops pose the biggest problem, because their make-up air requirements (the amount of air they draw) are extraordinary. Sometimes it is as much as 1,000 cubic feet per minute (cfm). I've visited many houses where the chimney backdrafts virtually every time the cooktop fan is operated.

I'm also seeing more powerful overhead range hoods. And some

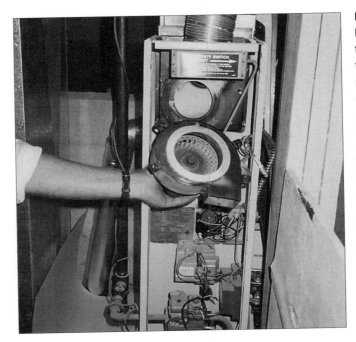

Figure 29. Induced-draft furnaces, such as this one, are not safe from backdrafting as is commonly thought. In this case, because of a misaligned blower gasket (at center) and unsealed flue collar, gases high in carbon monoxide were spilling into the house.

new clothes dryers exhaust at 250 cfm. That's about twice the previous norm! Unless a house is built like a sieve, the make-up air demands of such fans can be met only by a forced make-up air supply.

Exhaust-only ventilation systems. Finally, the increasing reliance upon exhaust-only whole-house ventilation systems poses a backdrafting threat. Until recently, the few whole-house exhaust fans in use were unlikely to exhaust more than half their specified capacity. However, the recent introduction of highly effective exhaust ventilators changed that. In combination with more powerful local exhaust fans and tighter

building envelopes, the backdrafting effect of these whole-house exhaust fans can be deadly.

Gas Furnace Problems

A 1984 survey of hundreds of houses suggested that 10% to 15% experienced furnace spillage at least once per year. Oil-fired systems spilled most frequently, but only for 15 seconds or so at the start-up of each operating cycle. Gas-fired systems spilled less frequently, but often for the entire five or six minutes of the cycle.

Gas furnace spillage. Fortunately, spillage from gas-fired furnaces or water heaters rarely poses a serious health hazard. In tighter houses,

spillage raises humidity and carbon dioxide (CO_2) levels above the norms recommended for indoor air, but seldom above what might be considered a health limit.

Natural gas combustion exhaust can contain nitrogen oxides, such as nitrogen dioxide gas (NO_2), which can damage lungs. Fortunately, NO_2 is unstable and is usually neutralized or diluted before it pollutes living areas. A gas range actually poses a much greater NO_2 pollution risk than a gas furnace, since people will be close to the source and exhaust hoods seldom capture more than 50% of stovetop exhaust.

The biggest spillage concern with natural gas furnaces is carbon monoxide (CO). This is rare but worrisome. A poorly tuned, broken, or dirty gas furnace *can* produce lots of CO (Figure 29). But even poor installation and maintenance won't ordinarily affect air quality unless spillage problems are also present. This is an unusual combination that can be avoided through regular maintenance, such as a furnace tune-up and spillage check every two to five years by qualified service people.

For most homeowners, then, the risk of backdrafting doesn't warrant major investments in elaborate ventilation systems; maintenance and safety tests will usually take care of the problem as long as the house does not get severely depressurized.

To give a little extra piece of mind, you can invest in a gas detector or CO alarm. A "dot" detector installs near likely spillage sites on furnaces or water heaters and changes colors when exposed to hot gases — usually from 138° to 160°F. These require frequent checking to be of any value.

Good CO alarms — either battery-operated, plug-in, or hardwired — are readily available from several manufacturers. These use a loud blare to warn homeowners of

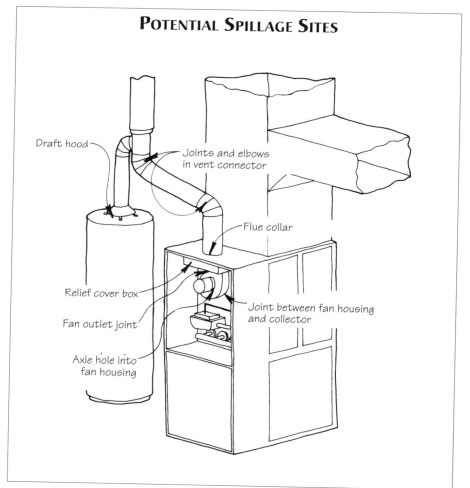

POTENTIAL SPILLAGE SITES

Draft hood

Joints and elbows in vent connector

Flue collar

Relief cover box

Joint between fan housing and collector

Fan outlet joint

Axle hole into fan housing

Figure 30. Even induced-draft furnaces have a surprising number of potential spillage sites. The so-called "spillage switches" on these units will shut off the furnace if the chimney is completely plugged, but they generally fail to detect the backdrafting or spillage common in normal use.

high concentrations of this dangerous gas. Make sure you get units that are certified by UL or the Canadian Gas Associations (see "Sources of Supply" at the end of the chapter).

Gas Furnace Solutions — Good and Bad

Eventually, changes to gas furnace design will probably solve the problem of spillage. So far, however, the more expensive alternatives have been disappointing.

Induced-draft furnaces. Also called ID or mid-efficiency furnaces, these appliances hold some promise. However, because of the way they are typically manufactured and installed, they offer little improvement over natural-draft appliances with regard to backdrafting.

An ID furnace has a little fan in the flue that induces a small draft to overcome the resistance of the more efficient heat exchanger. Theoretically, these furnaces should be able to withstand a normal range of house depressurization — up to about 20 pascals. (A pascal is a unit of pressure equal to $1/250$ of the pressure exerted by a 1-inch-deep column of water. For example, a 20-knot wind exerts about 10 pascals of pressure on the side of a house; on a very cold day, the warm air in your attic pushes through the cracks at about 3 pascals; hot chimneys usually have drafts of 20 to 30 pascals.)

Unfortunately, ID furnaces are not designed to resist the negative pressures found in many new homes. Flue gasses can spill out of leaky B-vents or around the blower housing (Figure 30). Where the furnace shares a common vent with a water heater, as is often the case, gasses will spill out of the water heater's flue pipe. Unless the manufacturer provides proof of increased resistance to negative pressures, it is wise to assume that an ID appliance is just as prone to spillage as a conventional one.

Water heaters are a concern, as well. Induced-draft models have all the same problems as ID furnaces.

Sealed combustion and condensing units. These days, many installers opt for sealed-combustion furnaces. These are virtually immune to spillage problems if properly installed, even with house depressurization as high as 50 pascals.

Sealed-combustion units are a good choice for new homes with down-draft grills or other big exhaust appliances, or for retrofits with chronic backdrafting problems.

Sealed-combustion water heaters are also available, as well as sealed-

---

A SIMPLE CHIMNEY BACKDRAFTING TEST

In general, houses with chimneys or furnace flues should avoid depressurization in excess of five pascals. To measure the amount of depressurization that will occur under "worst case" situations in a given house, follow the checklist below. You will need a "magnahelic" pressure gauge accurate within a low range and with a resolution of one pascal or less. Several companies make such pressure gauges, including Dwyer Instruments (Michigan City, IN; 219/879-8000; www.dwyer-inst.com), which has models of this type starting at $43.

For a more complete description of this test, obtain a draft copy of the Canadian General Standards Board Standard 51.71, available from Canadian General Standards Board (CGSB Sales Center, Hull, Quebec, Canada; 819/956-0425; www.pwgsc.gc.ca/cgsb).

(1) Prepare and calibrate the equipment.

- Turn off all fans.
- Turn off furnace and water heater.
- Close windows and exterior doors.
- Close interior doors leading to perimeter and basement rooms.
- Close fireplaces and wood stoves.
- Set up pressure gauge close to the chimney or flue you are concerned about.
- As per the gauge manufacturer's instructions, extend a hose to a sheltered position outdoors to get a pressure sampling there.
- "Zero" the pressure gauge.
- Observe normal fluctuations in pressure due to wind. If they are greater than two pascals, wait for a calmer period to do the test.

(2) Conduct the test and record pressure drop.

- Operate all exhaust fans (as well as any interlocked supply air systems), one at a time.

- Record level of house depressurization as measured on gauge.
- Operate any other fans that may be imbalanced, such as heat recovery ventilators, furnace blowers, etc.
- Record those levels of house depressurizations.

This will give you the basic depressurization levels you need. If a depressurization exists, you can try to locate the site of any spillage using the following test:

- Operate all the vented combustion appliances one at a time. While you have this depressurization in effect, check for flue gas spillage near the furnace, using either a smoke tube that creates "cool" colored smoke or a CO_2 gas analyzer.
- Return house to condition in which it was found — reset thermostats, turn off hot water taps if running, switch off furnace blowers and exhaust fans, etc.

—S.M.

combustion combo units that supply both hot water and space heating. Either option offers good protection against spillage.

Power venters can be a better option. An alternative in retrofits to installing an induced-draft or sealed-combustion furnace unit is to install a conventional unit and vent it with a "power venter kit." Such a kit lets you vent the furnace through any convenient external wall rather than a vertical chimney flue (Figure 31). For instance, it can be a horizontal "flue" of ductwork that exits a basement wall.

The units cost between $200 and $400 and come as a kit with controls and color-coded wiring included. The average gas fitter can install one without previous training. Two companies make them: Field Controls Company (Kinston, NC; 252/522-3031; www.fieldcontrols.com) and Tjernlund Products Inc. (White Bear Lake, MN; 800/255-4208; www.tjernlund.com). Field makes a unit that mounts outside the house; the external location ensures that any leakage from around the fan housing can't spill indoors.

Backdrafting in Oil Furnaces

The most toxic by-product of oil combustion is sulfur dioxide (SO_2) which, like the NO_2 from gas furnaces, is an acid gas that damages lungs. Fortunately, SO_2, unlike NO_2, carries a strong odor that makes even small quantities easily detected.

To protect against spillage from a conventional oil burner, the burner should be fitted with a "delayed action solenoid valve." This delays the flow of oil to the combustion chamber for about three to six seconds after ignition, giving the airflow within the burner time to set up a draft. This ensures that the oil is burned more completely, which reduces sooting and backdrafting, and also increases efficiency.

Delayed action solenoid valves cost under $100, and the increase in

---

TESTING FOR TIGHTNESS

Despite the growing importance of house airtightness, few builders actually know how tight they are building their houses. Until recently, the building community has tended to rely on subjective estimates of airtightness. Unfortunately, it is impossible to accurately estimate the tightness level of houses by visual inspection alone. And without knowing house airtightness, it is difficult to assess the need for, or to design an effective approach to, ventilation for good indoor air quality.

When discussing these issues, it is important to distinguish between two terms — *airtightness and natural ventilation.* The airtightness of a house is related directly to the cumulative size of all the holes and penetrations in the exterior building envelope. The natural ventilation rate is determined by the forces driving air in or out through the leaks in the envelope.

The easiest way to measure house airtightness is with a diagnostic tool called a blower door. This device consists of a powerful, calibrated fan that is temporarily sealed into an exterior doorway of a house. The fan blows air out of the house to create a slight pressure difference between the inside and outside. House airtightness is determined by the amount of air flow that it takes to maintain a 50 pascal (0.2 inches of water column) depressurization of the house. The tighter the house, the less air you need to exhaust in order to maintain the pressure.

It takes about 20 minutes to set up a blower door and do a test to document the airtightness of the building envelope. An experienced operator can use the blower door to get other important information about a house, such as an estimate of duct leakage or leakage between the living space and an unconditioned attic, as well as the location of air leaks in the building envelope. This information can help you assess the potential for backdrafting caused by exhaust fans.

In addition to knowing the airtightness of the envelope, it's also good to know the natural ventilation rate, because this is what determines how much indoor pollutants are diluted. While it doesn't measure this directly, the blower door test provides us with a measure of the total hole size in the exterior envelope. And that information can be used along with a simple mathematical model to provide useful estimates of the average annual natural infiltration rate of the house. This ventilation estimate can then be compared with published ventilation guidelines to help determine if additional mechanical ventilation may be needed.

— *Gary Nelson, Robert Nevitt, and Gary Anderson*

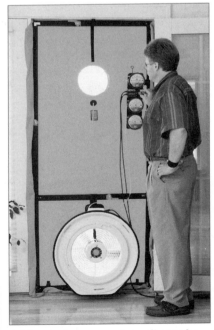

A blower door operator adjusts the fan speed to maintain a house depressurization of 50 pascals.

efficiency will pay for them within a couple of years. The flue pipe should have a high-quality barometric damper that is balanced and lubricated every year. Since even the best dampers leak, you should mount a smoke alarm on the ceiling directly over the damper to give warning if gases do spill for more than a few seconds at start-up.

A better approach is to forsake the conventional oil burner for a *high-pressure* oil burner. A high-pressure oil burner forces combustion air into the combustion chamber under pressure, so that the furnace burns with less excess air. This allows you to have a smaller chimney with less heat loss and higher efficiency. These units also withstand pressure changes up to ten pascals, and this prevents backdrafting and blow-outs within a normal range of chimney pressure fluctuations. They don't cost much more than conventional systems, and they eliminate the need for a barometric damper altogether. They also burn very cleanly. I've checked chimneys on these furnaces four years after installation and found them perfectly clean. Make sure to seal both the furnace or boiler and the flue pipe airtight at all joints.

Fireplaces

Fireplaces number fewer than furnaces, but their backdrafting record is worse. My 1986 field monitoring of fireplaces indicated that virtually every fireplace backdrafts or spills at least once per year, and that the typical unit spills for 1% to 2% of its operating time. This will happen most commonly at start-up and during stoking, and less often as the fire burns down. (This is less true for wood stoves, because their smaller, better-insulated flues are more resistant to pressure-induced spillage.)

Since fireplace spillage contains poisonous gases such as CO and cancer-causing substances such as benzene, backdrafting *always* poses a serious health hazard. CO concentrations in fireplace combustion gases run far above health limits, and they get worse at the end of burn, when backdrafting is most likely. From a rational point of view, the conventional fireplace doesn't belong in a modern home.

Of course, decisions about fireplaces are seldom rational. Since you can't know whether occupants will use a fireplace every day or only on Christmas, you must account for the worst case scenario, which is constant use.

Airtights not the answer. "Airtight" fireplaces — with airtight doors to the indoors and make-up air supplied directly from outdoors to the firebox — sound promising. Unfortunately, these designs depend heavily on the tightness of the fireplace doors, which fireplace manufacturers have yet to make airtight. As a result, when a house is depressurized by an exhaust fan or other force, these fireplaces act essentially as big make-up air ducts: air comes from the outdoor fireplace supply, through the fireplace, and into the house, bringing the toxic combustion gases with it.

Dual air supply even worse. Fireplaces designed to provide both outside and household air to the firebox pose a worse threat. The indoor supply, which is usually a vent beneath or alongside the doors, makes it even easier for the entire unit to act as a make-up air duct when the house is depressurized. These units pose a serious threat in any house that experiences even minor depressurizations.

Gas fireplaces. Note that the newly popular vent-free gas fireplaces effectively have a spillage rate of 100%, far outweighing the occasional spillage from most water heaters or furnaces. The latest versions are protected by an oxygen-depletion switch designed to guard against CO emissions. However, these still emit flue gases into the air, and are therefore banned in Canada and a number of municipalities in the U.S. and do not belong in a modern, tight home.

Many manufacturers now offer sealed-combustion gas fireplaces as an alternative. These are a good choice if house depressurization is a problem.

An alarm for every hearth. Given these hazards, a homeowner who plans to use a fireplace frequently should not only make sure the house has balanced ventilation, but should also install a CO alarm and a smoke alarm in the same room as the fireplace. If the alarms sound frequently, occupants will quickly learn to change their habits, or install a reliable ventilation system such as the one described below. For minor

Figure 31. Add-on power venters can help prevent backdrafting by pulling furnace or water heater exhausts out of the house. The Field Controls model, shown at left, typically vents out a side wall.

backdrafting problems, cracking a window may be a solution.

Testing for and Preventing Backdrafting

With airtight furnaces and fireplaces so elusive, what can you do to prevent backdrafting?

The best approach is to keep ventilation systems balanced and thereby avoid pressure-induced spillage: Design a house that lets fresh air intake match peak forced exhaust, and you'll avoid backdrafting.

When to ventilate. As a rule of thumb, you should provide additional fresh air intake to balance any single exhaust fan that blows more than one-half air change per hour. For example, in a 12,000-cubic-foot house (a 1,500-square-foot house with 8-foot ceilings), a 100-cfm exhaust fan would be the maximum unbalanced exhaust permitted, because such a fan blows 6,000 cubic feet per hour (100 cfm x 60 minutes). You can roughly figure a house's area by multiplying its square footage by 8, assuming the

ceilings are about 8 feet high.

The main problem with this method is that predicting the actual air-flow from exhaust fans is almost as tricky as guessing how tight a house will be. Manufacturers provide air delivery ratings, but actual flows vary depending on how much restriction is created by ducts, grilles, screens, and louvers. We tested all the ventilation devices in 200 houses; the measured air-flows generally ran at about half the ratings. So you can usually figure that an exhaust fan actually moves

EXHAUST FANS AND DEPRESSURIZATION: CRUNCHING THE NUMBERS

Exhaust fans, such as those found in bathrooms and above kitchen ranges, blow air out of the house. This can have the effect of depressurizing the house relative to the outside. Small bath fans — those in the 50- to 75-cfm range — are turned on for short periods of time and generally cause no problems. However, some range hoods — those with 200-cfm or larger blowers — may cause problems.

The level of negative pressure in a house is usually the main factor that causes backdrafting in natural-draft combustion appliances. Studies done for the Canadian Mortgage and Housing Corporation (CMHC) have found that typical natural-draft furnaces, boilers, and water heaters begin to have venting problems if negative pressures exceed about 5 to 7 pascals. (A pascal is a measure of air pressure equal to 0.004 inches of water column as measured by a manometer. A pascal is equal to about .02 pounds per square feet.) Conventional fireplaces were found to start having problems at only 3 pascals. In the summer, we see problems with backdrafting on natural-draft appliances at negative pressures of 3 pascals.

How much negative pressure is caused by exhaust equipment, such as kitchen and bath exhaust fans, depends on the tightness of the envelope and the flow rate of the fan. The graph (opposite) is a useful tool for understanding the relation-

ships between house pressure, tightness, and flow rate. The horizontal axis gives house pressure in cfm$_{50}$, as determined by a blower door. This is the flow rate, in cubic feet per minute, necessary to depressurize the house by a pressure of 50 pascals, and is a common standard for blower door testing. The vertical axis gives exhaust fan flow in cfm. The diagonal lines represent various levels of house depressurization measured in pascals.

Suppose we have a well-insulated new house that has been measured with a blower door to have a cfm$_{50}$ value of 1,200 (including leakage through the code-required combustion air inlet). This is about average for a typical new Minnesota house. We want to know if there might be a problem with the natural-draft gas water heater if we install a downdraft kitchen range fan rated at 350 cfm. We draw a vertical line up from 1,200 cfm$_{50}$ and a horizontal line from 350 cfm on the fan flow scale (in a solid rule on the chart). The diagonal line closest to the intersection of these two lines gives the depressurization level that would be caused by the operation of the downdraft exhaust fan in this particular house. In this case, we get about 8 pascals of depressurization — clearly a problem for the operation of the water heater, according to the work by CMHC. If some interior doors are closed, the part of the house that is open to the exhaust

fan could be depressurized even more.

We can also calculate the size of the fresh air inlet hole that would be necessary to limit depressurization to, say, 5 pascals, a level we might feel comfortable with. Starting at the intersection of the 5 pascal line and the 1,200 cfm$_{50}$ vertical line, draw a horizontal line (in a dotted rule on the chart) over to the fan flow scale. This tells us that at 5 pascals of depressurization, this house would leak at about 260 cfm. Therefore, in order to maintain 5 pascals' depressurization while the exhaust fan is operating, we would have to add 90 cfm of makeup air (350 − 260 = 90).

It turns out that an unrestricted hole between the outside and inside will leak at a rate in cfm approximately equal to the area of the hole in square inches times the square root of the pressure difference (in pascals). So

$$90 = \text{Area of vent} \times \sqrt{5}$$

$$\text{Area of vent} = 90 \div \sqrt{5} = 40 \text{ sq. in.}$$

This means that you would have to cut a 7-inch-diameter hole in the house to provide makeup air for the exhaust fan — hardly a practical solution. A better solution is to install a draft-assist fan on the water heater.

By Gary Nelson, Robert Nevitt, and Gary Anderson

about half its advertised rate.

Combined use of two or more smaller exhaust fans can cause problems. For example, a range hood, bathroom fan, and clothes dryer operating at the same time can produce up to 285 cfm in exhaust and a depressurization of 5 pascals or more. But these events are infrequent and of short duration, so they can usually be tolerated.

The "Chimney Backdraft Test." After construction you can run a more exact test to see if balanced ventilation is required. This test is described in "A Simple Chimney Backdrafting Test" (page 205). It takes only a few minutes and gives you hard information on which to base your ventilation decisions.

Supplying More Air

How do you meet the need for increased air supply? If you choose a balanced ventilation system such as a heat recovery ventilator instead of traditional exhaust fans, you may never have a depressurization prob-

lem. However, these systems are expensive to install and not really designed to provide makeup air, when needed.

Another option is to interlock an air supply fan to any exhaust fan(s) likely to depressurize the house so that whenever the exhaust fan comes on, the supply fan is switched on. The Air In-Forcer from Tjernlund or A Fan in a Can from Field Controls are packaged systems which accomplish this.

A simpler variation is to interlock the exhaust fan(s) with the thermo-

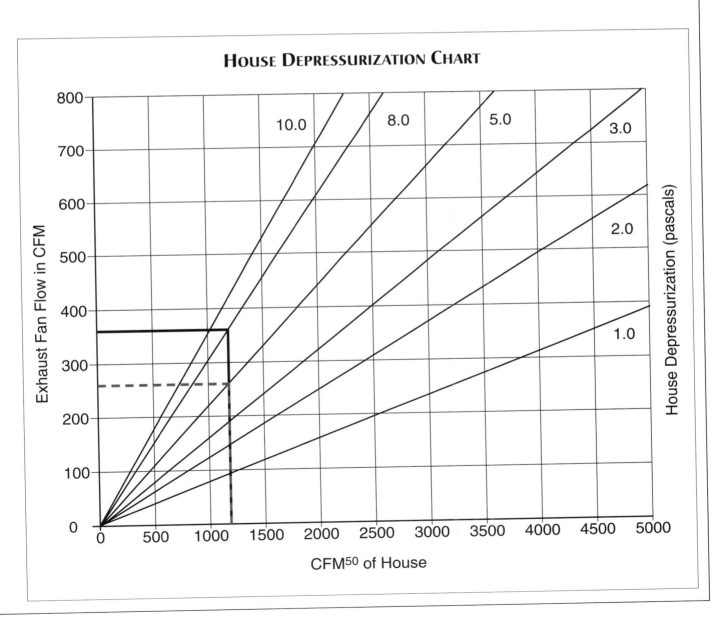

HOUSE DEPRESSURIZATION CHART

Exhaust Fan Flow in CFM (vertical axis): 0, 100, 200, 300, 400, 500, 600, 700, 800

CFM^{50} of House (horizontal axis): 0, 500, 1000, 1500, 2000, 2500, 3000, 3500, 4000, 4500, 5000

House Depressurization (pascals): 10.0, 8.0, 5.0, 3.0, 2.0, 1.0

stat so that the furnace is switched off whenever the exhaust fan is on. Although such interlock systems are technically feasible, they are not widely used.

The folly of more passive supply. One seemingly obvious solution to increasing air supply is to install a larger make-up air opening or another "combustion-air" duct. Unfortunately, passive air supply rarely does the job; or rather, it does it too crudely. For the typical house with an exhaust flow of 235 cfm, you would need an opening of 93 square inches to avoid excess home depressurization. Double that size if, as is almost certain, you'll be using a screened and louvered inlet. Such

massive openings inevitably get covered up by the house's chilly, incredulous occupants.

Connecting the make-up air supply to a return air plenum leading directly to the furnace may avoid such tampering, but this leads to a slew of other problems: high heating costs, cool drafts, condensation on furnace heat exchangers, and even frosty door hardware in freezing weather. (Using a motorized damper on make-up air openings can avoid some of these problems and reduce air entry into the house when the furnace is off.)

Despite these drawbacks, codes often require some type of passive air opening to supply combustion

air. But in limiting their attention to combustion air rather than total make-up air requirements, the codes miss the point. Almost any furnace will be able to draw sufficient combustion air through leaks, even in tight houses. The issue that should be addressed is not whether appliances have sufficient combustion air, but whether a house has sufficient make-up air to prevent backdrafting.

By Sebastian Moffatt, owner and manager of Sheltair Scientific Ltd., a Vancouver-based company that specializes in developing technology and testing buildings for health, safety, comfort, and energy efficiency.

SOURCES OF SUPPLY

Cast Chimney Liners

Ahrens Chimney Technique
Sioux Falls, SD
800/843-4417
www.ahrenschimney.com

North American Supaflu Systems
Scarborough, ME
800/788-7636
www.supaflu.com

Golden Flue
Ruther Glen, VA
800/446-5354
www.goldenflue.com

Solid/Flue
Grand Rapids, MI
800/444-3583
www.solidflue.com

Metal Chimney Liners

Chim Flex
Gaylord, MI
800/289-2446
www.chim-flex.com

Copperfield Chimney Supply
Fairfield, IA
800/247-3305
www.copperfield.com

Heat-Fab
Turners Falls, MA
800/772-0739
www.heat-fab.com

Metal-Fab
Wichita, KS
800/835-2830
www.mtlfab.com

ProTech Systems
Albany, NY
800/766-3473
www.protechinfo.com

Selkirk Corp
Richardson TX
800/992-8368
www.selkirkusa.com

Simpson Dura-Vent
Vacaville, CA
800/835-4429
www.duravent.com

Z-Flex
Bedford, NH
800/654-5600
www.z-flex.com

CO Detectors

North American Detectors Inc.
Markham, ON, Canada;
800/387-4219
www.nadi.com

Quantum Group Inc.
San Diego, CA
800/432-5599
www.qginc.com

CHAPTER 9

MOISTURE DAMAGE

- Mold, Mildew and Wood Decay

- Moisture in Wall Cavities: Case Studies

- Interior Moisture Problems: Case Studies

- A Rotting Timber Frame

- Wood Moisture Content & Interior Finishes

- Moisture Problems from "Dry Basements"

- Using Moisture Meters

MOLD, MILDEW AND WOOD DECAY

More than 5% of all construction lumber manufactured in the U.S. each year is used to replace wood that has decayed in existing structures. This need not be the case. Damage to wood-frame buildings by mildew, mold, staining, and decay is entirely preventable. Their presence points to design flaws, poor workmanship, and neglected maintenance.

The Culprits: Microorganisms

The microscopic organisms that cause mildew, mold, staining, and decay in wood belong to a huge group of primitive plants known as fungi. Unable to produce their own food, fungi feed instead on natural substances that make up organic materials such as leather, cloth, rattan, paper, and wood.

Mushrooms that spring from lawns and tree trunks are fungal "fruits." They release millions of dust-size "seeds" called spores that are scattered helter-skelter by wind. When conditions are right on the surfaces where they eventually settle, the spores germinate, sending out thread-like filaments called hyphae. Enzymes secreted by *hyphae* break down organic matter so fungi can use it for food.

Before fungi can colonize wood, four requirements must be met: an oxygen supply, temperature in the 40°F to 100°F range, sufficient moisture, and a food source (wood). Infection can be prevented by eliminating any one of the requirements. Obviously, it's hard to limit oxygen. Temperature control is tough too, since most living things thrive in this range. And even at subfreezing temperatures, many fungi don't die; they just go dormant.

Since you can usually control moisture to some extent, the most effective way to prevent fungal deterioration of wood is to keep it dry. Most fungi need a wood moisture content of at least 20% to grow. Since the moisture content of interior wood throughout most of the U.S. fluctuates between 6% and 16%, it's usually too dry for most microorganisms to get started.

In exterior or other situations where wood can't be kept dry, you can use naturally rot-resistant woods like western red cedar and redwood. Nature has partially protected these woods from fungi by depositing toxic extractives in their heartwood. But the supplies of naturally durable woods are shrinking, so to meet the demand, less naturally durable woods are impregnated with pesticides like CCA (chromated copper arsenate) that extend their service life by 30 to 50 years or longer.

Mildew

Mildew grows both inside and outside houses. Most mildews are black, but reds, greens, blues, and browns are possible. The familiar gray color of weathered wood is the work of mildew.

Masses of dark spores and hyphae give mildews their characteristic splotchy look. But although they discolor the surface they grow on, mildews have no appreciable effect on wood itself. Some mildews that feed on airborne organic matter can even grow on inorganic vinyl and aluminum sidings. Dew and rain supply the needed moisture.

Exterior mildew. Outside, mildews appear most often on unheated, projecting parts of buildings that cool quickly after sunset, like eaves, decks, and porch ceilings. North-facing walls and walls shaded by trees and other obstructions that restrict sunlight and airflow are also candidates. You often find mildew in the same places where dew forms. While mildew won't grow where siding crosses studs and other thermal bridges, mildew may thrive over the cooler, insulated bays between studs, where the dew persists to provide the needed moisture.

Interior mildew. Mildew occurs indoors most frequently in baths, basements, and other areas prone to high relative humidity. It also shows up in places with poor air circulation, such as behind furniture against exterior walls, and in closets and closed-off rooms. Mildew can form whenever the relative humidity of air near a surface exceeds 70%. This can happen when warm air near the ceiling cools as it flows down colder wall surfaces. The relative humidity of 70°F air, for example, rises from 40% to 70% when it's cooled to about 52°F.

Thermal bridges that lead to "hot spots" outside create "cold spots" inside where mildew can form. Exterior corners are notoriously mildew-prone because of poor air circulation inside and heat-robbing wind outside. In summer, water vapor from warm, humid air entering crawlspaces and basements below air-conditioned rooms may condense on cooler joists and subflooring, creating good conditions for mildew, as well as mold, stain, and decay. Moisture condensed as ice from heated air leaking into attics in winter likewise wets rafters and sheathing when it melts.

Stopping mildew. Not only is mildew unsightly, its spores and odors indoors can trigger allergic reactions. Fortunately, ridding wood of mildew is easy. But first, do a simple test to see if the splotches are mildew or just plain dirt. Place a drop of fresh household bleach containing sodium hypochlorite on the suspected area. The dark color of mildew will fade in a minute or two, while dirt is unchanged.

Once you've determined the stain is mildew, clean it by brushing or sponging the surface with a solution of one-third cup household detergent, one to two quarts household bleach, and two to three quarts of warm water. Or use commercial cleaners. Wear eye protection and gloves, and rinse surfaces with water.

Virtually all exterior finishes — paints, solid color and semitransparent stains, and water repellents alike — are susceptible to mildew. Oil-based formulations, especially those with linseed oil, are particularly vulnerable. Among water-based coatings, acrylic latexes have proven the most mildew-resistant. Defend against mildew on siding and trim by using only primers and topcoats that contain mildewcide, or by mixing in the add-it-yourself types that paint shops sell. Finishes with zinc oxide pigments also deter mildew. But beware: Finishes applied over mildewed surfaces that are recoated without first killing the fungus will soon discolor.

The amount of moisture generated inside a home may be beyond your control, but you can encourage use of the bath exhaust fan, for example, by wiring it to the room light switch or to a timer. Install louvered doors to ensure airflow in closets. Use a soil cover and vent and/or insulate crawlspaces as site and climatic conditions dictate. Always install a vapor retarder and use plenty of insulation in walls and attics, and provide adequate roof ventilation.

Molds

Molds need a wood surface moisture content of about 20% to get started. To provide that, simply surround wood with air at 90% relative humidity at any temperature from 40°F to 100°F, and presto! That's why

mold and mildew sometimes suddenly appear on furniture during the dog days of summer.

While most molds are green, black and orange molds are not uncommon. The color comes from spores strewn across the surface. Though hyphae reach deeper into wood, discoloration in softwoods tends to be limited to the surface of the sapwood. It can usually be planed, sanded, or even brushed off. Brown, gray, or black patches penetrate more deeply into hardwoods and can't be machined away. Discoloration aside, molds generally have little effect on wood's integrity.

Some molds are surprisingly tolerant of wood preservatives. This explains the fuzzy growths occasionally found between boards in banded

DETECTING DECAY

I use several methods when looking for decay in wood. When wood is suspiciously wet or discolored, but otherwise looks okay, I first determine its subsurface

moisture content with a moisture meter. If it's 20% or below, I know that there's no active decay present. If it's between 20% and 28%, existing decay can continue mer-

rily on its way. If it's over 28%, conditions are ripe for fungi to get started.

The pick test is also useful (see photos). I judge the soundness of the wood from the way a large splinter breaks when I pry it with an awl or ice pick. Sound wood emits a sharp crack as the splinter is pried up. The splinter is typically long, with one end still attached to the wood. Sometimes it breaks in the middle over the tool, but the fracture will still be splintery.

A splinter pried from wood with incipient decay lifts quietly from the surface and almost always fails directly over the tool, with both ends still anchored to the wood.

The pick test is highly subjective; natural characteristics of sound wood can produce misleading results. Accurate interpretation comes only with experience and consideration of other clues.

To find decay hidden inside timbers, I take a small-diameter boring and examine the shavings. Discolored, wet, and musty shavings signal decay. I always plug the hole with a preservative-treated dowel. — S.S.

Pick test. *A short splinter pried from decayed wood (left) typically breaks quietly over the tool with both ends still anchored. When pried from sound wood (below), the splinter cracks sharply, is longer, and remains attached at one end only.*

FUNGI FIELD GUIDE — A GUIDE TO FUNGUS IDENTIFICATION AND HABITAT

White Rot

Most common in hardwoods, giving them a whitish, gray, or yellow bleached appearance. Turns wood spongy and stringy.

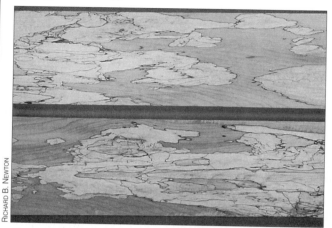

Partially decayed, or "spalted," rock maple. Spalted maple is prized by woodworkers for its figure.

Staining Fungi

Discoloration of wood in logs or freshly sawn lumber, primarily softwood. Can also occur on pine windows wet from condensation. Steel-gray to blue-black color, commonly called blue stain. Stain is indelible.

Eastern white pine lumber, sawn green during humid summer months, discolored by blue stain.

Note: All case studies photographed in southern New England.

Mold

Green, black, or orange discoloration on surface of wood. Can penetrate below the surface of hardwoods and cause permanent stain. Needs a surface moisture content of 20% to get started.

Location: *Douglas-fir floor joists in basement.*
Cause: *High humidity in basement.*

Mildew

Dark stains, usually black, on surface of wood. Needs 70% relative humidity at surface to grow. Primarily a visual problem. Will lighten from bleaching.

Location: *Cedar siding on shady side of house.*
Cause: *Persistent wetting from dew.*

Location: *Bottom side of roof sheathing, new home.*
Cause: *Dryer vented into attic.*

Brown Rot

The most common decay fungi in softwoods. Requires 28% moisture content to start, but once established, needs only 20%. Turns wood brown and crumbly, with cross-grain and cubical checking. May sprout cottony mycelia and mushroomlike fruiting bodies.

Location: *Sill in direct contact with concrete in 5-year-old home.*
Cause: *Untreated wood on concrete slab-on-grade.*

Location: *Behind shower stall in 22-year-old home.*
Cause: *No vapor retarder, no bath exhaust, cold outside wall corner.*

Location: *Crawlspace of 20-year-old apartment building.*
Cause: *Standing water and poor ventilation. Note mycelia (top) and fruiting bodies (above).*

Location: *Trim at entrance to 3-year-old home.*
Cause: *Splashing water from unguttered eaves two stories above. Exposed endgrain sitting on metal flashing.*

shipments of CCA-treated southern yellow pine. Molds die once lumber dries, but can be washed off beforehand with the same solution used for mildew.

Preventing mold. Flourishing in damp crawlspaces and basements and in poorly vented attics, molds form a living veneer on framing and sheathing. Prevention lies wholly in controlling air moisture levels and condensation potential through proper site drainage and dampproofing, and again, the proper use of soil covers, vapor retarders, insulation, and ventilation as required in your area.

Staining Fungi

Discoloration of wood by staining fungi happens almost exclusively in logs and freshly sawn lumber. As a precaution, rough lumber is often dipped in a fungicidal bath immediately after sawing.

Also called sap stains, these fungi are most troublesome in softwoods, where they cause a steel-gray to blue-black color commonly called blue stain. In hardwoods, staining fungi may create blue or brown hues. The stains result from dark hyphae that permeate sapwood in search of stored starches and sugars. You can often spot inactive blue stain in doors, millwork, and other pine products. Active staining fungi sometimes discolor the bottom rails and corners of pine windows that are kept wet by condensation. These stains are indelible and will not wash off.

In their search for food, staining fungi destroy certain wood cells. As a result, the wood becomes more permeable, and more susceptible to decay. Its strength and toughness are slightly reduced as well.

Decay Fungi

While discoloration by mildew, mold, and staining fungi is only an appearance problem, decay fungi threaten the structural integrity of wood. Aptly termed the "slow fire," these fungi eat the very cellulose and lignin of which wood cells are made.

Moisture content is the critical factor that makes wood susceptible to decay. It must exceed 28%, and liquid water must be present in cell cavities before decay fungi can gain a toehold. Once established, some fungi can carry on their destruction at a moisture content as low as 20%. When moisture content falls below this level, all fungal activity ceases. That's one reason why framing lumber is dried to 19% moisture content or less.

In its early, or incipient, stages, decay can be difficult to detect, even with a microscope, yet strength loss can still be appreciable. As the slow fire advances, wood's luster fades. Surfaces become dull and discolored, and a musty odor is often present. The rate at which decay progresses depends on moisture content, temperature, and the specific fungus.

It doesn't take a trained eye to recognize decay in its advanced stages. Wood is visibly discolored, spongy, and musty. Surfaces may be stringy, shrunken, or split across the grain. Cottony masses of hyphae called mycelia, as well as fruiting bodies, may be present. Decay extends deep into wood; strength loss is significant.

Brown rots and white rots. Decay fungi fall into three major groups: brown rots, white rots, and soft rots. Soft rots are rarely found inside homes, though they occasionally degrade wood shakes and shingles on heavily shaded roofs in wet climates.

Brown rots are so-named because infected wood turns dark brown. They usually colonize softwoods, consuming cellulose but hardly touching the darker lignin, which is the natural glue that holds wood cells together. Mycelia appear as white growths, either sheetlike or fluffy, on the wood's surface. Brown-rotted wood shrinks excessively and splits across the grain as it dries. The surface becomes friable and crumbly, and shows cubical checking.

Water-conducting fungi are a special type of brown rot that show up infrequently in the Southeast, Northeast, and Pacific Northwest. These fungi are unique in their ability to pipe moisture from the soil over long distances. They do this through rootlike fusions of hyphae called *rhizomorphs*, wetting otherwise dry wood in advance of their attack. Water-conducting fungi are sometimes called dry rot fungi. Unfortunately, this name suggests that dry wood can decay. Dry wood can't decay, period! What builders, inspectors, and homeowners alike routinely mislabel as dry rot is almost always, in reality, wood that got wet, rotted, and dried out before discovery.

Water-conducting fungi infect both softwoods and hardwoods. Their light-colored mycelia look like large, papery, fan-shaped sheets. Damp crawlspaces and wood in contact with the ground are avenues for entry.

White rots give wood a white, gray-white, yellow-white, or otherwise bleached appearance. They most often infect hardwoods, feeding on both cellulose and lignin. In advanced stages of decay, white-rotted wood is spongy, has a stringy texture, and lacks the cubical checking of brown-rotted wood. A thin black line often marks the advancing edge of incipient white rot in hardwoods. Ironically, this partially decayed, or *spalted*, wood is coveted by woodworkers for its unique figure.

Dealing With Decay

Like mold, mildew, and staining, existing decay can be stopped by drying up the moisture. But remember that to make the remedy permanent, you've got to cure the disease (water infiltration) not just treat the symptoms (mildew, mold, and decay).

Stopping decay. The first and most important step when you find decay is to figure out where the water is coming from. Check for the obvious — roof and plumbing leaks, and missing or punctured flashing. Look for stains and drip tracks caused by ice dams. Are the eaves wide enough to prevent water from cascading down sidewalls? Are gutters poorly maintained or missing? Do finish grades slope towards the foundation? Are foundation cracks admitting water? Is untreated wood in direct contact with concrete, masonry, or soil?

Check to see if crawlspaces have soil covers and if venting and/or insulation is adequate and properly installed. Look for adequate attic ventilation as well.

Peeling and blistering paint often signal inadequate interior ventilation or a missing vapor retarder. Water stains on framing and sheathing inside walls suggest condensation from excessive indoor humidity.

Once the source of water has been shut off, remove as much decayed wood as is practical and economical. Decayed wood absorbs and holds water more readily than sound wood, inviting further decay and insect attack. This is especially important with girders, columns, and other critical members whose load-carrying ability may have been compromised. There's no known way to accurately determine the remaining strength of decayed wood left in place. Cut back rotted members to sound wood, keeping in mind that difficult-to-detect incipient decay can extend well beyond visibly rotted areas.

When a partially decayed structural member can't be replaced, reinforce it with a sister anchored to sound wood. Let any rotted areas you don't remove dry out before making repairs. Otherwise, you're just adding fuel to the slow fire.

In damp crawlspaces or other places where water is likely to reappear, replace decayed members with preservative-treated wood. The major model building code agencies — BOCA, ICBO, and SBCCI — require that treated wood be used for sills and sleepers on concrete or masonry in contact with the ground, for joists within 18 inches of the ground, for girders within 12 inches of the ground, and for columns embedded in the ground that support permanent structures.

Borates. Dormant fungi can be reactivated when dry, infected wood is rewetted. Consider treating infected but otherwise serviceable wood left in place with a water-borne borax-based preservative that will not only kill active fungi, but will guard against future infection as well (see "Sources of Supply" at end of chapter). Borates have low toxicity to humans and are even approved for interior use in food processing plants. They don't affect wood's strength, color, or finishability, don't corrode fasteners, and don't outgas vapors. Widely used in treating new timbers for log homes, they're the preservative of choice for remedial treatment of wood in service. Because of the decay hazard posed whenever wood bears on concrete or masonry, solid borate rods are often inserted into holes bored near contact areas. Should wood ever get wet, the rods dissolve and ward off infection.

Epoxy. Sometimes replacing rotted wood isn't an option. In conserving historic buildings, for example, the goal is to preserve as much of the original "architectural fabric" as possible. Stabilizing deteriorated wood with epoxy is often the only choice. Epoxies consist of resin and hardener that are mixed just before use. Liquids for injection and spatula-applied pastes are available. After curing, epoxy-stabilized wood can be shaped with regular woodworking tools and painted. Epoxies are useful for consolidating rotted wood, restoring lost portions of moldings and carvings, and for strengthening weakened structural members. In the last case, they're used to bond concealed metal reinforcement inside holes or channels cut into hidden timber faces. Epoxies aren't preservatives and won't stop existing decay or prevent future infection. They can also be tricky to use; follow the manufacturer's mixing, application, and safety instructions to the letter.

By Stephen Smulski, president of Wood Science Specialists Inc., in Shutesbury, Mass., a consulting firm specializing in wood performance problems in light-frame structures.

Moisture in Wall Cavities: Case Studies

Moisture is one of the worst enemies of wood-framed buildings. The trend toward tighter, more energy-efficient houses has made it important for builders to understand how moisture behaves and to plan ways for the house to handle moisture. Increased insulation levels and better air-sealing techniques have lengthened the time needed for the air in these homes to be replaced by natural infiltration. As a result, water vapor from showering, cooking, plants, people, and pets lingers indoors longer than it does in older, leakier homes, while the moisture trapped in new framing lumber escapes more slowly. This paves the way for mildew, mold, decay fungi, and insects.

You can avoid these problems by using kiln-dried framing lumber and mechanically venting water vapor directly to the outside before it does any damage. As these three case studies show, failure to do so can lead to disaster.

Case 1: Indoor Humidity Causes Exterior Stains

A contractor was living with his family in an unsold spec house he had built ten months before. When numerous red-brown streaks appeared at random on the home's white siding in February, he complained to his supplier that the siding was defective. The streaks appeared on all sides of the house, but were worse around the windows and outside the master bath.

The contractor had sided the home with 1x6 clear heart, vertical-grain western red cedar bevel siding. The siding had been machine-primed on all sides with a stain-blocking primer and field-coated with two topcoats of a solid color exterior white stain. The wall construction was typical of a modern energy-efficient home: gypsum wallboard, a polyethylene vapor retarder, unfaced fiberglass batt insulation between 2x6 studs, ply-wood sheathing, an exterior air infiltration barrier, and the siding.

The dark streaks were what most contractors call "cedar bleed," though a more accurate term is "run-down extractive staining." It's a problem with redwood and red cedar, and shows up occasionally on Douglas fir and southern pine as well. Happening commonly during late winter, run-down staining occurs when liquid water — in this case water vapor from inside the home that leaked through wall cavities and condensed on the cold siding — wets the back of the siding for a prolonged period. Eventually, the water penetrates the primer, causing the wood's water-soluble extractives to leach out. The dark brown solution then seeps out from behind the siding through the overlap between courses, dripping down and discoloring the face of the courses below.

During my inspection, I found live mold on some joists and stair stringers in the basement. I wasn't too surprised, given the fact that basement relative humidity and wood moisture content (62% and 12%, respectively) were more typical of June than February. Relative humidity on the first and second floors (46%), was also much higher than the 25% to 35% typical for this time of year.

When I removed the siding in a heavily stained area, I found liquid water and extractive staining on its backside (Figure 1). Water also saturated the plywood sheathing behind the wet and stained air infiltration barrier. Siding, sheathing, and framing checked in at 33%, 50%, and 30% moisture content, respectively, instead of the 12% to 15% that I would have expected. Though I found no decay, conditions were ripe for rot. The reason rot hadn't yet taken hold was that it was simply too cold outside.

The cause of the wet siding was excessive indoor humidity. Sources included a humidifier on each of the

Figure 1. Water vapor from inside this new house (left) — caused in part by a humidifier on the forced-hot-air heating system, a dryer vented directly into the basement, and green framing lumber — leaked through the walls and caused extractive staining on the primed and painted siding (below).

home's two forced-hot-air heating systems, a clothes dryer vented into the basement, four bathroom exhaust fans vented into the attic, a recirculating-type kitchen range fan and, as shown by the S-GRN grade stamps, green framing lumber. Despite the weight of this evidence, the contractor insisted that the water vapor from inside his "tight" house couldn't be leaking through the walls. Not until I pointed out that there was no staining whatsoever on the attached garage did he finally come around.

The solution to the staining problem was simple: lower the indoor relative humidity. To do so, I recommended that the builder disconnect the humidifiers and vent the clothes dryer, bath exhaust fans and kitchen range directly to the outside. Stains could be removed later by washing the siding with a dilute solution of oxalic acid (available from paint or hardware stores) once the framing, sheathing, and siding had dried to below 19% moisture content. Repainting with a stain-resistant primer would complete the job.

Case 2: Bathroom Moisture Recipe for Decay

While renovating a bathroom in their 22-year-old home, the owners were shocked to find wet insulation, severely decayed framing and sheathing, and live carpenter ants behind the tiled shower stall (Figure 2). Tucked into an outside corner, two sides of the stall were against exterior walls. The walls consisted of floor-to-ceiling ceramic tiles set on mortar and metal lath, standard gypsum wallboard, unfaced fiberglass batt insulation between 2x4 studs, plywood sheathing, and wood shingles. The bathroom had a window, but no exhaust fan.

The shower pan and drain tested leakfree, and the owners recalled that the tiles and grout had only a few cracks. This told me that the cause of the problem was not liquid water

leaking into the walls. Instead, a construction error — omission of a vapor retarder behind the wallboard — had let water vapor diffuse into the wall cavity. Lack of an exhaust fan also allowed water vapor and liquid condensation generated by showering to persist in the bathroom. This increased the chance that the moisture would get into the walls

through hidden air leakage paths, then condense and freeze on the cold sheathing. When it melted in warmer weather, the liquid water increased the moisture content of framing and sheathing to the 28% threshold required for decay. Carpenter ants followed.

My diagnosis was confirmed by the run-down staining on the home's

Figure 2. The framing behind this shower stall (left) rotted because bathroom moisture leaked into the walls. The excess moisture also caused extractive staining on the home's siding (below). The solution was to add a bath fan that vented moisture directly to the outside.

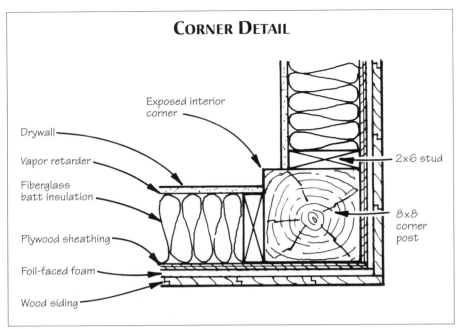

CORNER DETAIL

- Drywall
- Vapor retarder
- Fiberglass batt insulation
- Plywood sheathing
- Foil-faced foam
- Wood siding
- Exposed interior corner
- 2x6 stud
- 8x8 corner post

Figure 3. While remodeling their six-year-old timber-frame home, the owners found that the corner posts had decayed along the outside edge. The builder had boxed in the green timbers with framing and sheathing, holding the wood at a decay-susceptible moisture content for years after closing-in. Drying could only take place through the one exposed corner.

white shingles outside and below the second floor bathroom. The owners remarked that despite washing the streaks off each summer, they always reappeared the following spring.

To prevent future problems, I recommended that they add a vapor retarder to the warm side of the exterior wall and install a bath exhaust fan vented directly to the outside. Running the fan would reduce the amount of moisture infiltrating into the wall to a negligible amount.

Case 3: Green Timbers Spawn Decay

While adding a porch to their six-year-old hemlock timber-frame home, the owners found extensive decay in the corner posts. After removing more siding and trim, they found at least minor decay wherever the timbers contacted studs and sheathing.

The builder had framed conventional 2x6 walls between the posts and sheathed them with plywood.

From inside to outside, the walls consisted of gypsum wallboard, a polyethylene vapor retarder, unfaced fiberglass batt insulation, plywood sheathing, rigid foam insulation, and wood siding. The studs were fastened directly to the faces of the posts.

Built-in during construction, the source of the decay-causing moisture was the huge gallonage of water trapped in the green (water-saturated) timbers. In an effort to make the house energy-efficient, the builder had boxed the timbers in on three faces with studs, sheathing, and rigid foam (Figure 3). This had severely retarded the drying of the timbers. As a result, the wood stayed at a decay-susceptible moisture content for years after closing-in. The timbers were forced to dry through the one face exposed inside the home. Corner posts were especially slow to dry because of the tiny exposed surface area.

An 8-foot-long hemlock 8x8 contains about nine gallons of water

when green (about 97% moisture content). When it eventually dries to the 12% moisture content typical of framing in heated buildings, it will contain about one gallon of water. The other eight gallons will have been released into the air or the surrounding materials. The total water given off by a green frame counts in the hundreds of gallons, with the greatest release occurring during the first heating season. In fact, the owners of this home recalled a "Niagara Falls" of window condensation that damaged sashes, sills, and walls for the first three winters of occupancy. They actually put towels on the window sills to sop up the flow.

Fortunately, enough of the corner posts' cross-section was still sound enough to make reinforcement or replacement unnecessary. Following my recommendations, the builder replaced the decayed studs and sheathing, and treated the timbers with a waterborne borate preservative to kill existing decay and prevent future infection.

This problem could have been avoided. One option would have been to use partially air-dried timbers or to use salvaged timbers that had dried in place years before. Another would have been to use naturally decay-resistant timbers. Hemlock and red oak have no resistance to decay; white oak has very high natural resistance; eastern white pine has moderate resistance. You can virtually eliminate the decay risk of any species by applying foam-core stress-skin panels to the outside of the timber frame. This leaves three faces exposed on the inside, which provides an escape route for water and promotes faster drying.

By Stephen Smulski, president of Wood Science Specialists Inc., in Shutesbury, Mass., a consulting firm specializing in wood performance problems in light-frame structures.

INTERIOR MOISTURE PROBLEMS: CASE STUDIES

Moisture problems are caused by two culprits: a source of excess moisture and a cold surface. Solving the problem is just as logical: Identify and remove (or reduce) the moisture source, and warm the cold surface.

Most homeowners recognize that taking a long, hot shower is contributing moisture to the house, but there are lots of other sources that even many builders don't recognize. Big contributors include:

- firewood stored indoors
- unvented gas ranges
- power humidifiers
- cooking
- laundering and cleaning
- houseplants and aquariums
- poorly-drained foundations
- downspouts that are tied into footing tile
- capillary action through basement floors and walls
- uncovered or loosely covered dirt crawlspaces (1,000 square feet of uncovered earth in a crawlspace

can generate as much moisture as five power humidifiers, even if the ground appears dry!)

Moisture can enter wall and ceiling cavities through a number of air leakage points in conventional construction (Figure 4). Once inside the cavities, there are many cold surfaces on which the moisture can condense.

Cold interior surfaces generally have fewer causes: wind blowing through the insulation (windwashing), or misplaced and missing insulation (Figure 5). If indoor humidity is high, these cold spots will breed mold and mildew growth on the drywall or wallpaper.

In hopes of alerting builders who aren't up to speed on moisture control, here are three examples from

When double-glazed windows show this much condensation, humidity levels are too high and should be corrected by eliminating moisture sources and increasing ventilation.

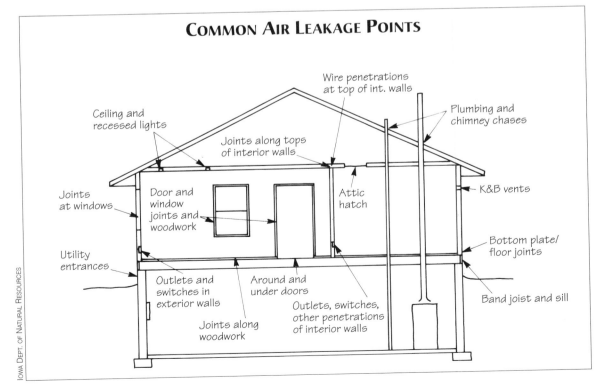

COMMON AIR LEAKAGE POINTS

Wire penetrations at top of int. walls

Ceiling and recessed lights

Plumbing and chimney chases

Joints along tops of interior walls

Joints at windows

Door and window joints and woodwork

Attic hatch

K&B vents

Utility entrances

Outlets and switches in exterior walls

Around and under doors

Joints along woodwork

Outlets, switches, other penetrations of interior walls

Bottom plate/ floor joints

Band joist and sill

IOWA DEPT. OF NATURAL RESOURCES

Figure 4. Moist interior air can enter wall and ceiling cavities through these common leaks in conventionally built buildings. The moisture can then condense and, in extreme cases, lead to structural decay.

COLD SURFACE CAUSES

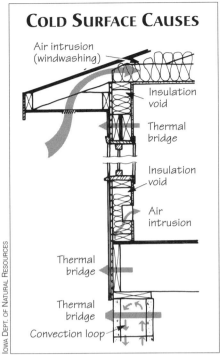

Iowa Dept. of Natural Resources

Figure 5. Insulation defects can cause cold spots on the interior surfaces of a home. Moist interior air can condense on these cold surfaces, causing mildew growth or rot.

CORRECT BAFFLE PLACEMENT

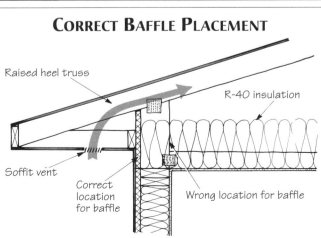

Raised heel truss

R-40 insulation

Soffit vent

Correct location for baffle

Wrong location for baffle

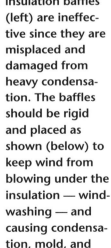

Figure 6. These insulation baffles (left) are ineffective since they are misplaced and damaged from heavy condensation. The baffles should be rigid and placed as shown (below) to keep wind from blowing under the insulation — windwashing — and causing condensation, mold, and mildew at the ceiling corners.

my consulting work. If you're still building with yesterday's technology, you may find yourself or a client in one of the following situations.

Case 1: Multifamily With Multi-Problems

My client was an apartment developer in a Midwest college town. He owned six identical, three-story apartment buildings each with 30 units. All had been built by the same builder using the same subcontractors. The three buildings that went up three years earlier had no problems, but the other three, built the previous year, were a mess.

There was mold growing on ceilings, walls, and sash, and the windows showed heavy condensation. As far as the owner was concerned, the culprit was a loose-fit poly vapor retarder on the ceilings — the only difference he could identify between the newer and older buildings. (It's pretty common for old-line builders to blame moisture problems on the presence or absence of poly in the ceiling.)

I found that all six buildings had a great deal of air leakage between units and between floors. The units with the highest moisture readings — 50% to 70% relative humidity in February — were mainly third floor apartments, indicating a strong stack effect.

The older apartments without problems were occupied by young working singles. They didn't cook much and seldom used the shower more than once a day. The attic insulation above these units was blown fiberglass.

The newer apartments with the problems were occupied by college students — two or three to a unit — who cooked at home and took several showers per day per unit. The range hoods in these units weren't ducted, and the bath exhaust fans weren't very effective. Aquariums were in style and every third unit had one.

The attics were insulated with blown-in cellulose, which forms a better air barrier than fiberglass. However, the insulating was poorly done since many of the infiltration stops (baffles) were improperly located flush with the inside of the wall (Figure 6). This created a cold ceiling corner and defeated the purpose of using raised-heel "energy trusses."

Most of the bath exhaust ducting in these "problem apartments" was exposed and uninsulated, and large chunks of ice blocked many ducts. Several birds were nesting in the wall grilles of the lower level bath exhausts. The new buildings pressure-tested 25% tighter than the older ones — indicating that the builder and subcontractors had progressed somewhat on the learning curve of energy-efficient building. But they had neglected to account for moisture.

The exterior walls consisted of steel siding, gyp board sheathing, 6-inch batt insulation, a loose-fit vapor barrier, and 1/2-inch drywall. After seeing icicles forming on the siding,

I was sure enough of what was happening in the walls that I cut a hole in the drywall from the inside of a third-floor unit and invited the owner to reach inside this exterior wall. He pulled out a handful of wet insulation.

An attic inspection showed that the stack effect had driven so much moisture up there that you could see the outline of the interior walls from above where the insulation had become soaked and had settled. So much for loose-fit ceiling vapor barriers.

The real impact of the moisture generated by cooking and showering wasn't apparent until the early evening hours when everyone got back from home and began showering and cooking in earnest. So I chose this time period to demonstrate to the owner how increasing the ventilation would solve the problem. Using the three existing 1,000-cfm attic exhaust fans, I opened the attic scuttles in the common hallways and stood back. Despite my 3,000-cfm ventilating effort, the moisture level rose 10%.

It was obvious that the building was tight enough that it needed continuous ventilation in each unit. Sure enough, a survey of the occupants revealed that over half rated their apartment air quality fair to poor.

My recommendations included correcting the obvious insulation and bath venting problems, as well as ventilating all third-floor units continuously with a 60-cfm roof-mounted exhaust fan. To reduce the stack effect, I suggested two American Aldes, humidity-controlled fresh-air inlets for each unit, and a time-delay switch on all bath exhaust fans that kept them running 15 minutes after the lights were switched off.

Case 2: Basement Moisture Causes Ceiling Stains

This was a two-year-old ranch house with a partial basement and partial crawlspace. It had a full brick exterior, 2x6 walls, foam sheathing, Tyvek, low-e windows, a loose-fit vapor barrier, and a high-efficiency furnace. The nicest home in town, it was built by a conscientious builder using conventional building techniques.

The owner called me in because he was concerned about ceiling stains around the three bath exhaust fans, and heavy condensation on the high-performance glass. To the owner's dismay, the first place I went was the basement and crawlspace. "My problem is in the attic," he said.

After noting a loose-fitting vapor barrier on the crawlspace floor, I removed one of the fiberglass insulation batts at the band (rim) joist. When the owner saw it was black with mold, he knew the attic was the least of his problems (Figure 7).

The home was pressure-tested at 2½ air changes per hour at 50 pascals with a blower door; pretty tight for a conventional builder. At two air changes or better I usually recommend continuous ventilation. At three to four air changes per hour, intermittent ventilation is usually sufficient. But this home was carrying 60% to 70% relative humidity in January, and the bathroom exhaust fans were all ducted into the attic. In addition, the homeowners had a large collection of house plants and a large aquarium. I recommended central ventilation, a sealed poly ground cover in the crawlspace, an air barrier at the band joist, and exterior ducting for the bathroom exhaust fans.

As it turned out, we solved another problem at the same time. Out of curiosity, I did a radon test before we started. The home had a radon level of 32 picocuries per liter (pCi/l) on top of the moisture problem. With the central ventilation and basement sealing, we were able to lower the radon level to an acceptable 4 pCi/l.

When we cut the hole through the wall to install the heat exchang-

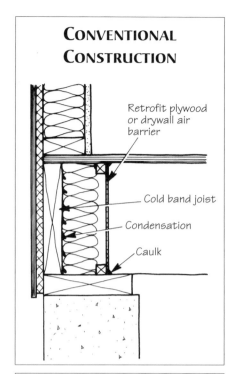

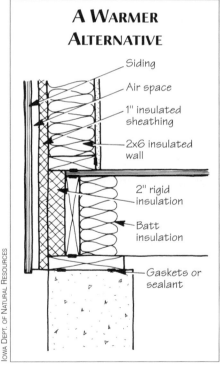

Figure 7. Conventional band or rim joists have cold interior surfaces that can condense moisture. The solution: Carefully retrofit airtight blocking between the joists (top) to keep moist air out. In new construction, insulate the band joist on the exterior (above) to keep the band joist warm.

HOUSEHOLD HUMIDITY SOURCES

Moisture Source	Estimated Amount (measured in pints)
Bathing *(excludes towels & spillage)*	
Bath	0.12/standard size bath
Shower	0.52/5-minute shower
Clothes Drying	
Vented outside	0+/load *(usually nil)*
Not vented	4.68 to 6.18/load *(more if gas dryer)*
Combustion *(unvented kerosene heater)*	7.6/gallon of kerosene burned
Cooking *(family of four)*	
Lunch	0.53 *(plus 0.68 if gas stove)*
Dinner	1.22 *(plus 1.58 if gas stove)*
Boiling — *10 minutes, 6" pan (plus gas)*	0.48 covered; 0.57 uncovered
Dishwashing by hand	
Dinner	0.68/family of four
Firewood storage	
Cord of green wood	400 to 800/6 months
Floor mopping	0.03/square foot
Gas range pilot light *(each)*	0.37-/day
House plants	
5 to 7 average size	0.86 to 0.96/day
Human respiration/perspiration	0.44/hour *(family of four)*
Saunas, steambaths, whirlpools	0 to 2.7+/hour
Ground moisture migration	
1,000 sq. ft. basement	0 to 105/day

Source: William Angell and Wanda Olsen, Cold Climate Housing Info. Ctr., Univ. of Minn.

er's air intake, we noted that the wall cavity was also saturated with moisture. With the full brick veneer and the vinyl-clad windows, the owner might not have known there was a problem until the walls began to fall apart from rot in five to ten years.

Case 3: New Furnace Catalyst Not Cause

This homeowner replaced his old fuel oil furnace with a new high-efficiency gas model. The first spring after it was installed, the paint on the exterior of the 27-year-old house began to peel and the windows were heavy with condensation. The homeowner filed suit against the mechanical contractor and the furnace manufacturer. The owner was convinced that the new furnace was "pumping moisture" into his home because he could see the water flowing out of the condensation line.

The insurance company hired me to sort out the facts and analyze the problem. I looked at a lot more than the furnace (Figure 8). I found poor site drainage away from the foundation, a sagging and leaking rain

Figure 8. These sources of excess moisture — a shower without an exhaust fan (left) and a bathroom exhaust vented into the attic (right) — are easy to fix if the homeowner and builder are aware of the damage they can cause.

gutter, a heavily used basement shower with no exhaust fan, a main-floor exhaust fan ducting into the attic, lots of house plants, a family with both a teenager and a baby (lots of showers and lots of laundry), and a clothesline full of wash hanging out to dry in the basement (they were proud of how much energy they saved by not using the dryer).

All of these moisture generating sources were in the home prior to the installation of the high-efficiency furnace, and the homeowner admitted that "the house never did quite dry out in the winter." But the old conventional furnace flue had been providing enough ventilation to partially relieve the problem. (A conventional furnace flue exhausts about 70 cfm continuously from a home, even when the furnace is not running).

A blower door test revealed that the house had 5.5. air changes per hour at 50 pascals pressure with the conventional furnace flue in place. The reading was 4.0 air changes at 50 pascals with the flue sealed. This difference in ventilation rates brought the relative humidity up to 68% — which was the primary cause of the paint peeling and blistering. Contributing causes were wind-driven rain that penetrated the siding, and deteriorating putty around the windows.

In this case, I suggested improving the site grading, repairing gutters and downspouts, adding an exhaust fan for the basement bath, and cutting down the basement clothesline.

These suggestions should also bring the humidity down to a level where the house can dry out season-ally, eliminating the flywheel effect of increasing the moisture each year by building on the previous one. The house was already experiencing a moisture problem; the new furnace merely accelerated it, making it surface sooner. As is often the case, the "last guy in" got the blame.

There's some truth to the old saying "They don't build 'em the way they used to." In fact, homes today are built much better, but that means less margin for error. Proper moisture control, good air barriers, and adequate ventilation are the keys to houses that are more comfortable and durable as well as cleaner, quieter, and healthier to live in.

By Bill Eich, a contractor who builds energy-efficient houses in Spirit Lake, Iowa.

A ROTTING TIMBER FRAME

"If you don't put in a vapor barrier, your house is going to rot away." You've heard this many times, but it's not so simple.

Thousands of insulated houses with no vapor barriers (or lousy vapor barriers such as kraft paper) have not rotted away. Furthermore, installing a sheet of poly in the wall is no guarantee against problems. Take for example, this rotting timber-frame house in southern Vermont.

The 1,800-square-foot, one-and-a-half-story Cape was four years old. The walls were framed with 8x8 timbers, which are exposed on the interior of the house. Between the 8x8s, the builder framed in with 2x4s to provide nailing and a place for fiberglass insulation. The frame was sheathed with 1-inch boards, then wrapped with 1-inch-thick, foil-faced isocyanurate, which was taped and caulked. Clapboard siding was installed over kraft paper.

Rotting Beams

The owner discovered the problem when a renovation contractor opened up the south side of the

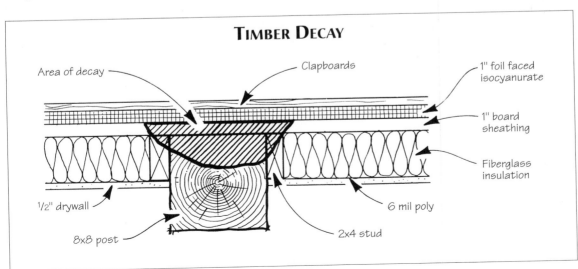

TIMBER DECAY

Area of decay

Clapboards

1" foil faced isocyanurate

1" board sheathing

Fiberglass insulation

1/2" drywall

6 mil poly

8x8 post

2x4 stud

Figure 9. Decay was concentrated on the outer portion of the timbers and the nearby sheathing and studs, as shown in the darkened area.

house in order to add a sunspace. He found extensive decay in and around the timbers. The rot occurred on the outer face of the timbers — up to 2 inches deep in some sections — and in the sheathing and 2x4s wherever they touched the timbers (Figure 9).

To learn more, the owner cut out sections of siding and sheathing on all sides of the house and found decayed wood on the north, south, and west sides (Figure 10). Only one hole was cut on the east side, and showed only minor damage.

There was decay on nearly all the beams looked at — high and low, on vertical posts, and on horizontal beams. Rot also occurred in the 2x4s that were directly nailed to the beams, and in the 1x pine sheathing where it touched the beams. No decay was found in the wall sections between the beams, or elsewhere —

although a thorough search was not made of all areas.

Looking Further

When I visited the house in November, I looked for evidence of high moisture levels. It was a sunny day in the 40s — too warm for condensation to form on the windows. But all the second-floor windows — and most on the first floor — were badly stained from pooling condensation.

The owner confirmed that condensation covered most of the windows for most of the winter. The sources of moisture were many. For the first two years, the house had a wet basement each spring. (This was finally cured by regrading around the foundation.) There were no bathroom or kitchen fans, and the dryer vented indoors. The house was heated mostly by a wood-fired furnace in the basement, which tended to keep the basement warm and drive any moisture upstairs. To this day, the basement houses wet firewood.

Up in the attic, the owner and I found black mold covering the underside of the sheathing on the north side. The wood felt wet.

What let moisture *into* the attic were eight recessed lights, along with the usual wiring, plumbing, and framing holes. The attic was vented with two large gable-end vents. Judging by the mold, however, the vents could not handle the excessive moisture load.

Surprisingly, the home's interior had no musty smell, and no obvious signs of water damage other than on the window sash. All the damage was "safely" hidden from view.

The Diagnosis

So what caused the problem? In short, a combination of green wood, a moist house, a cold-side vapor barrier, and a cold climate. The timber-frame, built of 8x8 hemlock beams, had been assembled green in the fall

Figure 10. The west face of the house (top) was cut open in four spots, all revealing severe decay of the timber frame and adjoining wood (above left). The southwest corner (above right) is shown up close.

and was closed in the next spring. Since wood does not dry well in the cold, it was probably still quite wet when wrapped in foam the following spring. The water in the green wood gave the decay fungi a head start the first year.

Why didn't the beams dry toward the inside of the house over the summer? They did — at least near the inside faces, which became severely checked. But when winter came, the high moisture levels in the house drove the moisture back into the beams toward the sheathing, where it condensed.

The large gaps in the 8x8s provided an easy path for moisture into the wood, which is quite permeable anyway. Moisture could also penetrate the wall along the sides of the beams. Other interruptions in the vapor barrier — at floors, ceilings, and electrical outlets — let more moisture into the wall cavities. The inside face of the foam was below the dew point of the moist interior air throughout much of the winter.

The exposed inside sections of the beams dried, but the wet outer sections festered. Enough water got into the wood each winter so that each spring temperatures caused decay before the wood could dry out. The foam kept the wood from drying outward, and kept the sun from drying the wood inward. By midsummer, perhaps, the wood fell below saturation levels, stifling decay

WHERE DOES THE DEW DROP?

To figure out how much insulating foam sheathing you should install on the exterior of a building, you need to know the dew point of the interior air during winter.

First look at the chart to figure out what the dew point is for a given air temperature and relative humidity. Say you have an indoor relative humidity of 50% at 70°F. On the horizontal scale, locate the temperature and move up to the curve that represents 50% relative humidity, as shown. Then move left to the saturation curve, and down to find the dew point temperature — 50°F in this case.

Moisture must condense on a solid surface (it won't condense in midair and is unlikely to condense in fiberglass), and the inside surface of the sheathing is where the condensation is most likely to occur. The objective is to put enough foam on the wall so its inside surface remains above the dew point (in this case, above 50°F) for the average winter temperature at the site.

You can find the temperature at any point inside the wall if you know the R-values of the wall insulations you are using. The temperature change through the wall is in direct proportion to that R-value. For example, for an average outdoor winter temperature of 32°F, the temperature inside the 1-inch foam sheathing in Wall A will

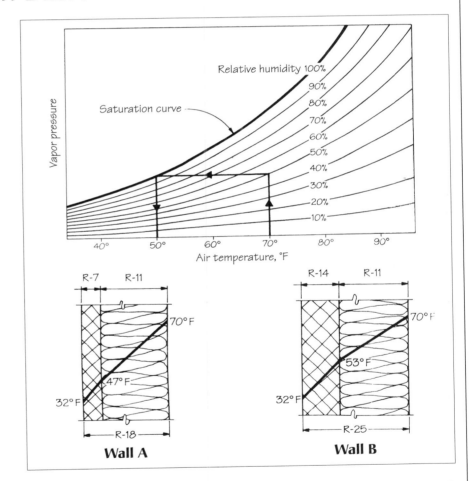

be $7/18$ (R-7 over R-18) of the way from 32°F to 70°F, or 47°F. This is below the dew point, so condensation is likely to form on the inside of the foam sheathing.

In Wall B, with 2 inches of foam, the temperature at the inside sheathing surface is $14/25$ of the way, or 53°F — safely above the dew point. This thicker insulating sheathing would be your safest bet in climates with an average winter temperature of 32°F or less.

growth. But the next winter the cycle would repeat.

The Treatment

To prevent further deterioration, the wood must be kept dry. A building consultant, Bill Lotz, recommended a three-pronged approach:

1. Keep household moisture levels down by adding fans and venting the clothes dryer outdoors.
2. Seal the checking in the beams and the gaps around the beams with caulking. Then seal the beams with a clear finish.
3. Replace the foil-faced sheathing at the beams with beadboard to allow some drying at these points.

It is possible that just reducing the moisture level would do the trick. In fact, most of the damage may have occurred in the first two years when household and wood moisture levels were highest. But several layers of defense is the best approach.

Conclusions

Up to a point, wood-frame houses are forgiving; they can safely store winter condensation and get rid of it in the spring. But if you push things too far, watch out.

This house violated too many rules. It combined too much moisture with too little ventilation, too cold a condensing surface, and too few opportunities for the wood to dry out. The moisture balance was tipped the wrong way, and the consequences were severe. But how far is too far? What precautions should you take?

If you like to live dangerously, you — or an engineer — can make an educated guess about how wet a given wall system will get in a given climate, and how fast it will dry. But there are always unknowns.

To play it safe and allow for a margin of error, you should design for dry wall and ceiling cavities. Keep the following points in mind:

- You can't control how a homeowner will run a house, but you can reduce the likelihood of high moisture levels. At a minimum, install kitchen and bath fans, continuous soffit and ridge vents, and build a dry foundation. Inform the customers that if they have condensation all winter long on double-glazed windows, they need to reduce moisture levels.
- A vapor barrier with gaping holes (like the beams and recessed lights) is no barrier at all. To keep moisture out of the walls and ceiling, seal all significant seams and holes in the air/vapor barrier. If you use recessed lights, put them in a dropped ceiling or use IC-type units.
- In cold climates, keep the exterior of the wall more permeable than the interior, or keep the sheathing temperature warm enough that condensation there is rare. In practice, this means don't use foil-faced exterior insulation at all, or use a lot of it — at least 2 inches. Better yet, put it on the inside.
- And for remodelers: Don't weatherize a house without solving moisture problems first.

By Steven Bliss, co-publisher and editorial director of **The Journal of Light Construction.**

Wood Moisture Content & Interior Finishes

Complaints about misaligned wood moldings, floor squeaks, and drywall cracks are like fingernails on a blackboard to a builder's ears. Callbacks can lead to customer dissatisfaction that will threaten a builder's reputation. Regardless of how you resolve these problems, you can always count on one thing: The cure will cost you money. Prevention is always the least expensive and most effective remedy.

Here is a selection of callback complaints that builders face over and over again. Each time the questions remain the same: What is causing this problem and how can it be prevented?

Gaps in the Floor Boards

Six months after a new home is occupied, large gaps may open up between the floor boards. The gaps are rarely uniform. Usually several individual boards appear to have shrunk significantly while large areas of flooring remain tight. The separations run in a connecting zig-zag pattern across the room.

Cause: Fluctuation in relative humidity causes wood to absorb and lose moisture and, consequently, to expand and contract. Wood shrinks and swells the most in the direction tangent to the growth rings (across a typical flat-grained board) and about half as much perpendicular to them.

Shrinking and swelling along the length of a board are insignificant.

Even if the flooring is delivered at a low moisture content and installed correctly, and the indoor humidity at the time of installation is kept at a reasonable level (between 40% and 60%), moisture can still be a problem. The floor can absorb moisture from the basement slab, fresh paint, and curing drywall mud. The wood expands as it takes on this moisture and the edges of the boards press against each other and compress. As indoor humidity drops, the boards shrink to a size smaller than their installed size — a condition known as compression set. Furthermore, polyurethane finish drips between the floor boards during finishing, gluing portions together, so areas of the floor shrink as a monolith. When this happens, it appears that only a few boards have shrunk, when in reality all the boards have swelled and then shrunk.

Cure: Contrary to conventional wisdom, leaving a 3/4-inch gap around the perimeter of the room does not solve the problem. Flooring nails would have to be sheared off or pulled out of the subfloor in order for flooring to fill the recommended 3/4-inch perimeter gap.

In this case, the only cure is prevention. Relaying the floor is the only fix.

To avoid similar problems with a new floor, only install wood flooring that has equalized to its in-use moisture content (see "Acclimating Wood"). Ideally, according to the National Oak Flooring Manufacturers Association, you should buy wood flooring at 6% to 9% moisture content. But even if the flooring arrives at the job site at 10% to 12% moisture content, it should still acclimate to job-site conditions in a few days, as long as indoor humidity at the site is controlled by mechanical ventilation and, if necessary, dehumidifiers. The floor may take on additional moisture from curing construction materials after you have left the job, but at least the chances for compression set are reduced. Advise your customers that continual ventilation during the first year after construction will reduce the swelling as long as no large sources of moisture are introduced into the home. Keep records showing the moisture content of the wood when it arrived and what the humidity conditions in the home were during storage and installation. Good recordkeeping will help reduce your liability when problems arise.

Miters Open Up

Often the miters on window and door casings are tight when you install them, but they open up at either the long point or the short point after you leave the job, so the angles look as if they were miscut.

Cause: A dry piece of wood casing, tightly mitered and installed during the winter months, can look much different during the summer months as the humidity in the home rises. Indoor relative humidity can drop to 20% during cold periods and rise above 75% during humid summer months. Under these conditions, the moisture content of the wood casings can swing from 4% to as much as 16%. A 6-inch-wide casing can expand more than 1/8 inch. Because wood swells by different amounts in each direction, mitered connections remain tight at the bottom, but separate at the top as the casing swells. Similarly, the miters open near the short points as the wood shrinks (Figure 11).

Cure: To prevent miters from opening up, first install high-quality wood casing that has an 8% to 12% moisture content. The easiest way to check the moisture content is with a moisture meter (see "Moisture Meter Basics," page 232). At the very least, acclimate the casing material to indoor humidity conditions. You

---

Acclimating Wood

The moisture content in woodwork is directly related to the relative humidity level inside a home. If the relative humidity rises, the wood will absorb water and swell. If the relative humidity drops, the wood will lose water and shrink. If the air remains at a fixed humidity level, the amount of moisture bound in the wood eventually stabilizes. At this point, the wood has reached its *equilibrium moisture content.*

The trick to keeping joints tight in finish woodwork is to use wood that has acclimated to indoor humidity levels. Finish stock should be brought into the house and stickered up to allow air to circulate around it. Wood that is brought from the lumberyard at an 8% to 12% moisture content should acclimate to job-site conditions in a few days. If the wood is at 15% to 18% moisture content, allow at least a week. To be sure, check the wood with a moisture meter periodically until it reaches its equilibrium moisture content. The table below shows typical equilibrium moisture contents over a range of indoor humidity levels.

Once the wood has acclimated, make every effort to stabilize the relative humidity level in the building, at least until you've applied a finish. — *P. F.*

Indoor Humidity vs. Wood Moisture Content

Relative humidity (%)	Equilibrium moisture content (%)
10	2.5
20	4.5
30	6.2
40	7.7
50	9.5
60	11.0
70	13.1
80	16.0
90	20.5

Note: The equilibrium moisture contents shown here are typical for most softwoods at 70°F. The moisture levels will fluctuate slightly, depending on wood species and temperature.

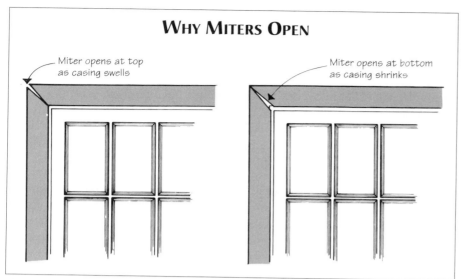

WHY MITERS OPEN

Miter opens at top as casing swells

Miter opens at bottom as casing shrinks

Figure 11. As indoor humidity fluctuates, wood casings shrink and swell, causing miters to open up. As the casing swells, miters separate at the top but remain tight at the bottom (left). As the wood shrinks, the opposite occurs (right).

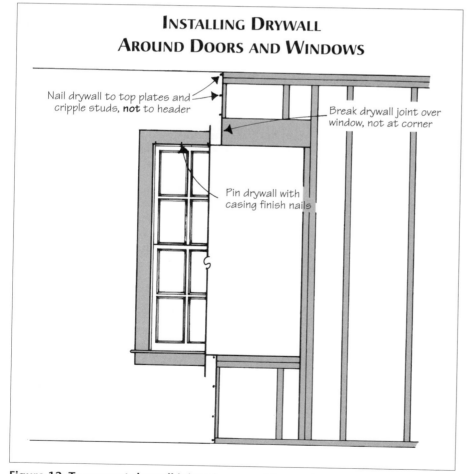

INSTALLING DRYWALL
AROUND DOORS AND WINDOWS

Nail drywall to top plates and cripple studs, **not** to header

Break drywall joint over window, not at corner

Pin drywall with casing finish nails

Figure 12. To prevent drywall joints from cracking at the corners of windows and doors, place the sheet so the joint falls in the center of the opening, and then cut out the waste. Also, do not fasten the drywall to the header, but use the interior casing to secure the loose edge of the drywall.

might try using biscuits at the joint. But beware that if the indoor humidity fluctuates too much, the wood will have to move somewhere. If the miters are held rigid, the casing may pull away from the window stool, warp, or, in extreme cases, split.

The best prevention is to educate your customers about controlling indoor humidity. Encourage them to maintain indoor humidity levels between 40% and 60% year-round. This range is healthy and will help keep your work looking good. Finally, be sure to lead your customer on a careful walk-through after the job is complete and point out the level of craftsmanship. Again, record and document humidity levels in the home and the moisture content of the trim stock during storage and installation.

Squeaky Floors

Squeaky floors rank high in nuisance value. Customers usually hold their complaints until the squeak has frayed their nerve endings. Then, when you attempt to fix it, they watch you like a hawk.

Cause: Squeaks result from wood rubbing against wood. Often the squeak occurs when a floor joist shrinks after it is installed. A space develops between the subfloor and the top of the floor joist, and when the homeowner walks over this spot, the subfloor moves against the joist and squeaks.

Cure: The best cure for floor squeaks is prevention. Use dry wood, keep it dry, and apply construction adhesive between all wooden surfaces. Also, use screws — not nails — to fasten subfloors and underlayment.

In theory, fixing floor squeaks is simple — stop the movement of the wood. But accomplishing this is often difficult.

If the squeaks are located in the first floor, you're in luck because you can usually get at the floor frame from the basement or crawlspace. One cure is to sister a length of 1x3 to the side of the offending floor joist. Holding it tight to the underside of the subfloor, attach the strip along the top edge of the joist using screws and glue. Make sure you also spread adhesive between the top of the 1x3 strip and the subfloor. The adhesive will help prevent future rubbing.

The solution is not so simple when the squeak is located on an upper level of a home. To fix these, you must add the extra step of opening and repatching the finished ceiling.

Cracked Drywall

Drywall cracks when the framing moves. This happens most often at the upper corners of windows and doors.

Cause: If the drywall joints fall at the edges of a window, the finished joint will crack when the header shrinks. Headers with a moisture content of 19% can shrink 1/4 inch across their width.

Cure: Don't break drywall sheets at the corners of an opening. Instead, lap the sheet over the corner so the joint falls in the center of the window or door span, and then cut out the opening (Figure 12). Also, do not fasten the drywall to the header. Screw the drywall into the cripples and wall plate above the headers. This lets the wallboard float down over the header. Use the interior window casing to hold the loose edge of the drywall secure.

Faux Truss Uplift

Have you ever seen drywall cracks at a ceiling corner or a center partition separate from the ceiling? This is often caused by truss uplift, but not always.

Cause: In many cases, the triple-2x12 girder in the basement that supports the floor joists is the cause (Figure 13). Since the beam is located directly beneath the center partitions and the partition sole plates are nailed securely to the deck, shrinkage of this beam can pull the partitions down-

ward, opening a crack at the ceiling. This happens frequently with lumber that is grade-stamped "S-DRY," meaning that it was surfaced at a moisture content of 19% or lower. Yet once the house is occupied and heated, the moisture content of the girder, joists, and partition studs can fall to 11%. The cumulative shrinkage of all these members can easily equal 3/8 inch.

Cure: While the cause is not true truss uplift, the effect is the same. Fasten trusses to partitions with hardware such as the Truss-Float-R (Stud Claw USA, 5370 Chestnut Ridge Rd., Orchard Park, NY 14127-3298; 716/662-7877), which allows the ceiling drywall and wall partition to float independently. Use dry framing lumber, especially for girders. Lumber stamped "MC 15" is a good choice.

The fix is the same as with truss uplift. Install a molding in the corner at the ceiling. Attach the molding to the ceiling only, allowing the wall to move.

By the way, this problem can occur in houses without roof trusses, too. To prevent this, break ceiling joists over a center bearing partition. As the partition settles, this break will act like a hinge, allowing the ceiling to drop as the center bearing shrinks.

Interior Doors Won't Close

The doors closed properly when they were installed, but after a couple of months the doors began to rub against the strike jamb and now they are too wide to be forced closed.

Cause: The doors have absorbed moisture, but to find the exact source requires a bit of investigation. Determine whether all doors have swollen or if just certain ones have, like the bathroom or basement doors. Isolated swelling suggests local humidity problems.

Cure: Wood doors should be delivered and installed at a moisture

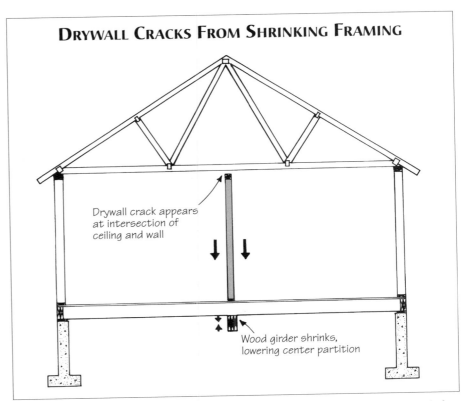

DRYWALL CRACKS FROM SHRINKING FRAMING

Drywall crack appears at intersection of ceiling and wall

Wood girder shrinks, lowering center partition

Figure 13. Drywall cracks at the ceiling can open up when the basement girder shrinks and pulls the partition downward. The only fix is to install crown molding over the crack. Attach the molding to the ceiling but not to the wall.

MOISTURE METER BASICS

There are two types of meters for measuring the moisture content in wood — *electric resistance* meters and *dielectric* meters.

Dielectric meters. Dielectric meters send out a radio signal that passes through the wood. The meter reads the return signal and measures either the power loss or the capacitance of the signal. These properties will vary depending on the moisture in the wood. Dielectric meters tend to be expensive ($300 and up) but they have one distinct advantage: You need only pass the device over the surface, so you can measure moisture content without damaging finished materials.

Electric resistance meters. In most cases, however, an electric resistance meter will be sufficient. You can tell an electric resistance meter by its two short, sharp metal prongs. To use the meter, stick these prongs about 1/4 inch into the back face of a board, which will leave two small holes. The meter passes a low-voltage electric current from one prong to another through the wood and measures the resistance. The wetter the board, the less resistance to the current it will have. Thus, an electric resistance meter is essentially an ohm meter, but instead of reading out in ohms of resistance, the meter translates the reading

An inexpensive electric resistance meter with a strong shell, such as this one from Veritas, is adequate for gauging the moisture content of lumber on site.

into percentage of moisture content. Readings will be slightly different for different species of wood; when you buy the meter, find out if there is some way to adjust for this.

There is a wide variety of electric resistance meters, ranging in price from $40 to $300. The less expensive models have built-in prongs, and read out at whole number percentages of moisture content. Most of these are only accurate between a 6% and 25% moisture content, but this is suitable for on-site use. Better low-end meters will provide a chart for calculating an adjustment for different wood species. The more expensive models have external electrode prongs that are connected to the meter by a cord, can be recalibrated for different species, and have a wider range of accuracy. For use on site, a medium priced ($140) meter with a durable shell is your best buy, as it will inevitably get dropped. For more information, see "Sources of Supply" at end of chapter.

— *Clayton DeKorne*

---

content between 6% and 12%. But even those doors can become unstable in houses with fluctuating humidity levels. For best results, doors should be sealed as soon as they are delivered (right after they are made would be even better). If the doors are prehung units, remove all the hardware and seal the undercut edge and all hardware cutouts, including hinge mortises and the inside of lock bores. Endgrain is very absorbent. An unsealed edge will suck up moisture rapidly under humid conditions. If doors arrive at the job site unsealed, check the moisture content by inserting the probes of a moisture meter into the endgrain. Then seal it when conditions are right.

To solve the immediate problem, plane the door to size and reseal the edges. Also, as with all wood movement problems, control the indoor humidity.

By Paul Fisette, a wood technologist and director of the Building Materials Technology and Management program at the University of Massachusetts in Amherst.

MOISTURE PROBLEMS FROM "DRY BASEMENTS"

We've known for a long time that much of the moisture that condenses on windows in winter, or promotes mold growth in summer, comes from damp basements or crawlspaces. With many indoor moisture problems, however, the source of the moisture is not so obvious. New research indicates that in many cases the basement or crawlspace is still at fault even though it appears to be dry.

Below-Grade Moisture Diffusion

At the University of Minnesota Underground Space Center researchers showed that "dry" basements can, in fact, contribute significant amounts of soil moisture to a home. Both surface water and deep ground water are sources of this moisture, which rises up by capillarity and evaporation into the sandy soil and then diffuses into the basement through the concrete walls and floor. The study also showed exterior wall waterproofing alone is only marginally effective at solving the problem.

The researchers built four test basements in a well-drained sandy site and over four months measured 36 and 50 gallons of moisture entry though a block foundation and a poured foundation, respectively. (Why more water entered through the poured concrete than the block in this test is unclear.)

The scientists installed 2 inches of Styrofoam on the outside of one of the foundations to test the effectiveness of exterior wall waterproofing. Contrary to expectations, the Styrofoam only slightly reduced moisture entry, from 36 to 30 gallons. An identical basement with *interior* foam insulation showed significantly better moisture control, with only 14 gallons measured.

The explanation, according to Minnesota researcher Louis Goldberg, is that much of the moisture enters up through the footings (Figure 14). Since interior wall waterproofing is inside the footings, it isolates the basement interior from the footings and the moisture. Exterior wall waterproofing, on the other hand, is outside the footings. For truly effective wall waterproofing, the footings must also be waterproofed. More on that later.

Below-Grade Moist Air Leakage

Underground air leakage into houses has become an important issue since radon was discovered in homes. But radon is just one component of soil gas. During winter, soil gas is usually saturated (100% relative humidity) with *water vapor*. Whenever a basement is at a lower atmospheric pressure than the surrounding soil (caused by exhaust fans, combustion appliances, or the "stack effect"), soil gas enters through cracks and penetra-

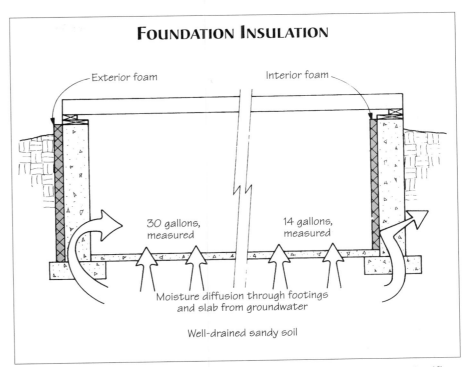

Figure 14. Researchers at the University of Minnesota discovered that significant amounts of moisture rise up into the wall through the footings. So placing the insulation on the interior surface is far more effective than on the exterior since the footings are then outside the waterproof layer.

tions and carries moisture into the basement.

In two Canadian test houses, 7.5 and almost 10 gallons of water per day, respectively, were drawn in through basement air leakage when the houses were depressurized with small (125-cfm) exhaust fans. These results indicate that foundations must be properly sealed against air leakage as well as moisture diffusion. Fortunately, many of the techniques used to seal a basement against radon, such as caulked control joints in slabs and airtight sump covers, will also help control water vapor.

Practical Underground Air and Vapor Barriers

As with above-grade air and vapor retarders, proper design is mostly common sense. The vapor retarder should be a durable, low-permeable material that covers most of the foundation on either the inner or outer surface. Neither concrete nor block is a good vapor retarder. Some type of membrane or parging must be applied.

The air barrier, on the other hand, should be continuous over the entire foundation. Concrete is a suitable air barrier as long as it isn't cracked and all seams and penetrations are sealed.

As with above-grade air and vapor barriers, a single material component, like sealed polyethylene sheeting or rigid foam, can serve as both an air and a vapor barrier. If poly is used on the foundation exterior, the plastic should be heavy-duty (minimum 6-mil) and preferably made for below-grade use. Recommended products include *Cross-Tuff* (Manufactured Plastics and Distribution, Inc., Palmer Lake, CO; 800/353-9345; www.mpdplastics.com), *Dura-Tuff* (Yunker Plastics, Inc., Elkhorn, WI; 800/236-3328; www.yunker-plastics.com), and *Tu-Tuff* (Sto-Cote Products, Richmond, IL; 800/435-2621). Another option is to build a stud wall on the interior and

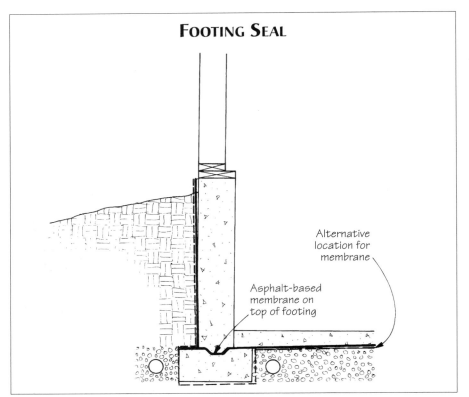

FOOTING SEAL

Alternative location for membrane

Asphalt-based membrane on top of footing

Figure 15. The best foundation air/vapor barrier is a continuous long-lasting membrane installed under the slab, over the footing, and up the exterior wall surface. An alternative is to install the membrane around the outside of the footing.

important to seal them against air and moisture leakage.

The Footings Question

The Minnesota research clearly suggests that homes can be kept drier by installing a waterproof layer either on top of or underneath the footings. One option commonly used by Swedish builders is to place the high-density polystyrene foam either on top of or underneath footings for thermal and moisture protection.

Despite engineering assurances and Swedish documentation, however, most U.S. builders will be reluctant to build a house on rigid foam. A more palatable alternative is a durable waterproofing membrane. W.R. Meadows, Inc. (P.O. Box 338, Hampshire, IL 60140; 800/342-5976) sells a line of specially reinforced asphaltic membranes for foundation moisture. The company recommends that the membrane be installed over the top of the footing and lapped up the exterior wall surface (Figure 15), but it can also wrap around the bottom of the footing.

By J.D. Ned Nisson, president of Energy Design Associates, a building systems consulting firm in N.Y.C., and editor of **Energy Design Update** *of Arlington, Mass.*

place the poly under the drywall as you would in a typical outside wall.

Block Foundations

Block foundations are more prone to moisture intrusion than poured foundations. Air circulation within the cores distributes moisture over the entire wall area. Blocks are also very porous to air. You can literally blow through most concrete blocks, so it is especially

USING MOISTURE METERS

I learned about wood moisture content the hard way. One hot, humid New England summer we laid down an absolutely gorgeous solid-cherry plank floor. But after just one winter's worth of dry central heating, the entire floor surface turned into a maze of ugly cracks and wide gaps between the boards. The client's response was none too pretty, either. In another home I worked on around that time, we installed an oak floor over a newly laid plywood substrate. Less than a month later we came back to a rip-

pled floor surface that resembled a mill pond on a breezy autumn day.

The demons that visited those projects were not hidden in the methods we used to put down the floor. Our installation techniques were fine. Nor can I pin the blame upon the woods themselves. Cherry and oak are generally well-mannered species. The fault lay in my ignorance of how wood moves in relation to moisture content, and in not having a couple of crucial instruments: an electronic moisture meter and low-cost digital hygrometer.

Identifying the Problems

In the case of the cherry flooring, although it was kiln-dried, it had probably soaked up a considerable amount of moisture between the time we had it delivered to the site and when we installed it (we stacked it in the client's garage over the summer). The moisture content of the floor boards likely grew to 12% or more, consequently expanding them in width and thickness. Once the floor was laid, the boards had no choice but to shrink and crack over the next winter as the home's heat-

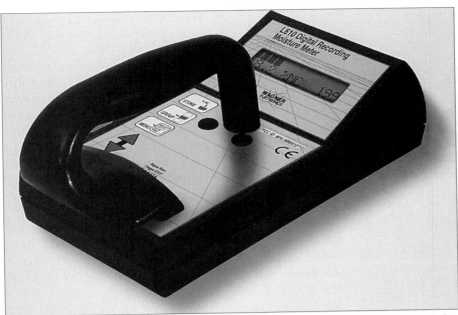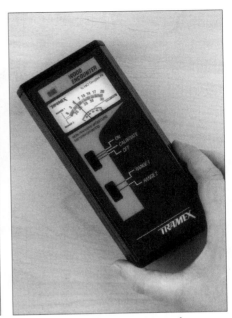

Figure 16. Dielectric meters don't require pushing pins in the material. Instead, you simply pass the meter over the surface. The section of material measured, however, must be at least as wide and thick as the electromagnetic field that the instrument emits.

ing system sucked the moisture out of the wood.

The rippling of the oak flooring, on the other hand, was a result of expansion. If I had the foresight (and the tools) to check the moisture content of the plywood subfloor, which I suspected may have been rained on, I probably would have discovered a level of 15% to 18% — not something I should have put dry wood on. It was only a matter of time before the drier oak sponged up some of this moisture (yes, even through the plastic vapor barrier) and cupped upward as the edges pushed hard against one another.

These days, I never lay down a wood floor without first using a meter to check the amount of moisture in the flooring and sub-flooring.

Meter Types

There are two main types of moisture meters: resistance meters and dielectric meters.

Resistance meters. Resistance-type moisture meters have two sharp metal prongs that pass a low-voltage electric current between them. The wetter a material is, the less resistance that material has to conducting the electric current. Thus, this type of moisture meter is similar to an ohm meter, yet it's calibrated to read a material's resistance as a percentage of moisture content. The range for most meters extends from 6% moisture content (fully seasoned wood in an arid climate) to 36% (unseasoned "green" wood).

To take a reading with a resistance meter, you insert its two electrodes (sharp pins) into the material and read the percentage of moisture content shown on the meter (or series of LED lights). Generally speaking, the deeper you insert the pins, the more accurate the reading will be. Don't prolong taking the reading with a resistance meter, however. As the current passes through the wood, a small amount of electrolysis begins to occur, which sometimes can create an artificially low reading.

Dielectric meters. Dielectric-type meters do not require you to push pins into the material (Figure 16). Instead, these instruments irradiate the material with a low-power (harmless) electromagnetic field that reads the apparent density of the material. Unlike resistance-type meters, which read the moisture of only the wettest fibers lying along a straight line between the two electrodes, the dielectric analyzes a broader area. While this helps ensure a more accurate reading, it can also work against you in some situations. A dielectric meter needs to be held to a mass at least as large in area as the electromagnetic field that the instrument emits. (The field of the Wagner L606, for example, is about 1³/4 inches wide by 2¹/2 inches long by ³/4 inches deep.) Resistance meters, on the other hand, can take a reading in nearly any size or configuration of material — you just need enough surface area to push in the two pins.

Using Moisture Meters

There are some tricks when using moisture meters to ensure that you get accurate, consistent readings. First, never be satisfied with a single reading on a board — you could be measuring a dry or wet pocket. Instead, always read a number of

Figure 17. With an inexpensive resistance meter that has short prongs, you will need to make a fresh cut at least 1¹/₂ inches in from one end (top). Or, drive a pair of finish nails to extend the prongs (center). Higher-cost resistance meters often have remote electrodes with interchangeable, insulated pins (bottom).

spots and average the results. It does not usually matter, by the way, if you take the readings with or across the grain. However, it may matter if the wood is rough-sawn — the up-raised fibers tend to dry out or absorb water more quickly than the fibers along a smoothed surface. Whether rough or smooth, always wipe away any standing surface moisture before taking a reading, and if possible, wait to allow the surface of the board to dry.

Measure at the core. If the board is thicker than 1 inch, you should take a reading at the core to see if it is substantially wetter than the surfaces.

With a resistance meter, you can do this in two ways: The first is to make a fresh crosscut to expose the interior of the board, then push the pins into the end grain. Unless the board has been exposed to rain, you need not make the cut more than 3 inches in from the rough end to get an accurate reading. The other option is to drive the electrodes through the face into the core of the board. If your meter has only short electrodes, you can drive a pair of finish nails into the core (set them in at the pin spacing) and take a reading off their heads (Figure 17). You should paint the nail shanks so the meter's current passes between the tips. The shanks of long-pin electrodes are usually insulated.

Because the field depth of most dielectric meters is about 1 inch, they automatically read to the core of a 2-inch-thick board. You'll need to measure off a fresh end grain cut if the board is thicker.

Taking readings of thin boards can be tricky with any type of moisture meter. Dielectrics cannot, for example, read any material less than about ¹/₂ inch thick. Even at this dimension you must be sure nothing sits directly behind the wood, as any type of material (especially metal) can throw off the reading. The trick to reading thin stock with dielectrics is to gather up enough stock to make a stack about ³/₄ inch high. The reading then automatically averages the moisture content of all the pieces.

Watch the variables. To ensure an accurate reading, you must take several variables into account (see "Getting Accurate Moisture Readings"). Most resistance meters are calibrated to a certain temperature setting and to one species (or to be more precise, to the specific gravity of that species). You then have to calculate the true reading by multiplying the number shown on the meter by an adjustment percentile taken from a chart to correct for temperature and species. Top-of-the-line resistance meters (such as Lignomat's Mini-Master and Lignomaster series) use microprocessors to automatically calculate these adjustments for you, once you've punched in numbers for the correct species and temperature.

Dielectric instruments are unaffected by temperature or humidity, which is a distinct advantage over resistance meters. But you must still make corrections from a chart for species (the Wagner models, for example, are calibrated to Douglas fir).

Measuring the moisture in plywood. Taking moisture content readings of plywood or other man-made wood products containing glues and compressed wood fibers is problematic. While many meter manufacturers can provide you with calibration tables for some of these materials, you might consider this simple, but accurate, approach instead: Measure a sample that you've thoroughly dried in an oven (you'll know it's dry when no more weight is lost after about 24 hours in a 220°F oven). The meter should read zero. If it doesn't, record the reading and add this number to correct each reading.

If you suspect that your meter is consistently taking untrue readings — or if a bone-dry sample doesn't read zero — you may need to send the instrument back to the manufacturer for recalibration. But first check the zero adjustment of the needle, the condition of the battery, and the cleanliness of the electrodes or sensor pad.

Measuring Moisture in the Air

For first-rate finish work, it's often not enough to just monitor the moisture in the wood, then slap the boards down when they've reached a suitable moisture content. You also have to make some attempt to monitor the moisture in the air on site while the wood is in storage awaiting installation.

To measure the moisture content of the surrounding air (the humidity level), I use a low-cost digital hygrometer. This tool can tell me what will happen to the wood when

GETTING ACCURATE MOISTURE READINGS

To ensure accurate readings in wood, watch out for these variables:

- *Species.* With either simple dielectric or resistance meters, you have to correct for the wood species. Simple resistance meters are calibrated to one species (typically Doug fir). For any other species, you have to calculate a true reading by multiplying by a number shown on a chart to correct for that species.
- *Temperature.* With resistance meters you also have to correct for temperature, using a similar chart. Dielectric meters are not as sensitive to different temperatures. However, if the wood temperature is below freezing, a dielectric meter may give a reading that erroneously adds 15% to the apparent moisture content.
- *Wild grain or knots.* Dielectrics are particularly affected by anomalous changes in the wood's density. Try to avoid knots and wild grain.
- *Surface moisture.* Always wipe the surface off and allow it to dry if possible. This is more of a problem with inexpensive resistance meters with short, uninsulated pins, because the meter will read the path of least resistance — in this case, saturated surface fibers. Better resistance meters (the Delmhorst with a 26 ES electrode, for example) have long insulated pins that eliminate this problem. Also, if wood is rough-sawn, the raised fibers absorb or lose moisture more readily than a smooth-surface board, producing untrue readings near the surface with resistance meters.
- *Finishes.* Some finishes and preservatives contain salts that can affect resistance meters. (Dielectric meters are unaf-fected by these salts.) To check if a finish is affecting the reading, dry a finished sample in the oven and then check it with the meter. If it reads wet, the finish has salt in it, so you won't be able to rely on a resistance meter.
- *Microenvironments.* Avoid taking readings of installed components — like flooring — in areas subjected to direct sun, heat outlets, or excessive dampness.
- *Readouts.* Resistance-type meters with LED readouts may be affected by ambient static electricity or electromagnetic fields. Near motors or wires carrying current, readings may fluctuate or two lights may come on at the same time. Move the wood away from the affected area and try again. Dielectric meters are unaffected by stray electromagnetic fields.

— J.T.

LOW-COST HUMIDITY METERS

Problem scenario: Homeowner calls builder, complaining of condensation dripping from "those crummy windows." Builder asks homeowner what the humidity in the house is. Homeowner reads 30% relative humidity from the brass dial humidity meter on the wall. So begins another moisture callback.

Since one primary cause of moisture problems is high indoor relative humidity, and since most "hardware store" humidity meters are notoriously inaccurate, the first step to resolve this problem should be a visit to the home with an accurate portable hygrometer. The problem is finding one.

Digital meters. A recent research project by Canada Mortgage and Housing Corporation (CMHC) showed that those digital units cannot always be relied on for accuracy.

CMHC tested three different brands: Bionaire, Micronta (made by Radio Shack), and Thermo-Hygro (made by Airguide, and sold under many other brand names). When placed in a calibration chamber, the Bionaire and Micronta units were accurate to within 5% of the humidity range from about 25% to 80%. But the Thermo-Hygro read up to 20% too high over the entire range.

According to an environmental consultant who has extensively studied these meters, most of the low-cost digital hygrometers, including all three in the CMHC tests, are produced by the same company. All three use the same *Shinyei* humidity sensor. The only difference between the various models is the packaging of the electronics.

In general, the Shinyei sensor is fairly accurate and reliable. The problem is in occasional manufacturing inconsistencies — now and then, you will get one that is way off. If you buy just one of these meters, there is no guarantee that it's accurate.

There are two solutions to this problem. The first is to have the meter checked against a calibrated hygrometer. The other is to test several units and look for agreement. If they all agree, they are probably accurate.

Mechanical meters. When all is said and done, a simple mechanical meter may be a builder's best bet. According to CMHC researchers, if you use a simple calibration procedure to verify the accuracy of a dial hygrometer, you have the best chance for getting an accurate reading.

The calibration procedure goes like this: Mix $1/2$ cup of table salt (sodium chloride) with $1/4$ cup water in a coffee cup. The salt doesn't have to dissolve, it just needs to be stirred so the water covers the salt. Then put this mixture with the dial meter in a Zip-lock bag (an airtight environment) and let it sit for about 8 hours so the temperatures of the mixture and the meter equalize. The salt mixture will create a climate with 75% relative humidity inside the bag.

If the meter does not read 75%, you can reset the dial position by either giving the indicator a delicate twist, or by adjusting a screw, if it has one. Some dial-type humidity meters have fancy cases that prevent you from moving the needle. So if a model doesn't have the screw adjust, it's better to steer clear of it.

This procedure will calibrate most mechanical meters to within ±5%, which is an acceptable degree of accuracy for most builders. The only meter the CMHC team was unable to accurately calibrate was the Taylor 6567. This model had problems below 40% relative humidity.

When reading the humidity level, according to CMHC, a builder is looking for broad differences — those between 20%, 40%, and 75%. Properly calibrated, a mechanical humidity meter will do this for you.

Adapted with permission from Energy Design Update, published monthly by Cutter Information Corp. of Arlington, Mass.

Digital hygrometer. *A simple electronic hygrometer can measure the relative humidity on site where trim stock is stored. Not all meters read accurately, however. Compare the meter to several others of the same make, or to a calibrated mechanical model, to make sure it reads accurately.*

it's placed in a certain environment. It's also useful as a troubleshooting tool in new and old houses, but you need to make sure you get an accurate one (see "Low-Cost Humidity Meters").

When measuring the humidity in the storage area, you want a relative humidity that's similar to what's inside the house — anything in the range of 30% to 50%. Most of all I want to avoid storing dry wood in a humid environment, or installing dry wood in an abnormally moist interior climate. If the wood measures 7% to 8% moisture content at 70°F on the moisture meter, for example, it will be perfectly stable in an environment that maintains this temperature at a relative humidity level of 35%. If the hygrometer reads a higher humidity level in the storage area or room in which the wood is to be installed, I can be sure that the wood will suck in some moisture and expand (and I can tell my client that). Changes in ambient relative humidity have a much greater effect on the moisture content in the wood than changes in temperature alone. On more than one occasion, my use of the humidity meter along with my moisture meter has nipped a potential problem in the bud — or explained the flowering of another.

By Jim Tolpin, a finish carpenter in Port Townsend, Wash.

SOURCES OF SUPPLY

Epoxy Resins

Abatron Inc.
Kenosha, WI
800/445-1754
www.abatron.com
LiquidWood, WoodEpox

Sika Corp.
Lyndhurst, NJ
800/933-7452
www.sikausa.com
Colma-Dur Gel, Sikadur Hi-Mod

Borax-Based Wood Preservatives

Chemical Specialties Inc.
Charlotte, NC
800/421-8661
www.treatedwood.com
Impel Rods

U.S. Borax Inc.
Valencia, CA
661/287-5400
www.borax.com
Tim-Bor

Nisus Corp.
Rockford, TN
800/264-0870
www.nisuscorp.com
Bora-Care, Impel Rods

Moisture Meters

Delmhorst Instrument Co.
Towaco, NJ
877/335-6467
www.delmhorst.com

Lignomat USA
Portland, OR
800/227-2105
www.lignomat.com

Wagner Electronic Products
Rogue River, OR
800/585-7609
www.wwwagner.com

Lee Valley & Veritas
Ogdensburg, NY
800/871-8158
www.leevalley.com

SDS Company
Paso Robles, CA
805/238-3229

Humidity Meters

Bionaire
El Paso, TX
800/788-5350
www.bionaire.com

Radio Shack
Fort Worth, TX
800/843-7422
www.radioshack.com
(or check the Yellow Pages for local listings)

Sonin, Inc.
Charlotte, NC
800/223-7511
www.sonin.com

CHAPTER 10

INSECT DAMAGE

- Wood-Destroying Insects

- Controlling Termites and Carpenter Ants with Borates

- Controlling Subterranean Termites

WOOD-DESTROYING INSECTS

One and one-half billion dollars is spent annually in the U.S. to treat, repair, and replace wood in buildings that has been damaged by wood-destroying insects. Recognizing damage is usually pretty easy, but figuring out who's responsible can be tricky. Since selection of the right remedial treatment depends on knowing who's responsible, it's important to identify the offenders.

With this primer on some of wood's six-legged pests, you should be able to figure out who's been eating you and your customers out of house and home.

Termites

With two thirds of the total annual infestation control bill spent on this insect alone, termites are by far the most economically damaging pest plaguing wood structures. Though more than 50 species of termites live in the U.S., about 95% of all damage is done by subterranean termites, which nest underground. Other termites of local significance include drywood termites found along America's southern border from California to Florida, dampwood termites of the coastal Pacific Northwest, and a recent exotic arrival in several Gulf states, the Formosan termite.

Lacking the natural antifreeze of other insects, subterranean termites cannot hibernate during freezing weather and must remain active year-round. Concentrated in the Southeast, they have expanded northward only since the early 1900s with the widespread adoption of central heating. These soil-dwellers live in large colonies whose six-legged citizenry is divided into castes of kings and queens, workers, and soldiers. Responsible for reproduction, kings and queens are black or brown, up to 1/2 inch long, and winged. Sterile, eyeless, and wingless, workers are white and 1/4 inch long (Figure 1). Rarely seen because they avoid light, workers maintain the nest and, in foraging for food, destroy wood. Some metamorphose into soldiers who fend off invaders with menacing mandibles.

After several years of colony growth, swarms of winged reproductives will emerge from the soil in spring, usually in daylight and after a rain, and fly off to establish a new colony. Termites stake out new territories based on their need for high soil moisture and a readily available source of wood from which they derive their diet of cellulose. Once a suitable site is found, reproductives shed their wings and reenter the ground.

In nature, termites feast on downed and dead trees and stumps

USDA

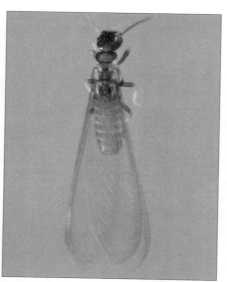
DOW ELANCO

DOW ELANCO

Figure 1. Termite workers (top left) are 1/4 inch long and wingless. They avoid light and thus are rarely seen. After several years of colony growth, winged adults (top right) emerge briefly and swarm to establish new colonies. Termites will tunnel in all wood products, except for PT, and can cause serious structural damage (above) — typically hidden below an unbroken wood surface.

and may forage for food 100 feet or so from their underground headquarters. In buildings, termites will attack virtually all wood- and cellulose-based building materials. In addition to structural lumber, plywood, flooring, and siding, I've found their damage in woodfiber insulation board sheathing, cardboard forming tubes, wastepaper-based cellulose insulation, and even the paper faces of gypsum wallboard. Though attracted to odors given off by moist or decaying wood, termites will attack wood at a moisture content as low as 8%, which is typical of the year-round average moisture content of indoor wood across most of the U.S. No species of untreated wood is immune from attack, but wood pressure-impregnated with CCA (chromated copper arsenate) preservative is an effective deterrent.

Termites usually enter structures through existing gaps at or below grade. If they can't find shrinkage and settlement cracks in foundations and slabs or gaps at electrical, plumbing, and septic penetrations, they build shelter tubes of soil and digested wood up the sides of exposed foundations to reach the wood above. Contrary to popular belief, metal shields inserted between foundation and sill won't stop termites from entering, as these beasties will simply build shelter tubes up and over such inconveniences. Shields, however, do force shelter tubes to be built where they are more easily visible, prevent termites

WOOD-DESTROYING INSECTS AT A GLANCE

	Preferred Wood Type	Preferred Wood Moisture Content	Emergence/ Bore Holes	Galleries and Frass	Possible Reinfest-ation	Typical Source of Infestation	Remarks
Termite	Softwood, hardwood, sapwood, heartwood, old wood, new wood*	>8%	Seldom seen; uses existing gaps, cracks	Messy, packed with excrema, soil, wood fragments	Yes	Enters heated buildings from soil	Seldom seen except when swarming; discarded wings indicate presence
Carpenter Ant	Softwood, hardwood, sapwood, heartwood, old wood, new wood*	>15%	Seldom seen; uses existing gaps, cracks	Clean with "sandpapered" walls; insect parts and shredded wood near nest	Yes	Enters heated and unheated buildings from soil	Often seen foraging in building though nest is in nearby tree or stump
True Powderpost Beetle	Hardwood, sapwood, new wood*	6% to 30%	Round, 1/32" to 1/8"	Loosely packed with very fine powder	Yes	Brought into buildings in infected furniture, flooring, firewood, etc.	Hardwoods coated with film-forming finishes safe from attack
Old House Borer	Softwood, sapwood, new wood*	10% to 30%	Oval, 1/4" to 3/8"	Tightly packed with fine powder and tiny pellets; walls with ripple-marks	Yes	Brought into buildings in infected new and salvaged lumber; can enter from outside	Larvae in wood make rasping, ticking, or clicking sound
Anobiid Beetle	Softwood, hardwood, sapwood, old wood, new wood*	13% to 30%	Round, 1/16" to 1/8"	Loosely packed with fine powder and tiny pellets	Yes	Enters damp areas like crawlspaces and basements from outside	Infestations develop slowly; 30 holes per sq. ft. indicates well established infestation

* "New wood" is less than ten years old; "old wood" is more than ten years old.

from entering sills directly through hollow masonry block foundations, and provide a capillary break between concrete and wood.

Poor building practices that invite termites include burying stumps, cutoffs, and other wood debris during backfilling, failing to remove

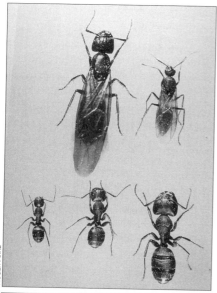

ROGER AKRE

DON JACKSON

Figure 2. Carpenter ant queens and males are winged and up to an inch long. Workers range from 1/8 to 1/2 inch long (top). Carpenter ants don't eat wood, but carve tunnels for nesting — preferring moist decayed wood or foam insulation. Tunnels in wood (above) run parallel to the grain.

wood or cardboard concrete forms, using untreated wood in ground contact, extending siding and trim to 6 inches above grade or below, and leaving soil exposed in crawlspaces. Termites' high soil-moisture needs can be met by omitting gutters and downspouts, backfilling with poor-draining soils, or failing to provide adequate foundation and site drainage.

Undetected, termite damage can lead to serious structural damage and even collapse. Because termites hollow out the interiors of wood members without breaking through the surface, there are few visible signs of their presence. Symptoms include blistered or puckered wood surfaces, crushed and collapsed wood at framing bearing points, and fine soil lining the edges of cracks in concrete and masonry. Termite-damaged wood resounds with a dull thud when tapped with a hammer. When broken open, termite galleries (tunnels) are characteristically messy and often filled with a mixture of fecal matter, soil, and chewed wood that looks like dried oatmeal. Because they prefer to tunnel parallel to the grain in the softer early wood portion of growth rings, damaged wood may appear as a series of concentric shells of late wood. In the absence of live insects, there are a few clues that reveal whether termite damage is ongoing. Clouds of swarming insects and piles of shed wings nearby strongly suggest it; shelter tubes that reappear after being destroyed confirm it.

Creating a toxic moat around your customer's castle by treating soil with a pesticide before footings, foundation, and slab are poured is the best defense against termite invasion in new construction. Infestations in existing buildings can be treated by pressure-injecting pesticide into the soil surrounding the foundation and beneath the slab. Though over-the-counter termiticides are available, treating

for termites is best left to reputable professionals.

Carpenter Ants

Carpenter ants, though found throughout the U.S., are primarily a problem in the Northeast and Northwest. Like termites, these colonial insects live mainly underground. Unlike termites, carpenter ants don't actually eat wood, but tunnel in it only as a place to live. The distinction may seem trivial, but it's not. CCA-treated wood, for example, while immune to termite attack, is still susceptible to carpenter ant destruction because they don't ingest the tainted wood.

Most of the many kinds of native carpenter ants are black or black and dark red. Kings and queens (reproductives) are winged and up to one inch long. Wingless workers are 1/8 to 1/2 inch long (Figure 2). Carpenter ants may nest underground, in live and dead trees, in stumps, in stored lumber and firewood, and inside wood buildings. Those nesting outdoors hibernate during freezing weather, while ants cozying up inside heated buildings may be active all year. Workers forage for food up to 150 feet from their nest. Plant juices, "honeydew" secreted by aphids, insects, and household food scraps make up the menu.

Winged carpenter ants swarm from mature nests in spring to establish new colonies, shedding their wings before nesting anew. Often mistaken for termites, and vice versa, it's easy to tell the two apart. Carpenter ants have two pairs of wings of unequal length, a constricted, hourglass waist, and "elbowed" antennae. Both pairs of termites' wings are the same length, and their waists and antennae straight. Color alone tells you that so-called "white ants" are actually worker termites.

Ants enter buildings via the same routes as termites, but they don't build shelter tubes. No untreated wood (not even CCA-treated wood) is safe from ant attack. These hexapods prefer wood whose moisture content is 15% or higher and are especially attracted to decayed wood. As owners of stressed-skin panel homes have learned, carpenter ants will also tunnel in the panels' foam cores. Panel makers now treat the foam with a pesticide and recommend that panel edges near grade be capped with a metal shield.

Carpenter ants excavate an irregular maze of tunnels in wood parallel to the grain, often following softer early wood. Fastidious in habit, their galleries are free of debris, with signature "sandpapered" walls. Extensive tunneling can weaken structural members, but ant infestations are usually detected long before damage becomes serious. A sure sign of activity is the coarse shreds of wood called frass, and occasionally insect parts, that workers dispose of through joints and cracks outside the nests as they tidy their tunnels. In established infestations, ants can sometimes be heard gnawing on wood.

Live ants seen inside a home may or may not mean the building is infested. If, for example, only a few ants show up each day and it's late spring or summer, they're probably workers on a foraging expedition from a nest in a nearby tree or stump. Don't overlook the possibility of ants escaping from firewood brought inside. However, if more than a few are appearing inside daily while the ground is still cold, then a nest hidden in a wall may have gotten the late winter sun's wakeup call. Consistently large numbers of ants seen inside during the winter or winged ants seen inside any time of year are sure signs of an indoor nest.

Inviting trouble spots include eaves and walls wetted by roof leaks, ice dams, condensation, and overflowing or leaky gutters. Plumbing leaks and within-wall condensation can raise wood moisture content to ant-attractive levels. Exposed soil, wood in ground contact, inadequate ventilation, and poor foundation and site drainage create crawlspace and basement moisture conditions that attract ants. Homeowners can attract ants by leaving crumbs about or by putting pet food in bowls outdoors.

Once a carpenter ant nest has been located, usually by observing the path by which foraging workers travel, it can be easily treated. When a nest behind a wall can't be precisely located, professional exterminators may resort to a "shotgun" approach, spraying pesticide through bored holes in hopes of hitting the hideaway.

Old House Borers

One type of long-horned beetle common in the mid-Atlantic states, the misnamed "old house borer," primarily infests wood that has been in service for ten years or less. This brownish-black 1/2- to 1-inch-long beetle has lengthy antennae and twin bumps on its thorax. But it's in the worm-like larval stage that this bugger does damage to attic framing, floor joists over crawlspaces and basements, and other softwood structural members (Figure 3).

After larvae emerge from eggs deposited in drying checks or joints between framing members, they immediately bore into wood. Homeowners may hear the faint ticking sound these white, up to 1 1/4-inch-long larvae make when tunneling. Though their attack is limited to

Figure 3. Old house borer larvae (at right) attack the sapwood of structural members. They may feed for three to seven years before emerging from 1/4- to 3/8-inch exit holes as adult beetles (at left).

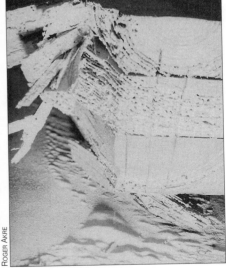

Figure 4. Powderpost beetles (left) are no more than 1/4 inch long, and are reddish-brown to black. The larvae attack only the sapwood of porous hardwoods, like oak, ash, and elm. Fresh frass the color of new wood indicates an active infestation (right).

Figure 5. Anobiid beetles (top) are $1/8$ to $1/4$ inch long. Attracted by moist conditions, they fly into the house and lay eggs in cracks and checks in wood (center). The larvae attack the sapwood of hardwood or softwood for three or more years, then emerge as adult beetles from $1/16$- to $1/8$-inch round exit holes (above).

the sapwood, it is so thorough that the wood beneath a thin, intact surface layer may be completely pulverized. Oval larval tunnels, running parallel to the grain and up to $3/8$ inch wide, are tightly packed with fine powder and rod-shaped fecal pellets. Walls are characteristically ripple-marked, looking like sand that's been lapped by waves. Larvae feed in wood for three to seven years before emerging as adult beetles sometime between July and October. Adults leave wood through $1/4$- to $3/8$-inch oval exit holes previously made by larvae. Occasionally exit holes are chewed through the materials covering infested lumber — wood sheathing, siding, flooring, and even gypsum wallboard. Exit holes are often the first and only sign of infestation seen by homeowners. Fortunately, the majority of infestations die out once adults emerge.

Most old house borer infestations are caused during construction of new homes when softwood lumber infected during drying or storage or salvaged wood is used. Beetles can infest or reinfest wood older than ten years, providing its nutritional content is still high and its moisture content exceeds 10%. Even professionals find it difficult to determine whether an old house borer infestation is active. Two sure signs of ongoing activity are the sounds made by tunneling larvae and the reappearance of fresh frass on cleaned surfaces. In the absence of exit holes, bulging or blistered wood surfaces over powder-packed tunnels indicate activity.

True Powderpost Beetles

Three distinct insects, true powderpost beetles, false powderpost beetles, and anobiid beetles, are collectively called powderpost beetles, because each reduces wood to a fine powdery frass. Of these, true powderpost beetles and anobiids are the more common.

True powderpost beetles occur throughout the U.S. and are second

only to termites in the dollar damage done. From residences in dead trees, they routinely infest hardwood logs and lumber at sawmills and storage yards. Reddish-brown to black, and at most $1/4$ inch long, occasionally-seen adults lay eggs only in the large early wood pores of ring-porous hardwoods, like oak, ash, and elm, that are less than ten years old (Figure 4).

After hatching, these larvae limit their attack to sapwood with a moisture content of 6% to 30%, where they tunnel extensively in search of stored starch. Hidden under a veneer of unaffected wood, galleries are loosely packed with talcum powder-like frass that sifts from drying checks and $1/32$- to $1/8$-inch round bore holes. Adults emerge from wood between April and September after one to two years. Infestations tend to die out naturally as the carbohydrate content of wood drops over the first few years, but reinfestation can occur if favorable food and moisture conditions persist.

True powderpost beetles most commonly enter homes as eggs or larvae in new hardwood flooring, furniture, and millwork. Tropical hardwood products are frequently a source of infestation because of inadequate wood storage and drying practices in the countries of origin. They may lurk in firewood, antique furniture, and tools recovered from unheated buildings. Hardwoods coated with film-forming finishes are safe from attack, as the coating clogs pores where adults lay eggs. In many cases, damage is limited to a single piece of flooring or trim, so removal of the affected item solves the problem. Adults and larvae can be killed by freezing or by heat-sterilizing wood at 135°F. If exit holes or adult beetles aren't seen within five years after a home has been built, chances are they'll never show up.

Again, it's difficult to gauge whether or not true powderpost beetle activity is ongoing. One way is to vacuum up all frass and mark existing bore holes. The reappearance of frass and new holes over the next few months confirms activity. Fresh frass is bright and cream-colored like new wood; old frass sifting from an inactive infestation is yellow or brown.

Anobiid Beetles

Anobiids, such as the common furniture beetle and the deathwatch beetle, also make their natural home in dead trees. While concentrated in the Southeast, their handiwork can be found in homes in the northeastern, north-central, and Pacific coastal states as well. The least discriminating of the powderpost beetles, anobiids attack the sapwood of softwoods and hardwoods, regardless of age. Attracted to wood with a 13% to 30% moisture content as well as decayed wood, anobiids most often infest framing in damp crawlspaces and basements.

Rarely seen, adults are 1/8 to 1/4 inch long and reddish-black to black (Figure 5). Eggs are deposited in drying checks, on rough-sawn lumber surfaces, and in joints. Tunnels excavated by larvae are loosely packed with fine powder and lemon-shaped fecal pellets that feel gritty when rubbed between the fingers. Adults emerge after three or more years from 1/16- to 1/8-inch round exit holes from which frass freely sifts. Anobiid infestations develop so slowly that the few exit holes present may go unnoticed for ten or more years. Thirty or more holes per square foot indicates a well-established infestation. Reinfestation is routine.

Unlike true powderpost beetles, anobiids rarely enter homes via infected wood. Adults fly in directly from the outside, invited by the moist conditions found in crawlspaces and basements lacking soil covers, proper ventilation, and foundation and site drainage. The same techniques for detecting and treating true powderpost beetle infestations are used for anobiids.

By Dr. Stephen Smulski, president of Wood Science Specialists Inc., in Shutesbury, Mass., a consulting firm specializing in wood performance problems in light-frame structures.

CONTROLLING TERMITES AND CARPENTER ANTS WITH BORATES

Borates are an ideal material for protecting buildings from carpenter ants, termites, and other wood-damaging pests. They are effective against a broad spectrum of pests and decay fungi, have no odor, do not discolor wood, and are no more toxic to humans than common table salt.

They also offer deep penetration of dry wood compared to other insecticides and are readily available from a network of pesticide formulators and distributors. Because they are so effective and so benign to the environment, the use of borates is growing rapidly.

Treated Wood Popular Abroad

If you were a builder in New Zealand, you would be legally required to use borate-treated wood for the house framework — a technique used successfully there since 1955. Framing lumber pressure-treated with borate is also readily available to builders in Hawaii and the U.S. Virgin Islands.

On the mainland U.S., however, borate-treated wood is available from only a handful of lumber companies around the country, primarily suppliers to the log-home industry.

Where borate-treated lumber is not available, another approach is to apply borates in the field during construction. This option is growing in use by licensed pest control operators (PCOs), largely due to the environmental concerns PCOs face regarding more toxic chemicals.

Common Uses of Borates

Borate is a generic term for compounds containing the elements boron and oxygen. Examples of borates include boric acid, borax, and disodium octaborate tetrahydrate (DOT). Boron compounds are pervasive in our daily lives. The average person consumes about 25 mg every day if following a balanced diet containing fruits and vegetables. Trace amounts of borates occur in eye washes, cosmetics, and mouth washes; large quantities are found in washing powders (20 Mule-Team Borax), and fire retardants.

Some people may be familiar with boron's pesticidal properties from their experience with various cockroach control products, which are essentially just boric acid. Mention Bora-care or Tim-bor, however, and a blank look results. EPA registration was granted for Bora-care, a glycol/borate formulation containing DOT, as an insecticide and preservative in 1989. Tim-bor, a brand name for DOT, was registered as a preservative in 1973 and as an insecticide in 1990.

How Do Borates Kill Insects?

Research suggests that borates inhibit enzymes that aid food breakdown in the gut of insects. In most cases, insects must ingest some boron from food or from cleansing themselves to be killed.

While a tiny amount of boron can kill individual termites, to repel them you need at least 1,500 ppm (about 0.9% boric acid on a weight to weight basis in wood). Minimizing damage from Formosan termites (found in Hawaii and Southern coastal regions) requires 3,500 ppm (2.0% boric acid).

Worker termites eating a small amount of boron live long enough to transfer boron-tainted food to other colony members by feeding soldiers, young, and reproductives. In this way the boron acts as a slow-acting toxic "bait," often eliminating most or all of a colony.

Thus, borates offer the same capability as the new termite baiting systems now being widely promoted without requiring expensive monitoring and repeat applications. In fact, a one-time application of borates to structures may permanently repel attacks by termites, wood-destroying beetles, and decay fungi as long as the borates are not subjected to persistent exposure to water.

How Do Borates Penetrate Wood?

Field-applied borates penetrate wood by a combination of absorption and diffusion. In diffusion, the chemical moves through the water in the wood from a high concentration on the surface to a lower concentration within. For effective diffusion to occur, the wood must be above the fiber-saturation point (about 25% moisture content). Complete, rapid penetration by diffusion requires unseasoned wood with 40%, and preferably higher, moisture content and several weeks of storage where drying of wood is restricted (such as tarping). Some borates also enter by absorption of water into the surface of the wood.

In new construction treated on site, borates will typically penetrate 1/8 to 3/8 inch beneath treated surfaces. Penetration will be somewhat deeper if the wood has higher than average moisture levels. Even without completely penetrating wood, borates may still effectively prevent insect attacks. Here's why.

The amount of boron in the outer layer of treated wood typically ranges from about 1,500 to 2,500 ppm — well above the levels needed to kill insects. Also, boron will continue to slowly penetrate the wood by diffusion, absorption, or movement across the wood surface (when wetted from condensation). The high humidity typically found in new homes the first year can work to your advantage here. Data also show that ends and backsides of studs may obtain borate even when not directly treated, although it is best not to cut any wood after treatment, since untreated ends would be exposed.

Borates also uniquely exploit termite feeding and foraging habits. Subterranean termites typically build tubes of soil to the wood being attacked. Because the termites keep the tubes and wood moist with water from the soil, borates quickly diffuse into the damaged wood and tubes.

WHERE TO TREAT WITH BORATES

For Carpenter Ants or Drywood Termites

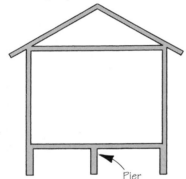

All exposed wood on interior and exterior walls, partition walls, crawlspace, and attic

Subterranean Termites (with Tim-bor)

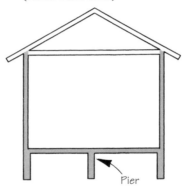

All exposed wood on interior and exterior walls, partition walls, and crawlspace

Subterranean Termites (with Bora-Care)

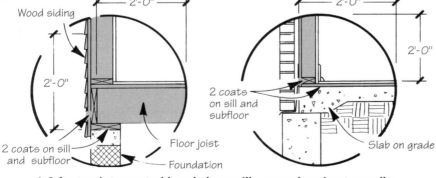

A 2-foot uninterrupted band above sills around perimeter walls; all wood 2 feet in from foundation wall or crawlspace perimeter; 2 feet around all piers, utility openings, fireplaces, and connections to porches and garages

Thus, many termites contact boron and are discouraged from building more tubes or feeding.

Limitations of Borates

One concern with borates is that they are soluble in water and can, therefore, leach out if moisture is present. This characteristic can be an advantage up to a point in that it helps you achieve better treatment of building timbers. However, it limits the usefulness of borates for exterior uses because extensive leaching would occur within a few years. Therefore borates should not be applied to exterior wood unless it is subsequently coated with paint, water repellent, or other covering. And although borates can be effectively injected in timbers with ground contact, they do not last long in that application.

The key uncertainty concerning borate treatment in new construction is how well it controls subterranean termites over the long term. Although testing and field experience over the past five to ten years is very positive, it does not go back far enough to be conclusive. However, with many documented failures of traditional soil treatments, many PCOs believe that the best approach available today is borate treatment of wood as a supplement to soil treatment with termiticide.

Borates are also proving themselves effective as a stand-alone pretreatment in new construction. If field experience with borates shows continuing success, increasing consumer demand may permanently change the traditional approach to termite prevention.

Regulations

The federal EPA requires that anyone who provides services or products which claim to prevent or control pests must use EPA-registered products or face stiff fines. Every EPA-registered product carries a label that specifies the pest and

application site, and PCOs are required to follow that label.

While some borate compounds are labelled for use against termites, other institutional barriers to their use exist. For example, in most Southern states and many other areas, certified termite treatment by PCOs is required to get building permits and financing from a bank. Termite treatments are inspected and enforced by structural pest control officials in about 35 states. In most cases, these regulators require soil treatment with termiticide around and beneath the foundation, as has been done for 50 years.

If code or loan officials in your area are uncertain about borates, you may sway them with the following facts:

- Bora-care literature states that it is "recognized by EPA as a primary termiticide treatment for both eliminating existing infestations and preventing future infestations."
- Tim-bor literature reports that it is used as a preventive treatment by PCOs.
- Traditional termiticide soil barrier treatments are frequently failing partly because termites can transport untreated soil to build "bridges" across these barriers. This has been verified by PCOs, regulators, and government researchers.
- Many PCOs currently supplement soil treatments with borate wood treatments.

Even with official approval, concerns about property value and potential liability will deter most builders in termite-prone areas from treating houses solely with borates. However, readers who live where termite-control regulations are limited or where carpenter ants cause more damage than termites should consider borates as a viable option. Anyone can use labeled or unlabeled products, including borates, to treat houses they are building for themselves or existing houses they own (see "Sources of Supply" at end of chapter).

Preventive Treatment of New Construction

I strongly recommend carefully reading labels and company literature for the major EPA-labeled borate pesticides whether you're hiring a PCO or applying the product yourself. Why? The labels and literature, especially from Nisus Corp., provide many details about the insects and their treatment. These

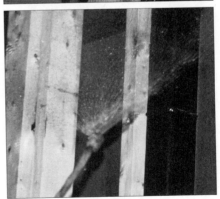

Figure 6. For an effective treatment against termites and carpenter ants, PCOs spray all framing and sheathing surfaces with a borate solution at the "dried-in" stage of construction (top). The low-pressure sprayer uses a wide nozzle to deliver a fan-shaped spray (above).

details cannot be adequately covered here and application directions differ for different products. Effective, long-lasting control of both carpenter ants and termites requires more than just spraying all exposed wood with borate.

Both ant and termite treatments should be done at the "dried-in" stage of construction when all structural wood and sheathing is installed and the roof is on, but before instal-lation of drywall, insulation, mechanical systems, and electrical wiring (Figure 6).

In general, all exposed wood, exte-rior and interior, should be treated with borate solution until thor-oughly wetted, using a low pressure sprayer. Tim-bor should be applied to all exposed wood for both ants and termites using a 15% solution (1½ pounds of powder per gallon of water). Bora-care is applied at a 1:1 dilution of the supplied concentrate with water for termites, and at a 2:1 dilution rate for ants.

Bora-care can be applied more selectively, according to research, because of its greater toxicity. Applications for termites can be lim-ited to the lower 2 to 3 feet of walls and a 2- to 3-foot-wide strip around the perimeter of crawlspaces and basement foundations and around piers (see "Where To Treat With Borates," page 248).

Both borate products should be applied twice to surfaces of wood members that are critical areas for termite attack and can only be treated on one side — such as band joists, box sills, sill plates, and girders (Figure 7). For slabs and basements, the soil around utility pipes and expansion joints must be treated with termiticide (Figure 8).

Dusts can also be used for pre-treatment, but these don't coat all wood surfaces as well as solutions, and tend to cake and lose effective-ness over time. A product such as Niban FG is better than straight boric acid, because it is coated for better moisture resistance. In gen-eral, dusts are better suited for treat-ment of ants in existing construction.

Builders and owners should work together for effective control of car-penter ants. Ants often have colonies outdoors and will forage into a house for food via openings around plumbing or wiring and will travel along these materials within houses thus avoiding treated wood. Therefore, effective control often requires bait applications to reduce outdoor populations. The product of choice is Niban Granular Bait which should be broadcast in a 2- to 4-foot band around the perime-ter of the house and around all logs, stumps, etc. (Figure 9). This prod-uct contains food attractive to ants and is coated to withstand up to 2 inches of water before losing effec-tiveness.

Figure 7. Areas prone to termite entry that can only be treated from one side — such as this band joist — should get two borate applications.

Figure 8. Borate treatment of the wood near these utility pipes provides extra protection. Traditional soil treatments are also recom-mended around such slab pene-trations.

Figure 9. To control outdoor populations of carpenter ants, broadcast bait around the perimeter of the building, and around nearby trees, stumps, and firewood piles.

COURTESY OF NISUS CORP.

Use in Existing Construction

PCOs have started using borates widely in existing homes over the past six to eight years and have generally given them favorable reports. Borates can often provide control when other treatments are not effective or are too costly.

In existing construction, PCOs can typically do a better job than contractors or homeowners because of their specialized equipment and familiarity with insect behavior. Application methods include sprays, injections, dusts, fogging, ultra-low volume mists, and in-foam carriers.

For example, PCOs can deliver borates in a foam carrier to treat otherwise inaccessible areas beneath beetle-infested hardwood flooring or drywood termite-infested window and door frames. For deep-seated termite or beetle infestations in large timbers, borate can be injected into holes drilled in the timbers. This technique is used with log homes where the timbers are too wet or too large for effective fumigation.

PCOs can also inject borates into posts, piers, and pilings with untreated centers which are vulnerable to termite damage. Untreated centers often result when large timbers are pressure-treated with preservatives such as CCA or creosote.

While surface treatments with borates are generally effective, they will not protect the interiors of wood pieces from the aggressive Formosan termite. Many PCOs also report better control of active infestations of termites with the borate/glycol formulation Bora-care than with water-based solutions, possibly because of the better coating of dry wood surfaces and the higher toxicity compared to pure DOT.

By Lonnie Williams, owner of Rich Mountain Wood Protection Services in Gulfport, Miss., and former research entomologist at the USDA Forest Service Wood Products Insect Research Laboratory.

CONTROLLING SUBTERRANEAN TERMITES

Subterranean termites are the most widespread and destructive termite group in North America. They are so-named because they excavate through the soil to reach wood in contact with the ground. To reach material above ground, they either move through connecting wood, or through earthen "shelter tubes" which they build over concrete, masonry, or other materials. Given the choice, subterranean termites will usually access above-ground wood through protected cracks and cavities, such as in concrete slabs and foundations.

Subterranean termites normally return to the soil periodically for moisture. However, if the moisture content of wood above ground level is high enough, they can survive and multiply indefinitely with no ground contact.

Eliminating conditions favorable to termites is an essential first step in long-term control. This entails reducing termites' access to food (wood), moisture, and shelter, which they need for their survival. The best time to address these concerns is during planning and con-

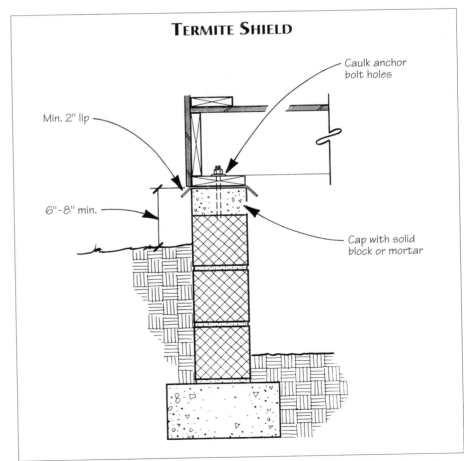

Figure 10. Metal shields force subterranean termites to build their tubes where they can readily be seen, but do not prevent infestations. To be effective, all joints and penetrations in the shield must be well sealed.

struction (see "Termite-Resistant Details," page 254).

Termite Shields

Metal termite shields are perhaps the oldest type of termite barrier and are widely used in the tropics and the southern U.S. The metal strips are installed on foundations, piers, pipes, and similar avenues of termite entry (Figure 10). They do not prevent termites from entering, but can be helpful in detecting infestations. Properly designed, installed, and maintained, shields force subterranean termites to build their tubes around the protruding edge and over the top of the shield where they can readily be seen.

To be effective, the ends of the metal strips must be firmly joined, either by soldering or by an interlocking mechanical joint. Some typical defects found in the shields include:

• Loose joints between metal sections
• Improperly cut and soldered corners where walls intersect
• Anchor bolt holes not sealed
• Insufficient clearance between the outer edge of the shield and adjacent woodwork or piping
• Shields less than 12 inches above grade
• Projecting edges that are bent, torn, corroded, or flattened against foundation
• High-risk areas such as filled porches left unprotected

Sand Barriers

About 40 years ago, researchers discovered that subterranean termites were unable to tunnel through sand if the particles were too large for termites to move with their mandibles, but small enough that termites could not crawl between them — in the range of 2.0 to 2.8 mm for most subterranean termites.

Sand and basaltic rock barriers are now routinely installed on new buildings and utility poles in Hawaii and Australia. Only a handful of U.S. companies outside Hawaii (mainly in California) are currently providing such treatments. Most of the jobs in California to date have been retro-fits in crawlspace homes.

Typically, a 4-inch-thick, 20-inch-wide layer of sand is blown inside the crawlspace along the foundation, and around piers and plumbing entries. Areas outside the foundation, under slabs, and within construction voids are still treated with conventional termiticide. Preliminary field trials have been encouraging but widespread use may not be practical in the U.S.

Barrier Treatment with Termiticide

Liquid termiticides have been the mainstay of subterranean termite control for more than 40 years. The goal of this approach is to provide a continuous chemical barrier in the soil surrounding and beneath a structure (Figure 11). Termites attempting to penetrate through treated soil are either killed or repelled.

Continuous coverage requires both horizontal and vertical barriers. Horizontal barriers are created under slabs, garages, patios, sidewalks, and other slabs abutting the

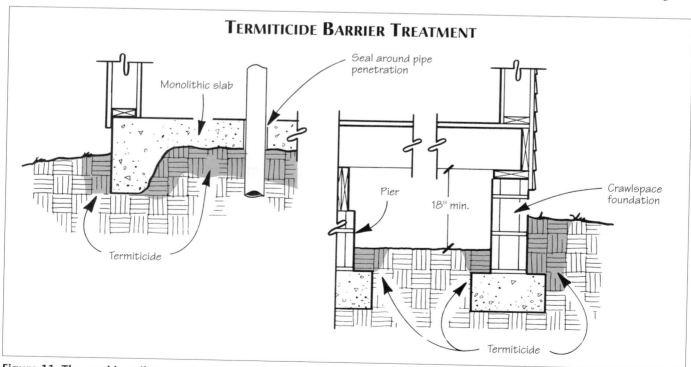

TERMITICIDE BARRIER TREATMENT

Seal around pipe penetration

Monolithic slab

Termiticide

Pier

18" min.

Crawlspace foundation

Termiticide

Figure 11. The goal in soil treatment is to establish an unbroken barrier around the structure. Horizontal barriers are created under slabs, garages, patios, driveways, and other slabs abutting the structure. Vertical barriers are required around foundation walls, piers, posts, etc., down to the footings.

structure. Vertical barriers are required around foundation piers, posts, filled porches, and chimneys down to their footings. The termiticide must be of sufficient concentration, applied at the proper rate (gallonage), and strategically placed to block all potential entry routes.

Comprehensive instructions for treating different types of construction can be found in the Approved Reference Procedures for Subterranean Termite Control (NPMA, Dunn Loring, VA; 703/573-8330; www.pestworld.org) and by referring to the directions on termiticide labels.

Pretreatment Vs. Retrofit

The most effective and economical time to apply a soil treatment is during construction — when termiticide can be precisely placed where it is needed below slabs, around pipes and utility conduits and along all sides of foundations and piers. A subsequent treatment along the foundation is needed after the final backfilling and grading.

Postconstruction treatment is complicated by many factors, including poor soil absorption, inaccessible areas, and a general inability to see where the termiticide is flowing. Many of the potential termite entry points are hidden behind walls, floor coverings, tubs, and other obstructions. The risk of puncturing and contaminating ducts, drains, and wells also increases with postconstruction applications. Due to all these factors, many more untreated gaps occur in the soil barriers — increasing the likelihood and need for retreatment.

Concrete Slabs

Concrete slabs present a number of challenges for treatment and have produced the greatest number of retreatments and damage-related claims for the industry. Termites enter slab-on-ground buildings through expansion joints, settlement cracks, posts, forms and grade stakes embedded in the slab, and around utility penetrations. Many of the interior entry points are hidden by floor coverings and other obstructions. Termites can also gain hidden entry by tunneling up the foundation under stucco, brick veneer, or wood siding at or below ground level.

Slab-related termite problems would rank even higher if "attached slabs" such as porches, stoops, garages, and additions were included in this assessment. Filled porches (raised slabs) are an especially common source of termite problems and a challenge to treat. Form boards, scrap lumber, paper, and other construction debris are often discarded here before the slab is poured. Besides being an attraction to termites, the hidden debris can obstruct the flow of termiticide.

The New Termiticides

For more than 40 years, the standard method of controlling subterranean termites was soil barrier treatment — Chlordane and Heptachlor were the dominant products for years until they were withdrawn from the market in 1987. USDA tests showed these compounds to last for more than 35 years in the soil. This characteristic made them very effective but was viewed negatively by environmental groups and regulatory agencies. Furthermore, the chemicals had been labeled possible carcinogens (based on lab experiments with mice) and often left detectable odors in houses that persisted for years.

The current generation of termiticide products are more expensive, shorter lived, and perceived by many to be less reliable than their predecessors. Presently nine products are being marketed for soil barrier treatments around and beneath structures. Six of these products are different types of synthetic pyrethroids, two are organophosphates, and the last and most recent (imidacloprid) is from a new chemical class called the chloronicotinyls. Other new products are undergoing tests throughout the country.

Some of the new products have lower acute toxicity to mammals than others, or are less likely to irritate the skin of applicators. Most have extremely low vapor pressures, resulting in virtually no indoor odors. All can be normally cleansed from surfaces with detergent and water. Because these products are relatively insoluble in water, they can

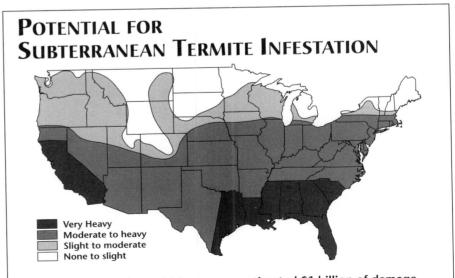

POTENTIAL FOR SUBTERRANEAN TERMITE INFESTATION

Very Heavy
Moderate to heavy
Slight to moderate
None to slight

Subterranean termites, which cause an estimated $1 billion of damage annually to U.S. homes, are found from New England to Florida in the East and from Washington to the Gulf of Mexico in the West.

be expected to remain largely in place in the soil following application. Although the new chemicals pose no known significant hazard to humans or pets, many are toxic to fish, necessitating extra care when treating structures adjacent to water.

Despite the handling and safety benefits, adjusting to the post-Chlordane termiticides has been a trying experience for many pest control companies. In comparison to Chlordane, the current products are more expensive to apply, yet less persistent in the soil. USDA studies suggest that these products should control termites for at least five years if they are applied at label concentra-tions. The actual length of control will depend on such factors as thoroughness of application, foraging intensity, and conducive conditions. Moreover, soil and climatic factors appear to have a much greater influence on the longevity of these products. What works well in one area may be an inferior product in another.

Application techniques. With any of the current chemicals, a continuous barrier is the key to long-term control. Once a group of foraging termites finds a gap of untreated soil and tunnels upward into the structure, other nest mates will follow their scented trail. One way to reduce untreated gaps is to use as many gal-lons of termiticide as the label and soil will allow. In one New England survey, researchers found that houses treated with over 200 gallons required far fewer retreatments than those that received less than 100 gal-lons. It is also important that the current termiticides be applied at their full labeled concentrations. Of course, high gallonage and concentrations are of little value if critical entry areas for termites are missed.

Use of foams. The most difficult area to accurately place termiticide is under slabs, which have historically produced the greatest number of retreatments and damage claims for the pest control industry. Liquid

TERMITE-RESISTANT DETAILS

Although there is currently no method to make a building "ter-mite-proof," there are ways to make structures less vulnerable to termite attack.

Wood-to-ground contact. It has been estimated that 90% of struc-tural termite infestations are the result of wood coming into contact with the ground. Keep wood siding, lattice work, door frames, and trim at least 6 inches above grade; 18 inches for horizontal structural members (24-30 inches in humid areas). Wood posts, stair carriages, etc., should never penetrate concrete floors. Set outdoor wood porches and steps on a concrete base at least 6 inches above grade (Figure A).

Where wood-to-soil contact cannot be eliminated, use preserva-tive-treated wood. However, be aware that termites can still enter the wood through cut ends and cracks and may also build tunnels over the surface.

Debris and vegetation. Remove cellulose materials such as stumps, scrap wood, form boards and grade stakes from under and around the building. Keep fire-wood and compost piles, as well as dense vegetation away from the foundation. Decorative wood chips and mulch should never contact wood siding or trim.

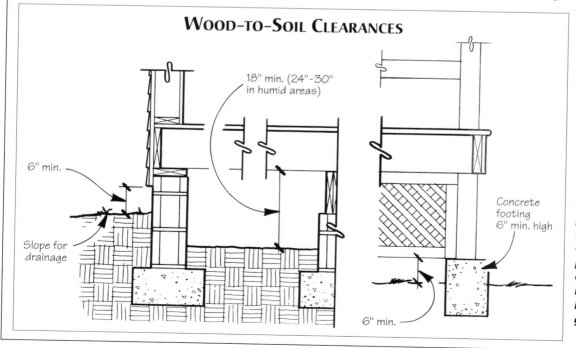

WOOD-TO-SOIL CLEARANCES

18" min. (24"-30" in humid areas)

6" min.

Slope for drainage

Concrete footing 6" min. high

6" min.

Figure A. Keep wood siding, lattice work, door frames, and trim at least 6 inches above grade; 18 inches for horizontal structural members (24-30 inches in humid areas). Wood posts, stair carriages, etc., should never penetrate concrete floors. Set outdoor wood porches and steps on a concrete base at least 6 inches above grade.

dilutions tend to disperse randomly under slabs resulting in inconsistent coverage.

One approach is to apply the termiticide as foam, which serves as a carrier to disperse termiticide laterally in the space that often exists between the bottom of the slab and the fill. Foam has proven useful in stopping termites from tunneling along the underside of slabs, within voids of concrete block or stone foundations, and behind brick veneer.

While it is not a panacea, foam can help deliver termiticide to hard-to-reach areas and has proven very effective in retreating chronically infected structures.

Wood Treatments

Wood can be treated for termites either as a preventive measure or to eliminate existing infestations. The best approach, where feasible, is to use preservative-treated lumber. Most termiticides used for soil treatment can also be applied to wood either by spraying, brushing, or injecting into voids and galleries of infested wood.

Products containing borates have certain advantages (see "Controlling Termites and Carpenter Ants with Borates," page 247). They are toxic to many species of wood destroying insects and fungi, and unless exposed to constant rewetting, maintain their preservative qualities for decades. In

addition, they are nonstaining, odorless, and low in toxicity to mammals (about the same as table salt), making them especially attractive for remedial treatment of wood inside homes.

Research and practical experience suggest that borate-treated wood is protected from subterranean termite attack, provided sufficient boron concentrations are achieved in areas where termites are feeding.

Termite Baits

Regardless of the amount of termiticide used, barrier treatments do little to reduce colonies in the surrounding soil. Termite baits are a whole different concept. With baits,

Moisture-related conditions. Termites are more likely to infest a structure if wood or surrounding soil is consistently moist. Slope finish grade, walkways, patios, etc., away from the building, and install and maintain gutters, downspouts, and splash blocks.

Moist crawlspaces also promote termite problems. To reduce humidity levels, cover the exposed soil with polyethylene or heavy roofing paper and install adequate foundation vents.

Problem building details. Certain construction details are conducive to termites. Dirt-filled porches, steps, patios, and similar raised attachments are responsible for a large percentage of termite infestations (Figure B).

Stucco extending below grade is another common source of hidden termite entry into buildings, especially in the South (Figure C). When stucco separates from the foundation wall, termites can tunnel upward undetected.

Foam insulation. When foam board insulation is installed below grade, termites may tunnel undetected through or behind it into the structure. The foam is of no nutritional value to termites, but apparently offers ideal nesting and tunneling conditions. Liquid termiticide cannot be applied remedially because the foam panels resist wetting. In light of these difficulties, many pest control companies refuse to treat structures with foam insulation or provide no guarantee. — *M.P.*

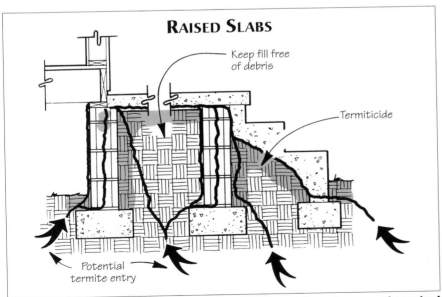

Figure B. Termites frequently enter buildings where porches, steps, or other raised slabs are attached. If such details can't be avoided, make sure all fill is free of debris and that soil and foundation voids are pretreated with termiticide.

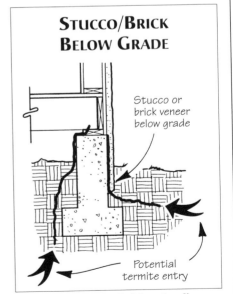

Figure C. Stucco or brick extending below grade is another common source of hidden termite entry.

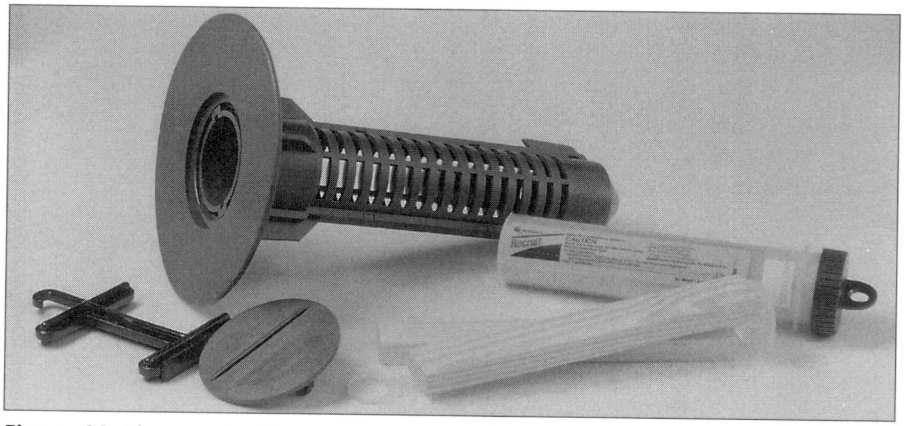

Figure 12. The new baiting systems coming on the market use slow-acting toxicants, which spread among termites by feeding and grooming. The Sentricon system shown above uses plastic monitoring stations (at left in photo) inserted in the soil — first with wood to lure termites, then with toxicant-laced baits (at right) formulated to eliminate entire colonies.

minuscule amounts of material are deployed like edible "smart missiles" to knock out groups of foraging termites. An aggressive baiting program seeks to achieve a termite-free zone around the structure through ongoing monitoring and rebaiting as needed.

Baits are being developed for both exterior and interior use, both below and above ground. Some may be used as comprehensive, stand-alone treatments. Others will be better suited for spot treatments of active infestations. While debates exist over which compounds and strategies are most effective, a variety of systems are now coming on the market. By the end of the decade, there could be almost as many termite baits as conventional termiticides.

Below-ground baits work by luring termites to feed on wooden stakes or other cellulose materials placed around the structure and/or around wood piles, stumps, moist areas, and adjacent to damage. Since termites cannot see or smell the bait, getting termites to find it requires planning and persistence, and can be a lengthy process.

One commercial system, called Senitron (DowElanco, Indianapolis, Ind.), uses a three-step process involving initial monitoring, delivery of the bait, and subsequent monitoring at three- to four-month intervals to guard against reinfestation (Figure 12). A portable computer and barcode scanner are used to input data at the job site. Researchers have confirmed the effectiveness of this type of system, but emphasize the importance of continued monitoring.

Baits are especially useful in chronic retreatment situations and where contamination is a risk. Difficult construction features, such as wells, plenums, sub-slab heating ducts, inaccessible crawlspaces, rigid foam insulation, stucco below grade, and rubble foundations, can all be treated with baits. As versatile as baits can be, however, they will not work by simply hammering a few into the ground and walking away. Success requires a thoughtful approach with diligent monitoring by crews knowledgeable about termite biology.

By Dr. Michael F. Potter, an urban extension entomologist at the University of Kentucky College of Agriculture in Lexington, Ky. Adapted from the eighth edition of The Handbook of Pest Control, *published by G.I.E. Publishing, Inc., Cleveland, Ohio.*

SOURCES OF SUPPLY

The following listing provides sources of borate products EPA-labelled for beetles, carpenter ants, and termites. To obtain Bora-care and Tim-bor, the two major products, call the manufacturer to find a local distributor.

Nisus Corporation
Rockford, TN
800/264-0870
www.nisuscorp.com
Bora-care, Niban Granular Bait, Jecta Diffusible Boracide

Perma-Chink Systems, Inc.
Knoxville, TN
800/548-3554
www.permachink.com
Shellguard Guardian

Sashco
Brighton, CO
800/767-5656
www.sashco.com
Penetreat Impel Rods

U.S. Borax
Valencia, CA
800/469-9094
www.borax.com
Tim-Bor Insecticide

NOTE: Two unlabeled products, chemically identical to Tim-bor Insecticide but less costly, are Solubor, a fertilizer-grade borate available from agricultural supply centers and Tim-bor DPT, available from Sashco. With either, follow label directions for Tim-bor Insecticide. Another option is mixing 1.2 parts borax and 1 part boric acid, yielding a similar compound.

CHAPTER 11

PLUMBING

- Plumbing Pitfalls for Remodelers
- Common Plumbing Service Calls

PLUMBING PITFALLS FOR REMODELERS

Relocating and adding to plumbing systems can be very expensive on a remodeling job. Since plumbing codes are stringent and complicated, it's always best to call in a professional plumber before giving a final estimate. Still, there are many red flags you can learn to recognize on an initial visit to a site. Sizing up the system can help you and your client plan well and avoid surprises.

For any plumbing system you should ask four basic questions:
- Has the existing plumbing caused hidden damage you will be responsible for once the job is started?
- Will your plumber be able to work with the existing plumbing, or will it be impractical to connect the new to the old?
- Will the existing system handle the increased demands of your remodeling work?
- Are there existing code violations your plumber will have to correct in performing the desired work?

All of these questions must be answered before you can compile accurate cost projections.

Hidden Damage

Water is a powerful force; it can carve rock, erode the earth, and destroy your remodeling budget. If you fail to disclaim unseen damage or don't notice evidence pointing to a problem, you could lose serious money.

In bathrooms, look for places where water may be getting behind and underneath fixtures (Figure 1). Check to see that the trim plates around faucets, drains, and overflow outlets are well-sealed with plumber's putty. Look at the caulking around tubs and showers; if it's dried and cracking, you may have rotted lumber in the walls or floors. Check around the base of the toilet. Water damage can be caused by faulty wax seals or condensation dripping off the tank — particularly where cold well water is used.

In the kitchen inspect every area you can gain access to. Whenever possible, go below all the plumbing fixtures and inspect the structure supporting them. This will often reveal subfloor stained by water.

Remove the access panel of the dishwasher if there is one and look under the appliance. Refrigerators with ice makers can leak and rot the floor underneath. Look also for any water heaters, washing machines, and well and water conditioning equipment that might be installed in the living areas of the house.

Assessing Existing Supply Lines

One of the main things to look out for, especially with an older home, is the type of water supply lines.

Figure 1. Water will penetrate the wall at the faucet handles (left) whenever the shower is used. The holes should have been covered with trim plates sealed with plumber's putty. The curling and torn linoleum around the toilet (below) indicates water damage to the underlayment, probably from a faulty toilet seal.

Galvanized. Galvanized water pipes are commonly found in older homes. Get rid of them; if you don't, you're asking for trouble (Figure 2). Galvanized pipe will gradually close up with rust and mineral deposits until, ultimately, pressure is reduced to a trickle.

Worn threads on galvanized fittings are a frequent cause of leaks. When working around old galvanized fittings, any significant jarring or vibration can cause the fittings to let go at any moment. If this happens to a riser hidden in a wall, it will cause a lot of trouble and expense to fix.

When tying into old galvanized pipe, you may want to protect yourself in the contract. If the client doesn't want to replace the galvanized piping and you have to tie into it, your plumber may have to remove several sections to find solid pipe to make a good connection. This will increase your costs unless your contract has a clause disclaiming responsibility for the condition of existing piping.

CPVC. Another type to watch out for is CPVC plastic water pipe. It's fragile and hard to work with. Also, do-it-yourself types like CPVC because it does not require soldering skills. They can cut it with a hacksaw and glue it together. If I see CPVC in a house my crew has to work on, I automatically increase the expected labor to allow for potential problems.

Polybutylene. This pipe is gray and very pliable, but unlike CPVC, "polybute" is very rugged. In freezing temperatures, it will expand to reduce the risk of splitting. When polybute was first introduced, there were problems with faulty connections, so you need to watch out for these. Remodeling plumbers like polybute because it can be snaked through walls without any concealed joints.

PVC. If you find PVC supply pipe, you'd better talk with your plumber. Most codes limit the use of PVC water distribution pipe to cold water. The code generally requires your cold water piping to be of the same material as the hot water pipe, and since PVC cannot be used for hot water, it's not suitable for residential use.

Copper. If you find copper supply line you're probably in good shape. It's easy to repair, add on to, and install.

Main shut-off. Locate and test the main water shut-off valve to see if it works properly. If water leaks past the valve, the plumber will have trouble soldering copper connections (the water turns to steam and causes voids in the solder joint). With CPVC pipe, water will prevent the glue from setting up properly. With polybutylene connections, a small amount of water will have no adverse effects on the connection.

Accessibility. Keep in mind that the plumber not only has to be able to see the plumbing, he will need room to work with it. In general, if you can easily put your hand around the water pipes, the plumber will be able to do his job. But if the pipes are tight against the subfloor, or notched into the top of floor joists, you may have to remove the floor to make a connection.

Placement of lines. In cold climates, pipes in attics, crawlspaces, and outside walls may freeze and burst if not insulated properly. In some cases, pipes in an outside wall may have been saved from freezing only because there was *no* insulation in the wall. In a house where you encounter distribution lines in an outside wall, make sure that you don't isolate the pipe by insulating on the wrong side — the insulation must not be between the pipe and the heated space.

Assessing Existing Drainage

Residential drains are typically installed with a grade of 1/4 inch per foot, and you'll have to maintain this pitch with any new lines. Make sure that any new drain pipe will not be lower than the existing pipe when it reaches the point of connection — an installed, sewage-ejector system can cost in excess of $1,000.

The plumber will need 18 to 24 inches of straight pipe to work with to cut a new fitting into the existing drain line. Also, make sure he has the room to install any new pipe and traps that may be necessary.

Cast-iron drain lines. Most of the main drain lines in older homes are cast iron, usually 3 to 4 inches in diameter. As long as these pipes are properly graded, they will give years of good service. Cast iron is generally easy to tie into, using a rubber coupling with stainless-steel hose clamps.

However, because cast iron can rust, the interior of the pipe becomes rough and can catch hair, grease, and other objects. Cast iron can also rust through from the inside. Rust stains on the outside of the pipe are reason for some concern.

Galvanized and lead drain lines. Galvanized and lead drain pipe are the ones to watch out for. Galvanized pipe is a metallic color, with heavy fittings at the connections. It was used as recently as 20

Figure 2. Galvanized supply lines should be replaced when found in older homes. The threads rust, causing leaks, and can eventually break off altogether if the pipe is jarred.

years ago for sink, shower, and tub connections (it's still code-approved for drainage). Over the years, it becomes restricted with rust and accumulated buildup of hair and grease (Figure 3).

As with galvanized supply lines, galvanized drains are prone to leaking because of rusted threads. This can cause water damage as well as health hazards, since sewer gas can escape. If the connections show a buildup of rust or a white efflorescence around the threads, the pipe will probably leak in the near future. Or the threads may simply break off when worked with. It's best to replace galvanized drain pipe.

In very old homes, you might find lead pipe and traps. These will be a dull gray color and very soft. The drains will rarely be straight and properly graded. When lead is bent, it creases and cracks and will leak. If the pipe runs through a spongy area of the floor, the effects of walking across the floor can take its toll on the soft material. When you see lead plumbing, plan to replace it.

Copper. You may find copper in the drain/waste/vent (DWV) system. Copper drains usually work very well and cause few problems, re-

Figure 3. Rust, grease, and hair completely clogged this galvanized drain pipe. The author attempted to unclog the pipe with a snake, but succeeded only in punching a hole through the blockage.

maining smooth and blockage-free. Except for rare circumstances, there will be no reason to replace a copper DWV system.

Plastic. Schedule 40 plastic pipe — either PVC or ABS — is now the most commonly used DWV material. Your plumber should have no problems tying into a correctly installed plastic DWV system.

Fixtures

It is not unusual to find odd-sized bathtubs and sinks. Trying to find a modern unit with comparable measurements may be impossible. If you have to alter the opening for a bathtub, it is best to know it before you submit your proposal.

When choosing a location for tubs or showers, provide an access wall for the faucet in case it ever needs to be replaced. Also, if you are replacing a bathtub with a shower, you'll need to increase the size of the drain. Bathtubs, even those with showers, require a 1½-inch trap and drain. Shower stalls, though, require a 2-inch trap and drain. This conversion may require removing the bathroom floor, or the ceiling below the floor.

If the customer wants to replace a lavatory or vanity with a pedestal sink, you'll have to relocate the plumbing; pedestal sinks require special spacing on the waste and water lines.

Assessing the Demand: Water Distribution

Undersized water pipe is a common problem. It was not unusual in the past for plumbers to install ½-inch pipe throughout a house. Unfortunately, this is not in keeping with current codes and creates problems. In a house with all ½-inch pipe, if someone is taking a shower when another fixture is turned on, they get drenched with cold or hot water. Adding another bathroom can make the water pressure even worse.

If you are unable to see what size the water pipe is, run a test. Turn the water on at full volume in the tub and notice the pressure. With the tub running, have someone turn on the kitchen sink. Then flush the toilet near the tub. Watch the pressure at the tub. If the house has more than one bathroom, try the test with both tubs running at full capacity. You may find some extreme differences between an upstairs and downstairs bath.

Sizing distribution lines. You should never have more than two fixtures being fed by a single ½-inch pipe. There should be at least a ¾-inch line up until the point of the last two fixtures. With a ¾-inch water service, most houses will have adequate pressure and be in code compliance.

Assessing the Demand: Drainage

The size of a house's building drain will be determined by the number of fixtures it handles. Most codes will not allow more than two toilets or bathrooms grouped on a 3-inch drain. A 4-inch drain can handle all ordinary residential demands.

Slow drains. When your work involves tying into the existing DWV system, you may become responsible for slow or clogged drains. Kitchen remodeling, for instance, may include the addition of a garbage disposal. When this device is installed, the existing kitchen drain may no longer be adequate.

To test a kitchen drain, fill the sink to the flood rim with water. If it is double-bowl, fill both sides. Release all the water at the same time. Repeat this procedure two or three times. Occasionally, if there is a clog down the line, a single bowl of water may appear to drain fine, even with the clog. By draining several bowls of water quickly, though, you'll discover the problem.

Check any fixtures your work may involve. Flush the toilet, fill and drain the tub, and test the lavatory. Follow this rule: If it has a drain, test it.

The absence of a vent can cause a drain to operate slowly. If you have a fixture that drains, but does so without force, it may need a vent. In any case, note existing drain problems and have the customer acknowledge the condition before you begin work.

Code Violations

Beware of existing code violations. If you alter existing plumbing, you may be required to correct all code deficiencies. Remodeling can expose all types of plumbing code violations.

Undersized distribution pipe. Undersized water distribution pipe is a common code problem. If the whole house is piped in 1/2-inch pipe, the plumber may connect to it, in most cases, without changing the existing pipe. However, if there is larger pipe available in an accessible location, the plumber will be required to make his connections to the larger pipe. This can mean running pipe for a much longer distance than you planned.

Unvented fixtures. Unvented fixtures are a frequent problem with older homes (most states require every fixture drain to be vented). If the drain goes straight down through the floor, the fixture is not properly vented and your plumber will have to install a vent for the new fixture being installed. Under remodeling conditions, you may be able to use a mechanical vent, a small plastic device that screws into a female fitting installed in the fixture drain line. Check with the local code official to see if mechanical vents are allowed.

Illegal traps. If the drain comes out of the wall into a "P" trap, you should be okay. If the drain comes straight up through the floor to an "S" trap, you have a code violation.

Drum traps, typically installed below the floor, are also prohibited in most states (Figure 4).

Illegal drains. Sink drains dumping into a sump-pump pit are in violation of code. If this condition exists, your plumber will have to tie the drain into the sanitary drainage system. This could result in additional costs of several hundred dollars.

Space requirements. If you are doing an extensive bathroom remodel, you may have to expand the size of the bathroom to meet modern code requirements. For example, the center of the toilet drain must have

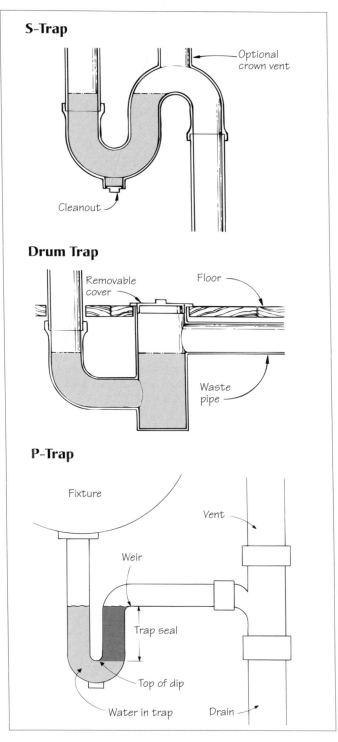

S-Trap

Optional crown vent

Cleanout

Drum Trap

Removable cover

Floor

Waste pipe

P-Trap

Fixture

Vent

Weir

Trap seal

Top of dip

Water in trap

Drain

Figure 4. The S-trap (top) does not meet code. Because it is unvented and has only a 2-inch water seal, it is likely to fail and release sewer gases into the home — even with the addition of a crown vent. The drum trap (middle) has a deeper water seal than the S-trap, but is still prohibited in most states. The modern vented P-trap (bottom) creates an effective seal to block gases from entering the home.

15 inches of clear space on each side and 18 inches of clear space in front.

Septic capacity. Another issue to consider, if you are adding space to a home, is whether the existing septic system will be adequate. Adding bedrooms may necessitate enlarging the septic system, which can cost several thousand dollars, depending on the soil type and the local code requirements. Locate and inspect the septic system. If you find the leach field to be soggy and saturated with liquid, the system may be defective. Strong odor in the air is another warning of a failed system.

Conclusion

Even if the plumbing you anticipate seems trivial, give the entire system a full inspection. A checklist is helpful. After a general walk-through, go back over the specific plumbing you plan to deal with. With the expense of plumbing work, this phase of your estimate deserves your concentrated attention.

By Dodge Woodson, a master plumber and general contractor in Topsham, Maine.

COMMON PLUMBING SERVICE CALLS

Over the years I have spent thousands of hours troubleshooting plumbing problems — everything from burst water mains to clogged stack vents on the roof. The problems are varied, and some are seasonal. But there are many that simply occur over and over. Here are a dozen of the most common ones.

Leaks Under the Kitchen Sink

Kitchen sink drain lines are arguably the most ill-conceived systems in American plumbing — they are simply designed to leak. Everything is held together with slip joints — those hand-tightened connections that come loose every time they're bumped. And since all the traps and drain lines are placed right up front, you can't help but bump them every time you reach into the cabinet (Figure 5). I would wager that at least 60% of those reading this book currently have a leak under the kitchen sink.

I used to hate working under the kitchen sink. I would fuss until I got the right no-leak combination, call it a day, and then someone would bump the trap or drainpipe and the leaks would start again. But that has all changed, ever since I figured out a drain-line configuration that works. Now remedying undersink problems has become a high-profit part of my business.

Strainers. Many leaks come from cheap strainers: The water leaks under the strainer's lip right down onto the outside of the drain lines. The fix is simple: I replace cheap strainers with high-quality ones — usually the Kohler 8801-CP Duostrainer, which is chrome-plated solid brass and has an O-ring on the strainer insert (Figure 6). The Duostrainer also has *cut* threads, like a threaded steel pipe, as opposed to the leak-prone rolled threads on cheap strainers. I also install my strainers with a Dow Corning 100% clear silicon sealant — never plumbers putty. (Even so-called nonhardening plumbers putty hardens and cracks.)

New drain lines. Under the sink, I throw away all the existing drain lines, all the way to the schedule-40 main drainpipe coming through the wall or floor. As a replacement, I use one of several methods, depending on the budget.

The best (and most costly) method is to move the trap and waste arm to the back wall of the sink cabinet so they won't get bumped (Figure 7).

Figure 5. A typical kitchen sink drain assembly, with its leak-prone slip fittings, leaves a lot to be desired. This two-sink setup has no less than six slip connections.

Figure 6. The author likes the Kohler Duostrainer for kitchen sinks — its cut threads are less likely to leak than the rolled threads on cheaper strainers.

Figure 7. For a leakproof drain and trap assembly, the author uses glued plastic fittings and places the pipes at the back of the sink cabinet. The rubber 90-degree elbows, attached with hose clamps, allow for quick disassembly.

Figure 8. For connecting a dishwasher, a double-Y fitting with a galvanized reducer in the center hub works well.

This only works in installations where the water lines are not in the way and the drain line is towards the back of the cabinet. Instead of thin-wall metal waste lines and slip fittings, I use 1¹/₂-inch glue-type schedule-40 plastic traps, pipe, and fittings (either ABS or PVC). I make an immediate right turn below each strainer with a flexible PVC 90-degree elbow (more on flexible PVC later) pointed towards the back wall. At the back wall I glue a 90 on each arm and connect the two waste arms together with schedule-40 plastic pipe and a 1¹/₂-inch double L, then drop straight down into a schedule-40 trap. (A trap with a built-in cleanout at the bottom is best.) If I'm slightly off-line entering the main drain, I'll use a 1¹/₂-inch flexible coupling.

Connecting the dishwasher drain. Whenever the under-sink lines need to accommodate a dishwasher drain hose, I use a double T or Y in place of the double L (Figure 8). Besides having drain inputs on both sides for the sink waste arms, these fittings have a center hub that points straight up. Here I glue a plastic threaded reducing bushing. I screw a galvanized reducing bushing into the plastic bushing, then a galvanized street 90, and finally a barbed fitting for the dishwasher hose to connect to.

Low-budget option. For a faster and less costly method, I use a waste assembly system that attaches straight to the strainers (Figure 9). This way I avoid those idiotic standpipes that place the drain lines and P-trap so low that they are assured of being constantly in the way. This assembly also has an attachment point for the dishwasher so I don't have to have another fitting, cutting out two more potential leak points. To minimize leaky slip joints and keep the P-trap off to one side, out of the way, I always use an end-outlet waste assembly as opposed to the more common center-waste.

Leaky traps. If I can't stop a trap from leaking, I replace it with a flexible PVC trap that fastens with stainless steel clamps. If I can't stop a leak from around the strainers threads, I install a flexible trap adapter. I also use the flexible drain and trap connector to connect onto the main drainpipe whenever the pipes are slightly out of alignment. These flexible PVC fittings are a little more expensive than rigid plastic, but they install quickly and are easy to disassemble if needed. I buy fittings made by Fernco Inc. (Davison, MI; 800/521-1283; www.fernco.com). These should be available at most professional plumbing supply shops. Another brand is available from Barnett, Inc. (Jacksonville, FL; 800/288-2000; www.e-barnett.com).

Clogged Kitchen Drain

Unlike in the TV commercials, my kitchen drain problems are always in the drain line and rarely in the trap. Sometimes kitchens are located on the opposite end of the house from

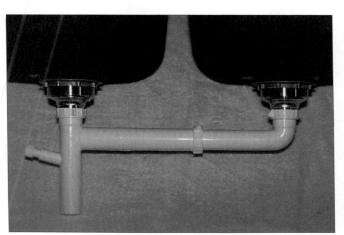

Figure 9. This less costly but improved drain configuration replaces the typical vertical standpipes — as well as their slip fittings — with screw-on elbows attached directly to the strainers. The only slip fitting is in a horizontal position, so it is less likely to leak.

the rest of the plumbing, resulting in a long kitchen drain line. If a shallow slope (1/8 inch per foot) has been used with 1 1/4- or 1 1/2-inch drain-pipe, it's only a matter of time until the drain will become totally clogged. In this case, it's actually much faster to replace the drain line than to try to clean out a 40-foot run of totally plugged pipe. I normally replace it with a 2-inch, or preferably, 3-inch drain with an increased slope (1/4 inch per foot minimum).

Slow Drain

Here the complaint is, "My kitchen sink takes forever to drain!" Again, if the pipe is almost totally clogged for a long length, I replace the entire pipe with a larger one. But sometimes there's a blockage at some point along the line. To diagnose an isolated blockage, there's a simple test that often works. First, drain all the water out of the sink and the

drain lines. Then run hot water into a bucket until the water coming out of the faucet is extremely hot. Once hot, let the water run into the sink drain until it backs up into the sink. Shut off the water and run your hand along the drain line. You'll feel the hot water (especially noticeable on metal drain lines) until you come to the clog — at that spot the pipe will feel cold. Cut the line there and clean it. Once it's clean, I install a cleanout at the cut.

Toilet Never Stops Running

There are three common problems that can cause a toilet to "run."

Refill valve. First is a faulty refill valve (Figure 10). The refill valve controls the flow of water entering the tank. Waterborne trash — such as powdered granite from drilling the well, pieces of rust flaking off galvanized pipes, or gravel from a water-main break — can get into the

turn-off mechanism and prevent the valve from turning off. Or the valve can simply wear out.

It will be obvious if the refill valve is faulty, because the water in the toilet tank will be flowing into the overflow tube — that 1-inch tube that sticks up in the center of the tank. I either replace the seals on the refill valve (Figure 11), assuming parts are locally available, or I replace the entire assembly — the more common fix.

You'll notice a small flexible pipe running from the refill valve into the overflow tube. This is called the refill tube — it puts water back into the bowl during the refill cycle. Make sure that this small pipe is not broken off and that it runs into the overflow tube.

Overflow tube. A second common problem, especially on older units, is the overflow tube itself. If the tube is brass, it may have corroded at the threads where it screws into the tank. Plastic tubes, on the other hand, sometimes crack along the side. If the overflow tube is damaged in any way, water will constantly flow through it into the bowl. A damaged overflow tube will have to be replaced.

Flush valve. A third possibility is that water is leaking out of the tank because of a faulty flush valve — the stopper that keeps the water inside the tank until the toilet is flushed. Replacing the flush valve, normally a rubber flapper or ball, will usually fix the problem. However, if the seat area under the flush valve has jagged edges, a new rubber flapper alone will not stop the problem. Instead, you'll have to use a special replacement unit with a putty seal that covers the rough seat area (Figure 12).

A minor but annoying problem is a flush valve stuck in the open position, so that you have to jiggle the handle to get the rubber seal to fall back into place. To solve this, re-adjust the linkage from the flush valve to the flush handle arm as necessary. Also check to see that nothing

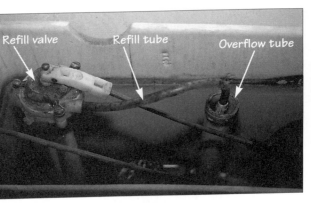

Refill valve   Refill tube   Overflow tube

Figure 10. The refill valve opens when the toilet tank empties. The refill tube shunts water back into the bowl via the overflow tube.

Figure 11. Sometimes replacing the seal in the refill valve can remedy a running toilet. More often, though, the entire assembly must be replaced.

is catching the flush valve and keeping it from dropping into place.

Water or Sewer Gas Leaking Around Toilet

If water or sewer gas is leaking out at the base of the toilet, it means the wax ring is not sealing the joint between the toilet "horn" and the toilet flange. In this case, I have to replace the wax ring, but I also have to figure out why the seal has failed; otherwise, the problem is likely to recur.

For instance, if the toilet rocks back and forth on the floor, the wax ring will compress, leaving a gap that water and sewer gas can escape through. Often, the toilet's attachment bolts have come loose or rusted through. Or sometimes the floor has rotted, causing the toilet to tilt to one side. I also often see closet flanges installed too low. The flange is suppose to be installed *on top of the finished floor* — not level with it (Figure 13). If the flange is too low, I may have to install two wax rings, one on top of the other, to obtain a good seal.

There are two types of wax rings (Figure 14). I use the type that has a built-in plastic funnel that goes down into the flange. The cheaper type is a simple wax ring. I never use this ring by itself — I've seen too many leaks with these. When extra height is needed, however, I'll use a plain ring in conjunction with the funnel type.

If the floor is rotted out, it has to be rebuilt. But before I remove a toilet to replace a seal, I always make sure that the water around it is not coming from condensation or a leaky water pipe.

Toilet Won't Drain or Drains Slowly

This is caused either by mineral buildup in the toilet itself or by an obstruction in the toilet or drain line. If the toilet is old and the problem has been getting worse over the years, it's probably from mineral buildup. In that case, a new toilet

will be needed. As for obstructions, I've pulled toys, wire baskets, plastic cups, toothbrushes, and other things too numerous to mention out of toilets. I've used everything from wire grippers and a closet auger to clothes hangers to fish things out.

If a toilet flushes fine for two or three times and then starts to have problems, there is probably a restriction in the sewer line. This could be caused by tree roots, foreign matter, or a shift in the sewer pipes in the ground. The solution can involve anything from cleaning the lines with a snake to digging up the yard and replacing old drain lines.

No Hot Water

This can be the result of a tripped breaker or blown fuse, a bad heating element, a faulty thermostat, or the

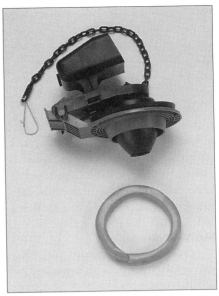

Figure 12. This flapper replacement kit comes with a putty ring for cushioning jagged edges in the outlet of the toilet tank, ensuring a good seal.

Figure 13. For a tight seal, the closet flange must be installed on top of the finished floor — not level with it, as is often the case.

Figure 14. When setting toilets, the author always uses a wax ring with a built-in funnel (left). A plain wax ring (right) may eventually leak.

water heater's overload switch. The problem with water heaters is not figuring out what happened, but *why* something happened. What happened will be obvious to a good plumber — but it may take a Sherlock Holmes to find out why.

As a remodeler, you can waste a lot of time trying to figure out what's wrong with a water heater. I wouldn't bother — call your plumber. But there are a couple of preliminary tests you can do before you make the call to give the plumber an idea of what's happening.

Look around the water heater for signs of leakage. Also, determine how old the water heater is. For electric heaters, check the breaker. If the breaker's tripped, reset it and see whether it trips again. If so, you may have an electrical problem. If the breaker's still open, find out whether there's no hot water at all, or only a

limited amount — a sign that the bottom heating element may be worn out while the top one is still working. Another quick test you can do is to raise the setting on the thermostat to see whether the heating elements come on. If they don't, it may mean the thermostat has worn out.

Beyond that, it's best to call a plumber.

Leaky Copper Pipes

Sulfur and excessive oxygen in the water can cause copper pipes to fail prematurely. Pinholes will appear, with a resulting spray of water. Installing a union or coupling at the hole will temporarily fix the problem, but the rest of the pipes will eventually fail. All the pipes should be replaced and water conditioning installed to prevent the corrosion from recurring. With really aggressive water, I usually rec-

ommend plastic (CPVC) or polybutylene supply lines rather than water conditioning.

Water Hammer

"It sounds like there's a jackhammer in the walls!" — a common complaint whenever metal supply pipes are installed along with fast-closing faucets and valves. Whenever any faucet, valve, or solenoid opens, the water rushes through the pipes to the outlet. Then, when the valve closes quickly, all that fast rushing water slams to a stop. But its energy is transferred into the metal pipes. From there it reverses itself and hits the opposite end of the water lines, then comes back again. The noise sounds as if someone is hitting the pipes with a hammer.

A common solution is to install an air column — a vertical pipe with a cushion of air in it — to dissipate the pressure of the rebounding water. This is not a good long-term solution, however, because the air that provides the cushion will eventually dissolve into the water and the problem will return. Special shock absorbers made by Sioux Chief Manufacturing (P.O. Box 397, Peculiar, MO 64078; 800/821-3944) are designed just to prevent this problem and should be installed at point of use and at the end of the plumbing line. Called the Mini-Rester, this patented shock absorber comes in many configurations for a variety of installations (Figure 15).

Leaky Faucets

Leaky faucets seem more common today than in the past. I suspect this is because there's an overabundance of cheap fixtures available in do-it-yourself stores. But if your customers pay their water bill on a per gallon basis, and especially if their sewer bill is based on water consumption, a small drip can be very expensive.

Some single-lever faucet designs use springs to help close the valve — the springs press little rubber seals

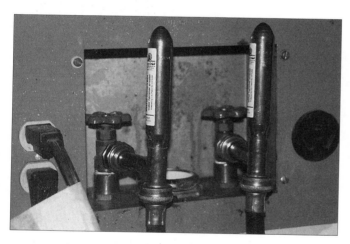

Figure 15. Water hammer arrestors — not simply vertical pipes filled with air — are the best way to prevent water hammer.

Figure 16. This Delta single-lever faucet repair kit includes new springs and gaskets (left); for other faucet designs, such as the Moen, the entire cartridge is replaced (right).

against a plastic seat (Figure 16). If the springs lose their tension over a period of time, or if they rust or get cut by debris in the water, they'll typically need to be replaced (as a temporary fix, I have been known to restretch the springs by simply pulling them apart with a pair of needle-nose pliers).

If the faucet is the type with a plastic ball — a poor design that never worked well — replace it with a stainless-steel one, which should be available at a plumbing supply house (Figure 17). If the faucet has a worn-out cartridge, replace that. If the faucet leaks around the handle only when the faucet is turned on, replace the appropriate gasket or O-ring. (If it's a cheap faucet, I simply replace it with a high-quality one. It costs more to maintain a cheap faucet than it does to install a good one.)

Older-style faucets have many replaceable parts — the stem assembly, the washer, and the seat itself. The stem assembly removes with a socket or crescent wrench, the washer with a screwdriver, and the seat with a hex wrench. Between all the old and new designs, no one can keep all the parts in stock. Therefore, when you can't find the part you need, you'll have to replace the faucet. Be sure to install one from a company that has been around a long time and has easily obtainable parts.

Low Water Pressure

When low pressure is the complaint, I ask several questions: Is the problem throughout the house, or only at one or two faucets? Or, is there a problem only on the higher floors of the house? Also, is the problem in both the hot and cold lines?

The most common complaint is low pressure on both the hot and cold sides at only one faucet. Usually the faucet screens are clogged with silt or sediment, although sometimes trash gets caught in the faucet body itself or at the stop valve beneath the sink. If the problem is throughout the house, don't forget the obvious — is there an in-line cartridge filter that is clogged with trash?

If the customer is on city water, I check the water pressure from the utility by cutting into the line where it enters the house and hooking up a pressure gauge. If the pressure is good coming into the house, then the problem must be within the pipes. I first check the faucet closest to the incoming main to verify its pressure, then work from there. In old homes, the galvanized lines are commonly choked with rust. New homes suffer more from incorrect supply line design, or from debris lodged in the lines.

When the pressure problem is only on the top floor, the house pressure must be raised. For city dwellers, I install a booster pump. In homes with wells, I simply raise the setting on the water tank's pressure switch and increase the air pressure within the tank (Figure 18).

Frozen Water Lines

If a water line freezes, it usually means the line was installed improperly. After thawing a supply line, I prefer to relocate it to within the heated space of the house. If the customer doesn't want to pay for that, I will install a UL-approved low-wattage heat tape.

If a drain line freezes, it's because it wasn't pitched properly. Water should never be in a drain line except when it's flowing through to the septic tank or sewer main. I have seen drain lines pitched uphill on which the owners installed heat tape to prevent freezing. Eventually, though, PVC or ABS drain pipe will start to deform and sag because of the heat.

Never use a welder when thawing metal water lines — it's a dangerous tool that can cause fires. For metal pipes, use a torch; for plastic pipes, a hair dryer will have to do. (Whenever I use a torch in a "tight" location, I always use a fiberglass fireproof backstop to prevent a house fire.) A sometimes faster

Figure 17. Some inexpensive single-lever faucets use a plastic ball to control water flow. This should be replaced with a stainless-steel ball like the one shown here.

Figure 18. There are two screws on a water tank's pressure switch. Turning the tall screw clockwise raises both the high and low cut-off pressures; turning the shorter screw clockwise raises only the high cut-off pressure.

option is to cut the frozen areas out and either replace them or take the iced-up pipe into the house and let it thaw out.

Different types of pipes respond differently to freezing. Galvanized pipe splits, and copper will either split or change diameter. With copper, I often have to cut away large sections of pipe to find a section that's not too deformed to accept a fitting. On occasion, I have had to use my flaring tool and squeeze a small section of copper pipe back to its original diameter so I could slip a fitting on. Plastic pipe cracks in long sections, while poly-butylene normally expands. Polybutylene will occasionally break, but freezing problems are minimal compared with other types of pipe. Polybutylene is also flexible enough that I can use pliers and gently squeeze the pipe to find the frozen areas — the pipe, which will normally compress when squeezed, remains inflexible when frozen. I find the frozen sections this way, and simply cut them out and replace them.

By Rex Cauldwell, a master plumber in Copper Hill, Va.

CHAPTER 12

ELECTRICAL

- Electrical Planning for Remodelers

- Rewiring Tips

- Common Electrical Inspection Failures

- GFCI Circuits

- Plug-In Electrical Testers

ELECTRICAL PLANNING FOR REMODELERS

Because most remodeling contractors are not electricians, this is an area where it's easy to overlook potential problems. By anticipating these problems, a contractor can avoid underbidding and, in some cases, simplify the work for the electrician. Below I'll look at some common problem areas where contractors typically underbid.

If the remodel requires any electrical add-ons, you should first look at the main service panel. Identify any existing problems within the panel and determine how much room is available for additional circuits. These panels will either be fuse boxes, circuit breakers, or a combination.

Fuse Boxes

If the main service panel is an old 60-amp fuse box, additional circuits probably should not be wired into it.

Although you may be adding a few receptacle outlets to an existing circuit, it's possible the additional load will be enough to overload the time-worn fuse box and cause a fire. Even if the fuse panel is 100 amps or more, it should be scrutinized thoroughly before any additional loads are added. Look for the following:

• Is there room for more circuits? Look for empty screws adjacent to the glass fuses. If there aren't enough empty circuits, an expensive service upgrade may be required. If there are empty screws, check the voltage on the screw terminals to verify that full voltage is present for the new circuits. Old fuse boxes are famous for loose, corroded connections, which allow only partial voltage to be available. This may be why there isn't a circuit presently using that connection.

• Are there two or more wires (circuits) under one screw and using one fuse? This situation normally occurs when a circuit is added to a panel that is already completely full, or when a circuit within the panel fails and a working circuit is doubled up to compensate. This is never allowed by code.

• Is the fuse amperage already exceeding the circuit maximum? For example, suppose a 30-amp glass fuse (colored green) is installed into a circuit wired with 12-gauge wire. The fuse won't open until 30 amps is exceeded, but the wiring starts overheating and burning at 20 amps. This commonly happens when circuits are overloaded and homeowners keep increasing the fuse size until the fuse finally holds. Watch out for this situation; it's a fire waiting to happen.

• Are there any hot spots on the fuse box that have melted and then solidified, or any discoloration due to overheating? Pull the main cartridge fuses out and the check the main prongs and the fuse itself for discoloration due to overheating. The plastic on the old fuse panels doesn't hold up well to heat. The most common problem in fuse panels next to oversizing fuses is meltdown.

Replacement is the best option. If budget permits, it's a good idea to recommend replacement of all older fuse panels with new circuit breaker panels. If you don't do this, you must assure yourself of the following: (1) that the fuse panel isn't already overloaded, (2) that it's in satisfactory condition for additional loads, and (3) that there is room for the additional circuits required for the remodel. Note any problems before work begins and add in the necessary extra money on the contract. Otherwise you may have to absorb the extra cost of correcting them

Figure 1. On its face the circuit-breaker panel seems to have room for extra circuits (left). Inside, though, the author found the panel completely full (right).

after the work begins. Whatever you do, don't ignore problems with the panel or you may end up in court.

Circuit Breaker Panels

Circuit breaker panels must also be carefully checked. You cannot tell if a service panel is full by observing the cover. There might be several blank knock-outs on the cover, but inside no empty slots for the breakers (Figure 1). Remove the cover to see if there is room for additional breakers. Also, look for damage to the hot buss. For example, either lightning or arcing in the box (from loose circuit breakers) can burn and deform the buss, making it physically impossible to pop in a new breaker.

Expensive breakers. Make note of the brand of service panel. Some manufacturers have gone out of business, which makes their breakers hard to find and very expensive. If you need a considerable number of these hard-to-find breakers, it could be less expensive to change out the panel to one that has readily available breakers.

Load Calculation

Once you have verified that the new circuits can be inserted into the panel, you must determine that the additional loads of these new circuits won't exceed the maximum load allowed for the service panel, main breaker, and service entrance wire. Just because there are physical openings for additional breakers doesn't mean the code allows them to be added.

Sometimes it is obvious that additional loads can be added. For example, a 200-amp box may have only one or two low-amperage double-pole breakers with a few 15 or 20 single-pole breakers. However, many times it is not so obvious. A 200-amp panel may hold up to a maximum of 40 circuits and have only 10 in it. Yet these 10 circuits could be pulling all the current the main breaker can hold.

To be absolutely certain, a house load calculation must be done. Page 761 of the 1990 National Electrical Code (NEC) or page 1103 of the NEC Handbook describes in detail how to do this. See also Sections 220-31, 220-30, and 220-35 of the NEC. Do not shy away from doing the load calculation. As a contractor you should know how to do it. If it seems overwhelming, hire a competent licensed electrician.

If the main panel has no main breaker, have a certified electrician verify the size of the service entrance wire and current rating of the service panel itself (the current rating for the panel will be indicated on a sticker inside the panel). Base the load maximum on that current figure (the lesser of the two if they differ).

Tying Into Existing Circuits

If you are adding only square footage without any fixed loads, and you intend to tie into an existing branch circuit, you must consider three items:

• First, what is the condition of the old wiring? Is it old knob-and-tube wiring, installed in the 1920s? Or ungrounded wiring, installed during the post-war building boom? In any case, if the existing wiring is ungrounded, the new wiring should run all the way back to the main panel to obtain a ground. Use a plug-in analyzer on a receptacle of the circuit that you are tapping into to verify that the existing wiring on that circuit is wired properly (Figure 2). Also, verify that the service has a service ground other than the house metal pipes. If none exists or the ground rod or ground connection is corroded beyond repair, a new house grounding system will need to be installed.

• Second, verify that the wire you are tapping into is of the proper gauge. If your renovation requires a 20-amp circuit, physically check the old wiring to make sure it is not 14 gauge (15-amp wire).

• Third, the load of the house increases by the additional square footage multiplied by 3 watts per square foot (NEC Section 220-3d). The increased house load must not exceed the house service load. Loads for additional circuits without any structural add-ons are also covered in the same section.

The bottom line here is not to tie into the existing house wiring unless you verify its gauge, that you are not placing too many receptacle outlets on one branch circuit, and that the existing wiring is in good condition and grounded. Be sure to add the new loads to the house load calculation to verify that the current is still under the amount allowed by the main service.

Service Main Panels Used as Subpanels

In the midst of renovation, it is not uncommon to change the existing service panel to a subpanel as a new and larger main service is installed. This situation is considerably more expensive than most contractors are led to believe.

You normally cannot use the existing three-wire service entrance

Figure 2. This three-prong outlet looks like it's on a grounded circuit, but when he used a simple plug-in analyzer the author found there was no ground wire present.

cable as the feed to the old panel. The feed from the new service entrance panel to the old main (now a subpanel) must be a four-conductor (or three-conductor with metal raceway) feeder (hot, hot, neutral, ground). The ground wire connecting the old panel to earth ground (ground rods, structural steel, etc.) as well as any ground wire to metallic plumbing pipes, must be disconnected from the old panel and run to the new one. In addition, as a newly created subpanel, it must have the neutrals (white wires) separated from both the equipment grounding wires (the bare wires coming into the box within the NM wire) and the box (the panel itself). All of these problems can translate into a significant cost.

Moving the Service Entrance Panel

If the service entrance panel needs to be moved away from the power company's meter base, the electrical inspector may require you to add an additional disconnect to the system immediately adjacent to the meter base. This is easy to overlook, but is costly to correct. The logic here is that it is dangerous to have the service panel too far from the meter base since the service entrance (SE) cable is not fused until it gets to the service panel. If a nail is driven into the SE cable between the meter base and the service entrance panel, it can cause a fire since there is no fusing to open the circuit. Therefore many inspectors require a disconnect immediately adjacent to the meter base. The cost is significant, so be sure to add it to the contract if the inspector in your area requires it.

Baseboard Heating

Baseboard heaters are normally installed whenever low initial costs are being considered. Because they are moderate in price and install quickly, they fit a limited budget. But

you need to watch out for some items that, if overlooked, can cause labor and material costs to skyrocket.

- Baseboard heaters cannot be placed under an electrical outlet. Lamp cords draped over the top of the heater could burn. In such locations, two smaller heaters may have to be placed on both sides of the outlet, staying several inches away from the receptacle. This small but significant problem increases material costs and may more than double the installation time. An alternative solution is to obtain baseboard heaters that have the outlets built in. However, you cannot use the 240-volt line that powers the baseboard for the 120-volt outlet. For that, a second cable or circuit will have to be installed. All existing receptacles immediately above the proposed heaters must be removed and blank plates installed.

- Baseboard heaters place heavy current loads on the service panel; 250 watts or approximately 1 amp per foot is typical for 240-volt heaters. Several baseboard units can create such a heavy load that the contractor must be certain that the service panel can handle it. A load calculation may be required for this situation to determine if an expensive service upgrade is required. Do not make the mistake of saying to yourself "that this little extra load doesn't matter since I am only adding one or two heaters." If the panel is already overloaded, the extra load that you add may be the straw that breaks the camel's back.

- Baseboard heaters install quickly only if the thermostats are located in the unit itself. If the owner wants the thermostats in the walls, labor and material increase tremendously. If the walls are plaster-on-lath, the thermostats should remain in the heaters or be wired using conduit. Cutting holes

in such walls risks cracking the plaster for several feet horizontally in both directions. Unless you have developed a method of sawing plaster-on-lath walls without cracking the adjacent plaster, I cannot emphasize too strongly not to try it.

HVAC

The most common electrical problem in hvac installations is overloading of the service entrance panel. As previously mentioned, just because there is room for the breaker doesn't mean the panel won't be overloaded when it's installed. If the service entrance is a 60- or 100-amp panel, it's probably not large enough. Be sure to allow enough money in the contract for the service upgrade. In addition, do not assume a 200-amp panel is large enough for the system, especially if an electric backup system is attached to the hvac unit. A load calculation should be done to verify that there is room for the extra load.

Though hvac units normally have the fusing requirements printed right on them, even experienced electricians can miscalculate hvac loads. For example, does the compressor run all the time the electric backup heat is running, or does it automatically shut off? The compressor can add 20 to 30 amps to the house load, but can be overlooked in the load calculation. If the load calculations are already close to the maximum the service panel will allow, the extra load from the compressor may trip the breaker.

Wherever the hvac unit is installed, code now requires switched lighting at the point of entrance. Don't forget to add it to the estimate. And make sure that you do not split the 240 volts supplied for the hvac system for the required 120-volt lighting (against code). Tap into another 120-volt line in the immediate area or run a separate circuit.

Kitchens and Dining Areas

The kitchen is usually the most miswired room in a house. A kitchen requires several circuits; if you're doing a kitchen remodel, make sure the service panel has room enough for any additional circuits you may need.

The NEC codes that apply to the kitchen also apply to the dining room, breakfast room, and pantry. If any renovation is to be done, the local inspector may require updating the wiring to current codes. This is extremely expensive as there are many code articles that apply. As a reminder:

- A minimum of two circuits (20-amp, 12-AWG wire) must feed the countertop receptacle outlets. The outlets must be no farther apart than 4 feet. I normally use the kitchen sink as a reference: to the left, one circuit; to the right, the second.
- All receptacle outlets within 6 feet of the kitchen sink (straight line distance) must have GFCIs (ground fault circuit interrupters).
- The lights must not be on same circuit as the kitchen/dining/pantry receptacle outlets. In addition, it is not good practice, and most of the time against code, to install the lights on the same circuit as the undercounter appliances.
- Additional circuits must be brought into the kitchen to power the fixed appliances such as the dishwasher, garbage disposal, compactor, etc., since these appliances cannot be powered by the kitchen/dining room/pantry receptacle outlets. Usually these appliances require their own separate circuits; be sure to read the instructions.
- An island is required to have receptacle outlets, and getting the wire there is sometimes labor intensive. How and where to place the receptacle without having a drawer slide into it is always a problem.

- The most common kitchen wiring error is installing the microwave on one of the kitchen receptacle circuits. The NEC doesn't specifically mention the microwave, but it does state that you must follow manufacturer's recommendations. Most manufacturers of medium and large microwave appliances require them to be put on a separate circuit. Read the instructions!

Porches

Open porches do not count in house loading, but specific codes do apply to special applications. If the owner wants electrical service on the porch area, and the porch is at or close to ground level, the receptacle outlets must have expensive GFCI protection. As before, verify that the branch circuit you are tapping into doesn't exceed the maximum number of allowed receptacle outlets, and that the house wiring is grounded and in good condition. In addition, if a door was added to the house to obtain entrance to the porch, a switched light must be added at the point of entrance. Walls that are to be removed normally have electrical wires inside, so be sure to allow finances to cover their splicing and relocation.

Garages

Do not make the error of bidding on a garage without the bid price reflecting the increased cost of GFCIs, which are required for general purpose outlets in garages. Dedicated and inaccessible receptacle outlets, however, are exempt; for example, receptacles for garage door openers, freezers, refrigerators, fans, etc.

If standard household receptacles are installed in the garage, be prepared for complaints. These receptacles are fine as long as heavy duty grounded cords aren't plugged in and out on a daily basis. Being made out of a brittle plastic, the grounding plug will break them apart in short

order if they are wiggled up and down as they are inserted and withdrawn. For such locations, it would be best to recommend to the owner the use of receptacles made out of nylon (about $6 apiece). If he refuses, he can't later complain to you about breakage.

Miscellaneous

Suppose your customers want to add one or two bedrooms to their house. Besides the required carpentry work, there are some code-required electricals that they'll have to have. Here are some items to watch for.

Smoke alarms. The new bedrooms will need hard-wired smoke alarms in the adjacent hallway. These can no longer be powered by batteries alone; I use hard-wired with a battery backup. If the bedrooms share the same hallway and are reasonably close to each other, one smoke alarm will normally suffice. However, if the renovation requires bedrooms that are separated from each other, you will need alarms for each. Further, the alarms will all have to be wired together so that when one sounds they all sound. Labor, as well as the wire itself, is not cheap. Don't be forced to "eat it" because you forget to "add it."

Closets. Closets are always problem areas. Closet lighting requirements (NEC Section 410-8) are extremely strict in the type and placement of the lights. Low-cost, bare incandescent bulbs can no longer be installed in closets. If the bulb is broken, the hot filament can fall on top of clothes or storage items and start a fire. Incandescent bulbs must be totally enclosed and be mounted at least 12 inches away from all clothes and storage items.

If fluorescent lights are to be installed in the closet, be sure the owner knows that these fixtures normally emit a 60-cycle hum. Also, NEC Section 410-8 applies severe restrictions to fluorescent lights as

Figure 3. When bidding a paddle fan installation, remember to include the cost of the extension pipe and a UL-approved electrical box to support the weight of the fan.

well. This article is far too complex to detail here, but it is imperative that it be understood by the contractor.

Recessed lighting. If the owner wants recessed lighting in the ceiling, be careful. Some recessed fixtures, especially the high wattage ones, cannot be placed next to insulation. Unless the light is rated "IC" (insulated ceiling) or equivalent, all insulation must be removed from the area determined by the requirements of that specific fixture. This means that if loose insulation is in the attic, barriers may have to be built around

the light to keep the insulation away from the fixture. Failure to do so may cause a fire. If you have to keep costs down, a low-voltage, battery-operated light fixture can be installed.

Switches. Be sure to ask how the client wants the lights switched. Switched outlets and three-way switching are much more expensive and labor intensive than standard switched lighting. You may assume the owners want a switched over-head light when what they really wanted was switched outlets. Do not put yourself in the position of having to pay for the increased cost of the latter because you didn't think to ask.

Dimmer controls. If the owner wants dimmer controls on his trac lighting, outside lighting, chandeliers, or any other heavily loaded lighting system, be wary. A standard low-cost dimmer is rated for only 600 watts. This limits the lighting to no more than four 150-watt bulbs. And there is no way to limit the amount of lights installed on a trac. Also, low-cost dimmers get hot with only a minimum load applied.

Don't assume you can use $5 dimmer controls and then find out later you really needed $50 high-wattage units. Question the owners to determine if they plan to add additional lamps at some time in the future. If you install the trac lighting with four 150-watt lights controlled

by a 600-watt dimmer and later the owners add a few more trac lights, the dimmer control could overheat and cause a fire. A 1,000-watt or larger dimmer has a heatsink located outside the wall which dissipates the heat and provides protection. But even with the expensive, high-wattage dimmers, the contractor should specify in the contract the maximum number of trac lights or floods allowed on the circuit if a dimmer is installed.

Ceiling fans. If the owners want one or more paddle fans, the contractor should realize that only UL-listed boxes may now be used for hanging them. These boxes are expensive, so be sure to include the extra cost (Figure 3). If the owner wants the fans on a variable speed control, make sure you use one that doesn't "sing," or complaints will follow. In addition, if the fan is hanging on a vaulted ceiling, an expensive extension pipe will be required to lower the fan so the blades won't hit the ceiling.

Splicing. When tying into existing circuits, splices cannot be covered up and left inside walls. All in-house splices are considered maintainable items, and access must be allowed. Splices are normally put in standard receptacle boxes with a blank plate.

By Rex Cauldwell, a master electrician and owner of Little Mountain Electric in Copper Hill, Va.

REWIRING TIPS

Rewiring old houses is not just a skill — it's an art. You have to be part electrician, part carpenter, part plasterer, and part magician. And like most magic, it's all an illusion. We can't always get wires to where we need them without disturbing the existing walls. The trick is knowing how to make it look like we weren't there.

Pulling Wires

To snake wires from one part of the house to another, I use $1/8$-inch-wide metal fish tape. It's stiff enough that I can shove it through some obstructions (like plaster buildup) and flexible enough to detour around others (such as blocking and cleats). It's usually easiest to pull the wires through the wall cavity in the

same direction that you fed the snake in. Since snakes come in 50- or 100-foot lengths, I often cut them shorter to avoid having to pull all of it up on a shorter pull. I recommend getting the longest snaking jobs done first in case you have to cut the snake shorter for another pull.

I store my snakes coiled up, so I have to straighten them before I start work. If the snake is still coiled, it will coil up inside the wall cavity.

On each end of the snake I bend a hook approximately 1 inch long and about 1/4 inch across. To attach three-wire Romex to a snake, cut through two of the wires at a 45-degree angle about 5 inches from the end (Figure 4). Bend the third wire through the hook on the end of the snake. Tape everything shut to avoid snagging inside the wall. If a pull is long or there is likely to be a lot of friction to fight, twist the wire around itself a few times before you tape it.

String. In straight chases or in balloon-framed buildings, it's often easiest to use a string and a slim weight. I can usually get the string to the bottom with just a couple of shakes. In difficult areas, it's a good idea to pull an extra string when you pull the wires — you may need it later.

Snake Grabber

With a little patience and finesse, one person with a "snake grabber" can do some of those difficult snaking jobs that usually take two people. This is a tool that I make from BX cable, aircraft cable, and a short length of fish tape (Figure 5).

To use the snake grabber, slide the cable end into a 3/8- to 3/4-inch-diameter hole, making sure the cable feeds into the wall. Pull the piece of fish tape toward you while holding the handle still, then twist the tape half a turn. The cables will now fill most of the bay.

Now stick your snake into the bay with an open hook on the end. Push the snake up and down in the bay until you hook the grabber. Pull the handle gently back to the end and gently guide the cable that is hooked on the snake out through the hole, pulling the snake out with it. (If your hole is bigger than 3/4 inch, be careful not to pull the grabber into the wall.)

The snake grabber obviously works better in an uninsulated wall, but I have had some success with it in insulated walls, too.

Using a Tone Generator

Sometimes when I am having difficulty locating a snake, I use my tone generator (Figure 6), which can locate a conductor or other metal object. To use the tone generator, I clip one of its leads to a snake I have fished up a wall. The tone generator causes the snake to emit an electronic tone that can be picked up by the tone amplifier. (An AM radio will also work adequately instead of a tone amplifier; for best results, tune the radio so that it's not on a station.) Hold the amplifier or radio near the area of the wall where you think the snake is. The tone will get louder as the receiver gets closer to the snake.

To help locate a wall from the cellar, I bend a piece of Romex in the shape of a T and clip the leads onto two conductors of the Romex. I place the T against the baseboard at the spot I want to locate. From the cellar I then use a tone amplifier to locate the T.

From the Cellar

Once you determine which walls you want the wires to run through, the next job is to find places in the cellar where you can drill access holes. Finding these walls can sometimes be a challenge, but there are usually clues — like pipes, heating ducts, and other wires — to lead you in the right direction.

When you're ready to drill, it's a good idea to post a "spotter" upstairs. The spotter rests a hand on the floor and baseboard near where you're aiming. If you miss the wall and the bit starts chewing into the baseboard, the spotter will feel the difference in the vibration and tell you to stop before you do any serious damage. Remember to drill slowly to give your spotter time to

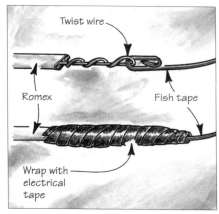

Figure 4. When attaching Romex to a snake for a long pull, the author makes a strong, twisted loop, as shown, and wraps the whole connection in electrical tape.

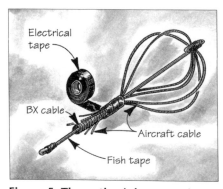

Figure 5. The author's homemade "snake grabber" uses aircraft cable inside a stud bay to help hook a snake that is probing the wall.

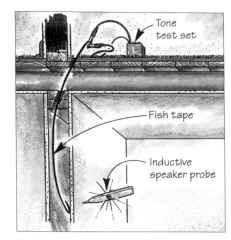

Figure 6. A tone generator turns a fish tape into a transmitter. Using a speaker probe (or radio tuned between stations), you can locate the tape inside a finished wall.

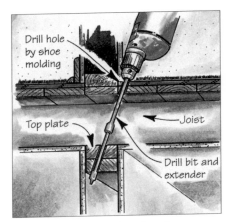

Figure 7. By removing the shoe molding at the edge of a carpeted room, you can drill an inconspicuous hole through the floor.

Figure 8. When an old sill is deeper than the wall, use a bit extender and drill at a shallow angle.

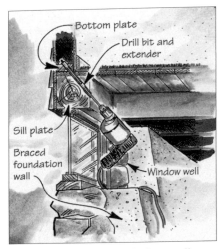

Figure 9. For old foundation walls that have been reinforced with concrete, a window well sometimes provides enough room for drilling.

react. If the wall cavity you're aiming for is near a doorway, the spotter can often feel both sides of the wall. Otherwise, I have the spotter feel the side that would be the most trouble to fix.

When a floor is going to be carpeted or covered with linoleum or tile, you can sometimes cut a hole in the floor to help gain access to an area. If a room already has carpeting, you can sometimes drill carefully at the edge of the carpet with a small feeler bit. Be extra careful not to snag a carpet thread while drilling. You can unravel a large section of carpet in just a few seconds if you don't pay close attention.

If the baseboard sits off the wall a little, you can sometimes drill a hole behind it with a small feeler bit to help locate the wall. You can also lift shoe moldings and carpet strips and drill where the hole won't be seen (Figure 7).

On an old wood floor that has not been refinished recently, there is sometimes a small crack between the boards that you can fit a small drill bit in to give you a reference point to help find the wall. Always remember to patch these small holes into the cellar. You don't want to create a draft.

Sill Drilling

It's easier to locate exterior walls, but before drilling, remember to take into account the width of the sill and the depth of the wall. In old buildings, the sills tend to be 6 to 8 inches wide, while the walls are typically $3^{1}/_{2}$ inches deep. So you have to drill at an angle through the sill to get inside the wall (Figure 8). Often, the easiest way to figure the angle is to find a wire or pipe already drilled at the necessary angle and try to duplicate the angle.

To further complicate the situation, many old foundations are made of stone. The stones protrude at irregular intervals, making it difficult to drill exactly where you wish. Also,

many old foundations have been braced by having another foundation poured inside the old one; this makes the foundation even deeper and more impossible to drill. When faced with this situation, you may be able to drill up at the window wells (Figure 9). This is very restrictive, but can sometimes solve the problem in a pinch.

Feeds to the Attic

Plumbing chases and chimney chases are the first places to look when trying to find a route for feeds to the attic. When these don't work, you should check to see if any closets line up from one floor to the next. You may be able to run a piece of pipe in the corner of the closet to pull your feeds through.

If there is an obvious way to get wires to the attic (such as a chimney chase or plumbing chase), I usually pull a few up there, then work down into the walls. It's also easier to find walls from the attic because they were often framed before the ceiling was covered. All you have to do is lift the insulation and look (Figure 10).

Notching

It's often necessary to make notches in the wall and ceiling to get around framing members. These should be as small and neat as possible.

The most common place I have to notch is where the wall meets the ceiling (Figure 11). Say I'm running a wire from a wall switch to a ceiling light. The goal is to get a wire from the wall bay up into the joist bay. Using a $^{1}/_{2}$-inch spade bit, I start at the corner and drill to find the bottom edge of the top plate. I then drill up from the corner through the plate into the joist bay.

You may also have to make notches to get from one stud (or joist) bay into the next. After finding the stud, I drill a 1-inch-deep hole in its center. I then drill at a tight angle

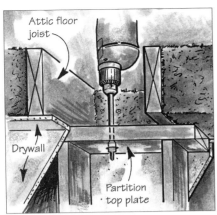

Figure 10. Finding partition walls from the attic is usually easy — just lift the insulation and look for the top plates.

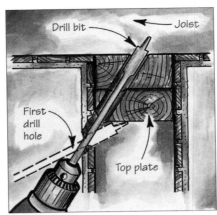

Figure 11. After drilling one hole to find the bottom edge of the top plate, you can drill at an angle that will pop the bit through the center of the wall in the attic.

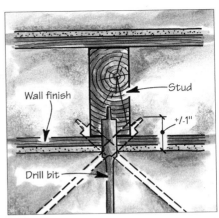

Figure 12. To run a wire across a stud or joist, the author drills three holes: one straight in, and one each at a tight angle into each bay.

in both directions to get access into both bays (Figure 12). This leaves only a small hole to patch.

Cutting in Boxes

After establishing where I want a box to be (Remember: Measure to the height of the other *boxes* in the room, not the cover plates!), I trace the outline of the box onto the wall. Then, depending on the wall finish, I often scribe the outline of the box with a razor knife. With wood paneling, scribing prevents splintering; if the wall is wallpapered, it prevents tearing. On a skim-coat plaster wall, scribing with a razor knife prevents the plaster edge from splitting and peeling away from the blueboard. Next, using a 3/8-inch spade bit, I drill out the corners of the box, then cut it out with a cordless jigsaw.

I carry two hole saws for cutting in round boxes: a dull one for cutting through plaster and a sharp one for cutting through wood and wood lath.

Plaster and Lath

Cutting rectangular boxes into true plaster and lath requires a little more work. After determining the approximate location of the box, I drill 1/8-inch holes about 1/4 inch

apart until I find the space between two pieces of lath. I work my way up until I find the next space, then I center the box on the piece of lath before tracing the outline of the box.

I drill out the corners, then I use the razor knife to scribe and completely remove the plaster. I like the cordless jigsaw for cutting lath because it vibrates the wall less than a keyhole saw. A recip saw or corded jigsaw will shake the wall to pieces. When using the cordless jigsaw, I never let the shoe touch the plaster. Any vibration will turn the plaster to dust.

To finish the cut, slide a screwdriver behind the middle piece of lath and hold the lath firmly between your thumb and the screwdriver. Then cut the lath on one side, leaving 1/4 inch uncut. This helps keep the lath from vibrating while you cut the other side.

After removing the middle piece, you can grab hold of the top and bottom pieces while cutting them out.

Metal Lath

My first impulse when I find out that a job has metal lath walls is to run away. After my heart stops pounding, I pull out my jigsaw with as many metal blades as I can find — I often go through two blades for

each box I cut in. The lath will also destroy a drill bit after a couple of boxes.

Another thing that makes working with metal lath walls more difficult is that you can't use a tone generator. If the energized snake touches the metal lath, the lath will become energized, making an accurate reading impossible.

Patching

Patching your holes may be the most important part of the job. A good patching job creates the illusion that you were never there. I like to patch holes as I go so I have time for another coat before going home. Go light on the spackle to avoid sanding.

For small holes, I use Onetime, a lightweight spackle from Red Devil that dries so quickly I can get a second or third coat on in the same day. For larger holes, I'll use a quick-drying mix-up powder like Durabond. This dries even harder and faster than spackle, giving me a solid base coat in a short time. The stuff dries in about 15 minutes, so mix up only what you can use quickly.

By Sean Kenney, a master electrician from Amesbury, Mass.

COMMON ELECTRICAL INSPECTION FAILURES

The *National Electrical Code (NEC)* says, "Electrical equipment shall be installed in a neat and workmanlike manner." This regulation is open to interpretation, and it means that, technically, the inspector can fail a job simply because the work looks sloppy. When asked about the first thing they look for when they inspect a job, most of the inspectors said the same thing: Neatness. In fact, sloppy work is a tipoff that the whole job needs some extra scrutiny (Figure 13).

Many electricians never realize how important neatness is because they aren't cited directly for a workmanship violation. Enforcing a workmanship violation can be difficult, but if the work is messy, inspectors say they usually have no trouble finding plenty of other violations to enforce.

Although neatness is subjective, there are certain guidelines to follow:

• Wires should be run in straight lines that are level and plumb.
• Romex should be unwound so it will lie flat without any twists.
• All electrical equipment should be installed level and plumb.

Keep Informed

Most code violations are caused by ignorance of the *NEC* or blatant disregard of the code. In many cases, it's a little of both.

The *NEC* is updated every three years, and it's difficult to keep up with all the changes. Many states require electricians to stay current by taking an update course during each code cycle. Many electricians don't bother to take the update course, however, until near the end of the cycle. By the time they learn about current changes, the code is about to change again.

Tub or Hot Tub?

Hydromassage bathtubs are a common source of code misinterpretations, because they are often confused with hot tubs. The rules for grounding and locating outlets and switches around hot tubs are much stricter than those dealing with hydromassage bathtubs.

According to the current *NEC*, "a hydromassage bathtub is designed so it can accept, circulate, and discharge water upon each use," and a "spa or hot tub is not designed or intended to have its contents drained or discharged after each use."

A bathtub with massage jets is clearly not a hot tub, yet many inspectors will require one to be wired as if it was. You won't achieve much, however, by waving the *NEC* in your inspector's face and arguing the point. Just find out what the inspector requires before you do the job.

"Accessible Outlet" Confusion

In garages, all receptacles on the ground level must be GFCI-protected — with two exceptions. No GFCI protection is required on "receptacles that are not readily accessible," or on a receptacle that is "located within dedicated space" and intended for use only with a single appliance.

The confusion lies in the phrase "readily accessible." If a receptacle cannot be reached without a ladder, few people would consider it readily accessible. Many inspectors, however, will require a GFCI-protected receptacle for a garage door opener receptacle because this is

Figure 13. Sloppy wiring like this is an invitation to an inspector to check the job very carefully for further violations.

Figure 14. An approval from Underwriters Laboratory is the accepted industry standard for materials used in electrical installations. But keep your eyes open — lots of home centers sell non-UL-listed equipment because it's cheaper.

often the "most accessible" outlet in the garage. Other inspectors consider it a dedicated, single-appliance receptacle and don't require a GFCI.

Using Improper Equipment

Listing services like Underwriters Laboratory (UL) examine and test electrical equipment to be sure it complies with the *NEC* and other appropriate standards. Violations having to do with product listings come in two categories: using unlisted products, and not using a product according to its listing.

Unlisted products. Keep your eyes open. Many supply houses and home centers carry products that are not listed by UL or other listing services (Figure 14). These products usually don't meet the standards set by the *NEC*. Their selling point is that they are usually much cheaper than their listed counterparts. These unlisted products most often turn up in very competitive markets where price is always a big issue.

These products can show up in a project for a variety of reasons. Sometimes it's just because the electrician didn't check the stock carefully; sometimes UL-listed stock is unavailable and the job needs to be finished. And occasionally an electrician will use unlisted products because of the cheaper price.

Many inspectors in my area keep an eye out for these unlisted materi-

---

FREQUENT VIOLATIONS

Stapling Romex. Romex must be secured within 12 inches of the box and every 4¹/₂ feet thereafter. Not securing Romex properly is one of the most obvious code violations. It's one of those "neat and workmanlike" violations that tip off an inspector to check everything carefully.

Outside receptacle. In new construction, some electricians will wire the outside receptacle from

Figure A. The PVC riser that carries the main service feed to a house's electric meter needs an expansion fitting near the ground. Without it, the movement from the freezing and thawing of the soil could crack the pipe.

the kitchen appliance circuit. This is a clear violation of the 1996 *NEC*. The outdoor circuit can come off of any other nearby circuit or be a homerun back to the panel.

Underground service riser. When running wires underground, many electricians forget to put clips on the conduit riser that houses the wire from the ground up to the meter socket. The riser must be secured within 3 feet of the meter socket. Some inspectors will pass a riser that's buried at least 2 feet deep — but some won't. The *NEC* says that you must clip the pipe to the house.

Many municipalities also require an expansion fitting on the PVC riser where it comes out of the ground to protect against ground movement damaging the equipment (Figure A).

Subpanels. Most electricians know that a subpanel must be

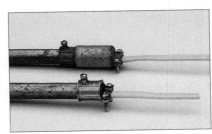

Figure B. When switching from one wiring method to another, code requires a changeover fitting (at bottom) or a similar transition fitting made from standard parts (at top).

wired using a four-wire feed rather than a three-wire feed, but many are still confused about where to connect the wires in the subpanel.

In the main panel, the ground and the neutral wires from each circuit are tied into a single neutral/ground bar. The subpanel has separate ground and neutral bars.

The ground bar must be bonded to the subpanel and the neutral bar must be isolated from the subpanel. The ground wire coming from the main panel will go to the ground bar and the neutral wire will go to neutral bar. All branch circuits will be tied in with the ground wires on the ground bar and the neutral wires on the neutral bar.

Circuits labels. The *NEC* says "All panelboard circuits and circuit modifications shall be legibly identified as to purpose or use on a circuit directory located on the face or inside of the panel doors." Many electricians fail to mark the circuit breakers after doing work.

Changeover fittings. When you switch from one wiring method to another, you must use a changeover fitting. The most common place this violation occurs is in the cellar. When using a piece of pipe as a sleeve for Romex, many electricians do not use a combination connector (changeover fitting) at the top of the pipe to secure the Romex to the pipe (Figure B). — *S.K.*

als and require the electrician to replace them with listed materials.

Ground clamps are a good example of an unlisted product which is inferior to its listed counterpart. UL-listed ground clamps are made of brass, while unlisted ground clamps are usually made of cast aluminum. If you tighten an aluminum ground clamp firmly, it can break later, even if everything looks okay when you install it.

Follow listing instructions. The *NEC* says, "... equipment shall be installed, used or both, in accordance with any instructions included in the listing or labeling."

The most common violation of this type has to do with circuit breakers. Many brands of circuit breakers are physically interchangeable, but don't be fooled: Just because it fits doesn't mean you can use it. The model number on the circuit breaker must be printed on the circuit breaker panel cover. Usually breaker panels will only accept breakers of the same brand.

Permits and Licensing

Some electricians will perform work without pulling the necessary permits. If the inspector discovers this, he will shut down the job and often fine the electrician. In many areas the electrician will have to pay double for the permit if he is caught working without one.

Most states also require one licensed electrician for every helper on the job; some require a master electrician to be present if there is more than one journeyman on the job.

Another common problem crops up when electrical work is performed by someone without an electrician's license, such as other tradespeople. Hvac contractors, remodelers, and alarm installers will sometimes do their own electrical work to save time and money. While nonelectrician tradespeople may know how to make something work electrically, they seldom know the codes involved. This can lead to some dangerous installations.

By Sean Kenney, a master electrician from Amesbury, Mass.

GFCI Circuits

Whenever a customer asks me to defend the need for GFCIs (ground-fault circuit interrupters), I recount the old movie scene where the radio falls — or is thrown — into a water-filled bathtub, swiftly electrocuting the unfortunate bather. I then explain that if the radio had been plugged into a GFCI receptacle, the bather would still be alive. This leads us to the ultimate purpose of GFCIs — the protection of life.

Do GFCIs work? Absolutely. These devices have saved countless lives and provide much needed protection for both the tradesman and homeowner.

If you are ever unlucky enough to receive an electrical shock, but lucky enough to have a GFCI in the line, it will feel like you're being stuck with a needle, then the GFCI will trip and open the circuit, stopping the current.

How GFCIs Work

In ordinary 125-volt residential circuits using NM (non-metallic sheath) wire, the amperage leaving the panel, usually through a black wire, must equal the amperage returning to the panel through a neutral, or white, wire.

A GFCI continually monitors the amount of current going to the load and compares it to that coming back. As long as the two are equal, the electricity is doing its work properly. However, if some of the electrons are missing and the current coming back from the load is less than that going to it, the GFCI will trip the circuit. The logic of GFCI design is that if the current is not coming back via the wiring, it must be going somewhere else. Often this "somewhere else" is to earth (ground) through a person holding a tool or appliance.

Here's an example from my own experience. I was using a drill that was plugged into an extension cord that, in turn, was plugged into a GFCI receptacle in my garage. The drill was old and the shell made out of solid metal. While I was using it, one of the wires inside the drill shorted to the metal case, which made it electrically hot. Since electricity can cause mus-cles to contract, my hand tightened around the metal handle so that I could not release it. The current was now leaving the service panel, traveling through the black wire of the house wiring to the GFCI, then through the extension cord into the drill. From the drill, the current was flowing through me to ground. This was a classic ground fault: The electrical short within the drill caused the current to pass through me to ground, rather than flowing back to the service panel via the white wire. The GFCI detected this imbalance and opened the circuit immediately, saving my life. My only discomfort was the pin prick feeling.

Split-second response. The time it takes for a GFCI to open a circuit will vary from manufacturer to manufacturer, but it should be no more than 1/30 of a second to comply with UL standards. The actual amount of current imbalance that the GFCI must detect before it trips is four to six milliamps (thousandths of an amp), also a UL standard. Theoretically, the average person can tolerate four to six milliamps of current for ¹/₃₀ of a second before his or her heart goes into fibrillation. (Fibrillation means that the heart goes out of sync; the result can be death.) With GFCI protection, you may still get a shock, but its duration will be limited to ¹/₃₀ of a second.

Why doesn't the circuit breaker trip? Most circuit breakers controlling general purpose receptacles will not trip until at least 15 or 20 amps of current flow has been exceeded. This amount of current is normally fatal. In order to protect against fatal shocks, you need a device on line, like the GFCI, that will trip before the circuit breaker can trip.

Common sense. Just because you are plugged into a GFCI doesn't mean that you can cast all common sense to the wind. You can still die if your body — your heart in particular — is placed between the incoming black wire and the outgoing white wire. In this case, your body is in series with the electrical current, just like a light bulb. As long as your body isn't grounded, you are no different to the GFCI than a normal working load (Figure 15). If you get caught in this situation, the GFCI will not trip because there is no current leakage to ground to create an imbalance…and you could be killed.

GFCI Types

For residences, GFCIs come in two types (Figure 16). One type looks like a receptacle. It has a test button on it and sometimes a light. The second type looks like a 15- or 20-amp circuit breaker with a test button on it. In both designs, the purpose of the test button is, when pressed, to place a current imbalance on the circuit. The GFCI should then trip if it is working properly.

Circuit breaker GFCIs. Use a GFCI circuit breaker only if all receptacles on the circuit require ground-fault protection. It fits into the service panel like a standard breaker but wires a little differently. Circuit

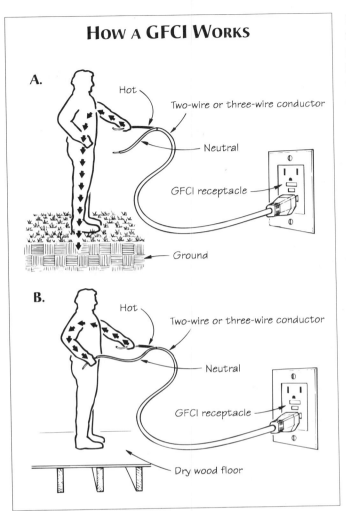

How a GFCI Works

A.

Hot

Two-wire or three-wire conductor

Neutral

GFCI receptacle

Ground

B.

Hot

Two-wire or three-wire conductor

Neutral

GFCI receptacle

Dry wood floor

Figure 15. A GFCI trips when it senses a current imbalance, protecting you from shock if you accidentally contact a hot conductor while you are grounded (A). If you come between a black and white conductor and are not grounded, however, a GFCI may not protect you (B), since there will be no current imbalance.

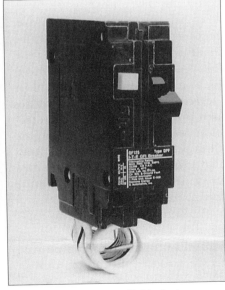

Figure 16. Residential ground-fault circuit interrupters are available in two types. Use receptacle-style GFCIs where possible for convenient resetting at the point of use (left). GFCI circuit breakers (right) protect an entire circuit but must be reset at the panel.

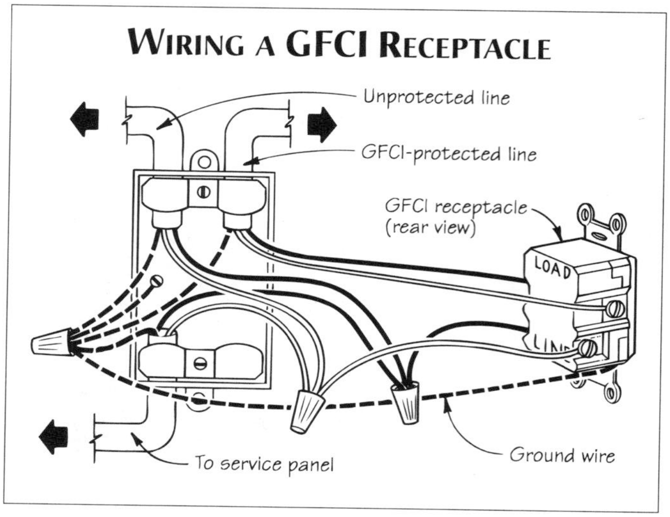

WIRING A GFCI RECEPTACLE

Unprotected line

GFCI-protected line

GFCI receptacle
(rear view)

LOAD

LINE

To service panel

Ground wire

Figure 17. To give ground-fault protection to downstream receptacles, you must wire them off the load side of the GFCI.

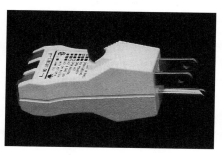

Figure 18. This plug-in tester can test a GFCI receptacle and any downstream receptacles it protects, but only in a grounded circuit.

breaker GFCIs have two main disadvantages: They cost more than receptacle GFCIs and are somewhat inconvenient. Because they're located in the service panel, the homeowner has to walk to the panel each time the GFCI trips the circuit.

Receptacle GFCIs are fed from the service panel through a standard circuit breaker. The GFCI receptacle is then placed at the point of use so that when it trips, the homeowner can immediately reset it without leaving the room.

I recommend using GFCI receptacles wherever possible inside the house, both for cost and convenience. However, the cost can escalate far above the cost of a circuit-breaker GFCI if you install them at several locations on a single circuit.

To power outdoor receptacles, however, I definitely recommend using a GFCI circuit breaker. Experience has shown that GFCI receptacles can have a short life span when located outside, even in watertight boxes. The boxes and lids may be watertight but they are not vapor tight. The water vapor seems to shorten the life of the electronics within.

Incorrect Wiring of GFCIs

A GFCI receptacle may be wired incorrectly by a homeowner or novice electrician. GFCI receptacles have a "line," or input, side and a "load," or output, side. The line side must be connected to the wiring that originates at the service panel. The load side must be connected to any downside receptacles that are to be protected (Figure 17).

Often a receptacle GFCI is wired incorrectly by pigtailing the downstream receptacles off the line side. These receptacles are now in parallel with the GFCI and are not ground-fault protected. Only those receptacles feeding out of the load side will be protected.

Remember to label any downstream receptacles as ground-fault protected. Use the stickers supplied with the receptacle expressly for this purpose. Inspectors often overlook this, but be sure to do it anyway. Without the label, the homeowner has no way of knowing that a particular outlet is protected.

It is also possible to wire a circuit-breaker GFCI incorrectly. However, the incorrect hookup would be immediately apparent if the "test" button doesn't trip the device. Under test, this type of device typically places an eight milliamp ground-fault on the circuit.

Testing

Always test GFCIs (using the test button located on the GFCI) immediately after installation. If you are at a site where you will be using a pre-existing GFCI to power your tools, always test it first to verify that the ground-fault protection is still working. It's possible to obtain 125 volts from a GFCI receptacle without its ground-fault protection working. Manufacturers normally request monthly testing of GFCIs.

Plug-in tester. Do not test a GFCI by shorting across the hot-to-neutral slots in the receptacle. This will not test the GFCI and may cause damage. Three-prong plug-in testers with a push button are specifically designed for the testing of GFCIs and are commonly available at most electrical supply houses. This type of tester typically places a .0068-amp current imbalance on the line to trip the GFCI. All electricians, contractors, and inspectors should carry and use these little testers (Figure 18).

You can also use a plug-in tester to test a GFCI that has several receptacles on its load side. First test the actual GFCI receptacle or GFCI circuit breaker. Then test the most distant receptacle working off its load side. The GFCI should trip when you push the button on the tester.

Testing GFCIs in an ungrounded circuit. Plug-in testers create an actual fault to the ground wire in a three-wire circuit, causing the GFCI to trip if it is working properly. However, this can lead to uncertain test results for a GFCI installed in an ungrounded (two-wire) circuit. The GFCI may actually work fine, but it will not respond to the tester since there is no ground wire to short to.

However, for UL-approved receptacle GFCIs, the test button on the device itself will still yield an accurate test. This is because the built-in test device works by taking some of the current from the black wire on the load side of the GFCI and shunting it back to the white wire on the line side to unbalance the circuit. This is, in effect, a ground-fault simulation rather than a true ground fault, but the imbalance effect is the same.

Code Requirements

The National Electric Code (NEC) defines where and how GFCIs should be used. Here are some of the more common regulations affecting residences. (Unless otherwise stated, "receptacle" refers to a 125-volt, single-phase, 15-amp or 20-amp standard residential receptacle.)

Kitchen. All countertop receptacles within a 6-foot straight-line distance from the kitchen sink must have GFCI protection. Since, according to code, two separate circuits must feed the countertop receptacles, I normally wire my kitchens with one GFCI circuit to the left of the sink and one GFCI circuit to the right (assuming the sink is in the center of the countertop). This normally separates the load evenly and, if I come back ten years later to troubleshoot a problem, I know exactly how the circuits are wired. I use GFCI receptacles, as opposed to circuit breaker GFCIs, since the former can be reset at the point-of-use in the kitchen. Countertop receptacles beyond the 6-foot limit, as well as other general use kitchen, dining, and pantry receptacles, can be wired into the line, or unprotected, side of the GFCI.

Bathroom. All receptacles installed in bathrooms must have GFCI protection. I always use receptacle GFCIs for reset convenience.

Garage. Every receptacle in a garage must have GFCI protection

Figure 19. GFCI-protected extension cords are recommended by OSHA for power tool use in outdoor or damp locations (at left). Another option is a portable plug-in GFCI (at right).

unless it is not readily accessible, such as a receptacle located on the ceiling for a garage door opener, or one serving a plug-in appliance occupying dedicated space, such as a freezer. Any 230-volt outlet is exempt, as is the laundry circuit.

Outdoors. All receptacles installed outdoors that are readily accessible and within 6 feet 6 inches of grade level must have ground-fault protection.

Unfinished basements and crawl-spaces at or below grade level. All receptacles installed in these locations must have ground-fault protection, except for:
- A single (not duplex or triplex) receptacle supplied by a dedicated branch circuit for a plug-in appliance such as a freezer or refrigerator
- A laundry circuit
- A single receptacle supplying a permanently installed sump pump

Job-site protection. In most areas of the country, builders are required to use a GFCI-protected temporary panel. This type of panel normally protects single-phase, 125-volt, 15-amp and 20-amp receptacle outlets. If you use a generator of five kilowatts or less, you may be exempt. (See Section 305(6)(a) of the NEC

for more information.) Extension cords with built-in GFCI protection are also available for job-site use and are recommended by OSHA (Figure 19).

Where Not to Use GFCIs

Even though it isn't against code, room lights should not be placed on a GFCI unless there is a specific need for doing so. The reason is simple: If the GFCI trips, you don't want to be left in the dark trying to find your way out of the room — especially in the bathroom, where the floor might be wet and slippery, with many objects to bump against or trip over.

Avoid this by wiring only the receptacles in the room, if you want them protected, off the load side of the GFCI, but put the lights on the line side.

Also, unless there is a specific reason, don't use a GFCI for equipment and appliances that cannot go without power for an extended time, such as a freezer or sump pump, since GFCIs are sensitive and are subject to nuisance tripping.

By Rex Cauldwell, a master electrician and owner of Little Mountain Electric in Copper Hill, Va.

PLUG-IN ELECTRICAL TESTERS

Plug-in testers are a safe, inexpensive way to troubleshoot 120-volt household circuits. By simply plugging in the tester, you get the results of a variety of tests, indicated by a series of three lights on the front of the unit. A key on the tester tells you what each particular combination of lights means.

Plug-in testers will work only with 120-volt receptacles. If a receptacle is incorrectly wired with 240 volts, the unit will be destroyed when it's plugged in. Most plug-in testers perform several standard tests; the most common are described below.

1. Correct Wiring

There's not a lot to say here — obviously, this is the reading you want — but there is one point that I can't stress enough. When wiring a receptacle, never use the push-in type connections that come on the backs of some receptacles. These are not reliable; they may work loose over time. Always use the screws; otherwise, a "Correct Wiring" indication one month may result in a dangerous situation the next month.

Loop the stripped end of the wire around the screw and tighten it snugly. Make sure you loop the wire so that it gets tighter, not looser, as you tighten the screw.

2. Reversed Polarity

I've been asked why this matters. "What difference does it make if you plug in a lamp and the current goes in the neutral leg and comes out the hot leg? The light bulb still comes on, doesn't it?"

Not long ago, a little girl in my home state put her tongue into the round metal bulb holder of a decorative electric candle — the kind you see in windows at Christmas. Even though the switch was off, the girl was electrocuted because the fixture had been wired backwards and the round cylinder that holds the bulb was hot.

On a recent service call, I was working on a pump in an underground concrete enclosure. The owner had switched off the power; I measured 0 volts from hot to neutral. But when I touched the neutral, I got a nasty shock that caused my elbow to smash into the concrete wall. Remeasuring, I read 120 volts from neutral to earth. On troubleshooting, I found that the receptacle the pump was plugged into was wired in reverse, so the neutral was hot. I went home with a sore, bruised elbow, but the situation could have been lethal.

If a branch circuit is wired backward, the same situation exists every time an appliance or light fixture is plugged in. Unfortunately, this is more common than you might think. In some cases, I have seen entire houses wired in reverse. The only remedy is to rewire.

3. Open Neutral

If the neutral is open, a plugged-in tool or appliance should not work. This presents no danger unless the user attempts to work on the tool or appliance while it is still plugged in. Since the hot is still connected, the user could provide a neutral path and get a severe shock. The same applies inside the receptacle — turn off the power at the panel before rewiring.

If you check the receptacle and the neutral is properly connected, you'll need to trace the wire back toward the panel, looking for a loose connection or a nail that has cut the wire. A loose or partially severed wire can cause a fire. Always leave the power off until you find and fix the problem.

4. Open Hot

An open hot is immediately obvious: None of the display lights on the tester will light. Turn the circuit off as soon as you've finished making the test; a loose or broken hot can start a fire.

If there is nothing obviously wrong inside the box, you'll have to look for a loose connection or severed wire somewhere in the circuit.

5. Open Ground

In this case, there is no ground connection at the receptacle, perhaps because it's a two-wire circuit, or because the ground wire has come loose, or because the installer cut the ground wire too short to make the connection. (Sometimes this is done on purpose because an untrained installer doesn't know what to do with the wire.)

An open ground gives the illusion of safety when actually there is grave danger. People see the three-prong

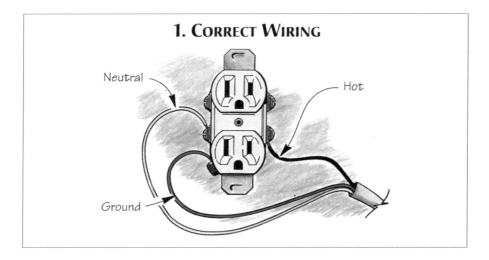

1. CORRECT WIRING

Neutral

Hot

Ground

receptacle and assume there's a proper ground. If a tool or appliance plugged into that receptacle develops a hot-to-ground fault, the user can get shocked and possibly electrocuted.

If in fact there is no ground on a circuit, the proper procedure is to use an older-type two-prong receptacle; that way, no one is misled into assuming there's a ground when there isn't. (Code also allows the use of GFCIs in this situation, though I don't like to use them without an actual ground connection.) If the ground wire was cut, you should rewire the receptacle with a properly connected ground.

6. Hot and Ground Reversed

An installer would have to be drunk to do this. This could only happen on a circuit with just one receptacle; otherwise, the breaker would immediately trip. Assuming the one receptacle, it's a potentially lethal situation. If an appliance like a clothes washer or electric drill is plugged in, its frame will be hot and will shock anyone that touches it.

7. Hot on Neutral With Open Hot

I've never encountered this situation and probably never will. It's basically a reversed polarity situation where the neutral has come loose. Even though the hot is on the neutral side, there is no return path to

2. REVERSED POLARITY

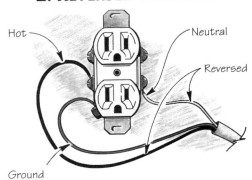

3. OPEN NEUTRAL

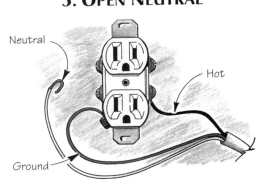

4. OPEN HOT

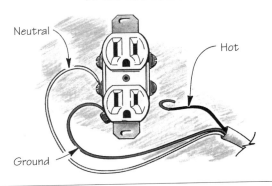

5. OPEN GROUND

6. HOT AND GROUND REVERSED

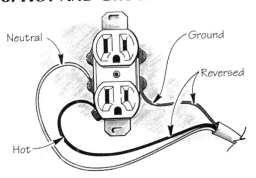

7. HOT ON NEUTRAL WITH OPEN HOT

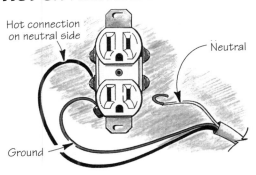

ADVANCED PLUG-IN TESTER

Industrial Commercial Electronics has taken the plug-in tester concept to a new level of sophistication with its SureTest line of "branch circuit analyzers." Besides the usual checks that common plug-in testers do, the SureTest ST-1D (the model we tested) will check for a bootleg ground, read line voltage, check for voltage drop, measure the load on the circuit between the receptacle and the panel, and measure the impedance of the building's grounding path. Considering the cost — less than $300 — the tool is great for anyone who needs to quickly and safely check a circuit.

Say, for instance, that you're adding on a home office for your client, and that the office will be stuffed with expensive, state-of-the-art electronic equipment — computer, fax machine, copier, etc. Despite assurances from the electrician, and despite the presence of plug-in surge protector strips at every receptacle, your client still wants evidence that the equipment is protected against power surges (either from the utility or lightning), and that neither noise in the lines nor power fluctuations will garble data. Unfortunately, there is no way for you to guarantee protection against lightning — the voltage from a near or direct hit is massive; and it's up to the power company to deliver continuous, good-quality electricity. But with the SureTest, you can be reasonably certain of the power quality within the house itself.

So you pull out the SureTest and plug it in a receptacle. The green lights tell you the receptacle is wired correctly; the digital display confirms that you've got 120 volts present from the utility. (Wild fluctuations in the reading would indicate that the utility is delivering poor-quality power.) You push the "display advance" button, and you get the voltage drop on that receptacle under 15-amp load (given as a percentage of 120 volts). Push the button again and you get voltage drop under 20-amp load.

For either size circuit, any drop under 5% is okay; above that, you may have a problem. Besides causing equipment problems, excessive voltage drop causes heat buildup in the wire and at connections, and can be a fire hazard.

Let's say you get a reading above 5%. Maybe this is because you've pulled the wiring for the addition off a lightly loaded preexisting bed-

room circuit, but the extra length of wire is creating too much resistance. So you rewire the circuit as a "homerun" back to the panel. Or maybe there's a bad connection at the receptacle that's causing the resistance. Either way, you locate the problem, fix it, and test again.

The next test is for excessive voltage between ground and neutral — an indication of how much noise is in the lines from the operation of other appliances on the circuit. For computer operation, a few volts is okay; for dedicated lines for faxes or copiers, no more than a few millivolts should be present. With this test, it's best to leave the SureTest plugged in overnight, or even for a few days. It will hold the peak reading that develops. That way, you can figure out how the intermittent operation of other appliances on the line — a hairdryer, a television, or a vacuum cleaner — might affect the circuit.

Push the advance button again and you get a reading of the load on that circuit, in amps, back to the panel (it's best to take this reading from the last receptacle on the circuit). This is a good way to check a dedicated circuit; if you get any reading at all, it may mean that the circuit shares a neutral. Again, the SureTest allows you to test for load over an extended period; just leave the device plugged in and it will record the peak reading.

A final test measures the resistance of the ground path in ohms — a very important test when it comes to sensitive electronic equipment. A low reading, preferably below .25 ohms, helps assure that excessive voltages that may develop in the line (from lightning or a power spike, for example) will be safely returned to ground at the panel without destroying equipment.

For more information on the SureTest ST-1D or other less expensive models, contact Ideal Industries (Sycamore, IL; 800/435-0705; www.idealindustries.com). — R.C.

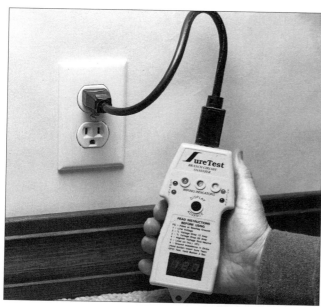

This branch circuit analyzer performs more sophisticated tests than a common plug-in tester. For example, it can check for false grounds and measure voltage and voltage drops.

complete the circuit. Appliances won't work when plugged into a receptacle wired this way.

GFCI Button

Many testers also have a GFCI test button. When the button is pressed, a simulated ground fault is placed on the line. A properly working GFCI will trip (assuming it's on a grounded circuit). You can also test GFCI-protected receptacles wired downstream from a GFCI receptacle (or circuit breaker). The simulated ground fault at the downstream receptacle should trip the GFCI receptacle.

Although GFCI receptacles will work on two-wire circuits, they can't be tested with plug-in testers, which work by creating an actual fault to ground. On two-wire circuits you have to use the test button on the GFCI receptacle itself.

Plug-In Tester Limitations

Be aware of what these testers cannot test for:

- *False, or "bootleg," ground:* This is where some idiot has jumped the neutral onto the ground connection of the receptacle (see illustration, above right). Why? Who knows? It might be an effort to fool an inspector into thinking a circuit is grounded when it's not. This is a very dangerous connection and can be life-threatening. Assuming something is plugged into that receptacle and turned on, this puts current on the grounding circuit in parallel with the neutral. That means anyone using an appliance anywhere on that branch would be in danger of shock.

- *Ground and neutral reversed:* This is rare because most people wiring a receptacle know that the ground wire is the bare wire. If it should happen, an appliance plugged into that receptacle will put current flow through the grounding wire instead of the neutral. This can endanger anyone who operates an appliance anywhere on that branch circuit. (It also endangers an electrician who is troubleshooting the circuit.)

- *Quality of ground:* This is a test to verify that the ground resistance path from the receptacle to the main panel is not only intact but is also a low-resistance path. This can only be done with a more elaborate plug-in tester (see "Advanced Plug-In Tester").

- *Any combination of defects:* If two of the tests share the same indicator light — for example, the open neutral test and the open hot test — you might think there is only

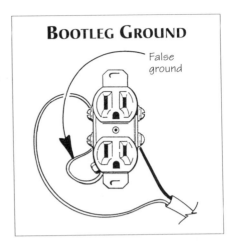

BOOTLEG GROUND

False ground

an open hot when the neutral is also open. Since the power is off to the receptacle (because of the open hot), there is no way for the tester to light the indicator for the open neutral. The solution is to remedy the open hot, then retest for other faults.

- *Check a standard two-prong ungrounded receptacle:* For this, you will need a more expensive test device, one with a retractable ground prong.

- *Check for voltage drop on the line:* Again, this is a job for the professional tester.

By Rex Cauldwell, a master electrician and owner of Little Mountain Electric in Copper Hill, Va.

INDEX